Behavior Change

Behavior Change

John R. Lutzker
Southern Illinois University

Jerry A. Martin
University of Minnesota

Brooks/Cole Publishing Company
Monterey, California

Brooks/Cole Publishing Company
A Division of Wadsworth, Inc.

Printed in the United States of America

10   9   8   7   6   5   4   3   2   1

Library of Congress Cataloging in Publication Data

Lutzker, John R   1947–
    Behavior change.

    Includes bibliographies and index.
     1. Behavior modification.   2. Psychology, Applied.
I. Martin, Jerry A., 1942–   joint author.
II. Title.
BF637.B4L87   153.8′5   80-20798
ISBN 0-8185-0420-X

Acquisition Editor: *Todd Lueders*
Manuscript Editor: *Sherman Butler*
Production Editors: *Marilu Uland and Patricia E. Cain*
Interior Design: *Ruth Scott*
Cover Design: *Stan Rice*
Typesetting: *Graphic Typesetting Service, Los Angeles, California*

For Sandra, Dov, and Tov—and Marti

FOREWORD

This book is an exciting and comprehensive presentation of the many new treatments developed so recently in the field known as applied behavior analysis. The book succeeds admirably in its broad coverage of topics, its scholarly and thorough documentation, its integration of findings, its inclusion of very recent findings, and its easy readability.

Not many years ago, the behaviorist view was considered a prototypic example of an intellectual dogma that was so overly concerned with methodology, scientism, antimentalism, and excessively precise quantification that it was irrelevant to the human situation and its ills. The salivation of Pavlov's dogs may have earned him the Nobel Prize and the lever-presses of rats in Skinner's box seemed to many a testimony to his skill as an animal trainer, but the extension to human problems of the findings of these experiments seemed metaphorical at best. The dogs' salivation and the rats' lever-pressing were designated as "responses," but what relevance could these responses have to the needs of society? The behaviorist tradition, however, has reached its culmination in the new field of behavior analysis. Behavior analysis is so diverse in its applications and concepts that it is more accurate to describe it as a newly emerged field than as a simple extension of behaviorism. For those scientists/professionals who value critical scientific evaluation, objectivity, standardization, and definitiveness of results to the same extent that they desire effective psychological treatments, applied behavior analysis provides a means of achieving both sets of values. We need not make a painful choice between the scientist's high standards and the professional's responsibility to provide sorely needed psychological services. Extrapolation has now become application, and the promise of behaviorism has been transformed into clinical treatment.

The guiding principle of this book is to describe the practical treatments for major human problems that have emerged from applied behavior analysis. Outcome, practicality, cost-benefit ratios, and degree of effectiveness have been used to determine which treatments are discussed. "What works?" is the question addressed in such diverse areas as alcoholism, marital disorder, classroom learning, child rearing, employee performance, fears, behavioral medicine, management and administrative practices, and depression, each of which is covered in depth, as are other problem situations. The behavioral literature in these problem areas is vast, but the authors have succeeded in providing information about the extent of the evidence while emphasizing those treatments that have proven to be effective and enduring. In most of these problem areas, effective behavioral treatments have been developed and often have been found to be more effective than the alternatives. In accordance with the behaviorist tradition, the authors' conclusions are closely tied to those studies that are most rigorously designed and definitive.

This book is exemplary as a vehicle for communicating the new behavioral treatments available for the many human problems with which practitioners must deal. Psychologists, social workers, counselors, and psychiatrists will find the description of treatments immediately useful. Since problems tend to occur together for individuals, families, and institutions, practitioners should find great utility in learning of the diversity of problems that now can be treated effectively from a unitary conceptual and methodological basis.

A great need exists for textbooks that are problem-oriented, rather than concept-oriented. The concept-oriented text dwells on history, names, definitions, comparisons of theories and concepts, and experiments crucial to a judgment of theories. But the student who uses such a text receives little information about what use can be made of these concepts in practicing the vocation that he or she will take on. The outcome-oriented text provides this needed emphasis on utility; for this reason, *Behavior Change* should be especially appropriate as a text in applied programs such as education, rehabilitation, psychology, social work, psychiatry, child development, and criminology.

The authors are to be commended for providing a treatment that is at once so meaningful, current, thorough, and readable.

Nathan H. Azrin

PREFACE

This book is about a set of principles and procedures that involve what B. F. Skinner of Harvard University calls the science of human behavior. The applications of this science, which we call *behavior change procedures,* have become apparent in virtually every conceivable area of human development and activity. The purpose of this book is to acquaint the reader with the basic behavior change principles, procedures, and methods for evaluating those procedures and to explore in depth the development of this broad field across 11 application areas: the environment, the working world, health care for adults, health care for children, the issues for normal and problem children, classrooms, severe disorders, personal problems requiring reduction of certain behaviors (such as eating, smoking, and so on), personal problems such as anxiety and depression, relationships and sexual behavior, and, finally, training and ethics.

We have tried to present an objective analysis of successes and failures in our review of the various applications and the particular research studies that comprise those applications. This is because behavior change professionals are wed to a scientific approach to the study and application of this technology to human behavior. We also hope that our obvious enthusiasm for this field comes through, which, if it does, will help make the book all the more readable.

Many books on behavior modification pay, at best, only casual attention to its nonclinical, nondeviant applications. The fastest developing applications of behavior change, however, are in environmental/ecological issues (Chapter 3), in the working world (Chapter 4), in health care (Chapters 5 and 6), and with normal children (Chapter 7). Thus, we have chosen to put these chapters in the beginning of the book. Such placement in no way diminishes the importance of chapters devoted to behavior change of problems and deviations. We hope that we have given a fresh look to these applications, for which we have provided up-to-date studies and coverage.

You will notice that in some chapters (such as Chapter 3, on the environment), we have provided more procedural detail than we have in other chapters (such as Chapter 4, on the working world). The reason for this difference is that the procedures in one area have been more varied than in another area. For example, behavior change procedures applied to the problems of litter control and energy conservation have been quite varied. On the other hand, the procedures used in business and industry have been fairly uniform. Thus, when covering this latter area, we have chosen to review the variety of settings, rather than the variety of procedures, since relatively similar procedures have been used to produce behavior change.

Behavior Change is appropriate for use in both undergraduate and graduate courses in behavior modification, applied behavior analysis, and behavior therapy. It should be useful in psychology, education, human development, rehabilitation, social welfare, medicine, nursing, and counseling. Professionals, we hope, will find it a useful reference source.

Several people who helped in a variety of ways deserve acknowledgment for their contributions in helping us come to fruition with this project. Our gratitude goes to the reviewers of the manuscript, Jon S. Bailey of Florida State University, Wayne R. Bartz of American River College, Frank Hovell of San Francisco State University, Brian A. Iwata of Johns Hopkins University School of Medicine, Jeanne S. Phillips of the University of Denver, and A. Robert Sherman of the University of California at Santa Barbara. The colleagues who provided valuable suggestions were Eric Errickson, Brandon F. Greene, Bill Hopkins, Judith M. LeBlanc, Gloria Leon, William H. Redd, and Pat Webber. Considerable assistance was provided by Nancy Huttig. The support of Jerome R. Lorenz of Southern Illinois University at Carbondale and Frederic J. Kottke of the University of Minnesota Hospitals is also gratefully acknowledged. Our parents, Abe and Anne Lutzker and John and Helen Martin, and our in-laws, Ed and Linda Zabel and J. Marshall and Cora Walker, have provided meaningful encouragement and support throughout our careers. Our wives, Sandra Lutzker and Marti Martin, have helped in countless ways. The people at Brooks/Cole Publishing Company have made writing this book a painless task, especially Marsha Baxter, Todd Lueders, Marilu Uland, and Sherman Butler. Finally, it would take up too much space to identify the contributions provided by the following people who, too, truly have our appreciation: Paula Davis, Mary Dolan, Granger Dinwiddie, Dee Glover, Connie Grangruth, Jung-Ae Hur, Shigeharu Ieda, George Kunz, Pam Levine, Anne Michalicek, Shirley O'Brien, Nancy Piper, Mary Polvinale, David Ritzman, Carole Sarnoff, Debbie Tertinger, Paula Whang, and Karen J. Zopf.

John R. Lutzker
Jerry A. Martin

CONTENTS

10 Personal Problems: Obesity, Smoking, Chemical Dependency 231

11 Personal Problems: Anxiety and Depression 265

12 Relationships and Sexual Behavior 288

13 Training, Ethics, and the Future 307

Behavior Change: History, Principles, and Processes

BEHAVIOR *therapy, behavior modification, behavior analysis,* and *contingency management* are among the labels that have been used to describe a set of techniques that, when applied to human problems, result in changes in behavior—hopefully, for the greater good. These techniques are founded in the rigorous methods of experimental psychology. Their practitioners are usually psychologists who have been trained specifically in their use, but they have also been used successfully by psychiatrists, physicians, sociologists, social workers, teachers, administrators, hospital staff, and parents. Their applications are now wide-ranging, dealing with a variety of human problems from littering to sexual dysfunction, from job productivity to alcoholism, in many areas of human activity both clinical and nonclinical. It has not always been so; early applications of the techniques seldom went beyond the laboratory, and present-day applications have been a long time coming.[1]

HISTORY

The earliest beginnings of the behavior change movement must be traced to the work on learning—in the late 19th century and early 20th century—of the Russian physiologists Sechenov, Pavlov, and Bechterev. In the early 1900s in the United States, the psychologist John Watson founded what came to be known as behaviorism. Watson rejected the study of the mind and called for psychology to focus on observable behavior. There followed in America important research on phobias by Mary Cover Jones in the 1920s and a treatment for bedwetting based on learning principles by Mowrer and Mowrer (1938). In a survey of the published psychological literature through 1938, Yates (1970) reports finding 28 different applications of learning to the treatment of problems.

Perhaps no single person has had as much influence upon behavior change applications as B. F. Skinner. He began his influential writings in the late 1930s, and their influence continues today. The next section of this chapter, which outlines the major behavior change principles, relies heavily on Skinner's writings. Also extremely important was the work of Joseph Wolpe in South Africa in the 1940s and 1950s. He first introduced one of the major behavior change techniques, systematic desensitization, which is still widely used for the treatment of a variety of neurotic disorders. At Maudsley Hospital in England in the 1940s and 1950s, Hans Eysenck led a group of researchers studying abnormal behavior. In addition to furthering the application of behavior change techniques, Eysenck led the attack on the weaknesses of other therapeutic approaches. In the United States, other psychologists developed behavior change techniques, including negative practice (Knight Dunlap) and conditioned reflex therapy (Andrew Salter). From South Africa, Wolpe and his former student, Arnold Lazarus, brought their behavior change techniques to the United States in the early 1960s. Using operant conditioning techniques, Skinner and Ogden Lindsley studied the behavior of psychotic patients at Metropolitan State Hospital in Massachusetts. A major center for the developing field of behavior change techniques with children grew at the University of Wash-

[1]For students interested in additional information about the development of behavior change applications, we recommend excellent books by Ullmann and Krasner (1975) and Kazdin (1978).

ington. There, gathered around Sidney Bijou, Donald Baer, and Jay Birnbrauer, were many young professionals who moved on to national prominence—among them, Todd Risley, James Sherman, Ivar Lovaas, Stephanie Stolz, Don Bushell, Billy Hopkins, Montrose Wolf, J. Robert Wahler, Vance Hall, and Warren Steinman. Other pioneers in the 1960s included Teodoro Ayllon, who with colleagues Jack Michael and Nathan H. Azrin applied behavior change techniques to psychiatric settings. Dr. Azrin went on to become, perhaps, the most prolific developer of new techniques in the entire field.

The group at the University of Washington began by examining the role of teacher attention on preschool children (Harris, Johnston, Kelley, & Wolf, 1964). They also produced some dramatic behavior changes in a severely disturbed boy (Wolf, Risley, & Mees, 1964). The other behavioral "fortresses" of the sixties were the Psychology Department at Arizona State University, where considerable work began in the treatment of developmental disabilities, and the Rehabilitation Institute at Southern Illinois University and Anna State Hospital in Illinois, where the early emphasis was on the treatment and training of psychotic and retarded individuals. Thus, behavior change applications—which today touch every conceivable aspect of human development—began with children and severely disturbed adults.

Dozens of other individuals have made important contributions to the behavior change movement. Although many of them will be credited throughout this book, there is not space to mention them all, just as it is impossible to do justice to the size of the present-day behavior change movement or numbers of individuals involved. The major professional group concerned with behavior change techniques is the Association for Advancement of Behavior Therapy (AABT), which has, currently, approximately 3000 active members. There are also a number of affiliated state and regional groups. Three other groups concerned with behavior change are the Behavior Therapy and Research Society, the Association for Behavior Analysis, and Division 25 of the American Psychological Association. The number of professionals outside these three groups who make regular use of behavior change techniques is not possible to know.

As the behavior change movement has grown, so have the number of books and scientific journals devoted to the subject. The major behavior change journals include the *Journal of Applied Behavior Analysis, Behavior Therapy, Behaviour Research and Therapy, Journal of Behavior Therapy and Experimental Psychiatry,* and *Behavior Modification.* Newer journals include *Behavioral Assessment, The Journal of Behavioral Medicine, Education and Treatment of Children,* and *Child Behavior Therapy.* Uncounted articles on behavior change techniques appear in other journals. In the next section we briefly describe the basic subject matter of these books and articles—the major principles underlying most behavior change techniques.

PRINCIPLES

Almost everything a human being does is somehow related, either directly or indirectly, to learning. A term less attractive than, but nonetheless synonymous with, learning is *conditioning.* Both terms mean behavior change. In this section we review the two ways of learning: operant conditioning and respondent conditioning. Because the major purpose of this book is to explore the applications, not the rationale, of behavior change principles, this review is not exhaustive. Several excellent sources that more thoroughly cover operant and respondent principles are suggested at the end of this chapter.

Operant Conditioning

In Chapter 7 you will read about the work of Yvonne Brackbill, who found that when an adult engaged in a variety of social responses whenever a baby smiled, the baby smiled more often (Brackbill, 1958). In the 1930s, B. F. Skinner found that pigeons would peck a lighted key more frequently when they received bits of grain for doing so. In Chapter 3 you will learn that children are more likely to pick up litter in a movie theater if they receive a free drink for doing so (Burgess, Clark, & Handee, 1971). These three examples demonstrate the principle of positive reinforcement: if a behavior is followed by a positive event, that behavior will recur more frequently than it did before the event was added to the environment.

Positive reinforcement is often defined in terms of rate; it may also apply to increases in percentage correct, duration of behavior, and distances. In the examples given above, the positive reinforcers were the food given to the pigeon, the social consequences provided to the infants, and the free drinks provided to the children in the movie theater. All of these "events" were added to the environment. They caused an increase in the rates of the behaviors (pecking keys, smiling, picking up litter) that they followed. Thus, positive reinforcement had occurred. It is important to remember that positive reinforcement is defined by its effects on behavior and by the way it is presented (that is, following the behavior). Once again: If an event is added to the environment contingent upon (following) a behavior and there is an increase in the subsequent rate of that behavior, positive reinforcement *has* occurred. Suppose, however, an event is added to the environment and there follows no increase—for example, a mother says, "Thank you for picking up your clothes" to a teenage daughter, and the daughter does not pick up her clothes any more frequently than usual (she still picks her clothes up only once a week)—then positive reinforcement *has not* occurred. We often hear students and professionals say, incorrectly, "I tried positive reinforcement, but it didn't work." By definition, positive reinforcement *always* works. A more accurate comment after experiencing a failure to increase a behavior is, "I thought that I was providing positive reinforcers, but what I added to the environment did not act as positive reinforcement."

There are two kinds of positive reinforcers. *Primary positive reinforcers* are those that can act to produce an increase in behavior without any previous experience with the reinforcer. For example, a hungry monkey may never have tasted a banana before, but when that banana is delivered contingent upon the monkey's pulling a lever, the monkey will probably pull it again. Similarly, a severely handicapped, brain-damaged child who is also hungry and has never had cheese before is more likely to try to imitate a sound if he or she has been given a bite of cheese for the effort.

Conditioned positive reinforcers are events that have no inherent reinforcing properties; their reinforcing value must be learned. For example, if you gave a dollar bill to a baby for smiling, you undoubtedly would not produce an increase in the baby's rate of smiling as a function of providing the dollar bill. If, however, you gave a college student a dollar bill every time he or she smiled, you would probably see one happy face! The reinforcing properties of a dollar bill must be learned. Many practitioners of operant conditioning have described social responses such as smiling at and talking to an infant as conditioned reinforcers. We believe that the evidence does not justify ruling out social consequences as, at least in part, primary reinforcers. To dichotomize primary and conditioned reinforcers seems to us academic; the essential elements in both kinds of reinforcers are that the consequence added to the environment is the event that produces behavior change, and that that change can be quantified.

Probably the two most common conditioned reinforcers you will find described in this book are money and tokens or points. In several chapters you will see that tangible cash rewards have acted as reinforcers or incentives for picking up litter, recycling resources, conserving energy, utilizing health facilities, and other activities.

Among the first to describe the use of tokens or points were Drs. Teodoro Ayllon and Nathan Azrin who, in the early 1960s, developed a sophisticated behavior management for hospitalized mentally ill women in Anna, Illinois. The women received token points in different quantities for performing a variety of habilitative behaviors such as socializing, grooming, and working. The women were able to exchange their points for privileges such as special dining arrangements and for a variety of events and sundry items from the hospital canteen. They were also charged points for engaging in inappropriate institutional behavior such as irrational talk. The system proved quite effective in changing the women's behavior. Similar token systems are described throughout this book for a variety of individuals and behaviors. Just a few examples are the training of positive behavior in predelinquent youth, compliance with dental and medical regimens in children, use in special education programs, and application in adult weight control. Tokens or points bridge the gap between the occurrence of appropriate behavior and the "back-up" of another positive reinforcer. Thus, token reinforcement represents an important form of positive reinforcement in the behavior change process.

Negative reinforcement is probably the most misunderstood concept in operant conditioning. Many people, quite inaccurately, equate negative reinforcement with punishment. Negative reinforcement and punishment are not the same processes. Positive reinforcement is produced by *adding* something to the environment; negative reinforcement is produced by *removing* something from the environment. Both positive and negative reinforcement produce an increase in behavior. Negative reinforcement accomplishes this increase by removing a stimulus from the environment contingent upon the behavior that has been targeted for increase. For example, a rat in a chamber suddenly receives a shock to its feet; it begins to hop around in pain and depresses a lever. When the lever is depressed, the shock stops. What behavior is likely to be increased? Of course, the rat will press the lever whenever shock is turned on. That is, when the rat feels the shock (the stimulus), the rat presses the lever (the behavior); the response rate is increased by the *removal* of the shock (stimulus).

Once again: negative reinforcement is the process by which the future like-lihood of a behavior being repeated has been increased by the removal of something from the environment. Another example of negative reinforcement is nagging—and how to relieve it. A 12-year-old boy, Richard, never takes out the garbage without being nagged. Every night his mother yells at him, "Richard, how many times do I have to tell you to take out the garbage?" Richard takes out the garbage, a response that *removes* from his environment his mother's nagging.

Much of our everyday behavior is maintained by the process of negative reinforcement. Two kinds of behavior lead to negative reinforcement. One is *escape*. In the examples above, both the rat and Richard engaged in a response in order to escape the ongoing presentation of the unpleasant stimulus. The other way to produce negative reinforcement is through *avoidance*. The rat can be taught to avoid the stimulus (shock) by continually pressing the bar and hence avoiding the presentation of that painful stimulus. Richard can avoid the unpleasant stimulus (nagging) by taking out the garbage before his mother yells at him. With these simple examples, you can think of the many behaviors you might engage in every day as a function of escape or avoidance, such as driving within the speed limit to avoid getting a ticket.

Behavior reduction.   Reinforcement procedures are a part of the basic tools of the behavior change process; so are behavior reduction procedures. (We use the term *behavior reduction,* rather than *punishment,* because it better describes the process and avoids the misunderstanding and emotion that seem inherent in the word *punishment.*) Just as the aim of reinforcement is to increase rates of behavior by adding or removing events from the environment, the aim of behavior reduction is to reduce unwanted behavior by adding or removing events from the environment.

When an event is added to the environment contingent upon a behavior and there is a reduction in subsequent rates of behavior, then behavior reduction has occurred. Common everyday examples are shouting "no" to the child reaching into the cookie jar or slapping the hand of a toddler reaching for a hot pot on the stove. Just as reinforcement is defined in terms of its effect on behavior, so behavior reduc-tion can be said to have occurred only if there is a decrease in the rate of the behav-ior. Therefore, if yelling "no" at the child for reaching into the cookie jar does not reduce future[2] reaching, then behavior reduction has not occurred. Thus, both reinforcement and behavior reduction are defined in terms of their effect on behavior.

Chapter 6 offers an example of a behavior reduction procedure that adds an event to the environment: an infant's life was saved when a nurse squirted lemon juice into the infant's mouth whenever she started to regurgitate her food. Painful electric shock has been used to reduce the seriously self-injurious behavior of severely brain-damaged children. Once again: behavior reduction can be achieved with the addition of a consequence to a behavior.

Among the most innovative behavior reduction techniques are overcorrection and positive practice (Foxx & Azrin, 1972). The basic components of these pro-

---

[2]The issue of future is critical because almost any novel stimulus such as yelling or even loud laughter is likely to suppress the ongoing behavior.

cedures are to restore a disrupted environment to its proper condition, to "overcorrect" the situation to ensure that the proper behavior has been learned, and to provide an alternative to inappropriate behavior. Many believe that the most important feature of overcorrection and positive practice is that they might involve *direct* teaching of appropriate behavior in addition to the reduction of inappropriate behavior. Many of the other behavior reduction techniques merely imply (indirectly) the appropriate behavior. In this book, you will see overcorrection and positive practice applied to toilet training normal and retarded children, to the teaching of sharing, and to other behaviors.

As we stated before, in addition to producing a reduction in behavior by adding something to the environment, behavior reduction can also be produced by *removing* something from the environment. The procedures involving removal that we will review here are timeout from positive reinforcement, extinction, and response cost.

Timeout from positive reinforcement involves either removing the individual from a reinforcing environment or removing the reinforcers from the individual. An example of the former method is the following situation: A 3-year-old child has been repeatedly told not to eat with her fingers at the dinner table. The parent briefly pulls the child's chair away from the table and says, "Gloria, you're not supposed to eat your meat with your fingers." The child is then required to spend a minute sitting away from the table, then is pushed back to the table while the parent says, "Now, show us how you can use your fork." Of course, it would also be important to praise Gloria frequently for eating properly. If this procedure worked to reduce Gloria's inappropriate eating with her fingers, then timeout from positive reinforcement can be said to have occurred—an instance of removing the individual from the reinforcing environment. An alternative to removing Gloria briefly from the table would be to place her dinner plate out of her reach for a minute—an instance of removing the reinforcers from the individual.

A common form of timeout from positive reinforcement is removal to another room in the house, such as a bedroom or bathroom. In schools or institutions, sometimes special rooms or areas are designated as timeout places. Usually, such a timeout is used for more serious behavior problems, although for years parents have sent children to their rooms for such things as "backtalk" or aggression toward a sibling, with some success if the measure is taken consistently.

Like the other procedures, timeout from positive reinforcement is defined in terms of its effect on behavior. For example, Solnick, Rincover, and Peterson (1977) found that an autistic little girl received positive reinforcement for tantrums by a brief timeout period, if she could engage in self-stimulatory behavior during the timeout. These researchers also provided data to demonstrate that a timeout effect was produced with a 16-year-old brain-damaged male only when "timein" was "enriched" with bright objects, toys, and music. When "timein" was "impoverished," inappropriate behavior was not reduced. This point cannot be stressed enough.

Extinction of a behavior—the ultimate reduction—involves withholding the reinforcers that maintain the behavior. For example, if a laboratory rat has been receiving food contingent upon its pressing a bar and that food is no longer delivered, the rat's rate of bar pressing will return to its pre-reinforced rate. And if—for a human example—Ella no longer wanted Wayne to phone her, she could have her roommate answer all calls and never again accept a call from Wayne. After a while, Wayne would surely stop calling. Extinction as a behavior change treatment technique is used less frequently than timeout or reinforcement, but it has been reported by some authors. Extinction is a difficult procedure that must be applied consistently and accurately.

Response cost is a fairly common behavior change technique that also involves removing something from the environment to produce a behavior reduction. A reinforcer (which often can be earned back) is removed contingent upon inappropriate behavior. That reinforcer or its backup might not be *directly* related to the behavior. For example, if you are stopped by a police officer for speeding and receive a $50 ticket, your speeding is likely to be reduced. How the loss of $50 "hurts" you or how it is necessarily related to driving is not particularly relevant. What does count is that your speeding habits have been reduced. Further, neither the police officer nor the judge has removed your ability to earn money; thus, you have an opportunity to earn $50 in whatever manner you usually earn money. Throughout this book, you will see several examples of response cost procedures, ranging from the removal of privileges to the removal of points or tokens (redeemable for privileges and other tangible reinforcers) in formal point systems or token economies. Judiciously applied, response cost can be a highly effective behavior reduction procedure that also runs little risk of producing negative emotions that might be associated with behavior reduction techniques.

Positive reinforcement also may be used as a behavior reduction procedure. Chapter 9 tells how DRO (differential reinforcement of other behavior) was used to eliminate exhibitionism in a 52-year-old retarded man (Lutzker, 1974). This was accomplished by providing social reinforcement (praise) on a regular basis at times when the man was *not* exposing himself. Thus, reinforcement was delivered for any behavior *other* than the targeted inappropriate behavior. Another good example of the successful use of DRO as a treatment strategy was provided by Iwata and Lorentzson (1976). They combined DRO with daily activities and timeout in reducing the seizure-like behavior of a 41-year-old male.

Inappropriate behavior may also be reduced by differential reinforcement of low rates of behavior (or DRL). An example of this technique was provided by Deitz and Repp (1973) who wished to reduce, but not eliminate, handraising of a special-education child. Another example of a behavior to reduce, but not eliminate, is the frequency with which a shy preschool child asks the teacher (as opposed to another child) to play with him.

Although all behavior reduction procedures run the risk of being misused and abused, and the further risk of producing unwanted side effects, there are numerous examples of their effective use—as this book will show.

Schedules.   The various ways to deliver reinforcement and behavior reduction procedures are called *schedules*. The five most commonly described and discussed schedules of positive reinforcement are presented here.

Continuous reinforcement (CRF) means that every *correct* response is reinforced. In the rat lab, CRF means that the rat receives food each time it presses the bar. In the special education classroom, CRF might mean that Sean is praised each time he correctly identifies the letter "A." CRF is the most effective schedule on which to teach a new behavior. It is also fairly easy to produce extinction of behavior maintained by CRF schedules.

Intermittent reinforcement means that not every correct response is reinforced. There are four kinds of intermittent reinforcement: fixed ratio (FR), fixed interval (FI), variable ratio (VR), and variable interval (VI). All four kinds are more resistant to extinction than behavior maintained by CRF. That is, once a behavior is learned, it is harder to get rid of if the reinforcement schedule is switched to an intermittent one. Try to picture yourself going to a soda machine every day. Your "history" with that machine is that it never fails you (CRF schedule). Whenever you put in your quarter, you get your soda. But then one day the machine fails you and "eats" your quarter! What then? You are likely to kick it, jiggle it, and maybe put another quarter into it. However, if it "eats" that and the next few subsequent quarters, you are likely to give up on that machine. If, on the other hand, your "history" with the machine is such that after it worked well for a while it began occasionally, but not always, to "eat" your quarters (an intermittent reinforcement schedule), you would continue to feed it quarters for some time if you did not know that it was unrepairable. In other words, your behavior is more resistant to extinction under an intermittent reinforcement schedule than under a continuous reinforcement schedule.

Fixed ratio (FR) means that reinforcement is delivered after a predetermined number of correct responses. An FR 8 schedule is one in which a point is given to Chan for each eight math problems done correctly in his fourth grade class. FR schedules of reinforcement produce steady (stable) rates of performance.

Fixed interval (FI) means that reinforcement is delivered for the first correct response after a set period of time has passed. For example, you receive a paycheck for going to the payroll window only on the 1st and 15th of every month. Because FI schedules usually produce less stable performance than FR schedules, a post-reinforcement pause is frequently observed on an FI schedule. That is, it is unlikely that you will go to the payroll window on the 16th of the month. An effect called scalloping also is frequently seen with behavior maintained by FI schedules. That is, as the predetermined interval draws close, the rate of the behavior begins to increase again. Nearly broke on the 29th, you go to the payroll window for an advance.

Variable ratio (VR) schedules of reinforcement require that reinforcement be delivered for different numbers of correct responses. A VR 10 schedule of reinforcement for our bar-pressing rat friend means that on the *average* food would be delivered for every tenth correct response, but the schedule is variable. That is, the rat may press the bar five times, receive food, fifteen times, seven times, and so on, for an average of ten responses per delivery of reinforcement. Variable ratio schedules of reinforcement produce high and stable rates of behavior.

Variable interval (VI) schedules of reinforcement involve the delivery of reinforcement for the first correct response after varying lengths of time. A VI 10″ schedule means that on the average reinforcement is delivered for a correct response after ten seconds have elapsed. Behaviors maintained on both VR and VI schedules are the most resistant to extinction—that is, compared to the other schedules, behaviors maintained on these schedules take the longest to eliminate or reduce to their operant levels.

Although we have begun to understand a great deal about learning from studying schedules of reinforcement in animal laboratories, we must speculate about human learning. Much less is known about complex schedules of reinforcement with humans because to isolate and control reinforcers in our lives is so difficult. Nevertheless, you will see schedules used with people (at least CRF and intermittent) mentioned several times throughout this book.

Two other methods of operant conditioning deserve review in this section: *stimulus control* and *shaping*.

Stimulus control.   College students typically behave quite differently with their friends at parties at school than they do with their parents at home. Two-year-old Malcolm never performs his cute "tricks" at his grandparents' house. A retarded child imitates his language sounds for the graduate student therapist he has been working with for the last few months, but not for the new psychology practicum student. What do these examples have in common? They all typify the principle of *stimulus control*. Behavior that is reinforced in the presence of one stimulus often does not occur in the presence of a different stimulus. A college student's party behavior is reinforced under the presence of common stimuli (called discriminative stimuli, or S^Ds). That same behavior is not reinforced by the stimuli at the parents' home. This condition is noted as S^Δ. Thus, the behavior of the college student at a party, Malcolm's "tricks," and the retarded child's language are governed by the process of stimulus control. Examples of this most important method of operant conditioning will be seen throughout this book.

Shaping. A fairly simple, yet very important, method of operant conditioning, shaping involves reinforcing successive approximations of a desired goal behavior until the goal is reached. For example, in teaching a child to swim, waiting to deliver reinforcement until the child gracefully swims across the pool would be most time-consuming and fruitless. Instead, what we do is reinforce small steps such as floating, kicking, arm movements, and so on, until the child can actually swim. As you will see, many behavior change programs utilize shaping as a major component.

Respondent Conditioning

In the early part of this century, the Russian physiologist Ivan Pavlov did his pioneering work on respondent conditioning. Most of his discoveries came from his study of the salivation responses of dogs. Later in the century, in 1927, John B. Watson and Rosalie Rayner showed how respondent conditioning affected human emotional learning. In an experiment that would be controversial today, they exposed a 9-month-old child named Albert to stimuli to which he had not shown any fear. In particular, they had Albert handle a white rat. Then on several occasions they sounded a loud noise. After a short while Albert began to fear rats and other furry objects. This experiment was a clear process of respondent conditioning. The rat initially was a neutral stimulus (NS). The loud noise was considered an unconditioned stimulus (UCS) in that it automatically produced an unconditioned response (UCR)—Albert's startled response. What Pavlov had discovered in his laboratory was that the repeated pairing of a neutral stimulus with an unconditioned stimulus produced a conditioned response (CR), thus making the formerly neutral stimulus a conditioned stimulus (CS). These findings lead to explanations about human emotional learning. Many behavior change applications you will read about in this book, especially those involving anxiety reduction and stress reduction, may be based, in part, on respondent conditioning.

In recent years, we have come to discover that the line between operant and respondent behavior is not as clear as it was originally thought to be. The roles of operant and respondent learning intertwine frequently in the control of an individual's behavior.

THE BEHAVIOR ANALYSIS PROCESS

Perhaps as important as the basic principles of behavior change are the series of steps used in problem solving by behavior change professionals. Zifferblatt and Hendricks (1974) have called these activities the *behavior analysis process*. This process is a scientific endeavor that may be used to solve personal, clinical, organizational, and societal problems. Without this empirical and scientific quality, behavior change principles would not have the impact on society they now have; with this rigorous behavior analysis process, however, behavior change principles have proven to be a significant influence on individual and societal problems.

Sequence of Steps

What is the behavior analysis process? Zifferblatt and Hendricks (1974) have noted that there is considerable controversy as to the exact components. However, we agree with them in delineating the following sequence of activities.

1. *Describe the Problem in Behavioral Terms.* This step requires that the problem be described in terms of observable, quantifiable behaviors, and not, as in other approaches, in terms of unobservable behaviors, traits, or hypothetical constructs.

2. *Conduct a Functional Analysis of the Problem.* This component consists of an analysis of both antecedents and consequences of the problem. Here the problem is viewed as part of a sequence of behaviors; that is, what is happening before and after the behavior occurs? Thus, it is important to identify both preceding and consequent behaviors as well as identifying the context or setting in which the problem is exhibited.

3. *Select the Target Behavior.* The selection of a behavior for change must be based on the functional analysis of the problem. Critical to this selection is the measurement process; the target behavior must be objectively and reliably measurable. Few human activities have been found unmeasurable. The method of measuring, or data collection, must be within the means of the behavior change professional or those involved with the problem, and it must not be too cumbersome or costly.

4. *Establish Behavioral Objectives.* Although the formulation of behavioral objectives is not always seen as a part of every behavior analysis process, we believe it to be very important. We recommend the writing of behavioral objectives because it helps to keep behavior change professionals accountable. There are many formats for writing behavioral objectives (see Houts & Scott, 1972, 1975; Thompson, 1978). We prefer the format that includes person or group, behavior, conditions, level of performance,

and date. For example: "Mary, when presented with a penny, a nickel, a dime, and a quarter will correctly identify a dime four times out of five by the end of the school year." "John, in routine daily living, will at all times participate in work and activities appropriate for his age and sex, rather than exhibit chronic pain behaviors, by the end of an eight-week hospital-based treatment program."

5. *Devise and Implement a Behavior Change Program.* Although these behavior change programs, more often than not, will involve one or more of the principles of behavior discussed, they may not always, despite the belief of many who see behavior change techniques as based purely on principles of learning. However, as many have noted (see Yates, 1970; Kazdin, 1978), the techniques of behavior change are based on principles derived from empirical research in psychology in general.

6. *Evaluate the Behavior Change Program.* The evaluation of behavior change programs is, perhaps, the cornerstone of the behavior analysis process. This evaluation usually consists of the collection of (baseline) data before the implementation of the behavior change program, the repeated collection of data during the implementation of the program, the further collection of data during other phases of an experimental design (the use of the experimental method and research designs is discussed in depth in the next chapter), and finally the collection of data at some follow-up date (for example, six months, one year) after the behavior change program has been terminated. Collection of all these data may be essential to the critical evaluation of any behavior change program. The collection of data provides the scientific basis upon which we evaluate behavior change applications. In this book we examine behavior change application to numerous individual and societal problems. Our judgment of these applications is based largely on adherence to the behavior analysis process we have outlined and upon the data this process has generated.

ACCOUNTABILITY

Aside from talk about the rising costs of goods and services, we have found that a major topic of discussion these days is accountability. It is not difficult to see the connection between rising costs and the demands that we be accountable for what we do on the job. We are living in a time when individuals are being asked to justify their actions in many segments of our society, including health and mental health care, educational systems, business and industry, and government. One way of justifying behavior is to measure the effectiveness of that behavior. Do the actions used have the desired result? It must be obvious that the *behavior analysis process* used in behavior change applications is inherently accountable. The analysis process generates data that enable anyone to judge the success or failure of a behavior change intervention. Although we have much to be proud of on this score, other issues surface in any discussion of accountability. For some of these issues, behavior change professionals have good answers; for others, solutions are still being sought.

One of the stickiest problems of accountability has to do with the selection of goals or behaviors for change. Frequently, behaviors that are a problem in one segment of our society are not seen as a problem in another. At other times, it may be difficult to determine whether a child has a problem worthy of behavior change or whether it is actually the parent, teacher, or staff who has the problem. We must ask who would benefit most from the change. Hopefully, the answer would be the child. Hawkins (1975) has discussed this issue in terms of the competencies of the behavior change professional. Obviously, if the behavior change professional is going to have a major voice in the selection of behaviors for change, then training and experience related to the behavior to be changed is imperative. For example, it would be absurd for a psychologist to make decisions about what motor behaviors should be changed in a child with cerebral palsy; such decisions should rest primarily with those who have specialized training, such as physicians or physical therapists. Another excellent discussion of goals or behaviors for change has been provided by Sulzer-Azaroff and Mayer (1977). Their concern is with goal conflicts among behavior change professionals, clients, staff or teachers, and others. Solutions to conflicts concerning behaviors to be changed may be solved through the following measures: (1) involving the client directly in the planning of behavior change programs from the beginning; (2) consulting with parents, guardians, and advocates from the beginning when children or individuals who have not been judged as competent are involved; (3) arriving at behavioral contracts through negotiation with all interested parties to alleviate many conflicts, to make explicit the costs and benefits to all parties, and to assure that participation is both voluntary and with informed consent; (4) finally, in some circumstances, forming a review committee in order to assure that the rights of individuals are protected and that proposed targets for behavior change are appropriate. This procedure is most common in institutional settings and when aversive and deprivation procedures may be used.

Related to the selection of behaviors for change are the concepts of *functional behavior change* and *social validity*. Occasionally, we have found that it is possible to change behavior only to the extent that it has minimal functional value. For example, a positive reinforcement program might be used to increase the percentage of math problems a third grader solves correctly from 50% to 57%. Although this change may be definite and replicable, few would argue that our behavior change techniques were of any use or value to this third grader. It is doubtful that his 7% increase in competence would change his life to any great extent. This question of *functional behavior change* arises in several chapters throughout this book.

Social validity (Wolf, 1978) concerns the social significance of goals or targets for behavior change. However, rather than ask whether the behavior change will prove functional or useful for the client, one must ask: (1) Is the goal or behavior change something society really wants? (2) Are the treatment procedures acceptable to the client, significant others in his or her environment, and consumers? (3) Are the consumers satisfied with all the results? Wolf and his colleagues (see Braukmann, Kirigin, & Wolf, 1976; Minkin, Braukmann, Minkin, Timbers, Timbers, Fixsen, Phillips, & Wolf, 1976) have pioneered research into the social validation of behaviors selected for change. While accountability in the choice of behaviors for change continues to be a problem for some, the approach to behavior change taken by proponents of the behavior analysis process has led the way toward increasing accountability.

We mentioned above that one element of accountability in goal selection is the competency of the behavior change professionals to make such a decision. A second accountability issue is the *competency of the behavior change professional to implement the program*. The problem has only recently begun to attract attention. Preliminary work has included the compilation of a list of some 50 behavior modification competency responses with specific accompanying criteria (Sulzer-Azaroff, Thaw, & Thomas, 1975), and a list of competencies required for the use of aversive and deprivation procedures (Grimm, Grimm, Reitz, & Thomas, 1976). An alternative to assessing the competency of behavior change agents is to use teaching or program packages that have been extensively field-tested and validated. Unfortunately, this alternative has seldom been attempted and may be beyond our present knowledge and technology. For the present, accountability of behavior change professionals may be best assured through competency-based assessment (also relatively untried).

Two final elements of accountability are assuring that behavior change is exhibited wherever appropriate and not just in a restricted setting, and that it is permanent. The former issue has to do with what is called *generalization*. Has the change in behavior generalized to settings (if appropriate) other than the one in which it was treated? In the early history of the application of behavior change principles, little attention was paid to this problem. It is difficult to know whether generalization was simply expected to occur naturally or change agents were so busy employing their new techniques that they neglected to think about generalization. Even an eloquent plea in the first issue of the *Journal of Applied Behavior Analysis* to program generalization rather than to expect it (Baer, Wolf, & Risley, 1968) went unheeded for many years. Only recently (see Stokes & Baer, 1977) have we come to a more intensive look at issues involved in training generalization. Unless we have changed behavior in all settings where necessary, we have done only part of our job as behavior change professionals. We must be accountable.

Likewise, we must reexamine previous behavior change programs. Until recently, we have not done this very often, or, if we have, the time lapse has been very short. When we have followed up our behavior change programs, we have not liked what we found (Azrin, 1978). Sometimes, initial successes have become long-term failures (see Spearing & Poppen, 1974; Kingsley & Wilson, 1977). Some of the more interesting follow-ups have been of several early, classic behavior change applications (Nedelmen & Sulzbacher, 1972; Sulzbacher & Kidder, 1975; Lovaas, Koegel, Simmons, & Long, 1973). Even here, we must say that results have been mixed. What does this mean for our use of behavior change techniques? Obviously, we must be more accountable, for if we set out to change a behavior, we usually wish to do so permanently. Thus, we need to investigate methods for assuring permanence. We (the authors) recommend a series of follow-ups with increasing time intervals between them. Whenever necessary, we (behavior change professionals) must be prepared to give "booster shots," to reapply behavior change techniques. With such an approach, we can provide the ultimate in accountability for a permanent change in behavior.

SUGGESTED READINGS

Catania, A. C. *Learning*. Englewood Cliffs, N.J.: Prentice-Hall, 1979.
Karen, R. L. *An introduction to behavior theory and its applications*. New York: Harper & Row, 1974.

Martin, G., & Pear, J. *Behavior modification: What it is and how to do it.* Englewood Cliffs, N.J.: Prentice-Hall, 1978.
Miller, L. K. *Principles of everyday behavior analysis.* Monterey, Calif.: Brooks/Cole, 1980.
Powers, R. B., & Osborne, J. G. *Fundamentals of behavior.* St. Paul: West, 1976.
Rachlin, H. *Behavior and learning.* San Francisco: Freeman, 1976.
Reynolds, G. S. *A primer of operant conditioning.* Glenview, Ill.: Scott, Foresman, 1968.
Sulzer-Azaroff, B., & Mayer, G. R. *Applying behavior-analysis procedures with children and youth.* New York: Holt, Rinehart & Winston, 1977.
Wenrich, W. W. *A primer of behavior modification.* Belmont, Calif.: Brooks/Cole, 1970.

REFERENCES

Azrin, N. *Behavioral methodology: Research design versus field testing.* Symposium paper presented at the 86th annual convention of the American Psychological Association, Toronto, 1978.
Baer, D. M., Wolf, M. M., & Risley, T. R. Some current dimensions of applied behavior analysis. *Journal of Applied Behavior Analysis,* 1968, *1,* 91–98.
Brackbill, Y. Extinction of the smiling response in infants as a function of reinforcement schedule. *Child Development,* 1958, *29,* 115–124.
Braukmann, C. J., Kirigin, K. A., & Wolf, M. M. *Achievement place: The researcher's perspective.* Paper presented at the 84th annual convention of the American Psychological Association, Washington, D.C., 1976.
Burgess, R. L., Clark, R. N., & Handee, J. C. An experimental analysis of anti-litter procedures. *Journal of Applied Behavior Analysis,* 1971, *4,* 71–76.
Deitz, S. M., & Repp, A. C. Decreasing classroom misbehavior through the use of DRL schedules of reinforcement. *Journal of Applied Behavior Analysis,* 1973, *6,* 457–463.
Foxx, R. M., & Azrin, N. H. Restitution: A method of eliminating aggressive-disruptive behavior of retarded and brain-damaged patients. *Behaviour Research and Therapy,* 1972, *10,* 15–27.
Grimm, J. A., Grimm, B. J., Reitz, A., & Thomas, D. R. *How to tell the good guys from the bad guys.* Paper presented at the Minnesota Association for Behavior Analysis Convention, Plymouth, Minn., 1976.
Harris, F. R., Johnston, M. K., Kelley, C. S., & Wolf, M. M. Effects of positive social reinforcement on regressed crawling of a nursery school child. *Journal of Educational Psychology,* 1964, *55,* 35–41.
Hawkins, R. P. Who decided that was the problem? Two stages of responsibility for applied behavior analysts. In W. S. Wood (Ed.), *Issues in evaluating behavior modification.* Champaign, Ill.: Research Press, 1975.
Houts, P. S., & Scott, R. A. Goal planning in mental health rehabilitation. Unpublished manuscript, Pennsylvania State University College of Medicine, 1972.
Houts, P. S., & Scott, R. A. Goal planning with developmentally disabled persons. Unpublished manuscript, Pennsylvania State University College of Medicine, 1975.
Iwata, B. A., & Lorentzson, A. M. Operant control of a seizure-like behavior in an institutionalized retarded adult. *Behavior Therapy,* 1976, *7,* 247–251.
Kazdin, A. *History of behavior modification: Experimental foundations of contemporary research.* Baltimore: University Park Press, 1978.
Kingsley, R. G., & Wilson, G. T. Behavior therapy for obesity: A comparative investigation of long-term efficacy. *Journal of Consulting and Clinical Psychology,* 1977, *45,* 288–298.
Lovaas, O. I., Koegel, R., Simmons, J. O., & Long, J. S. Some generalizations and follow-up measures on autistic children in behavior therapy. *Journal of Applied Behavior Analysis,* 1973, *6,* 131–165.

Lutzker, J. R. Social reinforcement control of exhibitionism in a profoundly retarded adult. *Mental Retardation,* 1974, *12,* 46–47.

Minkin, N., Braukmann, C. J., Minkin, B. L., Timbers, G. D., Timbers, B. J., Fixsen, D. L., Phillips, E. L., & Wolf, M. M. The social validation and training of conversational skills. *Journal of Applied Behavior Analysis,* 1976, *9,* 127–139.

Mowrer, O. H., & Mowrer, W. M. Enuresis: A method for its study and treatment. *American Journal of Orthopsychiatry,* 1938, *8,* 436–459.

Nedelman, D., & Sulzbacher, S. I. Dicky at 13 years of age: A long-term success following early application of operant conditioning procedures. In G. Semb (Ed.), *Behavior analysis and education—1972.* Lawrence, Kansas: University of Kansas, 1972.

Solnick, J. V., Rincover, A., & Peterson, C. P. Some determinants of the reinforcing and punishing effects of timeout. *Journal of Applied Behavior Analysis,* 1977, *10,* 415–424.

Spearing, D., & Poppen, R. The use of feedback in the reduction of foot-dragging in a cerebral palsied client. *Journal of Nervous and Mental Disease,* 1974, *159,* 148–151.

Stokes, T. F., & Baer, D. M. An implicit technology of generalization. *Journal of Applied Behavior Analysis,* 1977, *10,* 349–367.

Sulzbacher, S. I., & Kidder, J. D. Following up on the behavior analysis model: Results after ten years of early intervention with institutionalized, mentally retarded children. In E. Ramp & G. Semb (Eds.), *Behavior analysis: Areas of research and application.* Englewood Cliffs, N.J.: Prentice-Hall, 1975.

Sulzer-Azaroff, B., & Mayer, G. R. *Applying behavior-analysis procedures with children and youth.* New York: Holt, Rinehart & Winston, 1977.

Sulzer-Azaroff, B., Thaw, J., & Thomas, C. Behavioral competencies for the evaluation of behavior modifiers. In W. Scott Wood (Ed.), *Issues in evaluation in behavior modification.* Champaign, Ill.: Research Press, 1975.

Thompson, D. G. *Writing long-term and short-term objectives.* Champaign, Ill.: Research Press, 1978.

Ullmann, L. P., & Krasner, L. *A psychological approach to abnormal behavior* (2nd ed.). Englewood Cliffs, N.J.: Prentice-Hall, 1975.

Wolf, M. M. Social validity: The case for subjective measurement or how applied behavior analysis is finding its heart. *Journal of Applied Behavior Analysis,* 1978, *11,* 203–214.

Wolf, M. M., Risley, T. R., & Mees, H. Application of operant conditioning procedures to the behavior problems of an autistic child. *Behaviour Research and Therapy,* 1964, *1,* 305–312.

Yates, A. J. *Behavior therapy.* New York: Wiley, 1970.

Zifferblatt, S. M., & Hendricks, C. G. Applied behavioral analysis of societal problems: Population change, a case in point. *American Psychologist,* 1974, *29,* 750–761.

CHAPTER 2

Assessment and Evaluation

THIS chapter is devoted to two elements of behavior change applications that cannot be overemphasized: assessment and evaluation. In the first part of the chapter we look at how to determine whether there is a problem, whether it should be changed, and, if so, how it should be changed. In the last half of the chapter, we describe a number of ways to evaluate the success or failure of our behavior change programs.

ASSESSMENT

Numerous books are devoted to behavioral assessment (Hersen & Bellack, 1976; Ciminero, Calhoun, & Adams, 1977; Haynes, 1978; Cone & Hawkins, 1977), and two recent journals, *Behavioral Assessment* and the *Journal of Behavioral Assessment,* are concerned with this issue. Behavioral assessment of clinical problems currently receives much attention. Unfortunately, the same cannot be said of some of the nonclinical behavior applications covered in this book. We will, however, suggest a tentative strategy to follow when faced with nonclinical problems (and we believe it to be equally useful for clinical problems). Then we will focus on procedures involved in a thorough behavioral assessment of clinical problems. You will find that we are in agreement with psychologists who advocate a comprehensive behavioral assessment, rather than one limited to certain dimensions or domains. Behavioral assessment should draw heavily upon any aspect of psychology which has contributed to the problem area under study (Craighead, Kazdin, & Mahoney, 1976).

What is the purpose of behavioral assessment, and what is it? Actually, there are two major aspects: to determine the exact nature of a problem and to determine potentially useful strategies for altering that problem. Some writers (Ciminero, 1977) have considered evaluation of behavior change techniques as the third function of assessment, but we have chosen to view it separately. Our model for behavioral assessment of nonclinical problems (such as energy consumption by homeowners and absenteeism of industrial workers) is based upon recent attempts to intersect behavior change technology and ecology (Willems, 1974; Baer, 1974; Rogers-Warren & Warren, 1977; Lutzker, 1980). Table 2-1 is an outline, based upon the work of Ann Rogers-Warren (1977), of a set of guidelines to be used in assessing environments (behavior settings) when planning change.

Identification of the target behavior to be changed should consist of a precise, but comprehensive, behavioral definition that includes its topography (that is, what it looks like). An assessment of the behavior's function in the environment(s) where it is to be exhibited should also be conducted. Such an assessment may be useful when programming for response generalization and long-term maintenance of behavior change. Assessment of the physical setting should be made specifically with regard to the behavior to be changed. This would include persons present and how they are relevant to the behavior (for example, potential reinforcers). The physical properties (for example, room design, materials available, scheduling of activities, furniture) and their relation to the behavior should be examined. The physical setting should be examined in terms of stimulus control. Do certain physical components of the environment function as cues for the behavior to be changed? For

TABLE 2-1.

1. Identify the behavior to be changed.

2. Assess the environment (physical setting).
   A. What people are present in the physical setting?
   B. What are the important physical aspects of the environment?
   C. What are the antecedent stimuli (physical cues) for the behavior to be changed?

3. Assess the contingency environment.
   A. What are the consequences for the target behavior?
   B. Consider existing contingencies.

4. Determine what limitations the environment places on a behavior change application.

5. Are there environmental arrangements that might facilitate the behavior change?

example, Newkirk, Feldman, Bickett, Gipson, and Lutzker (1976) found that nursing home residents were more likely to attend activity sessions when the activities were held in a centralized location in the home.

Assessment should next proceed to an examination of the consequences of the behavior to be changed. Consequences should be functionally analyzed as to whether they are positive, negative, or neutral. At times there may be existing relationships in an environment which will overlap any behavior change program. These need to be assessed to determine whether they will in some way hinder the success of a behavior change program. For example, the mother-father relationship may be critical to the success of a behavior change program for one of their children. In a similar vein, all too often ignored is an assessment of constraints that a physical setting might apply to a behavior change intervention. Examples would be inability to control possible competing reinforcers or punishers, untrained or uncooperative persons, and arrangement of the physical setting. For example, a bedroom full of distracting stimuli such as a television, a record player, magazines, and so on, would undoubtedly be a poor recommendation for a place to study. Finally, one should determine whether there are environmental arrangements that might aid behavioral intervention. These arrangements might include emphasizing certain parts of the physical setting or merely altering existing contingencies of reinforcement. Behavior change programs that are more dependent upon rearrangement of the existing physical setting are probably more likely to support and maintain behavior change than are programs to which artificial ingredients (reinforcers, discriminative stimuli) have to be added.

While this approach to behavioral assessment comes from an attempt to synthesize behavioral technology and ecology (Rogers-Warren, 1977), we believe that it certainly has value as a guideline for the behavioral assessment of clinical as well as nonclinical problems.

In the next section of the chapter, we describe in considerable detail some of the procedures involved in behavioral assessment of clinical problems. As long as there is some disagreement about the scope and domain of such an assessment, we prefer to err on the side of too much information. Rather than restricting behavioral assessment to observable behavior, it may frequently be necessary to gather information from three separate channels (Lang, 1968, 1971; Cautela, 1968;

Hersen, 1976). The channels are motoric (for example, the actions or movements of a person), physiological (for example, a person's heart rate, blood pressure, and so on), and cognitive (for example, what a person thinks or says to himself). In behavioral assessment, causative, maintaining, and correlated variables should be exhaustively explored, for frequently the failure of behavior change programs may be due to inadequate or inaccurate assessment (Haynes, 1978).

One method of conceptualizing the information to be gathered during a behavioral assessment is the "SORC" model (Goldfried & Sprafkin, 1976). This is quite similar to the functional analysis of behavior approach (Peterson, 1968) or sequence analysis (Reese, Howard, & Reese, 1977). Situational antecedents ("S") of the behavior to be changed are evaluated. This involves a detailed analysis of the context (for example, time, location, people present, and so on) of the problem behavior. Such information can be useful to both a total assessment and to the planning of a behavior change program (Goldfried, 1977). Thus, it is critical to know about the settings and situations in which the behavior occurs. Organismic ("O") variables include a person's physiological makeup. Much of the general information a physician might obtain from a patient during an office visit might prove valuable to an overall behavioral assessment. Thus, dependent upon the problem behavior, a variable amount of this kind of information will be obtained (in fact, with some problems to be discussed in Chapters 5 and 6, it is frequently essential to have clients examined by physicians). Examples of the need for this component are determining whether an obese client for whom you were devising an exercise program had a cardiac problem, and discovering whether a child for whom you would like to use an edible reinforcement program had diabetes. In sum, physiological variables can have an important influence on behavior; thus, they must be assessed. The assessment of the problem behavior or *response* ("R") can be done in many ways that are discussed later in this chapter. Obviously, one may be able to assess only a *sample* of the problem behavior; however, we have a number of ways to make such an assessment with some reliability. Finally, in behavioral assessment, we want to look at the *consequences* ("C") of the problem behavior. Because many behavior change techniques are based upon operant conditioning principles, this assessment is extremely important. Like the assessment of antecedents, the assessment of consequences frequently leads directly to a plan for behavior change.

The "SORC" model for behavioral assessment differs from the others in the inclusion of "O" or organismic assessment. We believe that this can be an extremely important addition to the assessment of many clinical problems. Given that one is faced with a clinical problem and wishes to do a behavioral assessment and gather information about antecedents, organismic variables, the problem behavior, and consequences, how does one proceed? Although it was written some time ago, Kanfer and Saslow's (1969) strategy for behavioral assessment is the most comprehensive. An outline based on their approach is provided in Table 2-2.

It is obvious that, should a behavior change professional be able to gather all of the information asked for in Table 2-2, he or she would be extremely well prepared to plan a behavior change program. Not all of the information need be

TABLE 2-2.

1. *Preliminary Analysis of the Clinical Problem*
   A. Identification of behavioral excesses.
   B. Identification of behavioral deficits.
   C. Identification of behavioral assets.

2. *Clarification of the Clinical Problem*
   A. Who views the problem as objectionable?
   B. What are the consequences of the problem for the client and others?
   C. What would the consequences be for the client and others if the problem were altered?
   D. What are the antecedent conditions of the clinical problem?
   E. Would the client have *new* problems in living if the clinical problem were removed?
   F. Is the client able to help in the development of a behavior change program?
   G. What would the client and others *gain* if the problem behavior were changed?

3. *Analysis of Reinforcers*
   A. What kinds of reinforcers (for example, money, recognition, friendship, and so on) are most effective in initiating and controlling behavior?
   B. What has the client's experience been with each of these reinforcers?
   C. What groups or individuals exert the most control over the client?
   D. Does the client understand reinforcement contingencies?
   E. What are the client's major aversive stimuli?
   F. Would a treatment program require that the client *give up* current reinforcers associated with his problem?

4. *Developmental or Maturational Analysis*
   A. Biological Changes
      1. Does the client have biological limitations that may affect his problem behavior?
      2. When and how did these biological limitations or deviations develop?
      3. How would these limitations or deviations limit treatment?

   B. Sociological Changes
      1. Describe the client's present sociocultural milieu (for example, rural-urban, socioeconomic status, ethnic group, education, and so on).
      2. Are his attitudes and behavior congruent with his milieu?
      3. Have there been in his milieu any changes that might relate to his problem behavior?
      4. How does the client view the *cause* of these changes?
      5. Are the client's roles or functions different in different social settings?
      6. Can sociological factors be altered, if necessary, in a behavior change program?

   C. Behavioral Changes
      1. Before the onset of the current problem, did the client exhibit any deviations in behavior as compared to normal?
      2. Are there biological or sociological events which can be related to these deviations?
      3. What were the antecedent conditions for these deviations?
      4. Can the onset of these other problem behaviors be traced to a *model* in the client's environment?

5. *Self-Control Analysis*
   A. Are there any situations in which the client can control his problem behavior?
   B. What are those situations and how does he control his behavior?
   C. Have any problem behaviors been followed by aversive events and have these altered the frequency?
   D. Does the client's perception of his self-control correspond with observations by others?
   E. Can the patient's self-controlling behavior be used in a behavior change program?

6. *Analysis of Interpersonal Relationships*
   A. Who are the significant others for the client?
   B. Do certain people or groups facilitate problem behavior?
   C. What reinforcers can be identified in the client's close social relationships?
   D. What does the patient expect of his significant others?
   E. What do these people expect of the patient?
   F. Can those people who influence the patient participate in his behavior change program?

7. *Analysis of the Social-Cultural-Physical Environment*
   A. How does the client's behavior compare to the norms for this behavior in his social milieu?
   B. Are the norms for this behavior the same in the various environments (for example, home, work, school) in which the client participates?
   C. Are there in the client's environment limitations (for example, social, physical, economic, and so on) that limit his reinforcers?
   D. In which section of his environment is the client's problem behavior most obvious, most bothersome, or most accepted?
   E. Does the client's milieu approve of or permit self-evaluation?
   F. Does the client's milieu regard psychological intervention as appropriate for helping him solve his problem?
   G. Is there support in the client's milieu for changes in attitudes and values that might be required for successful intervention?

---

collected on every client and with every problem; Kanfer and Saslow (1969) have, rather, provided an *ideal* strategy for behavioral assessment, a strategy that need only be approximated. We cannot overstate the importance they place upon individuals in the client's milieu. Unfortunately, until recently, behavior change professionals have frequently ignored Kanfer and Saslow's emphasis on assessing these variables. As a result, we have struggled with the problems of generalization and long-term maintenance of behavior change (see Stokes & Baer, 1977). Too often in our behavioral assessment, we exhibit tunnel vision and focus on our client without proper regard to his or her functioning in the broader social, cultural, and physical milieu. We are pleased to note that the new series of books on behavioral assessment unanimously support thorough behavioral assessment and that other recent behavior change books (see Sulzer-Azaroff & Mayer, 1977) have addressed the practical issue of evaluating whether the client's milieu will be supportive of a behavior change program.

Methods of Behavioral Assessment

You now should have a fairly good idea of the kinds of information we think important to a behavioral assessment of a clinical problem. How does one collect all of this information? A number of different methods have been developed and all or some of them may be used in assessing any single problem. Basic to most behavioral assessment is the *interview*. Information of this type might be obtained directly from the client, from his family, from his friends, from teachers, and from other significant figures in his life. For the interested student, Linehan (1977) and Morganstern (1976) have written excellent descriptions of behavioral interviewing.

The *direct observation* of the client's behavior in the natural environment is a quite common (and perhaps most valuable) means of behavioral assessment. Much has been written about methods of direct observation (see Wildman & Erickson, 1977; Kent & Foster, 1977). Suffice it to say that a variety of procedures is available to enable behavior change agents to reliably assess (record) behavior in natural settings. This is not to say there are not problems such as reactivity (changes in behavior as a function of being observed) and observer bias; however, a discussion of these issues is beyond the scope of this book. The interested reader is referred to any of the excellent texts on behavioral assessment mentioned earlier in the chapter.

At times, direct observation of the client's behavior in natural settings may not be feasible. In these situations *analogue methods* may be used. These are techniques that simulate the "real world" in the behavior change professional's office or setting. These may be "structured" where the client is instructed to do something very specific, such as for a mother to play "crazy eights" with her noncompliant child, or "unstructured" where a mother may be instructed merely to play with her noncompliant child in any way she chooses. While somewhat less satisfactory than direct observation in the natural environment, extremely useful information can be gathered this way. Students with an interest in analogue measures might wish to examine reviews by McFall (1977) and Nay (1977).

For some problem behaviors, *physiological assessment* (for example, blood pressure, heart rate, skin temperature) may be useful. This is particularly true of the health-related behaviors discussed in Chapters 5 and 6. Physiological assessment is likewise important in the treatment of anxiety and fears, as you will learn in Chapter 11.

Standardized tests of intelligence, achievement, and personality are not frequently used as a part of a behavioral assessment. However, we have found them to be particularly useful at times in working with children and with certain adult problems such as chronic pain and depression. More frequently used are *checklists or questionnaires*. With handicapped children or adults these might be any of a number of developmental or behavioral checklists (see Walls, Werner, Bacon, & Zane, 1977), while with adults, checklists might be used to assess possible reinforcers (see Cautela & Kastenbaum, 1967). Questionnaires have been used to assess such things as assertiveness (Rathus, 1973), depression (Beck, 1967), and marital adjustment (Locke & Wallace, 1959). Haynes (1978) has written a very useful discussion of questionnaires, while Walls et al. (1977) have contributed a comprehensive evaluation of available checklists. One final method of behavioral assessment is self-monitoring (Watson & Tharp, 1977). We can ask our clients to observe and record their own behavior. Obviously, there are problems with the accuracy of this technique (it should be noted that sometimes behavior will change *merely by asking the clients to self-monitor their own behavior*). Much has been written about problems of self-monitoring and possible solutions (see Mahoney, 1977; Bellack & Schwartz, 1976). In sum, we are of the opinion that self-monitoring can be useful as a part of a behavioral assessment, but we would not want to rely on it alone.

We have presented seven different methods for collecting information as a part of a behavioral assessment. With such comprehensive information, one should be able to design and implement a behavior change program. We next turn to methods for evaluating our behavior change programs. Evaluation through the use of research designs is a critical component of the behavior change approach presented throughout this book. In our presentation and evaluation of behavior change applications throughout the remainder of this book, we will be looking for the presence of data based on scientific evaluation to substantiate the effectiveness of the various procedures. Thus, knowledge of these fairly simple research designs is critical to your understanding of this process.

EVALUATION

Observational Recording. We have mentioned that in order to proceed with the behavior change process that which we want to be changed must be measured or recorded. How is this done? First, behavior is *operationally defined.* This means that we describe the target behavior (the behavior selected for change) in measurable components. For example, instead of saying that we want to modify young Roland's bad temper, we would say that we want to reduce the number of tantrums Roland has per day. A tantrum may further be defined as crying, thrusting arms and legs, and screaming for any period of three continuous seconds or more.

After target behavior has been operationally defined, there are several ways that it can be measured. One easy way is *event recording.* This simply means that we count each occurrence of the behavior. In the case of Roland's tantrums, we might have his mother mark on a piece of paper or chart every time he throws a tantrum according to the operational definition.

Permanent product is another fairly simple strategy of observational recording. For example, in several of the litter control studies reviewed in Chapter 3, the amount of litter placed somewhere or gathered was actually weighed. Another example of permanent product would be to have an agoraphobic (someone who does not like leaving home) present the therapist with a theater receipt, thereby verifying newly developed freedom from the phobia.

One of the most commonly used methods of observational recording is *interval recording.* With interval recording, a specific amount of time, say, 30 minutes of a math class, is divided into smaller intervals, such as 30 seconds. Thus, there would be 60 30-second intervals during the observation time in math class. One or two observers would then continuously observe behavior throughout this period. The observer(s) might record in one of two ways. The first way is occurrence/nonoccurrence recording whereby once the target behavior is recorded within the interval, no further recordings are made during that interval. The other way is to record the frequency (event) of the behavior within each interval. This, of course, means constant recording throughout the entire interval. While interval recording has the disadvantage of requiring constant observer attention, it offers the advantage of quite accurate measures that can be readily compared between or among observers, a process we call *reliability.*

Time sampling is an excellent observational technique for recording behavior over a long period during the day. With time sampling, observers note the occurrence or nonoccurrence of a behavior only at the end of a specific interval. For example, in Chapter 9 we discuss the case of an institutionalized man who exposed himself many times a day. The staff was instructed to observe whether or not the man was exposing himself at the end of 10-minute intervals throughout six hours of the day. Thus, while a considerable amount of data were collected each day, comparatively little staff time was taken up in observational recording.

Occasionally, we might want to know most about the temporal aspects of a behavior. In this case, we use *duration recording* as our technique. An example of duration recording might be how long a child stays on a two-wheel bike before falling or how much time a previously impotent man can maintain an erection. One of the best summaries of observational recording methods is provided by Miller (1980).

Reliability is another important concept in the evaluation of behavior change programs. Reliability recording symbolizes the behavior change professional's dedication to accountability. Very briefly, reliability consists of the amount of agreement between two or more observers on the behavior being recorded. The importance of high reliability figures (calculated in a variety of ways) is the demonstration that the results of the measurement process are not the potentially biased view of one individual. Good reliability figures indicate that we can have some trust that the data reflect what did occur according to the operational definitions. This belief in reliability in no way implies a personal, ethical, or moral indictment against a single observer. It reflects a mistrust of the ability of any one individual not to be unintentionally influenced by a host of variables that might cause mistakes. Many researchers have actually focused their interests on the study of reliability of observations and have found that even two observers, recording behavior independently (without information as to what the other observer is recording), are subject to a variety of environmental influences that affect the veracity of their records. This kind of research is exemplary of the constant rigor applied to the science of behavior change and has led to recommendations on how other researchers can achieve even more accurate behavioral measures.

RESEARCH DESIGN

Another critical feature of the behavior change strategy is the proper evaluation of procedures to assure us that our treatment or environmental manipulation was truly responsible for the change we observe. Probably the most common strategy for such an evaluation is something we call a *reversal design*.

Almost all behavioral research and evaluation strategies begin with a baseline period. This means that data are gathered on the target behavior for a period of time with no treatment in effect. The use of baseline measures is critical for the determination as to whether measurable change has occurred. The baseline data are usually gathered until they show stability; that means that they are not clearly ascending or descending. Let's say that we have operationally defined verbal contributions in the classes of a shy college student, Margie, and somehow we are able to place observers in all of Margie's classes. The hypothetical data in Figure 2-1 show that without treatment, over time, Margie's verbal classroom contributions seem to be increasing; thus, it would be inappropriate for us to offer any treatment or training to Margie at this time. On the other hand, the data in Figure 2-2 show that the frequency of Margie's classroom contributions seems to be going down. We had better wait to see whether this may be due to some extraneous variables (for example, she might have laryngitis) before we begin a treatment phase. The data in Figure 2-3 are relatively stable; that is, they show no particular trend up or down, but do show that Margie is a relatively infrequent classroom participant. By the way, we often label baseline conditions "A."

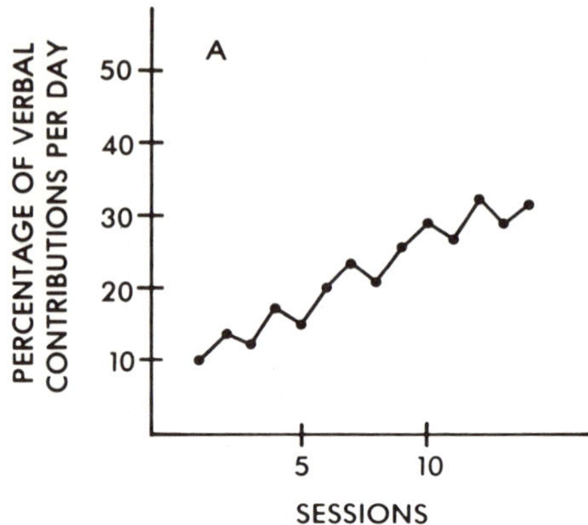

FIGURE 2-1.   The rate of Margie's verbalizations in class is going up.

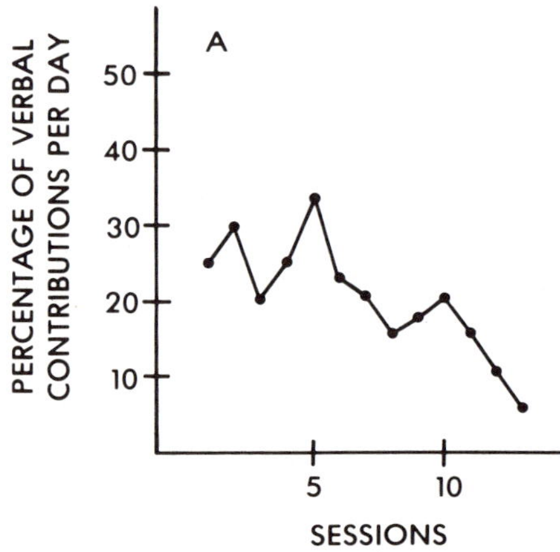

FIGURE 2-2.   The rate of Margie's verbalizations in class appears to be going down.

Since Margie has said that she wants to become a more frequent classroom participant, let's say that we have developed a treatment plan whereby she role-plays speaking in class with two dormitory friends. Whenever she does make a classroom contribution she gives herself ten points in a little notebook. For every fifty points she earns in this simple token economy, she selects from a variety of self-administered privileges and "goodies" that she is using as token "back-ups" such as a movie, a walk in the park, and a long-distance phone call. Figure 2-4 shows that our treatment of practice and a token reinforcement program appears to have been quite effective in increasing the frequency of Margie's classroom

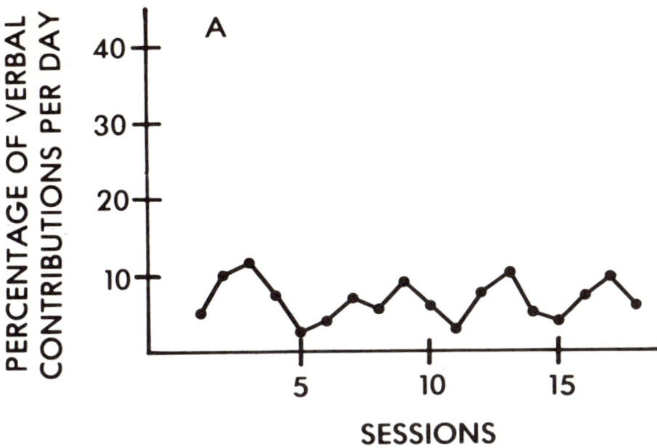

FIGURE 2-3. The baseline rate of Margie's verbalizations in class appears stable.

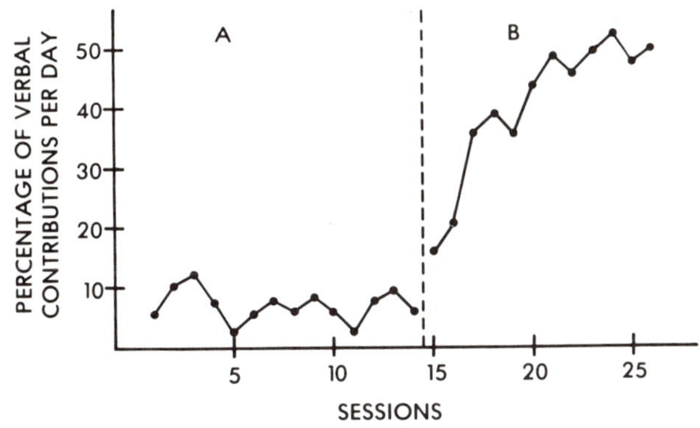

FIGURE 2-4. Between baseline (A) and treatment (B) there is a clear increase in the rate of Margie's verbalizations in class.

contributions. We frequently label the treatment condition "B." Thus, a design which utilizes only one baseline and one treatment condition is called an "AB" design.

Early in the history of behavior modification we were often satisfied to accept AB designs as evidence that behavioral treatment programs were responsible for some dramatic changes in behavior. But it is always possible that some important event in the life of the subject associated in time with our treatment was responsible for the behavior change and not our treatment at all. Perhaps when we introduced practice in speaking in class and the token program to Margie, she also got a new boyfriend. Further, her boyfriend improved her self-image so much that she began speaking more frequently in class. How can we determine whether Margie's behavior change resulted from our treatment or some other variables? Take the treatment back out for a while. Reverse—or withdraw, as Hersen and Barlow (1977) have said—the situation to the baseline conditions. If the behavior then returns to a rate similar to what it was during baseline, then we have much stronger evidence that it was our treatment that was responsible for the change. Of course, we never want to leave our subject back at baseline ("ABA"), so we reintroduce our treatment program. If the behavior returns to a desirable level, we have all the more strengthened our demonstration of its effectiveness and left much less to speculate about what caused the change. Figure 2-5 shows this happy state of affairs for Margie. (This would be called an "ABAB" design.) It also shows that follow-up data were taken six weeks and three months after the end of formal treatment. We find that Margie is still participating in class at a rate greater than during either baseline phase. In fact, since this kind of behavior change often comes under the control of "natural" contingencies such as the satisfaction of no longer being shy and some positive feedback to Margie from her professors, before the formal termination of treatment we would have programmed for it to be faded out. First, we would have suggested gradually fewer practice sessions until they were no longer necessary. Then we would have had Margie change the token system until it was gradually faded out.

There are variations in reversal designs, many examples of which you will find throughout this book. We will briefly mention two of them here. First, while we also call a reversal design a form of "single-subject" design (utilizing only one subject such as Margie), single-subject design logic is often applied to grouped data. That is, baseline data are gathered on more than one subject and averaged; treatment (the same treatment) is applied to all members of the group (individually or as a group); then there is a return to baseline, a return to treatment, and a follow-up.

The other variation that deserves some attention here is *component analysis,* or breaking down a treatment "package" into its parts to see whether one component

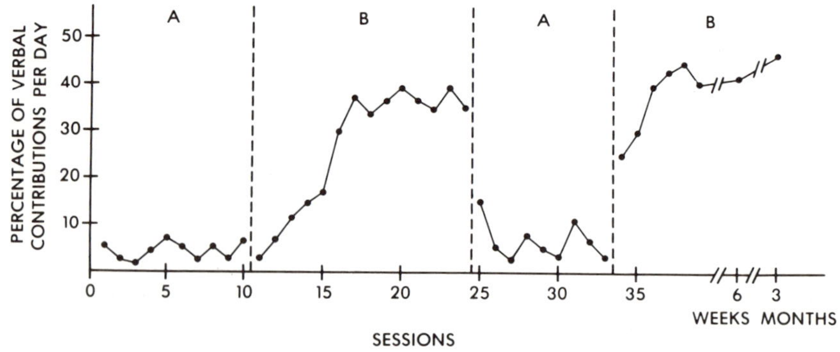

FIGURE 2-5.   It is clear that the treatment program (B) is responsible for the increases in Margie's rates of verbalizing in classes.

is more effective than another. In Margie's treatment, for example, there were really two components, practice and reinforcement. To do a component analysis, we might have done "ABA," then "C," which might have been practice without reinforcement, then back to "A" then to "D," which would have been reinforcement for speaking in class, but no practice. This analysis could have any number of results. We might discover that both components alone are relatively equally effective, that neither stands well alone, or that one component is more effective than the other. Although component analyses can yield some valuable information, they can be time-consuming and still leave unanswered questions about, for example, the effects of sequence. That is, once you break a "package" into components, one component must precede another, thus creating a particular sequence of events. It may be possible that *the sequence itself* is responsible for the observed behavior changes. There are actually ways to control for this phenomenon, too, but they are beyond the scope of this discussion.

Multiple baseline designs are another very commonly used strategy in single-subject research. The special advantage of the multiple baseline design is that it usually does not require any reversal condition, but it does, nonetheless, still manage to demonstrate experimental control. As with the reversal design, the multiple baseline design helps eliminate extraneous variables as possible explanations for successful behavior change.

The three most common kinds of multiple baseline designs were first described in one classic report by R. Vance Hall, Connie Cristler, Sharon Cranston, and Bonnie Tucker (1970) of the University of Kansas. In the first of three experiments, these researchers modified the tardiness from lunch and morning and afternoon recess of children in a fifth grade classroom. The data in Figure 2-6, which also show a brief reversal period, show that whenever a chart (called the Patriots' chart, which listed the names of punctual students) was introduced, punctuality improved. As you can see in Figure 2-6, the multiple baseline shows its effect by staggering the introduction of treatment over time. The treatment is not introduced in one setting until some change has occurred in the other setting. The data from the noon break and the two recesses show clearly that the Patriots chart was responsible for the change. This is an example of a multiple baseline across settings.

In the second experiment, we see a demonstration of a multiple baseline design across subjects wherein treatment is introduced in each successive subject as each subject shows stabilized improvement. Figure 2-7 shows that being required to stay after school for poor performance on French quizzes was a successful treatment in improving the performance of three tenth-grade students.

The third multiple baseline design is across behaviors. In Figure 2-8 we see that three home chores of a ten-year-old girl were sequentially modified when an early bedtime contingency was imposed for failure to spend the criterion amount of time on the activities: clarinet practice, her Campfire project, and reading.

As with the reversal design, multiple baseline logic can be applied to grouped data representing any number of individuals. It is a widely popular design within the behavior change field because of the advantages we have mentioned here and its demonstrated utility.

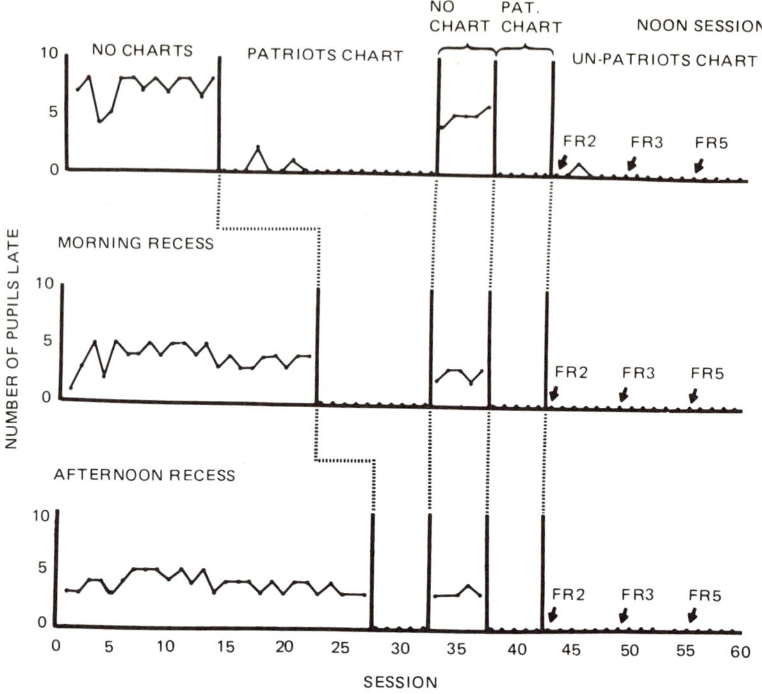

FIGURE 2-6.   A multiple baseline design across settings. A record of the number of pupils late in returning to their fifth grade classroom after noon, morning, and afternoon recess. *No Charts:* baseline, before experimental procedures. *Patriots' Chart:* posting of pupils' names on "Today's Patriots" chart contingent on entering class on time after recess. *No Chart:* posting of names discontinued. *Patriots' Chart:* return to Patriots' chart conditions. *Un-Patriots' Chart:* posting of names on "Un-Patriots'" chart contingent on being late after recess (FR2) every two days, (FR3) every three days, and (FR5) every five days. (From "Teachers and Parents as Researchers Using Multiple Baseline Designs," by R. V. Hall, C. Cristler, S. S. Cranston, and B. Tucker, *Journal of Applied Behavior Analysis*, 1970, 3, 247–255. Copyright 1970 by the Society for the Experimental Analysis of Behavior, Inc. Reprinted by permission.)

Two other experimental designs, examples of which are cited in other chapters, deserve our brief attention. Sometimes it is not practical or possible to repeat baseline or treatment conditions successively over days. Also, sometimes we might want to evaluate several treatment components that, as we mentioned, can pose questions of experimental confounds because of sequence. The *multielement baseline* design handles these problems well. In this design, a different treatment or baseline is offered each session or within sessions. For example, Martin (1977) wanted to know which of three kinds of feedback (ignore, reprimand, or praise)

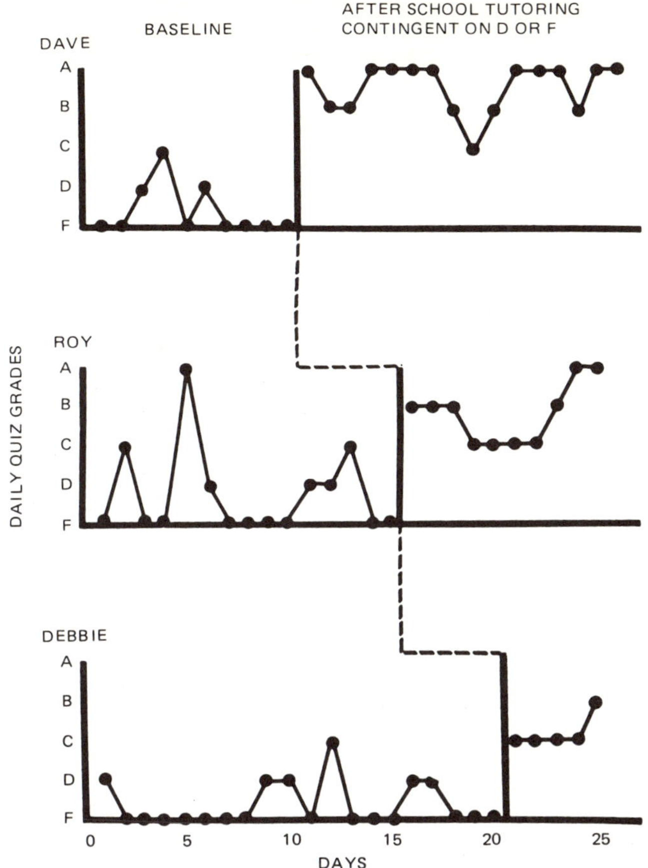

FIGURE 2-7.   A multiple baseline design across subjects. A record of quiz score grades for three high school French class students. *Baseline:* before experimental procedures. *After-School Tutoring Contingent on "D" and "F" Grades:* pupils required to stay after school for tutoring if they score "D" or "F" on daily quizzes. (From "Teachers and Parents as Researchers Using Multiple Baseline Designs," by R. V. Hall, C. Cristler, S. S. Cranston, and B. Tucker, *Journal of Applied Behavior Analysis,* 1970, 3, 247–255. Copyright 1970 by the Society for the Experimental Analysis of Behavior, Inc. Reprinted by permission.)

children preferred and which caused them to work at the highest rate when working on simple tasks. In daily sessions, children received all three kinds of feedback. The data were graphed according to each form of feedback so that any obvious trends would surface. As you can see from Figure 2-9, the children worked harder whenever they were reprimanded; however, it turned out that they never chose a task for which they had been reprimanded, a rather clear expression of preference. Martin (1978) has also pointed out the clinical utility of multielement baseline

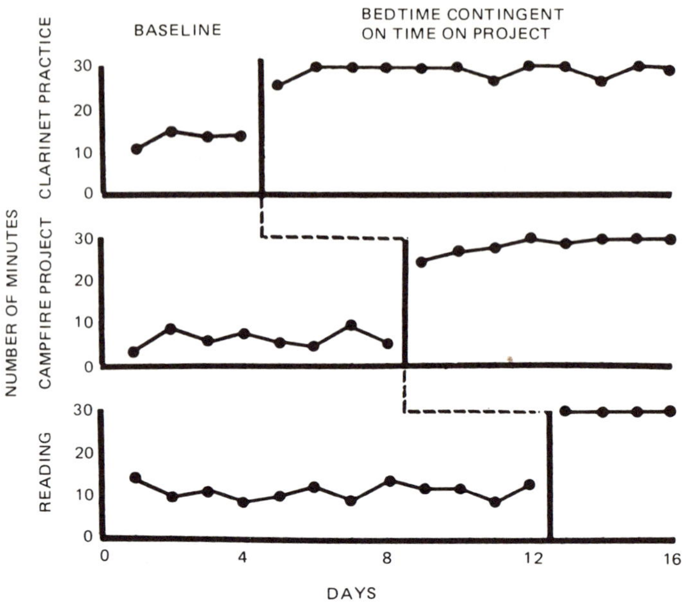

FIGURE 2-8.   A multiple baseline design across responses. A record of time spent in clarinet practice, Campfire honors project work, and reading for book reports by a 10-year-old girl. *Baseline:* before experimental procedures. *Early Bedtime Contingent on Less Than 30 Min. of Behavior:* 1 minute earlier bedtime for each minute less than 30 engaged in an activity. (From "Teachers and Parents as Researchers Using Multiple Baseline Designs," by R. V. Hall, C. Cristler, S. S. Cranston, and B. Tucker, *Journal of Applied Behavior Analysis,* 1970, *3,* 247–255. Copyright 1970 by the Society for the Experimental Analysis of Behavior, Inc. Reprinted by permission.)

designs. He has used it to determine which reinforcers will be the most effective in a clinical intervention with children.

Of course, if you have had any exposure to statistics or experimental psychology, you are familiar with group designs. Any number of books can give you a solid background in group design. Our purpose in mentioning them here is to be sure that you understand the concept of a control group.

Let us say that on the basis of several case studies we are pretty sure that we can produce a significant weight loss in normal adults by one intense one-hour session using a variety of behavioral techniques. Let us say that we call this treatment Behavioral Rapid Weight Loss (BRWL). To demonstrate its effectiveness, we would offer BRWL to 50 people. But how do we know BRWL is responsible for weight loss? Maybe any approach taking an hour's time is equally effective. Maybe one hour of nondirective counseling is just as effective. Further, maybe time alone helps people lose weight. In order to test these notions, we would put 50 people who are matched as well as possible on the basis of demographics such as age, race,

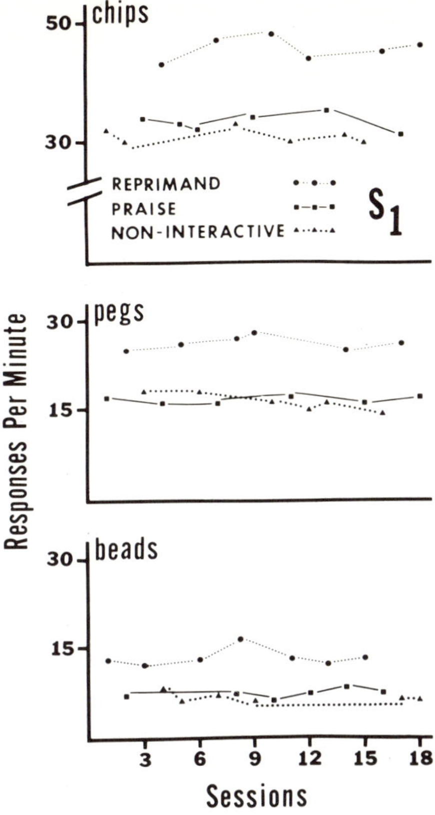

FIGURE 2-9.   An example of a multielement baseline design. Responses per minute for subject 1 on each of the tasks across sections. *Circles:* sessions when tasks were associated with verbal reprimands. *Squares:* sessions when tasks were associated with verbal praise. *Triangles:* sessions when tasks were associated with a noninteractive adult. (From "Effects of Positive and Negative Adult-Child Interactions on Children's Task Performance and Task Preferences," by J. A. Martin, *Journal of Experimental Child Psychology,* 1977, *23,* 493–502. Reprinted by permission of the author and the publisher, Academic Press, Inc.)

socioeconomic status, and weight in another group that receives one hour of nondirective counseling for weight loss. Further, we utilize a control group of 50 matched individuals who are on what is known as a waiting list control. These people will be weighed before and after, but will receive no treatment. At the end of the study the results are compared statistically to see whether one treatment is superior to another or to nothing (the control group). Hersen and Barlow (1977) have identified three reasons for using group statistical designs: (1) for actuarial purposes—that is, to determine what percentage of a sample of subjects is affected by a given treatment; (2) for comparison purposes, to compare kinds of treatment with one another; and (3) for evaluation purposes, to determine the effectiveness of the modification of group behavior.

Many experimental psychologists use group research design as their *modus operandi*. The behavior change professional tends to prefer a group design only after replicating a treatment using single-subject designs several times and desiring to demonstrate the broad applications of the treatment or to do a large-scale comparison with some other treatment. We will refer to the results of several experimental group designs throughout this book.

CONCLUSIONS

Assessment is a newly recognized tool for behavior change professionals to use to improve the quality of their behavior change programs. Several dimensions of the environment should be assessed in order to give the behavior change professional the clearest picture of how to proceed with a successful change program. Perhaps the most important assessment is the examination of generalization. The next ten years will produce a particular focus on assessing and programming generalization.

The hallmark of the behavior change approach is direct observation of behavior. Several methods are available to the behavior change professional, each method having special advantages depending on the behavior of interest.

Accountability is also a major feature of the behavior change approach. Both single-subject logic designs and group experimental designs provide the behavior change professional with a means of demonstrating that the change observed is due to the procedures used, rather than to some extraneous factor.

Now, on with the applications.

REFERENCES

Baer, D. M. A note on the absence of a Santa Claus in any known ecosystem: A rejoinder to Willems. *Journal of Applied Behavior Analysis,* 1974, *7,* 167–170.

Beck, A. T. *Depression: Causes and treatment.* Philadelphia: University of Pennsylvania Press, 1967.

Bellack, A. S., & Schwartz, J. S. Assessment of self-control programs. In M. Hersen & A. S. Bellack (Eds.), *Behavioral assessment: A practical handbook.* New York: Pergamon Press, 1976.

Cautela, J. R. Behavior therapy and the need for behavioral assessment. *Psychotherapy, Research and Practice,* 1968, *5,* 175–179.

Cautela, J. R., & Kastenbaum, R. A. A reinforcement survey schedule for use in therapy, training, and research. *Psychological Reports,* 1967, *20,* 1115–1130.

Ciminero, A. R. Behavioral assessment: An overview. In A. R. Ciminero, K. S. Calhoun, & H. E. Adams (Eds.), *Handbook of behavioral assessment.* New York: Wiley, 1977.

Ciminero, A. R., Calhoun, K. S., & Adams, H. E. (Eds.). *Handbook of behavioral assessment.* New York: Wiley, 1977.

Cone, J. D., & Hawkins, R. P. (Eds.). *Behavioral assessment: New directions in clinical psychology.* New York: Brunner/Mazel, 1977.

Craighead, W. E., Kazdin, A. E., & Mahoney, M. J. *Behavior modification*. Boston: Houghton Mifflin, 1976.

Goldfried, M. S. Behavioral assessment in perspective. In J. D. Cone & R. P. Hawkins (Eds.), *Behavioral assessment: New directions in clinical psychology*. New York: Brunner/Mazel, 1977.

Goldfried, M. S., & Sprafkin, J. N. Behavioral personality assessment. In J. T. Spence, R. C. Carlson, & J. W. Thibault (Eds.), *Behavioral approaches to therapy*. Morristown, N.J.: General Learning Press, 1976.

Hall, R. V., Cristler, C., Cranston, S. S., & Tucker, B. Teachers and parents as researchers using multiple baseline designs. *Journal of Applied Behavior Analysis,* 1970, *3,* 247–255.

Haynes, S. N. *Principals of behavioral assessment*. New York: Gardner Press, 1978.

Hersen, M. Historical perspectives in behavioral assessment. In M. Hersen & A. S. Bellack (Eds.), *Behavioral assessment: A practical handbook*. New York: Pergamon Press, 1976.

Hersen, M., & Barlow, D. *Single case experimental designs*. New York: Pergamon Press, 1977.

Hersen, M., & Bellack, A. S. *Behavioral assessment: A practical handbook*. New York: Pergamon Press, 1976.

Kanfer, F. H., & Saslow, G. Behavioral diagnosis. In C. M. Franks (Ed.), *Behavior therapy: Appraisal and status*. New York: McGraw-Hill, 1969.

Kent, R. N., & Foster, S. L. Direct observational procedures: Methodological issues in naturalistic settings. In A. R. Ciminero, K. S. Calhoun, & H. E. Adams (Eds.), *Handbook of behavioral assessment*. New York: Wiley, 1977.

Lang, P. J. Fear reduction and fear behavior: Problems in treating a construct. In J. M. Schlien (Ed.), *Research in psychotherapy*. Vol. III. Washington, D.C.: American Psychological Association, 1968.

Lang, P. J. The application of psychophysiological methods to the study of psychotherapy and behavior modification. In A. E. Bergin & L. L. Garfield (Eds.), *Handbook of psychotherapy and behavior change*. New York: Wiley, 1971.

Linehan, M. M. Issues in behavioral interviewing. In J. D. Cone & R. P. Hawkins (Eds.), *Behavioral assessment: New directions in clinical psychology*. New York: Brunner/ Mazel, 1977.

Locke, H. J., & Wallace, K. M. Short marital adjustment and prediction tests: Their reliability and validity. *Marriage and Family Living,* 1959, *21,* 251–255.

Lutzker, J. R. Deviant family systems. In B. B. Lahey & A. E. Kazdin (Eds.), *Advances in clinical child psychology,* Vol. III. New York: Plenum, 1980.

Mahoney, M. J. Some applied issues in self-monitoring. In J. D. Cone & R. P. Hawkins (Eds.), *Behavioral assessment: New directions in clinical psychology*. New York: Brunner/Mazel, 1977.

Martin, J. A. Effects of positive and negative adult-child interactions on children's task performance and task preferences. *Journal of Experimental Child Psychology,* 1977, *23,* 493–502.

Martin, J. A. *Using the multielement research design in applied settings*. Symposium paper presented at the 86th annual convention of the American Psychological Association, Toronto, 1978.

McFall, R. M. Analogue methods in behavioral assessment: Issues and prospects. In J. D. Cone & R. P. Hawkins (Eds.), *Behavioral assessment: New directions in clinical psychology*. New York: Brunner/Mazel, 1977.

Miller, L. K. *Principles of everyday behavior analysis* (2nd ed.). Monterey, Calif.: Brooks/ Cole, 1980.

Morganstern, K. P. Behavioral interviewing: The initial stages of assessment. In M. Hersen & A. S. Bellack (Eds.), *Behavioral assessment: A practical handbook*. New York: Pergamon Press, 1976.

Nay, W. R. Analogue measures. In A. R. Ciminero, K. S. Calhoun, & H. E. Adams (Eds.), *Handbook of behavioral assessment.* New York: Wiley, 1977.

Newkirk, J. M., Feldman, S., Bickett, A., Gipson, M. T., & Lutzker, J. R. Increasing extended care facility residents' attendance at recreational activities with convenient locations and personal invitations. *Journal of Applied Behavior Analysis,* 1976, *9,* 207.

Peterson, D. R. *The clinical study of social behavior.* New York: Appleton-Century-Crofts, 1968.

Rathus, S. A. A 30-item schedule for assessing assertive behavior. *Behavior Therapy,* 1973, *4,* 398–406.

Reese, E. P., Howard, J. S., & Reese, T. W. *Human behavior: An experimental analysis and its application.* Dubuque, Iowa: Brown, 1977.

Rogers-Warren, A. Planned change: Ecobehaviorally based interventions. In A. Rogers-Warren & S. F. Warren (Eds.), *Ecological perspectives in behavior analysis.* Baltimore: University Park Press, 1977.

Rogers-Warren, A., & Warren, S. F. *Ecological perspectives in behavior analysis.* Baltimore: University Park Press, 1977.

Stokes, T. F., & Baer, D. M. An implicit technology of generalization. *Journal of Applied Behavior Analysis,* 1977, *10,* 349–367.

Sulzer-Azaroff, B., & Mayer, G. R. *Applying behavior analysis procedures with children and youth.* New York: Holt, Rinehart & Winston, 1977.

Walls, R. T., Werner, T. J., Bacon, A., & Zane, T. Behavior checklists. In J. D. Cone & R. P. Hawkins (Eds.), *Behavioral assessment: New directions in clinical psychology.* New York: Brunner/Mazel, 1977.

Watson, D. L., & Tharp, R. G. *Self-directed behavior: Self-modification for personal adjustment* (2nd ed.). Monterey, Calif.: Brooks/Cole, 1977.

Wildman, B. G., & Erickson, M. T. Methodological problems in behavioral observation. In J. D. Cone & R. P. Hawkins (Eds.), *Behavioral assessment: New directions in clinical psychology.* New York: Brunner/Mazel, 1977.

Willems, E. P. Behavioral technology and behavioral ecology. *Journal of Applied Behavior Analysis,* 1974, *7,* 151–165.

CHAPTER 3

The Community and the Environment

As we saw in the first chapter, the applications of behavior change principles and procedures have gone beyond the treatment of clinically deviant behavior. This extension of nonclinical behavior change is perhaps best exemplified in behavioral community change. Behavioral community change is the application of behavior change procedures and behavior analysis to environmental-ecological and consumer problems. Some of these problem areas are litter control, public transportation, reduction of lawn trampling, the purchasing of returnable drink containers, recycling, energy consumption, refuse packaging, and gasoline consumption.

FIGURE 3-1. An example of attempts to change peoples' littering habits. "Iron Eyes" Cody, the famous "crying Indian" used in the Help Fight Pollution campaign. (Used by permission of The Advertising Council, Inc.)

Most of these problems are quite literally among the most important of our times. We are constantly reminded that we must find new sources of energy, and that, in the meantime, we must drastically cut back our gluttonous use of resources while we search for new resources. As we consider current problems, new ones always manage to appear. In 1977, California and other parts of the United States suffered from severe drought. Water conservation became a necessity. Today, we are trying to conserve oil and gas. How can we learn to sacrifice, to cut back our energy and water consumption? Is information—that is, propaganda—sufficient to change our behavior? Is punishment or the threat of punishment (for example, fines for littering, higher costs for overconsumption of electricity) effective in changing our behavior? Or is reinforcement (incentives, lotteries, rewards) a solution? Behavior change professionals have been conducting research since 1970 in an attempt to answer some of these questions. In this chapter, we will look at recent studies that have attempted to provide practical solutions to these problems. As you will see, some of the earliest studies in each area of behavioral community change tended to be simple, in that they examined a problem such as littering in an easy-to-study, and perhaps not greatly socially significant, setting such as a movie theater during a children's matinee. These studies, however simple they may have been, provided the methodological trial bases for continued research, and litter research now has been conducted in zoos, stores, a football stadium, and a U.S. Forest Service park. Like other kinds of research, litter research basically has followed a sequence from simple to complex, and it is this sequence that we examine in this chapter. We also make some projections as to where this research will lead in the attempt to improve our world.

LITTERING

Litter is a serious problem. It is ugly. It is a potential health hazard. It is something we do not wish our children to do. It is flagrant disrespect for the environment. Who are litterbugs? Nearly everyone; however, a survey in 1968 (Public Opinion Surveys, Inc.) concluded that adults between the ages of 21 and 35 are twice as likely to litter as adults over 35. Men litter more than women, and residents of rural communities litter more than urbanites. Children, however, are hardly exempt. While it might be somewhat useful to collect demographic data on litterbugs through direct behavioral observation—that is, find out who they are, not by surveys but by observing—such information seems secondary to simply finding ways to effect behavior change in large numbers of people in order to help reduce pollution problems.

One of the earliest studies done to examine how littering might be modified was reported by Marler (1970). He conducted research for two weeks in a National Forest. Three different treatments were applied to three different campgrounds. Campers entering one campground received a leaflet with a "positive" theme—that is, the leaflet advised the campers that picking up litter could prevent injuries to people. Campers entering another campground received a more personally threatening theme on their leaflets. This message stressed that picking up litter might prevent injuries to *them*. Finally, campers at the third campsite received leaflets that were considered neutral—that is, the message stated simply that litter is dangerous. All three leaflets included some facts about litter as a problem. A control group comprised other campers who received no leaflets. Cleanliness ratings of the campsites were used before and after campers had been at their sites to compare treatments. The personally threatening message was the most effective in producing clean campsites. Ninety percent of campers who received this message cleaned their campsites or did not contribute new litter. The other campers who received the more positive and the neutral messages, and the control group campers who did not receive any message, did not do as well in keeping their campsites clean.

A quick conclusion would be that personally threatening or negative information about litter might be effective in reducing it. However, there are some problems with this research that necessitate that we be guarded in our conclusions.

Marler distributed questionnaires to all of the campers and found that of those who received the questionnaires, no matter which treatment or control group they were in, only 60% read the leaflets. Thus, perhaps the results were merely accidental; perhaps only people likely to litter read literature on it; or perhaps only people who were already concerned read the leaflets. In their review of consumerism studies, Tuso and Geller (1976) point out that results such as Marler produced from his questionnaire point to the fact that "if antilitter messages are to be workable solutions in the fight against litter, there must be some assurance that the messages will reach the population" (p. 6). Finally, ratings as were used in this study are probably a better measure when combined with some direct measure of amount of litter than when used alone as was done here. Subsequent studies, which we review later in this chapter, made use of more sophisticated measurement techniques.

Further, research at a junior museum trail (LaHart & Bailey, 1975) showed that terse lectures and instructions were effective in persuading children to avoid adding to litter, but not effective in getting them to pick it up. Since the trend in behavior modification is, wisely, to avoid punishment or negative techniques alone in trying to change behavior, perhaps it is fortunate that Marler's results seem somewhat equivocal. Nonetheless, his study was an important beginning in the examination of techniques for modifying people's littering habits.

Two movie theaters showing children's matinees served as settings for the next important study in litter control techniques. The study (Burgess, Clark, & Hendee, 1971) examined several methods to induce children to pick up litter in the theaters. The techniques compared were the use of extra trash cans (often the proposal of city councils in attempts to reduce street litter), the showing of an antilitter cartoon before the feature presentation, and the distribution of litter bags to the children as they entered the theater. In one condition of the study, the children were told how to use the litter bags (verbal instruction); in the two reinforcement conditions, the children either were offered 10¢ for each bag of litter they collected, or received a free movie ticket for filling a litter bag. The amount of litter in the theaters during the experiment was counted and weighed in the trash cans after each movie.

Not surprisingly, the most effective treatments were the 10¢ rewards and the free movie tickets. When these reinforcers were offered, the children picked up 95% of the litter in the theaters. The condition in which the children were shown (prompted) how to use the litter bags was the next most effective. The children in this condition reduced daily litter by 57%, not nearly as much as when the rewards were offered. The other treatments showed negligible change over baseline rates of litter removal by the children in the theaters during those conditions.

Thus, in their study, Burgess et al. (1971) showed that reinforcement techniques were clearly more effective than prompting or propaganda (the antilitter cartoon) in causing children to pick up litter in two movie theaters. Not answered by this research was whether these procedures were cost-effective; that is, would the theater managers find these techniques more economical than employing sanitation crews to clean the theaters? Certainly the distribution of free tickets would not be particularly cost-effective for management and would probably not be the treatment of choice over time. Nonetheless, the Burgess et al. (1971) study clearly showed reinforcement procedures to be effective with children in promoting litter pickup. The failure of the cartoon in producing litter pickup by the children is something of which we particularly need to take heed.

A National Forest campground also served as the setting for Clark, Burgess, and Hendee (1972) to examine the role of reinforcement on children's litter collecting. During the study, the experimenters "planted" 160 pieces of litter in eight designated areas on two successive Thursdays and Fridays. During the weekends, baseline observations were made by actually counting the amount of "planted" litter still present. On the second weekend, seven families were asked by an experimenter (who, with permission, had dressed as a forest ranger) if their children could participate in a litter-control program. The children who agreed to participate (26 of them) received comic books, junior ranger badges, or gum for collecting litter. Each child was provided with plastic bags for depositing litter. There was a tremendous reduction in litter during the "reward" weekend as compared with the previous "baseline" weekend. The kind of litter collected most frequently by the children was bottles, which had the further incentive of being returnable for cash refunds. Unfortunately, no formal data were collected on the amount of litter added by the children who served as subjects, or by other campers. Casual observations, by the experimenters, noted that litter increased overall during both weekends. Thus, even the children in the study who might have picked up large quantities of "planted" litter could have still added their own litter. It is conceivable that agreeing to participation is a sign of predisposition not to be litterbugs and therefore the rewards might have been superfluous. The study could have been improved if between the baseline and reward conditions there had been a condition in which families were told that litter was a problem and the amount of litter picked up by children was going to be counted. It is possible that this information alone might have increased litter pickup by some children. Another weak point in this kind of research is that it did not determine whether there was any durable change in litter pickup when rewards were offered—that is, would the children pick it up *only* when rewards were offered or, over time, could rewards become more infrequent (the principle of intermittent reinforcement) and continue to result in litter pickup? This latter proposal surely seems the more desirable outcome.

Another litter study in a natural setting was conducted by Powers, Osborne, and Anderson (1973). They provided data on procedures to induce the pickup of "unplanted" or indigenous litter by campers and hunters in a Forest Service campground. This study not only offered improvement over the earlier studies because the litter was indigenous; it also offered other methodological improvements as well as cost-effective techniques. Placed in the observation areas were two litter stations that had a large trash barrel on either side and a compartment for plastic litter bags in the center. During the baseline condition, a sign on the front of each station contained instructions to fill a bag with litter, tie it, and deposit it in a trash can. Also, the instructions asked that name cards be filled out and deposited in the card container. A reversal design (Baseline, Treatment, Baseline, Treatment) was used to evaluate the reinforcement procedures, which involved a choice between immediate cash rewards of 25¢ per bag deposited or a chance for a weekly $20 lottery prize.

Two kinds of measurements were used to examine the amount of litter deposited. One was the number of litter bags actually deposited in the trash barrels, and the other was item counts in three observation areas. Figure 3-2 shows that there was a dramatic reduction in litter deposited during the two treatment-reward conditions. Metal litter decreased by 55% and paper litter decreased by 20%. The lottery was the reward of choice by 73% of the participants in this study.

The Powers, Osborne, and Anderson (1973) study is particularly important for at least two reasons: First, it further substantiates the value of reinforcement procedures in reducing littering. Second, it demonstrates that people can be induced to pick up indigenous litter in a natural setting. In this case, a lottery system was

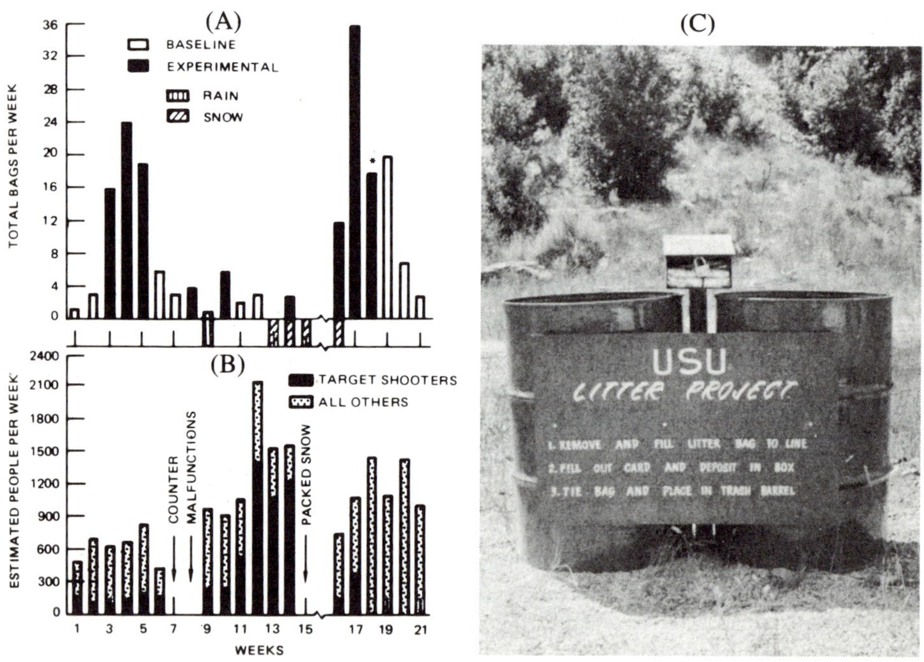

FIGURE 3-2. (A) The number of litter bags filled each week. The asterisk indicates publication of U.S. Forest Service orders prohibiting shooting in the area. (B) The estimated number of weekly users of the canyon and the proportion of those who were target shooting. Data points for weeks 7, 8, and 15 were not included because of nonfunctioning equipment. (C) The litter barrels as they appeared in the U.S. Forest Service Campground. (From "Positive Reinforcement of Litter Removal in the Natural Environment," by R. B. Powers, J. G. Osborne, and E. G. Anderson, *Journal of Applied Behavior Analysis*, 1973, 6, 579–586. Copyright 1973 by the Society for the Experimental Analysis of Behavior, Inc. Reprinted by permission.)

used with considerable effectiveness, thus obviating the cost and effort of providing direct tangible consequences to each litter depositor contingent upon his or her behavior. Perhaps the only major weakness of the study was the lack of long-term follow-up of the reward procedures. Would returning campers, hikers, hunters, and fishers continue to "compete" to win the lottery, or would repeated failure to win (extinction) cause them to lose interest and thus stop picking up litter? Only future research can answer this question.

An excellent, methodologically strong study was reported in 1973 by Kohlenberg and Phillips. Litter reduction and pickup was produced in visitors to the Seattle Zoo. The reinforcement procedures were free zoo admissions. Researchers in this study recorded the number of litter deposits made in a specified trash can during 20-minute intervals, eight hours a day. Data were also collected on the approximate ages of the litter depositors. The experimenters even compared parking lot receipts (as a measure of attendance at the zoo) to weather reports to make sure that reductions in litter were not simply a result of poor attendance because of poor weather. The data indicated that a contingency (the free admissions) resulted in increased rates of litter depositing. The authors point out an important esthetic advantage to reinforcement programs in litter control. That is, if a crew is hired to come in to clean up litter, an area is clean for only a while, but becomes progressively dirtier and uglier until the next cleanup. However, when reinforcement procedures are in effect as they were in the zoo, the area stays clean all the time.

Another example of the questionable effects of propaganda or "education" appears in the work of LaHart and Bailey (1975), who, at a junior museum and nature trail in Tallahassee, Florida, compared five groups of children who were exposed to five different conditions. These conditions were (1) a simple statement that littering was a problem, (2) specially prepared educational materials on littering, presented before the children came to the museum, (3) a five-minute lecture on littering, (4) instructions not to litter, (5) a statement that they could earn a badge for picking up litter. As in other studies reported here, the trail was "salted" with litter. The experimenters also weighed the total litter after the children left to measure how much litter the children added. Data showed that only the incentive condition resulted in any of the "salted" litter being picked up. The statements preceding the trail tour and the lecture were effective in preventing the children's adding litter.

The results of this study are at once encouraging and discouraging. The encouraging aspect is that once again we see simple, low-cost incentives being effective in inducing children to remove litter. The discouraging part is that some children added new litter. Perhaps a combined contingency whereby they received badges only when they both picked up litter and refrained from adding new litter would have solved this dilemma. Not surprisingly, the "educational" attempts to produce litter pickup were not effective. Despite these mixed results, much advertising for the "public good" and most attempts to produce "moral" behavior depend upon lectures, propaganda, or questionably functional educational materials.

Perhaps one of the most interesting and difficult settings for a litter control study was used by Baltes and Hayward (1974) in the football stadium at Pennsylvania State University. Six sections of the stadium were used for comparison: two sections for baseline (no technique), and one section each for positive reinforcement, positive prompting, negative prompting, and the mere presence of plastic litter bags. Every third person who entered the four treatment sections of the stadium became a subject. In the positive reinforcement condition, subjects were given plastic litter bags with labels stating that the bag might be exchangeable for a prize if it was turned in after the game. The positive prompt involved the distribution of the bags on which the labels urged participants to provide good examples (models) to others and reduce cleanup costs by proper disposal of the litter bags. In the negative prompting condition, the labels warned that "litter can hurt" and "others will disapprove of your littering." After the game, the experimenters collected the litter left on the ground in each row of the stadium and weighed the collected litter (excluding bottles). All treatment conditions were superior to baseline (untreated areas of the stadium) in producing litter pickup. Although it might be easy to conclude that the less expensive techniques, which did not offer rewards, were effective and thus are "treatments of choice," much of the other litter control literature reviewed in this chapter runs contrary to this notion. Since a football stadium is such a relatively closed and supervised (police and ushers) setting compared to the U.S. Forest parks and zoos, it is possible that people simply complied to antilitter requests as a function of suspected observation or sanction.

Litter is frequently a serious problem in urban areas. Chapman and Risley (1974) report a well-controlled and methodologically "tight" study done in the yards of 25 homes in an urban, high-density neighborhood. The subjects were children who resided in a housing project in Kansas City, Kansas. A baseline condition involved a verbal appeal to pick up litter; a reinforcement condition involved promising the children 10¢ for each bag of trash they returned. Weeks of payment and no payment were altered (reversal design) to examine the role of payment. In the last condition, children were assigned particular yards and were paid their 10¢ only when the yard had been cleaned to a specified criterion. The payment per yard was the most effective condition in this study; however, the results were not long-lasting. The other payment conditions produced considerable litter deposited and returned, but the experimenters suspected that the children took other litter out of trash cans to fill their bags rather than pick it up from the ground. Verbal appeal was not effective. Perhaps longer-term results would have occurred if the experimenters had switched to intermittent schedules of reinforcement by not paying for each bag returned, but rather for every few bags returned. A lottery might also have been effective.

A multiple baseline design was used by Hayes, Johnson, and Cone (1975) to reduce a littering problem in four areas of a "camplike" federal prison. In this study litter counts were made on ten lawns, which were consolidated into four observation areas. The experimenters placed marked litter in Area 1. Inmates were told that they could voluntarily pick up litter and were provided with bags and a special trash can. The presentation of a bag with marked litter earned 25¢ or a "special privilege." This technique was sequentially applied to the other areas. The inmates did not know the marking system, so they went about picking up all kinds of litter. The Hayes et al. study shows another creative method for trying to produce maximum performance (a high volume of litter removal) with procedures as time- and cost-efficient as possible.

The research on litter control to date reviewed here shows some improved methodological development and practical techniques. Some studies that took place in environments where individuals know that paid cleanup crews are used (football stadia, theaters) may produce questions of overall importance (Bailey, in press). Nevertheless, these studies were important in showing what kinds of procedures might be effective and followed by studies in more natural settings. And we typically find that some treatments work in some settings and not others, with some individuals and not others. Working for a singular solution to a complex problem such as littering would undoubtedly not be fruitful.

Another weak point in most of the litter studies to date is lack of long-term follow-up. Over time, would reinforcement procedures continue to help keep littering at a minimum in natural settings? This question can be answered only by further research.

One behavior change technique that seems especially useful and has been reported only once (Geller, Chaffee, & Ingram, 1975) is the use of competition. In a study we will review below, competition helped in inducing recycling in college dormitories. As we will see in Chapter 8, the Good Behavior Game, which makes use of pseudo-competition, has been very effective in classroom behavior management. The Good Productivity Game (see Lutzker & White-Blackburn, 1979, Chapter 4) also used pseudo-competition to increase work output in employees of a rehabilitation industry. Perhaps this technique should be explored in litter control and other community environmental research.

RECYCLING

In an attempt to reduce our enormous waste of resources, recycling programs have been developed, particularly with paper products, bottles, and cans. Getting people to participate in recycling programs has been disappointing. Like so many things that may be good for us or our environment, recycling involves engaging in behavior that results in few immediate payoffs. Some people may feel good conscience when they participate in a recycling program, but most people can find a variety of excuses why they do not participate. Like the litter study, research with recycling has been fairly limited, but some encouraging signs have appeared.

The earliest reported study on recycling was by Geller, Wylie, and Farris (1971). They used reinforcement and prompting techniques to increase the purchase of returnable bottles by customers in two supermarkets and a smaller convenience store. Returnable glass bottles, of course, are recycled; nonreturnable bottles are not recyclable, which makes for a drain on resources. After six days of baseline measures in the stores (simply counting the purchases of the two kinds of bottles), treatment began. One research assistant gave handbills to customers as they entered a store, one assistant recorded the kind of bottle purchased as customers checked out, one assistant thanked customers who purchased more than 50% of their soft drinks in returnable bottles, and a fourth assistant tallied the kinds of bottles purchased on a poster near the exit. Thus, the customers received a treatment "package" in an attempt to increase their purchase of recyclable containers. They were prompted (the handbills), publicly accounted (the recording of the purchase), rewarded (the "thank you"), and given feedback (the poster). Unfortunately, the only clear effects were seen in the convenience store where the percentage of customers who purchased returnable bottles increased by 20% over baseline. No similar results were found in the larger stores.

The authors point out that the prompt had a weaker probability of success in the larger stores because customers probably spend a longer time shopping there than in the convenience store. Why the other components of the treatment package were not more effective in the larger stores is up for speculation. But, as we have seen, the use of feedback, or intangible consequences ("thank yous"), undoubtedly has a lower probability of success than the use of meaningful incentives. In a study reported two years later (Geller, Farris, & Post, 1973), however, three different treatments produced clear successes in increasing the purchase of returnable bottles in a convenience store. The three treatments were compared to a baseline condition during which no efforts were made to influence customers' purchasing habits. The three effective treatment conditions were (1) a handbill prompting returnable bottle purchases, (2) a handbill and a poster (as in the previous study), and (3) group pressure where four assistants surrounded the poster to stress the importance of the project. No treatment condition was more effective than the others, but all were at least 20% more effective than baseline.

The disappointing feature of this study, perhaps, was the amount of effort, time, and personnel required to produce a change in purchase habits. More economical procedures must be examined. *Neither of these bottle-recycling studies reported the number of bottles returned.*

The recycling of newspapers is another kind of program for which we need to find ways of increasing participation. Individual and group reinforcement contingencies were effective in promoting newspaper recycling at a college campus. Residents of six dormitories were participants in the study reported by Geller, Chaffee, and Ingram (1975). The dorms were matched into three pairs according to the number of residents—that is, three male dorms were matched with three female dorms of comparable size. In each pair, three experimental conditions were alternated. The conditions were baseline, contest, and raffle. Each condition was in effect for two weeks. The critical measure in this study was the number of pounds of paper delivered by each dorm resident (measured after each delivery by two research assistants). The contest, which lasted for two weeks, involved competition between dorms in each matched pair. Posters announced that the dorm that delivered the most paper would win $15 for the dorm treasury. The raffle condition involved the distribution of coupons to each resident who brought paper to the collection room at designated times. Monetary prizes averaging $8, four per week, were provided by local merchants. Both the contest and raffle conditions were effective in dramatically increasing the pounds of paper delivered over baseline conditions, when students were simply asked to contribute to the recycling program. This study provides support for three treatments: (1) reinforcement, which was implicit in the two treatment conditions, (2) competition, and (3) lotteries, in promoting recycling programs. The authors do not discuss the costs and benefits of the program; one wonders how long merchants would continue to support such a program generously. One way to guarantee merchant support might be to locate recycling stations in their stores. Thus, for a small contribution on the merchants' parts for the reinforcers, they might simultaneously increase business—a nice combination of ecological spirit and profit motives.

In a very similar study, Witmer and Geller (1976) once again found a raffle to be very successful in facilitating paper recycling among college dormitory residents. In this study, the contest had some effect, flyers had no effect; and students whose rooms were closest to the collection center showed the greatest participation.

Perhaps the greatest weakness of the recycling studies is the use of small, "closed" natural settings rather than large, "open" ones—that is, the best results we examined appeared in small convenience stores and in college dormitories. Very encouraging in the paper-recycling studies was the use of raffles to promote behavior change. Raffles are cheaper and easier to dispense than one-to-one reinforcement programs. A final consideration worth noting regarding the bottle-purchasing studies is that the ultimate answer may lie in simply outlawing the manufacture of nonreturnable bottles, as has been done in Oregon. This is certainly an effective behavior change technique.

TRANSPORTATION

Part of our efforts in energy conservation are concerned with trying to have people use their own cars less in an attempt to get them to use more energy-economical systems of transportation such as public transit, car pools, and nonpolluting transportation such as walking and bicycling when possible.

A unique study, in which bus ridership was dramatically increased on the campus of Pennsylvania State University, was reported in 1974 by Everett, Hayward, and Meyers. These authors made use of a token reinforcement system to accomplish their goal of increased ridership. Two experimental buses, identifiable by their large red stars, were used in the study, which encompassed several days of baseline, treatment, baseline ("ABA"). During the treatment ("B") condition, passengers were given tokens (a real switch for old streetcar riders!) when they entered the bus after they paid the regular 10¢ fee. The tokens could be exchanged on campus and in the stores of local merchants for such things as record discounts, free pizza slices, soft drinks, and the like. The token system increased ridership over baseline ("A") by over 150%. One serious problem was noted, however, in that many people who normally walked began using the bus. On the other hand, many people who had been using their cars also started riding the bus. It is unfortunate that careful measurement of car use was not accomplished in this study, but it is another promising example of a method for changing people's unsound environmental practices. Again, here we see local merchants participating for community good and, hopefully, for their own good business.

Once more on a college campus, gasoline consumption (car usage) was reduced through reinforcement for alternative transportation usage. From the campus of the University of Maryland, Baltimore County, Foxx and Hake (1977) involved students in two psychology classes in their study. The students were divided by class into two groups. The experimental group was offered cash prizes, tours of a mental health facility, car-servicing privileges, and university parking stickers for reducing their driving. The control group received no such inducements. Subjects in the experimental group first received baseline (no inducements), then treatment (the inducements), then baseline and treatment again. The experimenters were careful in taking special precautions to reduce odometer tampering since the odometer readings were the critical dependent measures in the study. Students in the experimental group reduced their driving by 20% over their own baseline rates. The students in the control group showed no such reduction. While the 20% reduction by the 12 experimental subjects meant a savings of 170 gallons of gasoline, the authors do not address the overall issue of cost-effectiveness and practicality of the reinforcement procedures. It is not clear how much time, cost, and effort were involved in producing the 20% reduction in driving by the experimental subjects.

The two transportation studies we examined here hold some of the same promises and pitfalls as the early litter studies. It is clear from the results that people (college students) can be induced to use their cars less. However, both the studies were done on college campuses where controlling reinforcement contingencies and measuring behavior are easier than in our communities with daily clogged freeways. We are certain, nonetheless, that research in behavior change techniques in transportation will extend to larger and more natural settings and that cost-benefit analyses will be made. Although energy conservation efforts over the years may require sacrifices, if they can significantly reduce pollution and energy consumption, they will be worth the cost.

UTILITY CONSERVATION

Brownouts and blackouts of the 1970s were harsh reminders of our need to conserve our gas and electric resources. Winett and Nietzel (1975) compared the effect of information and the effect of incentive in an attempt to reduce energy consumption among volunteer households in a Kentucky community. The study involved 31 households in which regular electric or natural gas bills were paid. Before baseline data were collected, the experimenters administered questionnaires aimed at assessing attitudes and knowledge of ecological issues. In addition, past utility bills were collected in order to provide a general picture of the usage histories of the 31 households. During the eight weeks of the study, meters were read by the experimenters each Thursday between 6:00 and 8:00 P.M. Baseline measures were collected for two weeks, at which point the households were matched according to their current utility consumption. Households were then randomly assigned to one of two conditions for four weeks. The information condition involved the distribution of a pamphlet that detailed procedures for reducing energy consumption. Each household in this group was also provided with record sheets for logging its own meter readings. The households assigned to the incentive group also received the detailed manual and data sheets, but were informed that cash awards proportionate to the size of their energy-saving efforts were available. Reductions in consumption of 5–10% from baseline earned $2; reduction of 11–20% earned $3; and reduction of over 20% earned $5 for the participating households. Bonuses of $25 and $15 were made available to the best and second-best energy-reducing households. The incentive group reduced electricity consumption by 15% more than the information group. There was no reduction in natural gas consumption. After two months, households in the incentive group were still using less electricity than households in the information group. We can only speculate as to the reason that consumption was reduced for electricity and not gas. If the homes were heated by electricity, turning down one's thermostat was easier than adjusting gas-run water heaters or reducing hot water use. In any case, this study presents another example of the poor record of information or propaganda when compared to incentives or feedback contingencies for significantly affecting people's behavior.

Cash awards were found to be superior to feedback and information in reducing electricity consumption in four married student households in a housing complex at West Virginia University (Hayes & Cone, 1977). The households in this study did not pay their own utility bills; thus the cash awards were not confounded with savings that resulted from lower bills. Consumption was monitored by the experimenters for five months, January through May, by special watt-hour meters that allowed separate monitoring of each apartment. Household members did not have access to the meters. A combined multiple-baseline–return-to-baseline design was used to assess the relative effects of the three conditions (cash awards, feedback, information). Initially, six families were monitored, without their knowledge, from 11 to 14 days. One family had such low consumption rates that they were dropped from the study. Another family refused to participate in the remainder of the study. Formal baseline data came from the four remaining households after they were informed that their electricity usage was being monitored. Using a multiple baseline design, cash awards were introduced after varying lengths of baseline data from the four households had been collected (from 8 to 13 days). The amount of the cash awards depended upon the amount of energy conservation a family demonstrated from baseline rates. A reduction of 10–19% from baseline meant a $3 cash award, a 20–29% reduction meant a $6 award, a 30–39% reduction meant a $9 award, 40–49% earned $12, and for reductions of 50% or more, the households received $15. This program was in effect for one week in two of the four apartments. A reduced payment was used in subsequent weeks for two of the four households. Thus, the separate effects of information and payments was compared in two households to feedback and payments in two other households. The information condition meant that those two households received a poster listing common electrical appliances and the amount of energy they consumed. Also, the poster contained information on ways to reduce energy consumption. This information was not unlike the kind of literature gas and electric companies might include along with their monthly bills.

For household residents in the feedback condition, daily data in the form of costs (rather than kilowatt hours) were presented to them on their use of energy.

The results of the study showed that when the full payment schedule was in effect, energy consumption was reduced considerably. Feedback alone resulted in moderate conservation; information alone was basically ineffective.

This study, once again, shows the powerful effect of reinforcement contingencies in controlling consumer behavior for the public benefit. Once again, however, this study is merely a demonstration study; it leaves open the questions of cost-benefit analysis and impact of such procedures on large numbers of energy users.

Another problem in energy consumption is "peaking." Peaking is the use of large amounts of electricity at a particular time of day, which causes ineffective, costly, and potentially dangerous stress on power plants. Kohlenberg, Phillips, and Proctor (1976) studied three families in an attempt to modify peaking. The study took place during a three-month period from January through March.

A recording device was installed in each home to measure power use. The families were not permitted access to the device so that feedback would not influence them during baseline. Consumption was recorded in 96 15-minute intervals. Use in a particular interval was considered a peak when the amount of energy consumed exceeded by ten the largest 15-minute totals. An information condition similar to those previously described was implemented after baseline. During this two-week phase, families were given a presentation on the peaking problem, were requested to avoid peaking, and were given 100-watt light bulb equivalents for electrical devices in their homes. During the third condition, feedback that involved a signal light to warn families when they were peaking was instituted. Conceptually, this signal light is not unlike devices installed in automobiles to remind the driver to avoid speeding. After the feedback condition, a return to baseline was instituted for two weeks. After the second baseline period, feedback was reinstituted, previous use data were provided to the families, and the families were told of an opportunity to earn monetary rewards for reducing peaking. The rewards involved rebates of cash amounting to *double* the electricity bill for a 100% reduction in peaking and proportionally smaller awards for smaller reductions. As in the other studies, the results showed that information alone did not reduce peaking. While some reduction in peaking occurred during the feedback condition, a considerable reduction in peaking occurred during the incentive condition.

Once again, we have little information overall about the practicality of incentive procedures, but the data seem to indicate rather clearly that the traditional kinds of attitude-changing or educational approaches to producing behavior change in the consumer are not effective. Industry and government must combine efforts to implement effective, cost-efficient programs that benefit consumer and business alike; these efforts will require considerable research.

MISCELLANY: FROM TELEPHONES TO GARBAGE

As we have seen, to date most of the research using behavior change techniques in the community has been in conservation. Recent research, however, has indicated fascinating and practical applications to important day-to-day problems. Behavior change procedures have been applied to an analysis of free Found ads in community newspapers, the packaging of refuse, and journal reshelving in a university library.

In a study entitled "Finders Keepers?: An Analysis and Validation of a Free Found Ad Policy," Goldstein, Minkin, Minkin, and Baer (1978) used a multiple baseline design to show that when newspapers stopped charging for Found ads in their classified sections, the number of Found ads placed dramatically increased. The authors of this study point out that Lost ads greatly outnumber Found ads in newspapers, probably in no small part because the altruistic gesture of placing a Found ad is punished by having to pay for it. This is a reasonable, if partial, explanation for the discrepancy; the other, obvious explanation is that some lost items are never found because of theft and other reasons.

Using multiple baseline logic across three community newspapers, the researchers had the newspapers introduce free Found ads sequentially across time as stable higher rates of their placement began to appear. In addition to making the Found ads free, the newspapers allowed them to be called in over the telephone, while Lost ads had to be submitted in writing. Finally, each newspaper agreed to provide daily notification of the free Found ads to its readers. As you can see in Figure 3-3, there was a tremendous increase in the number of *free* Found ads placed whenever the free Found policy was introduced. Follow-up data after three months showed that the increased rates of placement were maintained. The number of Lost ads placed during the same period had remained relatively stable. A telephone survey indicated that 43–46% of all Found items were recovered by their owners through the ads in the three newspapers. When respondents were asked if Found ads *should* be free, almost all said yes. Thirty-seven percent said that they had placed the ad only because it was free.

An important question is whether the altruistic behavior of the newspaper publishers would continue, since such a change in policy might cause them to lose a small amount of revenue. Probably the most reliable empirical measure to answer this question is to determine whether the papers continued the free Found policy after the study was formally terminated. The papers did, in fact, continue the policy. Furthermore, a business manager of one of the newspapers reported that readers frequently remarked that they approved of the policy change that had been made concerning the ads. Thus, the manager felt that the good public relations generated by the free Found policy more than paid for the nominal cost to the newspaper for running the ads.

Although the Goldstein et al. study is really very simple, it is a good example of the use of behavior change procedures and design to examine a community/consumer issue and manipulate behavior for the community good.

Stokes and Fawcett (1977) conducted a study that resulted in a municipal policy change after the positive results were noted by the city's Sanitation Commission. The research was accomplished with the cooperation of the local Sanitation Workers Association and city management personnel in a midwestern city with a population of 50,000. The experiment was conducted with 183 single-family residences. The experimental areas were on either side of a major street, 94 residences on the west side and 89 on the east side.

Refuse was left for pickup by residents either at the curb in front of their house or in alleys behind the houses. Frequent packaging violations that had been

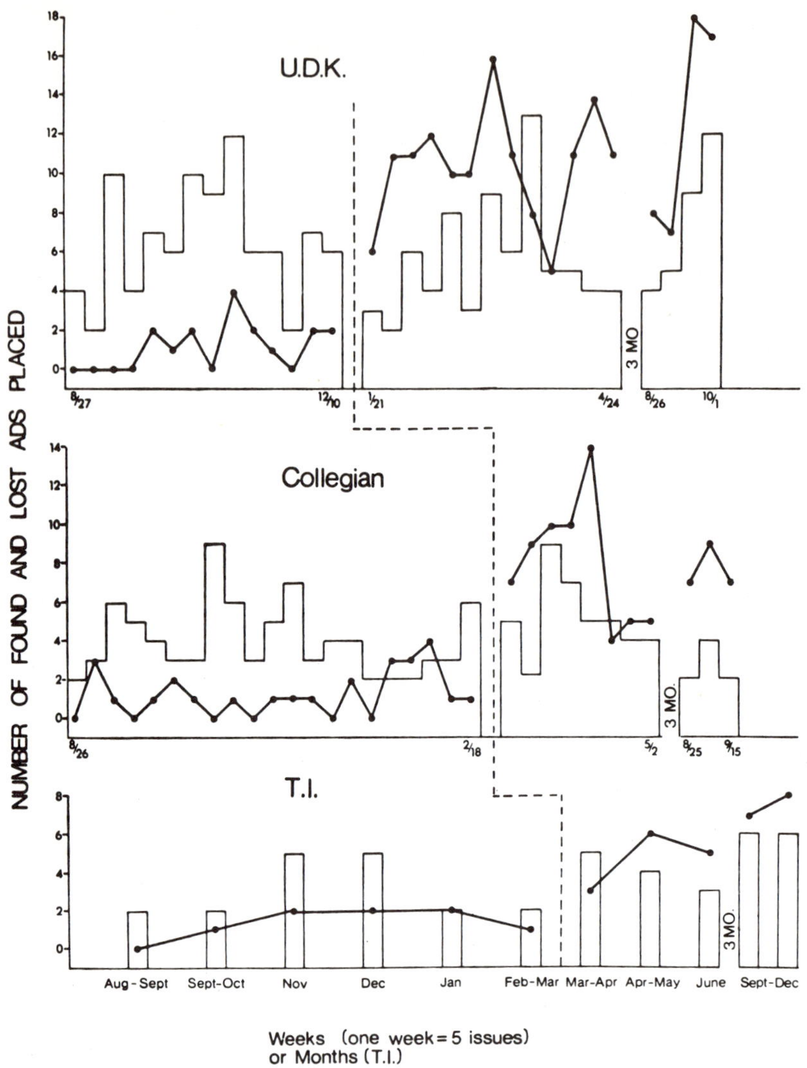

FIGURE 3-3.   Rates of Lost and Found ads for the three newspapers. One week equals five consecutive issues. Each T.I. data point represents five consecutive Thursday issues. (From "Finders Keepers?: An Analysis and Validation of a Free Found Ad Policy," by R. S. Goldstein, B. L. Minkin, N. Minkin, and D. M. Baer, *Journal of Applied Behavior Analysis*, 1978, *11*, 465–473. Copyright 1978 by the Society for the Experimental Analysis of Behavior, Inc. Reprinted by permission.)

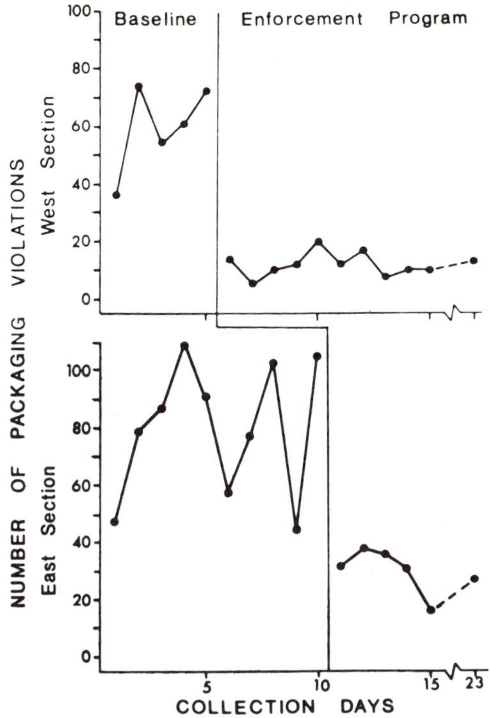

FIGURE 3-4.   Daily number of packaging violations in the west and east neighborhoods. (From "Evaluating Municipal Policy: An Analysis of a Refuse Packaging Program," by T. F. Stokes and S. B. Fawcett, *Journal of Applied Behavior Analysis*, 1977, *10*, 391–398. Copyright 1977 by the Society for the Experimental Analysis of Behavior, Inc. Reprinted by permission.)

a problem were counted during baseline. From a car, an observer looked for the following violations:

1. refuse container more than 6 ft from the curb or alley line
2. overfilled refuse containers
3. untied or torn refuse bags
4. unacceptable refuse containers such as cardboard boxes or wicker baskets
5. uncut or untied yard trimmings
6. loose litter, trash, or garbage on the ground near the refuse container

A multiple baseline design with treatment first being implemented on the west side of the street and later on the east (see Figure 3-4) showed the positive effects of the treatment program. The treatment involved instructions and feedback about packaging and contingent collection of properly packaged refuse. A letter of instruction signed by the city manager and the superintendent of sanitation was sent to each experimental household after the last day of baseline.

The letter advised the families of the city's intent to enforce packaging standards (which were provided along with the letter). In addition, the letter included a sample "violation" tag that would be attached to refuse not picked up by sanitation crews because of packaging violations. The tag indicated what kind of violation had occurred. Figure 3-4 shows that this enforcement "package" greatly reduced the number of packaging violations. Some social validation data further indicated that the sanitation crews were very pleased with the new program in that they felt that refuse was better packaged and easier and safer to collect. An assessment of resident complaints showed that, during the experiments, complaint records among those 193 families were not different from complaint records for the rest of the city.

Perhaps one of the most important results of this study was that the city adopted the program as general sanitation policy to be implemented throughout the city. These results, along with those from the free Found ads study, are especially encouraging. It seems that, when large-scale behavior change programs are practical and inexpensive, they have a high probability of being used by appropriate agencies.

The only experimental flaw that we might find with this otherwise innovative study by Stokes and Fawcett (1977) is that it is not clear whether the whole treatment "package" or just particular parts of it were responsible for the results obtained—for example, would a strongly worded letter (or threat) from the city manager and sanitation director be sufficient to cause a change in refuse-packaging habits? Much of the literature we have examined in this chapter would lead us to conclude that it is unlikely that the letter alone could produce such an effect, but given the way the study was carried out we can conclude only that the whole treatment was effective without knowing about the "parts." This flaw could have been remedied, in part, by following the baseline conditions with one or two letters providing packaging instructions and a statement of the city's interest in reducing refuse packaging violations. We might predict a transient effect—that is, a temporary decline in packaging violations. If that was the case, then—in the same manner as in the study—the rest of the treatment package could have been introduced. If, then, the durable changes had appeared as they did when the study *was* run, it could be concluded that indeed the *enforcement* component was more effective than the instructions. Similarly, we could examine the individual effects of the tags as compared with the contingent pickup of correctly packaged refuse. In any case, this study is a good example of practical application to a consumer problem of behavior change procedures that produced subsequent durable change in the community.

We have seen that behavior change procedures can be applied to a variety of problems in several new research settings. One problem that occurs frequently in libraries is the lack of reshelving by users—that is, when someone takes a book or journal off a shelf, he or she most often fails to return it. Failure to reshelve journals in a university library causes a buildup, which means problems for both the staff and the potential users. In fact, failure to reshelve has been described as the single most time-consuming component of the entire library circulation process.

The problem of journal reshelving was tackled by Meyers, Nathan, and Kopel (1977), who conducted a study at the Library of Science and Medicine at Rutgers

University. This study was conducted quite similarly to some of the energy consumption studies we have examined, in that after baseline an instruction condition was instituted, followed by token reinforcement, instructions again, and token reinforcement again. As in the other studies, instructions were first used to see whether failure to demonstrate the behavior under study was due simply to ignorance, in which case instructions alone should produce some significant changes in behavior.

Library staff members were the primary observers in this study. They were provided with detailed instructions on how to count the number of unshelved journals. Other staff members occasionally did the same count independently from the other observers as a measure of reliability. The Pearson product-moment correlation was a very respectable 0.87.

After 13 days of baseline, which showed low rates of reshelving, the instructions condition was begun. This involved the use of large, conspicuously placed signs (in 15 locations) that said, "Please Reshelve Journals." After 13 days of instruction that showed little change in reshelving, the token economy was instituted. During this condition, instruction signs were replaced with signs that said, "Free Food, Movies, Photoduplication, and more. For each bound journal you reshelve, you are entitled to a blue token. Blue tokens can be found in boxes throughout the floor. Then exchange blue tokens for red tokens at the centrally located table. The red tokens then can be used to obtain various items. Check the token exchange list for details." Several university businesses had agreed to accept the tokens in exchange for goods and services. These goods and services included movie tickets, hamburgers, cigarettes, photoduplication, bowling, sweets, and chances at a $25 raffle. Obviously also in effect here was an honor system, since students could pick up tokens without really doing any reshelving. The corroborative measure, however—their actual rate of reshelving—let the experimenters know that dishonesty was not a frequent problem.

Both token reinforcement regimens drastically increased the amount of reshelving done by the library's users. A concern that we have repeatedly brought up in this chapter is one of cost-benefit analysis. The two token phases in this study cost $213. The hiring of an extra staff person who would have been required to do a job (in terms of amount of reshelving) equal to that done by the library users during the token phases would have been $245 for the two-week period. Whether more long-term costs would "pay for themselves" was not determined. The library kept up the token system, however, for 11 months after formal termination of the study. Also not determined was how long other university agencies would continue to support the token economy when the direct benefit to them might not be observable—for example, while the university center where tokens were redeemable for bowling is financed under an overall university budget (as in the library), both units operate independently, under their own budgets, within the overall university budget. Thus, simply, the center might get tired of using its budget to control a library problem. Of course, this problem could be resolved by budget shifts.

The only major experimental question we have about this study is that it fails to discuss the quality of reshelving, which is a serious issue. Did users reshelve just anywhere to get their tokens, or did they do it accurately? Since the library continued to use the system, it might be presumed that reshelving was fairly accurate. Further research in this area should surely focus on quality measures as well as quantity.

In a study that provided not only an important community service and experimentally compared three treatments, Reiss, Piotrowski, and Bailey (1976) provided also the cost-effectiveness information we have been suggesting is so important. The study involved encouraging low-income parents to seek dental care for their children.

Three experimental treatment groups were compared, utilizing 180 children from a rural elementary school. The treatments compared were (1) one prompt, (2) three prompts, and (3) one prompt plus money incentive. The one-prompt treatment was a note to the parents, sent home through the children, that notified the parents of the outcome of dental screening performed on the children. The note made specific recommendations for parental follow-up. The three-prompts condition involved the same note as in the one-prompt treatment, plus a telephone call, plus a home visit by a dental hygienist. The school personnel who made the phone calls asked several questions: Did the parents receive the note? Did the parents make contact with a dentist and make an appointment? When was the child's last dental visit? Who is the child's dentist? The third treatment was one prompt plus a $5 incentive. This treatment included the same note home plus a "dental coupon" when it was verified that the child made a visit to the dentist's office. The one-prompt-plus-$5-incentive treatment was the most effective. The three-prompt treatment was also quite effective, while the one-prompt (note only) condition was relatively ineffective.

Of particular interest are the results of the cost-effectiveness data. All materials or personnel that were used for treatment were included in the computation of costs. The "cheapest," but also least effective, treatment was the one-prompt, which cost 88¢ per family to execute. Perhaps surprisingly, the one-prompt-plus-$5-incentive treatment was next best in terms of cost-effectiveness, with an average of $6.21 per family. The three-prompt condition, which, remember, included some visits, cost $19.75 per family to run. Thus the treatment of choice would seem to be the incentive condition. If health agencies are seriously concerned with the public's use of their services, they might look toward the Reiss, Piotrowski, and Bailey (1976) study for some possible answers.

CONCLUSIONS

In this chapter we have seen behavior change procedures applied to a variety of consumer and ecological problems. The data seem consistent in showing us that instructions, education, propaganda, and feedback are not nearly as effective in producing behavior change as rewards, reinforcers, and incentives. Not clearly demonstrated by most of the studies reviewed in this chapter is the large-scale practicality of some of the procedures, and whether they are financially viable. Furthermore, none of the studies have determined whether and to what extent the results are generalizable: Will people who have been reinforced for picking up litter in a campground pick up litter on their own from the sidewalk of their Main Street?

Will people who have seen the positive effects of journal reshelving or conserving energy in their homes encourage their friends to do the same? Future research must address these issues to determine whether behavioral researchers' techniques are impractical and cumbersome.

Energy conservation and the other problems examined in this chapter are real everyday problems that need quick solutions. As has been pointed out repeatedly in recent years, we may all be running out of time if these problems are not solved soon. Unfortunately, politics enters the picture, as it does with most problems of a community level. No matter which side of the political fence one may be standing on, one cannot ignore the role of politics. Energy packages that include components of reinforcement and punishment have been proposed. Rebates for the purchase of small cars have been proposed; higher taxes on bigger, gas-guzzling cars have also been proposed. Like too many parents, teachers, and others, Congress tends to accept the idea of punishing the consumer (by supporting the tax) but to reject the idea of reinforcement (by turning down the rebates). Until the utility of reinforcement procedures can be demonstrated, we may be perennially thwarted in our attempts to implement large-scale behavior change. Nonetheless, the research reviewed in this chapter should provide considerable hope that we are moving in good directions. If we feel confident in making any accurate prediction in this book, it is that the 1980s will see considerably more and better behavioral research in the area of community and the environment.

REFERENCES

Bailey, J. S. *A handbook of research methods in applied behavior analysis.* New York: Plenum, in press.

Baltes, M. M., & Hayward, S. C. *Behavioral control of littering in a football stadium.* Paper presented at the 82nd convention of the American Psychological Association, New Orleans, 1974.

Barrish, H., Saunders, M., & Wolf, M. Good behavior game: Effects of individual contingencies for group consequences on disruptive behavior in a classroom. *Journal of Applied Behavior Analysis,* 1969, *2,* 119–124.

Burgess, R. L., Clark, R. N., & Hendee, J. C. An experimental antilitter procedure. *Journal of Applied Behavior Analysis,* 1971, *4,* 71–75.

Chapman, C., & Risley, T. R. Antilitter procedures in an urban high-density area. *Journal of Applied Behavior Analysis,* 1974, *7,* 377–383.

Clark, R. N., Burgess, R. L., & Hendee, J. C. The development of antilitter behavior in a forest campground. *Journal of Applied Behavior Analysis,* 1972, *5,* 1–5.

Everett, P. B., Hayward, S. C., & Meyers, A. W. The effects of a token reinforcement procedure on bus ridership. *Journal of Applied Behavior Analysis,* 1974, *7,* 1–9.

Foxx, R. M., & Hake, D. F. Gasoline conservation: A procedure for measuring and reducing the driving of college students. *Journal of Applied Behavior Analysis,* 1977, *10,* 61–74.

Geller, E. S., Chaffee, J. L., & Ingram, R. E. Promoting paper recycling on a university campus. *Journal of Environmental Systems,* 1975, *5,* 39–57.

Geller, E. S., Farris, J. C., & Post, D. S. Prompting a consumer behavior for pollution control. *Journal of Applied Behavior Analysis,* 1973, *6,* 367–376.

Geller, E. S., Wylie, R. G., & Farris, J. C. An attempt at applying prompting and reinforcement toward pollution control. *Proceedings of the 79th Annual Convention of the American Psychological Association,* 1971, *6,* 701–702 (Summary).

Goldstein, R. S., Minkin, B. L., Minkin, N., & Baer, D. M. Finders keepers?: An analysis and validation of a free found ad policy. *Journal of Applied Behavior Analysis,* 1978, *11,* 465–473.

Hayes, S. C., & Cone, J. D. Reducing residential electrical energy use: Payments, information, and feedback. *Journal of Applied Behavior Analysis,* 1977, *10,* 425–436.

Hayes, S. C., Johnson, V. S., & Cone, J. D. The marked item technique: A practical procedure for litter control. *Journal of Applied Behavior Analysis,* 1975, *8,* 381–386.

Kohlenberg, R., & Phillips, T. Reinforcement and rate of litter depositing. *Journal of Applied Behavior Analysis,* 1973, *6,* 391–396.

Kohlenberg, R., Phillips, T., & Proctor, W. A behavioral analysis of peaking in residential electrical energy consumers. *Journal of Applied Behavior Analysis,* 1976, *9,* 13–18.

LaHart, D. E., & Bailey, J. S. The analysis and reduction of children's littering on a nature trail. *Journal of Environmental Education,* 1975, *7,* 37–45.

Lutzker, J. R., & White-Blackburn, G. The good productivity game: Increasing work performance in a rehabilitation setting. *Journal of Applied Behavior Analysis,* 1979, *12,* 488.

Marler, L. A study of antilitter messages. *Journal of Environmental Education,* 1970, *3,* 52–53.

Meyers, H., Nathan, P. E., & Kopel, S. Effects of a token reinforcement system on journal reshelving. *Journal of Applied Behavior Analysis,* 1977, *10,* 213–218.

Powers, R. B., Osborne, J. G., & Anderson, E. G. Positive reinforcement of litter removal in the natural environment. *Journal of Applied Behavior Analysis,* 1973, *6,* 579–586.

Public Opinion Surveys, Inc. (1968) *Who litters—and why.* Available from Keep America Beautiful, Inc., 99 Park Avenue, New York, NY 10016.

Reiss, M. L., Piotrowski, W. D., & Bailey, J. S. Behavioral community psychology: Encouraging low-income parents to seek dental care for their children. *Journal of Applied Behavior Analysis,* 1976, *9,* 387–397.

Stokes, T. F., & Fawcett, S. B. Evaluating municipal policy: An analysis of a refuse packaging program. *Journal of Applied Behavior Analysis,* 1977, *10,* 391–398.

Tuso, M., & Geller, E. S. Behavior analysis applied to environmental/ecological problems: A review. *Journal of Applied Behavior Analysis,* 1976, *9,* 526.

Winett, R. A., & Nietzel, M. T. Behavioral ecology: Contingency management of consumer energy use. *American Journal of Community Psychology,* 1975, *3,* 123–133.

Witmer, J. F., & Geller, E. S. Facilitating paper recycling: Effects of prompts, raffles, and contests. *Journal of Applied Behavior Analysis,* 1976, *9,* 315–322.

CHAPTER 4

The Working World: Business, Industry, and Government

THIS chapter reviews behavioral approaches to problems and issues in business and industry—in such problem areas as safety, performance, administration, theft reduction, productivity, management-employee relations, and so on. The world of business and industry is a "natural" for behavior change procedures because that world understands data and, of course, the use of data is the foundation on which behavior change procedures are built.

PERFORMANCE

One of the earliest reports of behavioral approaches in the business world was the article "Conversations with B. F. Skinner" in the 1973 issue of *Organizational Dynamics* that discussed the applications and effects of positive reinforcement at the Emery Air Freight Company. At Emery, the use of reinforcement techniques saved the company $650,000 annually. Those kinds of data make business people happy. One of the goals was to encourage employees to increase their use of containers. Emery's best expectations were exceeded, in that use of containers increased from 45% to 95%. Tardiness also was greatly reduced during the treatment period. The whole program was based on positive reinforcement techniques and allowed for considerable employee feedback. Behavioral procedures involving positive feedback, specification of desired behaviors, and careful record keeping were the key factors in this pioneering effort.

Productivity has been increased in several other settings. A study (Kim & Hammer, 1976) on the effects of performance feedback and goal setting on productivity and satisfaction was conducted at a large midwestern telephone company affiliated with the Bell System. The subjects were 113 blue-collar, unionized employees. The objective performance measures were cost performance, absenteeism, and safety. This study was a group design in which three groups of employees received three different treatments. One group received extrinsic feedback, which involved information provided to the workers by the foremen as to how many workers met the weekly goals. Further, the foremen praised performance that exceeded the previous week's levels. The second group received intrinsic feedback. This involved having the employees rate themselves on their efforts as a function of data provided to them by the foremen. The third group of employees received both extrinsic and intrinsic feedback. A control group of employees received goal-setting instructions only.

The results showed that the control group (goal setting alone) improved somewhat in performance, but both extrinsic and intrinsic feedback greatly enhanced performance (statistically significantly over baseline and over the control group) in those groups. There was no statistical difference between the extrinsic and intrinsic groups. Thus, this study showed that a relatively simple system could be used to greatly enhance performance.

Performance improved in two small businesses, a neighborhood grocery store, and a downtown game room following application of behavioral strategies with individual employees (Komaki, Waddell, & Pearce, 1977). In the first study, employees of the neighborhood grocery store were provided with goals described in observable terms and their performance was repeatedly monitored. A multiple baseline design across employee responsibilities demonstrated that the consequences (time off with pay, feedback, and the self-recording procedures) as a "package" were effective in improving performance by a range of 30% to 50% in the three categories to which the "package" was applied. Further, the employees stated that they preferred the objectivity of the "new" system and liked the reinforcers. Despite the time off, the procedures were cost-efficient because of the increased productivity. A similar set of procedures was effective in increasing by almost 40% the performance of an attendant in a game room in a downtown area of a metropolitan city.

Miller (1978) has described several examples of the use of behavior change procedures to improve performance. In one study, Miller details the problem the finishing department manager in an apparel manufacturing plant had with a sampler (an employee who completes a daily statistical quality control report) who was not getting his reports done on time. A simple program consisting of goal setting, feedback, and reinforcement reduced the average amount of time it took the employee to complete the reports from 100 minutes to 10 minutes, a tremendous reduction.

Again, praise and public feedback were responsible for reducing the problem of high bobbins in a yarn mill. If a bobbin on a spinning frame is not pushed all the way down on a spindle, it causes tangles, waste, lower winder efficiency, and lost time in clearing the tangles. The problem was reduced by about 75%. The employees reported that they appreciated the positive comments their supervisors were providing and enjoyed trying to beat the goals. Off-quality performance in yarn packing was reduced from 218% to 0.8% through goal setting, public posting of feedback, allowing time off for meeting goals, and assigning extra time for not meeting goals. Shaping performance through personal approval as a reinforcer increased operating efficiency in an abrasives plant by 81.3%. A senior employee had spent an excessive amount of time in nonproductive activities prior to the program, which was implemented by his foreman. Finally, in this series of case reports, Miller (1978) again describes the use of standards, feedback, and praise for improvements that increased by 30% a secretary's attending to her tasks in a business office.

Throughout this book we have made reference to token economies or point systems, which, when used consistently and contingently, produce desired behavior change. Roger D. Bourdon (1977) of J. P. Stevens and Company described the use of a token economy to encourage management performance improvement. The task at hand was to train management personnel at two plants with a total of 1500 employees in the use of behavioral procedures. The management personnel were taught to use a contingent point system for efficiency, quality, attendance, and waste. They were also taught how to set goals and run the point system on the basis of operationally defined goal behaviors and performance. The reinforcers were both tangible and intangible. The tangible reinforcers were items of value from $7.50 to $25 that were listed in a catalog and were available for varying amounts of points earned and saved by the employees. The intangible reinforcers were the social exchanges between management and line staff and, among the line staff, boasting about performance and points earned. The results showed considerable improvement in all four areas. Bourdon, however, cautions about two prerequisites that he feels are necessary for programs such as this to be effective: one is for managers to be willing to try something new in the first place, the other is a complete commitment by the plant managers in supporting the effort. This latter prerequisite might be difficult to accomplish in many settings.

As we have seen, reinforcement procedures have been used on a variety of industrial problems. Runnion, Johnson, and McWhorter (1978) used procedures similar to those described above to reduce the length of time trucks spent at each mill while transporting goods between 58 plant locations of a textile company. The average turnaround time was reduced from 67 to 38.2 minutes. Emmert (1978) compared group feedback to individual feedback by first-line supervisors in increasing performance of four separate crews in a glass manufacturing plant. Both kinds of feedback produced increased performance, but the individual feedback appeared more functional than the group feedback. Monetary refunds were used to increase the frequency of field staff telephone calls to the home office (Kreitner & Golab, 1978). A combination of instructions, group and individual feedback, and social reinforcement was found to be the best method of increasing and maintaining the completion of graphs by staff members in a human service setting (Shook, Johnson, & Uhlman, 1978). Similar procedures were used in reducing waste in a production department of a camera and film company (Eldridge, Lemasters, & Szypot, 1978).

Not only has performance of "normal" industrial employees been increased by behavior change procedures, but there have also been improvements in performance in employees in rehabilitation settings. Goal-setting and reinforcement procedures very similar to those described above in industrial settings were utilized as early as 1969 by Zimmerman, Overpeck, Eisenberg, and Garlick. They increased work rates and units completed per hour of over 20 handicapped employees of a sheltered workshop. The employees' handicaps included mental retardation, neurological impairments, auditory and speech problems, emotional disorders, and orthopedic problems.

Work output was increased by over 100% in four severely and profoundly retarded employees of a rehabilitation industry (Lutzker & White-Blackburn, 1979). Their productivity in removing nails and sorting boards was increased by a procedure called the Good Productivity Game, for which they earned points for reaching criterion levels of performance. The points were backed up by a variety of privileges such as time off, candy, and soft drinks. Both the employees and the managerial staff voiced considerable approval of the Good Productivity Game, which the management continued to use after the formal experiment was concluded.

Thus, here we have seen behavior change technology applied to a variety of subjects and settings in the increase of industrial performance. One concern of ours in the studies described here, however, is lack of long-term follow-up data. How long high productivity can be maintained by using simple contingencies has yet to be documented.

Tardiness and Absenteeism

One of the earliest and most thorough reports of the use of reinforcement procedures in increasing punctuality of industrial workers was provided by Jaime A. Hermann and his colleagues, Ana I. deMontes, Benjamin Dominguez, Francisco Montes, and B. L. Hopkins (1973). The study took place in a plant in Mexico where toilet fixtures were made. Twelve employees who had shown chronic tardiness were targeted as subjects. A small bonus system was offered for each day the employee was on time. No bonus money was available for tardiness. Six of the subjects were exposed to the reversal experimental design which included baseline, bonus, baseline, bonus, baseline, and bonus. The other six employees constituted a control group and thus received no treatment. There was a dramatic reduction in tardiness in the six employees whenever they received bonus money for their punctuality. The control group showed no such improvements. Hermann et al. (1973) recognized the potential impracticality of large-scale daily bonus systems for punctuality. They further suggest that once punctuality came under the control of a bonus system, the bonus system could be provided on a more intermittent basis. Importantly, the study proved to be cost-efficient in that it was less expensive for the company to provide small monetary bonuses than it was for them to lose the amount of production time that they had been losing with their employees who had shown chronic tardiness. Their study is another instance of a pioneering demonstration of the application of behavior change procedures to a novel problem area. These authors did not address whether punctual employees were perturbed over the formerly tardy employees' receiving special benefits.

Absenteeism in blue-collar workers was significantly reduced in a manufacturing and distribution plant (Pedalino & Gamboa, 1974). Using an "ABA" design, they compared a group of employees with groups in four adjoining plants and demonstrated behavior change techniques to decrease absenteeism in the treatment group, but not in any of the comparison groups. The treatment was a lottery incentive system. The lottery was called a "poker game." Each day when an employee *came to work* and was *on time* a card was drawn by the employee from a deck of cards. At the end of the week (thus requiring a full week's attendance) the employee with the best poker hand won $20. When it was in effect, the lottery was successful in reducing absenteeism. The project was not continued because of an impending union contract renegotiation, but again a novel set of procedures showed some very hopeful results. It would be interesting to learn what union officials felt about the lottery.

A lottery system for reducing employee absenteeism was also reported by Wallin and Johnson (1976) and was shown to save a small company $3,109.11 in a one-year period because of the reduction in the sick-leave expenditures.

A large-scale study in the reduction of industrial absenteeism was conducted by Robert W. Kemper of the Western Electric Company and R. Vance Hall of the University of Kansas (1976). They applied their program to 7500 production workers in two factories of a large manufacturing company. Employees at 13 other plants served as comparison groups. A multiple baseline design across the two experimental plants showed the effectiveness of the intervention system used to reduce absenteeism. In addition to the significance of this study being enhanced by the large number of subjects, it is also most important to note that the *intervention phase in Plant "A" lasted a year and a half and in Plant "B" it lasted one year.* The intervention system used was called an Attendance Management System (AMS). With consultation from the researchers, the AMS was primarily designed by a plant manager. A variety of nonmonetary privileges was used in the AMS. These included freedom from a requirement to punch the time clock, earned time off without pay, temporary immunity from discipline, and reduction in position on the disciplinary ladder. In Plant "A" the average percent of absenteeism dropped from a baseline of 5.0% to 3.4% during AMS. In Plant "B" the baseline ranged from as low as 5% to as high as 13%. During AMS, the range was from 6% to 7.5% with the mean around 6.2%. No similar reductions in absenteeism were seen in the control groups. The AMS was subsequently utilized with equal success across the comparison plants.

Miller (1978) has also provided a series of reports on improving attendance. A textile firm in North Carolina was experiencing a rate of absenteeism that it considered unacceptable. A simple program of visual graphic feedback and social reinforcement provided by supervisory staff improved attendance by over 8% over a two-month period and saved the company $9,000 annually. Similar procedures were used to increase efficiency and attendance and reduce labor turnover at a weaving mill. Graphic feedback and social reinforcement also reduced tardiness in employees of an upholstery plant. An obvious advantage of these kinds of procedures is the comparative ease with which they can be introduced and taught to other people.

Finding international replications of behavior change procedures, we note a study reported by Christoper Orpen of the University of Witwatersaand, South Africa (1978). He describes the use of small monetary bonuses, in a manner very similar to that used by Hermann et al. (1973), to increase attendance in 23 female factory workers. Finally, a nearly cost-free procedure has been described by Lamal and Benfield (1978). They utilized self-monitoring on arrival time at the workplace and percentage of time spent working by a draftsman. The draftsman's behavior changed dramatically whenever self-monitoring was instituted, and his improvements maintained after an 11-week follow-up. More studies are, of course, needed to see whether self-monitoring and perhaps group self-monitoring would have any large-scale practicality.

SAFETY

For both humanitarian and economic reasons, industry is interested in the safety of its employees. The humanitarian reasons are obvious; no one wants to see someone else get hurt. The economic reasons involve the costs in actual dollars and in performance and efficiency that are created by industrial accidents.

A personal safety program using a behavioral approach was first described by Mirman, Ritschl, Hall, Sigler, and Hopkins (1976). A large chemical plant with 120 employees had requested assistance in reducing a high rate of lost time due to injurious accidents. A multiple baseline design across one-half of the plant employees at a time was used to evaluate an incentive program and supervisory training in positive and corrective feedback. The incentive system was called Protective Poker and was very similar in logic and design to the Pedalino and Gamboa (1974) study which used a poker-game lottery incentive to reduce absenteeism. At the end of each week employees who had a perfect safety record that week drew a hand from a deck of cards. Ten winners were then chosen on the basis of the ten best poker hands. The back-up reinforcers for the winners included such things as Green Stamps, tickets to sporting events, dinner tickets, money, and amusement park tickets. In addition, supervisors participated in a separate monthly incentive program contingent upon their unit's severity rate of accidents being below a predetermined low. The supervisory training consisted of two two-hour sessions on how to administer and log positive and corrective feedback on workers' safety behaviors. The results showed the program to be effective in reducing the severity and frequency rates of lost-time injuries. As in the studies we have seen above, the company was willing to pay for incentives that amounted to less than the cost of the injury time off.

The wearing of ear protection in a high-noise-level area is a Federal requirement; nonetheless, only 14.5% of the employees in a high-noise area of a textile plant in North Carolina were wearing their earplugs despite the fact that earplugs were regularly supplied by the company to the employees (Miller, 1978). After baseline data were gathered, the department manager called the employees into his office to explain the importance of wearing the ear devices. He then explained the meaning of a graph of baseline data, how this "information" phase worked, and publicly posted the graph. The feedback produced a moderate, but not criterion, increase in the wearing of earplugs. Later, doughnuts and other tangible, edible reinforcers were added to the feedback procedure. This raised the wearing of earplugs to nearly 100%. The manager was very pleased with the results and continued to vary the kinds of edible reinforcers used in order to prevent a satiation effect.

Once again, a multiple baseline design was used to evaluate the effects of pinpointing and reinforcing safe performance in a food manufacturing plant (Komaki, Barwick, & Scott, 1978). The design went across the wrapping department and the makeup department in a wholesale bakery. The intervention procedure consisted of an explanation and visual slide presentation of correct safety performance and daily graphic feedback on safety performance. Improvements of over 20% to nearly perfect safety performance were achieved in both departments. In addition to the staggered introduction of intervention procedures within the multiple baseline design, the effect of the education and feedback intervention was also demonstrated by a brief reversal during which the procedures were removed and safety performance began to fall. Employee reaction was so favorable to the intervention that they actually applauded and cheered good data when they were posted.

Hermann (1977) conducted two experiments that examined the effects of a safety program on the accident rates of automobile workers. Two safety indices were used to determine the effectiveness of the program: an index of medical accidents and one of disabling accidents. In the first experiment, the intervention program included the workers' participation to detect unsafe conditions, correction (in an overcorrection-like manner—that is, the repeated, rapid-succession demonstration of the appropriate behavior) of unsafe conditions, a job-safety analysis performed by a safety engineer, weekly safety audits carried out by the safety engineer, talks with the workers about safety, and group recognition of safety achievements by the workers.

A multiple baseline design across two departments was used to assess the effects of the intervention. The intervention was introduced in the cleaning department and later in the molding department. A significant reduction in medical and disabling accidents occurred in both departments; the accident indices were lower than during the baseline conditions. A similar study, which yielded similar results, was then executed in the engine-casting plant and the hub- and drum-casting plant. In both studies, not only was the frequency of accidents reduced during intervention conditions, but there was also a reduction in the severity of the accidents. The basic advantage of these studies is that they showed that existing personnel could combine readily available safety practices to improve safety performance of auto workers.

Dr. Beth Sulzer-Azaroff of the University of Massachusetts (1978) has also described some simple, nonintrusive, cost-effective ways to reduce hazards in 30 university research laboratories. Building inspections had indicated the presence of various mechanical, chemical, and electrical hazards. Across subjects, multiple baseline designs evaluated the effects of periodic inspections by safety officers who provided written feedback about and suggestions on how to improve the hazardous conditions. The programs were effective in all of the laboratories.

STAFF AND MANAGEMENT BEHAVIOR

As we have seen, simple feedback procedures have been shown to be effective in improving performance, attendance, and safety in industrial employees. Tardiness at professional committee meetings involving a pediatrician, a nurse supervisor, a social worker, a recreational therapist, a special education principal, the director of in-service training, a secretary, and a psychologist was also reduced by presenting individual graphic feedback to each member of the committee (Favell, 1973). The feedback, in reducing the tardiness of the committee members, allowed the committee to get more work done in a meeting. Thus, we see that line staff are not the only people modified by feedback. In this case, professional staff showed behavior change and expressed an appreciation for it.

You will see several examples throughout this book of the use of behavioral strategies to examine existing practices or policies. For example, Quilitch (1975) compared three staff-management procedures, two of which are common techniques used by administrators. The administration of a mental health institute wanted to see the retarded residents involved in more activities on their wards. Thus, Quilitch examined the procedures across four wards containing 95 residents. After baseline data were collected on the number of residents seen engaging in activities, a memo from the administrator was sent out instructing staff to lead daily recreational activities. Memos, of course, are one of the most frequently used techniques of administrators in attempts at changing the behavior of their employees. The results showed the memo to have virtually no effect in increasing activities, so a workshop was provided to the staff. The workshop concentrated on teaching staff to lead activities. During and after the workshop the staff expressed considerable enthusiasm for what they were learning and vowed that they would use what they had learned in leading considerably more activities for the residents. Again, the results showed *no changes* in the staff's actual behavior. Finally, the administrator assigned staff activity leaders and provided performance feedback to the staff by publicly posting the daily average number of active residents on each of the four wards under study. During this condition, which lasted as long as a month and a half, the number of residents engaged in recreational activities increased by more than 400%. The administrator then adopted similar scheduling and feedback procedures to maintain activities on all wards in the institute. Here we see an example of utilizing behavioral measurement procedures and design to evaluate administrative procedure and its effect on staff (and thereby, resident) behavior.

A common need in business and human service settings is for groups of individuals to solve problems. Often the process of trying to solve problems *leads* to interpersonal problems in the group rather than solutions to the problems brought before the group. At Florida State University, Richard V. Briscoe, David B. Hoffman, and Jon S. Bailey (1975) trained a community board to solve problems. In their report they point out that,

> in recent years, many federally funded programs designed to help the poor (Head Start, Community Action, Model Cities . . .) have required the participation of low-income parents, clients, and residents in decision-making roles. This has usually taken the form of service on advisory or policy boards, often with low-income parents and community representatives constituting over 50 percent of those decision-making bodies (Hoffman, Jordan, & McCormick, 1971). More often than not, such participation has been ineffective. Marshall (1971) found that . . . representatives of the poor saw themselves as ineffective, as did non-poor board members. Many resigned in frustration and bitterness [pp. 157–158].

To try to avoid this kind of frustration, Briscoe et al. (1975) trained nine lower socioeconomic adults who were participating as policy board members in a federally funded rural community project to make behaviorally defined statements to increase problem-solving behaviors in board meetings. Using a multiple baseline design across subjects and skills, these researchers analyzed three behavioral categories: (1) stating the problem, (2) finding solutions to the problem, and (3) implementing action to the solution. The training involved modeling and videotape feedback. Problem-solving responses during board meetings increased for subjects following training and remained higher than baseline when follow-up observations were made. It is likely that this model will be used by other agencies and businesses as a way to teach problem solving.

MORE "REAL-WORLD" APPLICATIONS

Two of the most important studies in the work environment area were conducted by Dr. Nathan Azrin and his colleagues. The original study (Jones & Azrin, 1973) took place in a rural county in Southern Illinois. Two experiments were involved. The first was a survey evaluation of current job-finding methods of 90 graduate students at a large state university. The results showed that by far (66%) the majority of the respondents to the survey found jobs through a friend, relative, or acquaintance. Fifteen percent found jobs by applying without any prior information about them, 8% through a public employment agency, 5% through "help wanted" advertisements, 2% through "employment wanted" advertisements, and 2% through private employment agencies. While these percentages seem generally representative of how most people find jobs, the figures were probably disappointing to federal and state agencies that try to help people find the jobs.

Experiment 2 was conducted by Jones and Azrin to see whether an information-reward procedure would be effective in filling jobs and therefore reducing unemployment. The subjects of the experiment were all unemployed persons in the county who were registered with the Illinois State Employment Service. The job-producing effectiveness of two kinds of newspaper advertisements was compared. Both ads solicited job-opening information, but the experimental ad offered a $100 reward for information that resulted in a job for one of the registered persons. The ads were nearly identical in listing what kinds of applicants were available (for example, stenographer, sales clerk, truck driver, and the like) and whom a prospective employer should contact. The reward ad, however, included the information about the $100 job-locator fee to be paid to anyone providing an applicant information that led to a job. When someone did provide job information, he or she was given further information about the reward. Information providers were told that the applicant must be hired before the providers would be paid, that $25 would be paid after the applicant was hired, and that three weekly $25 checks would be paid contingent upon the applicant's staying on the job for each of three subsequent weeks. The results are shown in Table 4-1. As can be seen, the reward ad produced eight times as many filled jobs as the no-reward ad. Furthermore, a cost-benefit analysis was conducted. The reward ad cost the agency $130 per placement (filled job). This was figured by dividing the number of placements into the cost of the

TABLE 4-1. Comparison of the Reward Advertisement and No-Reward Advertisement Procedures in Locating Job Openings and Facilitating Actual Placements.

	No-Reward Ad (First Week)	Reward Ad (Second Week)	No-Reward Ad (Third Week)
Number of calls received	2[a]	14[a]	0
Number of job-openings reported	2	20	0
Number of applicants sent for interviews	1	19	0
Number of applicants actually hired	1	8	0
Number still working after 1 month	1	8	0

[a]One call was refused because the job was outside the appropriate geographical area.

From "An Experimental Application of a Social Reinforcement Approach to the Problem of Job-Finding," by R. J. Jones and N. H. Azrin, *Journal of Applied Behavior Analysis,* 1973, *6,* 345–354. Copyright 1973 by the Society for the Experimental Analysis of Behavior, Inc. Reprinted by permission.

ad plus the $100 reward. The average cost per placement for the no-reward ad was $470 (the cost of the ad divided by the number of placements). Jones and Azrin further point out that a private agency would have charged around $500 to place a person.

While the use of the kinds of rewards described above worked well and appeared to be fairly cost-effective, Dr. Azrin and his colleagues, T. Flores and S. J. Kaplan, advanced the job-finding process further by creating an even more practical approach called the Job-Finding Club (1975). As in others of Dr. Azrin's programs described throughout this book, in this program Azrin and his colleagues looked at unemployment behaviorally, analyzed the requisite behaviors for getting a job, and went about teaching all of the necessary skills and setting up an environment conducive to the intended outcome—that is, reduced unemployment.

Several components were developed. A *group meeting* was organized in order to make the clients feel that they were not "in it alone." Like members of weight-loss groups, the club members were able to provide encouragement for good role-playing, provide leads to jobs, and share other experiences related to job-seeking. The group also provided for multiple partners for role-playing. A *buddy system* was also instituted within the group meeting. This allowed for more individualized encouragement.

Motivation was provided by recruiting the help of the family in providing encouragement, providing testimonials from successful job seekers, and providing encouragement from the group and the counselor. Further, the club provided special ways of using want ads, telephoning, constructing resumés, the contacting of friends, and so on. In a comparison to a group of job seekers not using the job club, the job club members found considerably more jobs. Further, their average starting salary was 72¢ per hour more than the salaries of job seekers not in the club.

The advantages of an approach like this should be obvious. Unemployment among the Job-Finding Club members was dramatically reduced and many of the negative side effects of unemployment were undoubtedly prevented.

Probably the most important element of behavior change procedures is reliance on data. Important decisions in many walks of life are made frequently on the basis of a quantitative analysis. A major issue in the past several years, and one that often produces considerable emotional reactions when discussed, is the problem of crime and how crime prevention should proceed. Often, federal or local governments create large agencies or promote local efforts at crime reduction and prevention. Probably more often than not, these efforts are based on less than scientific calculations. In 1975, some researchers in Tennessee (Schnelle, Kirchner, McNees, & Lawler, 1975) used as much experimental rigor as possible to provide social evaluation research for comparing two police patrolling strategies. The analysis took place in several zones of Davidson County, Nashville, Tennessee, which had a population of 449,000. The first analysis was conducted in order to evaluate the effect of a 35-member specialized burglary patrol. This is known as a saturated patrol procedure—that is, putting extra patrols in a particular neighborhood in order to be on the lookout for burglaries. A time-series analysis (daily data taken over several weeks) showed that there were no reductions in burglaries that could be attributed to the special burglary team. In a second evaluation, a multiple baseline design was used to examine the effects of a special walking patrol. This analysis showed that this patrol produced an increase in the number of crimes reported, but not in the number of arrests made. Thus, our daily lives can be affected by research strategies that have the potential of yielding very important, socially significant information to agencies such as police.

In a later study (1977) Schnelle, Kirchner, Casey, Uselton, and McNees monitored the effect of increased police patrols on the report of crime in four patrol zones. Overall patrol movements were increased four times above normal levels. Slow patrols, on which the police car is driven less than 20 mph, were increased by 30 times their normal rates. A multiple baseline design showed an increase in the reporting and occurrences of crimes such as robbery, burglary, and aggravated assault during night patrols, but not during day patrols. When the saturated patrols were removed at night, there was an increase in crimes. The authors of this study had some interesting speculations as to why the results occurred as they did. Home burglaries are the prevalent daytime crime, whereas business burglaries occur at night. Patrolling businesses at night is easier than patrolling homes during the day because there are fewer obstructions such as bushes in front of businesses, there are fewer distractions for the patrolmen at night, and business establishments are grouped closer together than homes. Despite the partly encouraging results of this study, cost-effectiveness was a concern of the department. It was suggested that more cost-efficient procedures be examined.

The Metropolitan Nashville Police Department continued its evaluation of crime prevention programs. Schnelle, Kirchner, Macrae, McNees, Eck, Snodgrass, Casey, and Uselton (1978) reported an experimental and cost-benefit analysis of a helicopter patrol in a high-crime area. The helicopter was used to patrol two different zones of the city over two 12-day periods from 9 A.M. to 5 P.M. each day. Baseline data were gathered in the zones normally patrolled by cars when the helicopter patrol was not in effect. The data showed that the helicopter patrol was effective in reducing the number of burglaries during the experimental periods. The cash costs of the helicopter patrol were compared to the costs of the usual routines. An attempt was also made to include in the analysis the social and "security" effects of the helicopter patrol. All things considered, the cost-benefit analysis showed the helicopter to be the recommended patrol procedure. More data are, of course, necessary before conclusions of this sort can be generalized to other crimes or cities. A social validation might be in order here also; that is, the citizens could be polled as to whether they wanted extra noise and possible privacy disruptions from the helicopter as a means of reducing burglaries.

The acceptance of a behavior change technique comes when it has been demonstrated to be practical and successful when applied repeatedly, and when it is used with a large number of individuals. A study in which, perhaps, the greatest number of subjects ever participated was reported by A. John McSweeney (1978). The subjects were the 1,385,000 residents of greater Cincinnati, Ohio. In the time period of 1962 to 1976 the Cincinnati Bell Telephone Company collected data on the usage of local and long-distance directory calls. Over a baseline period (1962 to mid-1973), the average number of daily calls for local directory assistance was around 80,000. In mid-1973, a response-cost procedure was introduced whereby a local directory assistance caller was charged 20¢ per call for that service. From 1973–1976, the average number of local directory assistance calls dropped by approximately 60,000 per day. Throughout the entire 14-year period the use of long-distance directory assistance calls (which were not punished by the 20¢ response cost) remained stable (see Figure 4-1). The cost-efficiency data showed that consumers averaged about 65¢ overall savings on their monthly bills, and businesses saved approximately $1.25 on their monthly bills because of the reduced use of expensive directory assistance calls. The author of this study points out that response-cost procedures might be very effective in situations where costly or precious services or commodities are being overconsumed.

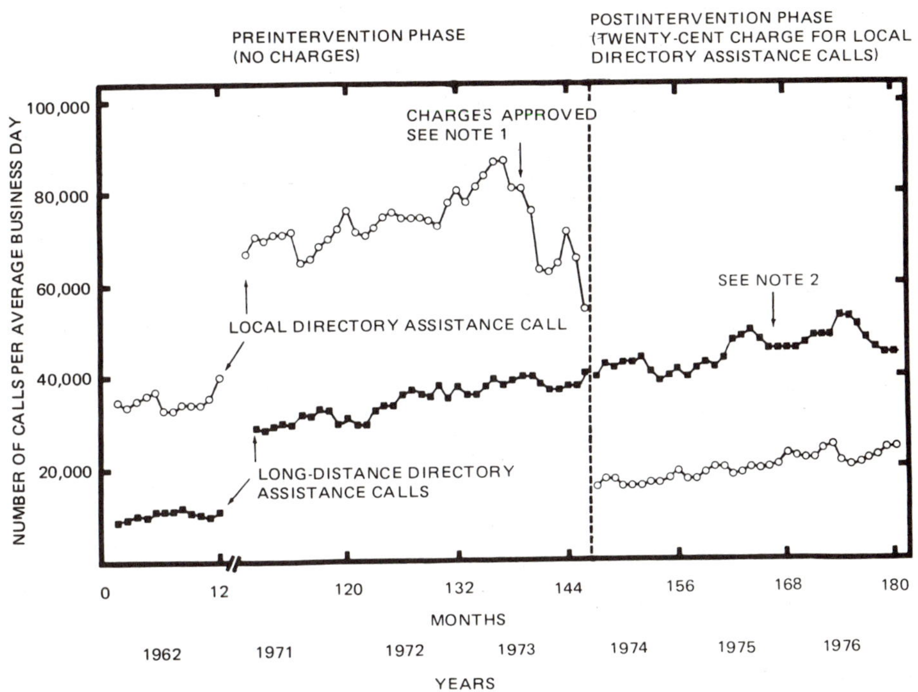

FIGURE 4-1.   Number of local and long-distance directory assistance calls placed per average business day before and after charges were introduced. (From "Effects of Response Cost on the Behavior of a Million Persons: Charging for Directory Assistance in Cincinnati," by A. J. McSweeney, *Journal of Applied Behavior Analysis*, 1978, *11*, 47–51. Copyright 1978 by the Society for the Experimental Analysis of Behavior, Inc. Reprinted by permission.)

Shoplifting is one of the most frequent crimes in the United States. It is very costly to business and, of course, ultimately it is the consumer who pays, literally, for shoplifting. Providing information through signs was a strategy used by McNees,

Egli, Marshall, Schnelle, and Risley (1976) to reduce shoplifting in a department store in Murfreesboro, Tennessee. In the first of two studies, 25 items from each type of merchandise in the store were selected as key items. A code letter on the price tags—which were removed by cashiers—helped provide data on the key items that were legitimately purchased as compared to those that were marked in stock, but disappeared. Baseline data on the items sold and missing were collected for 26 days. After baseline, five signs (containing four messages) were posted in the store. The signs said, "Shoplifting is stealing, shoplifting is a crime, shoplifting is not uplifting, and shoplifting helps inflation." The reversal design showed that the signs were functional in reducing, but not eliminating, shoplifting. After the first study, the authors concluded, ". . . it appears that the placement of anti-shoplifting signs in the department may have produced a decrease in shoplifting without affecting sales rates. If similar changes were present with a larger sample, the procedure would probably be recommended as being both inexpensive and useful" (p. 402). Thus, a second study was conducted in which colored, rather than letter-coded, tags were used to distinguish types of merchandise, easier tracking procedures were utilized, and three groups of merchandise instead of two were targeted. Signs that said, "ATTENTION SHOPPERS AND SHOPLIFTERS: The items you see marked with a red star are items that shoplifters frequently take," were placed on clothing racks and walls. This procedure virtually eliminated the shoplifting of the specially marked items. Sales data showed that the procedures did not adversely affect sales. These latter data, of course, are the kind that store-owners would need to see.

Cash awards have been used to try to encourage employees to submit their ideas for solving organizational problems. One potential problem with systems such as this is that most suggestions receive no response, and extinction of the responses may occur in many individuals. Also, some systems may not be able to afford or might not be allowed to use cash awards to reinforce employee suggestions. As we have seen repeatedly in this chapter, in work environments, simple feedback can be effective in producing productive behavior change. Once again, we see feedback used (Quilitch, 1978) to reinforce the submission of written suggestions by mental health employees. A suggestion manager posted each submitted suggestion publicly, along with her answer, within two days of its receipt. Eighty employees submitted 76 suggestions over the 32 weeks of the study. A "BAB" design was used whereby data were first collected for a few weeks under a "posting" condition. For six weeks in the "A" condition, no feedback was provided. Feedback was then reintroduced in the second "B" condition. Considerably more suggestions were made during the posting and feedback conditions. Anecdotal reports from staff suggested that the system improved morale.

CONCLUSIONS

The application of behavior change techniques to work environments is showing signs of being a major contribution to the working world. The use of data and controlled designs are understandable to the business world, which relies on data to evaluate its accomplishments. More and larger-scale demonstrations of cost-effective successes of implementations of behavior change programs in business are in order before we conclude that we have revolutionized the business world. However, our contributions in such diverse areas as textile plants, mental hospitals, department stores, and police departments suggest that we may be on our way to applications in other working environments about which we have not yet even thought.

REFERENCES

Azrin, N. H., & Besalel, V. B. *Job counselor's manual: A behavioral approach to vocational counseling*. Baltimore: University Park Press, 1980.

Azrin, N. H., Flores, T., & Kaplan, S. J. Job-finding club: A group-assisted program for obtaining employment. *Behavior Research and Therapy,* 1975, *13,* 17–27.

Bourdon, R. D. A token economy application to management performance improvement. *Journal of Organizational Behavior Management,* 1977, *1,* 23–37.

Briscoe, R. V., Hoffman, D. B., & Bailey, J. S. Behavioral community psychology: Training a community board to problem solve. *Journal of Applied Behavior Analysis,* 1975, *8,* 157–168.

Conversation with B. F. Skinner. *Organizational Dynamics,* Winter 1973, 31–40.

Eldridge, L., Lemasters, S., & Szypot, B. A performance feedback intervention to reduce waste: Performance data and participant responses. *Journal of Organizational Behavior Management,* 1978, *1,* 258–266.

Emmert, G. D. Measuring the impact of group performance feedback versus individual performance feedback in an industrial setting. *Journal of Organizational Behavior Management,* 1978, *1,* 134–141.

Favell, J. E. *Reduction of staff tardiness by a feedback procedure.* Paper presented at the annual meeting of the American Psychological Association, Montreal, Canada, 1973.

Hermann, J. A. Effects of a safety program on the accident frequency and severity rate of automobile workers. Unpublished doctoral dissertation, University of Kansas, 1977.

Hermann, J. A., deMontes, A. I., Dominguez, B., Montes, F., & Hopkins, B. L. Effects of bonuses for punctuality on the tardiness of industrial workers. *Journal of Applied Behavior Analysis,* 1973, *6,* 563–572.

Hoffman, D. B., Jordan, J. S., & McCormick, F. *Parent participation in preschool daycare* Monograph No. 5, Atlanta, Ga.: Southeastern Educational Laboratory, 1971.

Jones, R. J., & Azrin, N. H. An experimental application of a social reinforcement approach to the problem of job finding. *Journal of Applied Behavior Analysis,* 1973, *6,* 345–353.

Kemper, R. W., & Hall, R. V. *Reduction of absenteeism: Results of a behavioral approach.* Paper presented at the annual conventions of the Midwestern Association of Behavior Analysis, Chicago, May 1976, and the American Psychological Association, Washington, D.C., September 1976.

Kim, J. S., & Hammer, W. C. Effect of performance feedback and goal setting on productivity and satisfaction in an organizational setting. *Journal of Applied Psychology,* 1976, *61,* 48–57.

Komaki, J., Barwick, K. D., & Scott, L. R. A behavioral approach to occupational safety: Pinpointing and reinforcing safe performance in a food manufacturing plant. *Journal of Applied Psychology,* 1978, *63,* 434–445.

Komaki, J., Waddell, W. M., & Pearce, M. G. The applied behavior analysis approach and individual employees: Improving performance in two small businesses. *Organizational Behavior and Human Performance,* 1977, *19,* 337–352.

Kreitner, R., & Golab, M. Increasing the rate of salesperson telephone calls with a monetary reward. *Journal of Organizational Behavior Management,* 1978, *1,* 192–195.

Lamal, P. A., & Benfield, A. The effect of self-monitoring on job tardiness and percentage of time spent working. *Journal of Organizational Behavior Management,* 1978, *1,* 142–149.

Lutzker, J. R., & White-Blackburn, G. The good productivity game: Increasing work performance in a rehabilitation setting. *Journal of Applied Behavior Analysis,* 1979, *12,* 488.

Marshall, D. B. *The politics of participation in poverty: A case study of the Board of Economic and Youth Opportunities Agency of Greater Los Angeles.* Berkeley: University of California Press, 1971.

McNees, M. P., Egli, D. S., Marshall, R. S., Schnelle, J. R., & Risley, T. R. Shoplifting prevention: Providing information through signs. *Journal of Applied Behavior Analysis,* 1976, *9,* 407–416.

McSweeney, A. J. Effects of response cost on the behavior of a million persons: Charging for directory assistance in Cincinnati. *Journal of Applied Behavior Analysis,* 1978, *11,* 47–51.

Miller, L. M. *Behavior management: The new science of managing people at work.* New York: Wiley, 1978.

Mirman, R., Ritschl, E. R., Hall, V. R., Sigler, J. R., & Hopkins, B. L. *Personal safety program: A behavioral approach to industrial safety.* Paper presented at the annual conventions of the Midwestern Association of Behavior Analysis, Chicago, May 1976, and the American Psychological Association, Washington, D.C., September 1976.

Orpen, C. Effects of bonuses for attendance on the absenteeism of industrial workers. *Journal of Organizational Behavior Management,* 1978, *1,* 118–124.

Pedalino, E., & Gamboa, V. U. Behavior modification and absenteeism: Intervention in one industrial setting. *Journal of Applied Psychology,* 1974, *59,* 694–698.

Quilitch, H. R. A comparison of three staff-management procedures. *Journal of Applied Behavior Analysis,* 1975, *8,* 59–66.

Quilitch, H. R. Using a simple feedback procedure to reinforce the submission of written suggestions by mental health employees. *Journal of Organizational Behavior Management,* 1978, *1,* 155–163.

Runnion, A., Johnson, T., & McWhorter, J. The effects of feedback and reinforcement on truck turnaround time in materials transportation. *Journal of Organizational Behavior Management,* 1978, *1,* 110–117.

Schnelle, J. F., Kirchner, R. E., Jr., Casey, J. D., Uselton, P. H., Jr., & McNees, M. P. Patrol evaluation research: A multiple-baseline analysis of saturation police patrolling day and night hours. *Journal of Applied Behavior Analysis,* 1977, *10,* 33–40.

Schnelle, J. F., Kirchner, R. E., Jr., Macrae, J. W., McNees, M. P., Eck, R. H., Snodgrass, S., Casey, J. D., & Uselton, P. H., Jr. Police evaluation research: An experimental and cost-benefit analysis of a helicopter patrol in a high crime area. *Journal of Applied Behavior Analysis,* 1978, *11,* 11–21.

Schnelle, J. F., Kirchner, R. E., McNees, M. P., & Lawler, J. M. Social evaluation research: The evaluation of two police patrolling strategies. *Journal of Applied Behavior Analysis,* 1975, *8,* 353–366.

Shook, G. L., Johnson, C. M., & Uhlman, W. F. The effect of response effort reduction, instructions, group and individual feedback and reinforcement on staff performance. *Journal of Organizational Behavior Management,* 1978, *1,* 206–215.

Sulzer-Azaroff, B. *Behavioral ecology and accident prevention.* Paper presented at the 86th annual convention of the American Psychological Association, Toronto, August 1978.

Wallin, J. A., & Johnson, R. D. The positive reinforcement approach to controlling employee absenteeism. *Personnel Journal,* August 1976.

Zimmerman, J., Overpeck, C., Eisenberg, H., & Garlick, B. Operant conditioning in a sheltered workshop: Further data in support of an objective and systematic approach to rehabilitation. *Rehabilitation Literature,* 1969, *30,* 326–334.

CHAPTER 5

Health Care: Adults

THE major health care problems of adults are a function of their lifestyles. We eat too much, and we eat the wrong foods; we consume too much alcohol; we smoke too many cigarettes. We are sedentary almost to the point of going out of our way to avoid exercise. Americans have only recently become aware of the health-related dangers of stress and the need to develop skills for coping with life crises. Poor habits, the stress of our industrialized society, and a myriad of environmental conditions (air pollution, carcinogenic agents, and so on) all combine to make our country seem an unhealthy place to live. The application of behavior change techniques to these problems is just beginning, and we are discovering how difficult it is to change long-standing habits. A major problem is getting every one of us to assume responsibility for his or her own health-related behavior. That is quite a task; we examine it in this chapter.

The health care problems of our country have become enormous, in terms of both numbers of patients served and cost. In 1965, $39 billion and only 5.9% of our gross national product (GNP) were devoted to health care. Ten years later those figures were $119 billion and 8.3% GNP (Knowles, 1977a). In 1979, it was predicted that the total would be $206 billion and 9.1% of our GNP (Health costs: What limit?, 1979). Somers (1976) has stated that close to one million Americans die prematurely each year from causes primarily related to their style of life. These include deaths from heart disease, accidents, cirrhosis of the liver, suicide, and homicide. It is obvious that if significant changes could be effected in health-related behaviors, longevity could be increased and ultimately health care costs could be reduced.

In this vein, it has been shown that life expectancy and better health are significantly related to seven simple but basic health habits (Breslow, 1973; Belloc & Breslow, 1972). These are as follows:

1. regular meals three times per day and no snacks
2. having breakfast every day
3. a moderate amount of exercise two or three times weekly
4. seven to eight hours of sleep each night
5. not smoking
6. not being overweight
7. abstinence from alcohol or only a moderate intake

Knowles (1977b) has gone so far as to say that 99% of us are born healthy and become sick only as a result of personal misbehavior and environmental conditions. Lewis Thomas (1977) has estimated that at least 75% of the patients seeking help in doctors' offices or clinics have complaints or ailments for which no organic explanation can be found. Obviously, *stress* plays an extremely important role in disease and an individual's perception of his own health (Knowles, 1977b).

These findings point to the conclusion that the health care of our country must broaden its base to include elements of health beyond the traditional biomedical or disease model. Engel (1977) has suggested the adoption of a biopsychosocial model that takes into account, in addition to biomedical components, the patient, the social context in which the patient lives, and the health care delivery system. All of these components must be utilized to understand the determinants of a patient's disease and to devise rational patterns of treatment and health care.

Given that environmental events play critical roles in the disease process, it follows that alteration of these events through behavioral procedures where possible would seem promising. The maladaptive health-related behaviors that lead to disease should be potential targets for behavioral procedures. Likewise, behavioral procedures could be used to reinforce and thus strengthen more adaptive health behaviors. Areas such as compliance with medical regimens, health education, and self-monitoring of health-related behaviors also seem likely targets for behavioral procedures.

The application of behavior change procedures to the problems of health care make up a new field, which has been called behavioral medicine. There is currently considerable controversy over an exact definition (Schwartz & Weiss, 1978a, 1978b; Pomerleau, 1978; Matarazzo, 1979); however, we find ourselves most sympathetic with the views of Pomerleau and Brady (1979). Behavioral medicine can best integrate behavioral and biomedical science knowledge through the use of behavior analysis, behavioral assessment, and behavior change principles. In behavioral medicine these principles and procedures are used in the prevention, diagnosis, treatment, and rehabilitation of disease or physiological dysfunction.

Interest in behavior analysis and health care is growing, as is demonstrated by the formation of a Special Interest Group within the Association for the Advancement of Behavior Therapy, the publication of the *Behavioral Medicine Advances,* the formation of a limited membership Academy of Behavioral Medicine Research, and the formation of the Society of Behavioral Medicine, an open membership organization for researchers and clinicians within behavioral medicine. A *Journal of Behavioral Medicine* has been founded and now coexists with journals such as *Biofeedback and Self-Regulation* and *Psychophysiology.* A number of behavioral medicine centers and clinics have developed around the country—at Harvard Medical School, Johns Hopkins University School of Medicine, University of Mississippi Medical Center, University of Pennsylvania School of Medicine, Stanford University, and Yale University (Weiss, 1978).

In this chapter and the next, we look at some of the applications of behavior change techniques to the health care problems of adults and children. A word of caution is necessary. Assessment of illness and disease in an individual is a complex affair. It is one that should include a physician with, perhaps, additional input from other allied health professionals. Only when this assessment has been done—and, perhaps most safely, only with continuing consultation with a physician—should behavioral intervention with health-related behaviors proceed. Obviously, behavioral intervention is most appropriate in cases in which more traditional medical procedures have been exhausted. It is extremely important to rule out all patients whose complaints are clearly of organic or physiologic origin; after proper screening and medical assessments, remaining patients should undergo a thorough behavioral assessment as described in Chapter 2.

BIOFEEDBACK

Before starting to look at health care problems, we must take time to briefly define and discuss biofeedback, which is one of the major behavior change procedures associated with health care problems. Biofeedback gives an individual immediate feedback about a physiological response that would not normally be discriminated. Special instruments have been developed to measure such physiological information as heart rate, blood pressure, muscle activity, skin temperature, and the electrical activity of the brain (see Table 5-1). These indexes of physiological functioning have long been viewed as reflexive or respondent behaviors not subject to voluntary control. Research to the contrary began to appear throughout the 1960s in experiments with animals (see Miller, 1969) and humans (see Fowler & Kimmel, 1962; Shapiro, Crider, & Tursky, 1964). In the typical biofeedback procedure, information about the physiological activity is fed back to the person. This information may be visual (flashing lights, a meter reading, digital numerical information) or auditory (tones which may vary in frequency, pitch, or loudness). Subjects are generally told such things as "Make the lights flash," "Try to raise the meter reading," or "Try to make the tone louder."

TABLE 5-1. Biofeedback Applications.

Types	*Uses*
Heart rate	Tachycardia
Blood pressure	Hypertension
Electromyogram (EMG)	Muscle contraction headaches, neuromuscular reeducation
Skin temperature	Migraine headaches
Electroencephalogram (EEG)	Seizures

From the early biofeedback research of the 1960s boomed a new specialty and an industry complete with gadgets and cookbooks on how to do it (Obrist, 1976). Unfortunately, the excitement and enthusiasm was scientifically premature. Numerous writers have surveyed and evaluated the biofeedback literature. Most have come to the conclusion that at this time biofeedback can be of significant benefit to only a few clinical problems (see Blanchard & Young, 1974; Blanchard & Epstein, 1977). Furthermore, biofeedback has rarely been found to be superior to other behavior change techniques (Shapiro & Surwit, 1979). Overall, generalization beyond the biofeedback training setting has seldom been demonstrated; long-term follow-ups have not been conducted; results have not been *clinically* significant; and the research designs used have been very poor.

This is not to say that biofeedback does not have much promise for the future. Rather, research should be done to determine whether biofeedback is superior to no-treatment control groups, attention-placebo groups, and to a control group that receives false feedback (or feedback contingent upon physiological activity in the opposite direction from that desired). This research is needed if we are to determine whether *feedback* is the critical element in biofeedback research, for it may be that some other more general, nonspecific elements (for example, "attention," "belief in biofeedback") are responsible for the changes in biofeedback studies. Blanchard and Epstein (1977) have noted that *relaxation* may account for the successful results obtained in many biofeedback studies and in clinical practice.

You will find in this chapter that relaxation has been used to treat many health care problems. Stress may play a major role in a variety of health care problems, such that any one of several methods of achieving relaxation may prove a successful treatment. As previously mentioned, most types of biofeedback produce a relaxed bodily state. Other methods include progressive relaxation (taught through initially tensing muscles and then releasing the tension) as developed by Jacobson (1938); autogenic training (a passive method that produces relaxation through the use of self-suggestions) as developed by Schultz and Luthe (1969); and meditation as developed by many different religious groups and more recently popularized by Herbert Benson's "relaxation response" (1975).

We are cautiously optimistic about the future of biofeedback as a behavior change technique. All of the needed scientific evidence is not in yet, and you should be aware of that. Throughout this chapter we will try to point out those health care problems where biofeedback may or may not prove an effective behavior change technique.

CARDIOVASCULAR DISORDERS

In 1974, cardiovascular disease accounted for 39% of the total deaths in the United States (Thomas, 1977). Some 24 million Americans are reported to suffer from hypertension, with high blood pressure being the primary cause of death in 60,000 Americans each year. Hypertension has been identified as a significant factor in the approximately 1.5 million heart attacks and strokes suffered each year by United States citizens (Knowles, 1977b). It is little wonder that Knapp and Peterson (1976) have called cardiovascular disease the number one health care problem in our country.

Perhaps the most visible application of behavior change techniques to cardiovascular disease has been that of biofeedback. Major efforts have been directed toward altering heart rate and blood pressure. Blanchard and Epstein's (1977) review of heart rate biofeedback has pointed out numerous methodological flaws in most of the research. Most of the work has looked at only a few individual patients or has not compared treatment or control groups, and so it is too soon to draw any firm conclusions. Engel (1977) has reviewed a number of his own excellent studies on operant control of heart rate and has come to a similar conclusion. Further, he raised the interesting question of the cost-effectiveness of behavior versus medical intervention. Similar caution was advised by Blanchard and Epstein (1977) concerning direct blood pressure biofeedback. In general, most studies have lacked proper experimental controls and there are no adequate follow-up data.

Results have been more encouraging in ventures other than direct feedback of blood pressure. Patel (Patel, 1973; Patel & North, 1975; Patel, 1975a; Patel, 1975b) has conducted an impressive series of studies demonstrating that a combination of passive relaxation, meditation (yoga), and galvanic skin potential biofeedback (electrical activity of the skin) are effective in lowering blood pressure in hypertensive patients. Effects were maintained in follow-ups after nine months. Using EMG (electromyogram) biofeedback (muscle activity) and autogenic training, Love and his associates (Moeller & Love, 1974; Love, Montgomery & Moeller, 1974) have found significant decreases in blood pressure maintained for periods extending to one year. It should be pointed out that other investigators, using combinations of progressive relaxation training, autogenic training, and meditation (see Byassee, Farr & Meyer, 1976; Wallace & Benson, 1972) have reported that drops in blood pressure have not been maintained on follow-up. In conclusion, the research with hypertensives is inconclusive. Many researchers have combined several methods and so component analyses are necessary. Likewise, control groups may be essential because of likely placebo, suggestion, or other nonspecific effects (Byassee, 1977; Pomerleau & Brady, 1979). Quite possibly, the most critical variables may be early detection, compliance with medical regimens, and the teaching of self-control procedures. The latter two topics are discussed later in this chapter, with regard to health care in general. Hypertension has been called a "silent killer" because many adults do not know they have high blood pressure until they become seriously ill. Indeed, the disease may be easier to treat the earlier it is detected (see Obrist, 1976). Public health efforts are being channeled toward this end. Additionally, blood-pressure measuring instruments now can be found in many drugstores and shopping centers.

Before leaving cardiovascular disease, we should mention other behavioral efforts. One has involved the use of behavior change methods to alter behaviors highly correlated with cardiovascular disease. Typical of these programs is the effort of Meyer and Henderson (1974) to alter weight, smoking habits, diet, physical activity, and cholesterol and triglyceride levels in subjects with risk of heart disease. Although mixed results were obtained on the completion of the study and on three-month follow-up, preventive programs such as this have much promise. Suinn (1975, 1977) has developed a similar program to alter Type A behavior that has been linked to cardiovascular disease (Friedman & Rosenman, 1974). Suinn (1977, p. 55) has characterized Type A behavior as "an eagerness to compete, self-imposed deadlines, desire for recognition, physical and mental alertness, quickness of mental and physical functioning, and an intensive drive towards self-selected but poorly defined goals." His methods include the use of relaxation to manage stress and the learning of new behavior patterns. Initial data from this program are mixed but encouraging (Suinn & Bloom, 1978).

Raynaud's Disease is a cardiovascular disorder that has received some attention from biofeedback researchers. This is a disease of painful "cold" hands and feet resulting from spasms of the small vessels in the extremities (Surwit, 1978). Skin temperature biofeedback has been used in attempts to treat this disease (see Schwartz, 1973; Jacobson, Hackett, Surman & Silverberg, 1973; Surwit, 1973; Blanchard & Haynes, 1975). Because of methodological problems, it is probably too soon to draw any firm conclusions about several successes obtained thus far with biofeedback. In fact, a recent doctoral dissertation (Guglielmi, 1979) that made use of double blind controls failed to demonstrate a significant biofeedback treatment effect. Additionally, Keefe, Surwit, and Pilon (1980) reported no difference in treatment outcomes when comparing skin temperature biofeedback, autogenic training, and progressive relaxation. Patients improved with each of the three procedures.

NEUROLOGICAL DISORDERS

Behavior change professionals have worked, with some success, with a wide variety of neurological problems that plague a large segment of our society. These include epilepsy, insomnia, and headaches.

Epilepsy

Epilepsy refers to chronically recurring seizures and has been managed medically by anticonvulsants and neurosurgery (Bird, 1978). It is important to note that even though epilepsy has been successfully treated with behavior change techniques, it cannot necessarily be inferred that the disorder was learned (Adams, 1976). Mostofsky (1972) has reviewed the different behavioral procedures that might be applicable to the treatment of epilepsy. He has placed an emphasis upon the reduction of psychological stress, which might trigger seizures. Thus, the route many investigators have taken with adult epileptics has been to teach them relaxation techniques. Parrino (1971) has used relaxation training in combination with the presentation of graded series of anxiety-provoking situations (this procedure, developed by Joseph Wolpe, is called systematic desensitization) to reduce the number of seizures in a 36-year-old male. This man had 95 seizures the day before his admission to the hospital. Therapy sessions were held twice weekly during 15 weeks of hospitalization. As the result of the systematic desensitization procedure, the number of seizures while in the hospital dropped from a high of 43 per day to 10 per day. Outpatient therapy sessions followed and eventually there was a gradual reduction to no seizures. A five-month follow-up indicated that the man was free from medication and seizures.

The use of electroencephalogram (EEG) or brain wave biofeedback may hold great promise for the treatment of epilepsy. Initial work in this area was conducted by Sterman and his associates (Sterman, LoPresti & Fairchild, 1969; Sterman, MacDonald, Feinstein & Berntsen, 1976). They found that conditioning of 12–15 cycles per second (cps) EEG rhythm led to increased seizure thresholds in animals. This led to an examination of the effects of EEG biofeedback of 12–14 cps rhythm (sensorimotor rhythm) on the seizure activity of humans. The biofeedback training procedure has proven quite successful in decreasing the frequency and intensity of seizures in a small group of patients (Sterman, 1973; Sterman & Friar, 1972; Sterman, MacDonald & Stone, 1974). More recently, Lubar and his associates (Seifort & Lubar, 1975; Lubar & Bahler, 1976) have replicated the findings with a larger number of patients. Most of these studies have made use of good single-subject reversal or withdrawal designs; thus, there is strong evidence from a series of case studies that sensorimotor biofeedback can be effective in the treatment of a variety of seizure disorders. It should be pointed out that these changes were achieved after many months (as many as nine) of training and that long-term follow-up data are still needed.

Insomnia

The inability to sleep or remain asleep is a serious problem that bothers all of us some of the time and approximately 25 million Americans all of the time. Over $100 million is spent on drugs to alleviate insomnia, yet most of these medications have no effect after several weeks and there is a real danger of chemical dependency (Brody, 1977). The use of behavior change techniques in the treatment of insomnia has focused mainly on problems associated with initial sleep onset. It is important to keep in mind that there are considerable individual differences in the amount of sleep an individual needs and the latency to sleep onset. Borkovec (1977) has collected data on latency to sleep onset from 480 college students; these findings are presented in Table 5-2. In a behavioral assessment of insomnia, one must be careful to rule out possible biological causes for insomnia. These include drug dependence, sleep apnea (cessation of respiration), bodily movements of unknown origins, and so on. Insomniac patients who show obvious life-stress problems may not be good candidates for problematic treatment unless there is also a simultaneous treatment of the other problems—for example, if a person is stressed because of poor interpersonal relationships at work or because of an inability to organize his or her life, then the behavior change professional would want to intervene with a treatment program for these problems in addition to a behavior change program for insomnia.

TABLE 5-2. Distribution of Reports of Latency to Sleep Onset (in Minutes) and the Percent within Each Latency Category Reporting That Latency to Represent a Sleeping Problem.

Latency to Sleep Onset	*Percent Reporting This Latency*	*Percent Reporting a Latency Problem*
0–5	10.6	0.0
6–10	19.4	0.0
11–15	21.7	2.9
16–20	17.1	9.8
21–25	2.7	84.6
26–30	13.3	42.2
31–45	9.2	36.4
46–60	4.4	71.4
61–90	1.5	85.7
91 +	0.2	0.0

From "Insomnia," by T. D. Borkovec. In R. B. Williams and W. D. Gentry (Eds.), *Behavioral Approaches to Medical Treatment*. Copyright 1977, Ballinger Publishing Company. Reprinted with permission.

Behavioral treatment of insomnia has consisted primarily of the use of progressive relaxation training and stimulus control methods. Borkovec (1977) has summarized his work of over four years with 250 sleep-disturbed clients. In six outcome studies, progressive relaxation training proved significantly better than no-treatment, placebo, and other control procedures. As the result of three to four relaxation training sessions, average sleep onset decreased from 41 to 19 minutes at four-month and one-year follow-ups. Haynes, Sides, and Lockwood (1977) have recently explored the use of EMG biofeedback as an adjunct in the treatment of sleep-onset insomnia, but found relaxation training alone just as effective.

The use of stimulus control procedures in the treatment of insomnia has been primarily used by Bootzin (1972, 1973). Focus is placed on breaking the chain of non-sleep behaviors associated with insomnia. Bootzin (1973) has presented the following six instructions:

1. You should lie down to go to sleep only when you are sleepy.
2. The bed is to be used only for sleep (or sexual activity). It is not a place to read or eat.
3. Get up and leave the bedroom if you cannot go to sleep. You can stay up as long as you wish. The goal is to fall asleep quickly, so if you are not asleep within 10 minutes, get up.
4. Repeat step 3 above as often as necessary if you cannot go to sleep.
5. Get up at the same time each day no matter how much sleep you get. Use an alarm if necessary.
6. Never take naps during the day.

With subjects who averaged 90 minutes to sleep onset, an average improvement of 74 minutes was reported within four weeks. The results may be comparable to those achieved through progressive relaxation. Borkovec (1977) has stated that stimulus control techniques may be more cost effective for the medical practitioner since a full course in relaxation training requires nine sessions (of up to an hour each). Stimulus control instructions can be presented in a few minutes of a single office or clinic visit. However, Borkovec has acknowledged that the stimulus control procedure may be of limited application, since relaxation techniques may be used by insomniacs in a variety of tension-producing situations. Relaxation, in effect, may produce a more generalizable effect and thus greater psychological adjustment. Additionally, the role of exercise and physical activity needs to be investigated.

Headaches

Brown (1977) has noted that some 50% of the world's population suffer from headaches. She has listed three fundamental causes of headache including muscle tension, vascular headaches as the result of known causes such as food and barometric changes, and vascular headaches of unknown origin. Quite naturally, it would seem, behavior change professionals have used several relaxation techniques as major methods for treating muscle tension headaches.

Blanchard and Epstein (1977) and Blanchard and Young (1974) have critically reviewed the literature on the use of EMG biofeedback in the elimination of headaches. They concluded that EMG biofeedback training sessions combined with at-home relaxation exercises lead to decreases in the frequency of tension headaches; however, they noted that the necessity for biofeedback as a part of this package was unsubstantiated. Cox, Freundlich, and Meyer (1975) have found that laboratory relaxation training (without EMG feedback), plus home relaxation exercises, was equivalent to the same procedure with added EMG biofeedback. Further, Otis and Turner (1975) have reported that, through error, muscle tension headache patients were given feedback when EMG activity *increased* rather than *decreased* and that frequency of headaches *still decreased*. To further complicate things, Hutchings and Reinking (1976) have reported results contradictory to those obtained by Cox, Freundlich, and Meyer (1975). EMG relaxation training was found superior to relaxation training alone. It can only be concluded, as Blanchard and Epstein (1977) have done, that the specific, active role that EMG biofeedback plays in the reduction of muscle tension headache is unknown at this time.

A second method for treating headaches has been through the use of skin temperature biofeedback (handwarming). This procedure has been used with migraine headaches thought to be vascular in origin. Again, Blanchard and his associates (Blanchard & Young, 1974; Blanchard & Epstein, 1977) have systematically reviewed this literature and have concluded that, as a result of recent research, temperature biofeedback can be beneficial to individuals suffering from migraines. A laudable study was that conducted by Wickramasekera (1973) with two single migraine sufferers. They were first treated with EMG biofeedback with no results. The two patients were then seen in weekly sessions for three weeks to obtain a baseline on headache activity (frequency and intensity). Then, a temperature feedback training procedure was initiated and continued for 11 weekly sessions. Figure 5-1 shows the results of the biofeedback training. Headaches were essentially eliminated in both patients. Although the frequency of consumption of analgesics (pain relieving drugs) was not altered during treatment, at a three-month follow-up the consumption was significantly reduced. This study has special merit because

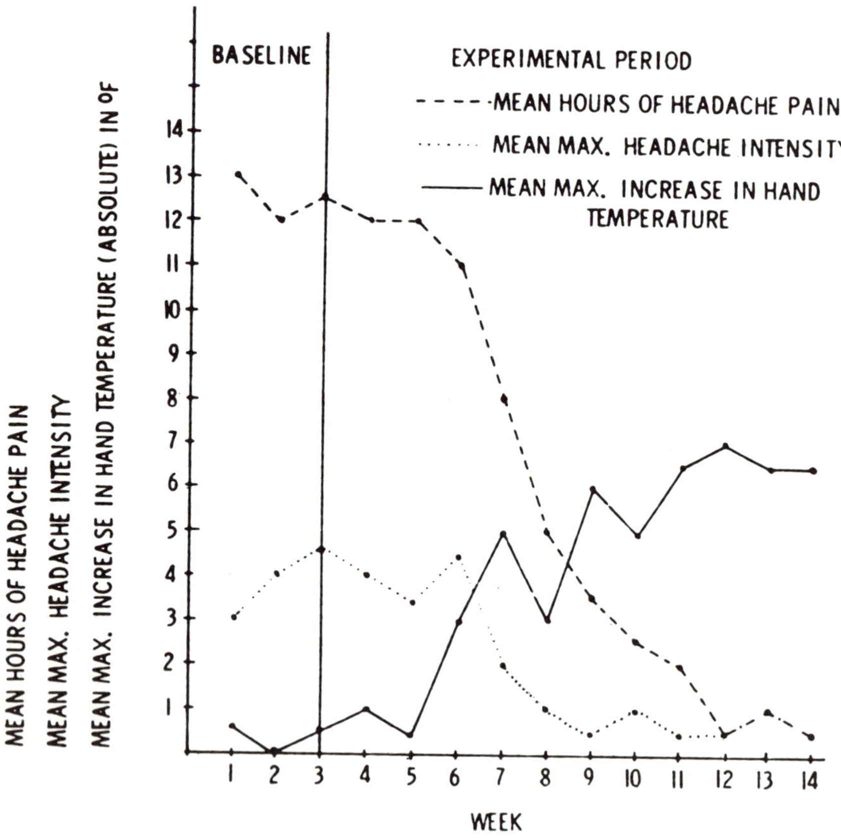

FIGURE 5-1. Data on M showing changes in headache duration, intensity, and absolute hand temperature. (From "Temperature Feedback for the Control of Migraine," by I. E. Wickramasekera. In *Journal of Behavior Therapy and Experimental Psychiatry*, 1973, 4, 343–345. Reprinted by permission of Pergamon Press, Ltd.)

it addresses the placebo effect of biofeedback. No changes resulted from the EMG biofeedback which preceded temperature feedback.

More recently, Kewman and Roberts (1979) have conducted a double-blind study (the subjects were unaware of the specific experimental procedure to which they were exposed, and the research assistants present during biofeedback training were unaware of the subjects' task) of the effects of skin temperature feedback on migraines. Subjects were trained either to raise (the usual treatment procedure) or lower their skin temperature. A third group of subjects merely kept records of their migraine activity (self-monitoring). No differences were found between the three groups at the end of the study. All three groups reported significant improvements on a number of measures related to migraines. Kewman and Roberts (1979) attribute the results of this study to nonspecific factors such as placebo (subjects expected to improve) and regression toward the mean (patients with problems such as migraines tend to seek help or volunteer for studies at times when their problems are at their worst; thus, improvement during the course of a study or over time may actually be due to natural fluctuations in the severity of the problem). Consistent with these findings is the research of Lake, Rainey, and Papsdorf (1979), who found self-monitoring of migraines to be as effective as skin temperature biofeedback, skin temperature biofeedback combined with rational emotive therapy, or EMG biofeedback training.

A number of other behavior change procedures have been used with some success in the treatment of migraines (see Lutker, 1971; Mitchell, 1969; Reeves, 1976). Relaxation training has been a component of most of these procedures. Thus, at this time the question of which behavior change techniques are most appropriate for headache patients remains unanswered. Contradictory evidence exists concerning the use of biofeedback. More studies comparing different techniques are needed. Additionally, long-term follow-up data are essential.

RESPIRATORY DISORDERS

A limited amount of research has been conducted on the use of behavior change techniques with adults who have respiratory disorders. This paucity of research is unlikely to change significantly with regard to asthma because current evidence indicates that psychological or behavioral difficulties play little or no part in the precipitation of asthma attacks (Creer, 1978; Alexander & Solanch, in press). This is in marked contrast to an earlier focus on the behavioral aspects of asthma (see Turnbull, 1962; Wohl, 1971). A number of investigators (Moore, 1965; Sergeant & Yorkston, 1969; Rathus, 1973; Sirota & Mahoney, 1974) have reported improvements in the frequency of asthma attacks. Relaxation has been a common component in most studies; however, no study has yet demonstrated a clinically significant change documented by the measurement of lung functioning. Because this is the only method by which the improvement of asthma can be reliably assessed, Alexander (1979) has recommended that behavior change professionals abandon their attempts to alter lung function via psychological means and concentrate on other difficulties experienced by asthmatics. These include the anxieties and fears associated with asthma attacks, adjustment to living with asthma, and compliance with medical regimens.

Chronic coughing is a respiratory problem that might prove more amenable to behavioral treatment. Alexander, Chai, Creer, Miklick, Renne, and Cardoso (1973) used shock avoidance to treat a 15-year-old boy with this problem. A more positive approach to this problem has been provided by Munford, Reardon, Liberman, and Allen (1976) in their work with an adolescent female diagnosed as having a "hysterical neurosis." Not only did she have a baseline rate of coughing of 40–50 coughs per minute, but she had also been mute for over two years. The girl had to consume over two gallons of water per day to prevent drying of her respiratory tract. She could eat relatively normally, but avoided meats and similar foods because she feared that she might aspirate. Previous attempts at treatment included psychotherapy, sleep therapy, hypnotherapy, and acupuncture. A trial of contingent electrical aversive conditioning also failed. The girl was finally hospitalized and treated by contingency management procedures. Since coughing was highly correlated with attention from others, the staff implemented an extinction procedure. They also determined that coughing allowed the girl to escape anxiety-producing situations such as school and interpersonal contacts. Thus, social interaction was shaped with the use of contingent points awarded as part of the ward token economy. Social interactions were moved from the ward, to the total hospital, to the home community, and finally to the girl's peer group. The mutism was also treated by a shaping procedure, and, after six weeks of hospitalization, she was speaking fluently at discharge. A follow-up after 20 months revealed that the girl was symptom-free.

GASTROINTESTINAL DISORDERS

Several gastrointestinal problems have been treated by behavioral procedures. These have, however, been mainly case studies; systematic research in this area has only recently begun. Functional diarrhea has been altered by several investigators using biofeedback. Furman (1973) treated five patients with varying degrees of the problem. Audio feedback and contingent encouragement was given patients for correctly increasing or decreasing peristaltic activity (monitored by placing an electronic stethoscope on the patients' abdomens). Only five 30-minute training sessions were necessary for patients to obtain at least partial bowel control. Engel, Nikoomanesh, and Schuster (1974) used a similar procedure with six patients who had suffered from incontinence for over three years. Balloons were placed in the patients' rectums at external and internal anal sphincters. In two-hour training sessions, patients tried to establish sphincter control. Feedback was provided both visually and verbally, based upon pressure changes in the balloons. Training sessions were about three weeks apart and all six patients completed training within four sessions. Four of six patients were still continent upon follow-up. A total of 40 patients have now been treated by this procedure (Cerulli, Nikoomanesh, & Schuster, 1976), with impressive follow-up results: approximately 70% have markedly decreased or eliminated their incontinence as a result of biofeedback.

Limited research has been conducted on behavioral treatment of constipation in adults (not an inconsiderable health problem, according to television commercials). Quarti and Renaud (1964) have conducted a behavioral analysis of constipation and described a treatment program based on conditioning (that is, pairing

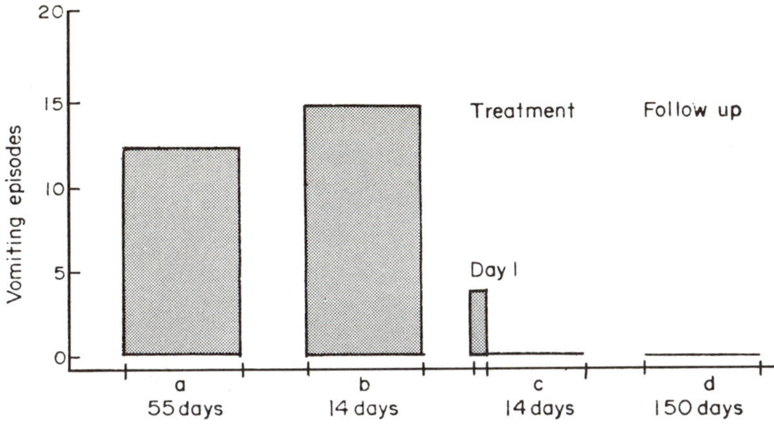

FIGURE 5-2.   Average number of daily vomiting episodes. (From "The Counter Conditioning of a Vomiting Habit by Sips of Ginger Ale," by J. Morgan and J. S. O'Brien. In *Journal of Behavior Therapy and Experimental Psychiatry*, 1972, 3, 135–137. Reprinted by permission of Pergamon Press, Ltd.)

a mild electrical stimulus with defecation) and the gradual withdrawal of laxatives. Certainly this is an area in need of further work.

Youell and McCullough (1975) have reported on the application of behavioral principles to the treatment of a 22-year-old female who had averaged one colitis attack per day. Symptoms included abdominal cramps, rectal spasms, and diarrhea. Treatment focused on developing coping strategies to deal with stressful events that usually led to the attacks. Weekly treatment sessions ended after 14 weeks with no attacks occurring for the past four consecutive weeks. Intermittent follow-up occurred for 49 weeks with colitis attacks occurring during only one week.

Frequent vomiting exhibited by a 60-year-old woman was treated with behavioral techniques by Morgan and O'Brien (1972). The woman had vomited 10–15 times per day over a 10-week period. She had lost 18 lbs and physicians were unable to determine any organic cause for vomiting. Treatment was described as a counter-conditioning procedure in which the patient was instructed to take one sip of ginger ale every 15 minutes while awake. Ginger ale in these small amounts would produce digestive responses which would be incompatible with the digestive response necessary for vomiting. Results of this program may be seen in Figure 5-2. She vomited only four times on the first day of treatment and never vomited thereafter. The woman was also free from vomiting at a five-month follow-up.

REHABILITATION

Rehabilitation is concerned with rendering disabled individuals' lives as independent and socially useful as possible (Michael, 1970). To achieve this, an interdisciplinary health care team is needed. Successful rehabilitation depends not on the individual work of many separate disciplines but, rather, upon the *cooperative* efforts of a large number of professionals. The principal problems faced in rehabilitation include chronic and disabling pain, spinal cord injury, cerebrovascular accidents, arthritis, amputations, and traumatic physical injuries. The dollars lost owing to the inability of disabled adults to work and the dollar cost of providing direct physical care to the disabled would seem to indicate that successful rehabilitation, which leads to greater independence, would be a very cost-effective endeavor.

Chronic Pain

In 1977, *Newsweek* magazine (Clark, Gosnell, & Shapiro, 1977) reported that individuals with chronic back pain account for more than 18 million physician office visits per year. Chronic pain costs at least $10 billion per year in the use of medications, surgical procedures, and time spent away from jobs. Dr. Wilbert Fordyce and his associates at the University of Washington Medical School have developed an extremely effective and provocative treatment program for those with chronic pain (Fordyce, Fowler, Lehmann, DeLateur, Sand, & Trieschmann, 1973; Fordyce, 1976). Fordyce has conceptualized pain as a behavior and, as such, subject to the laws of learning. Many pain behaviors (such as verbalizations or grimaces) can be looked upon as operant behaviors that are maintained by their consequences—either positive or negative reinforcers. Pain behavior may be positively reinforced by attention and concern from family or friends. Pain may be negatively reinforced whenever a person is enabled to escape or avoid unpleasant jobs or responsibilities.

Fordyce's treatment program consists of some rather simple manipulations of the pain patient's environment. First, environmental events that may positively reinforce pain behavior are identified and then eliminated. In general, this means that *all* pain behavior is ignored. Second, a gradual increase in physical activity is prescribed. Rest becomes contingent upon completion of physical activity rather than pain. Finally, there is a gradual decrease and eventual elimination of analgesics and other drugs. Medication may reinforce pain behavior because of both chemotherapeutic relief and social attention. Thus, medications are placed in a masking vehicle ("pain cocktail") and administered on a time-contingent, rather than pain-contingent, basis. The amount of medication in the vehicle is then gradually reduced. Obviously, the success of this entire program is contingent upon the informed consent and cooperation of the patients.

Fordyce's program is hospital-based and has proven extremely successful. Staff involve both the patient and the patient's family in treatment, as they must be trained to continue the therapeutic program upon the patient's discharge from the hospital. Typical of Fordyce's successful program are the data presented in Figures 5-3 and 5-4 (Fordyce et al., 1973). Described are 36 patients who suffered primarily from chronic low back pain. They had had pain from 4½ to 30 years and none had worked in over three years. The inpatient program lasted for an average of seven weeks, with varying amounts of outpatient treatment follow-up. While the figures

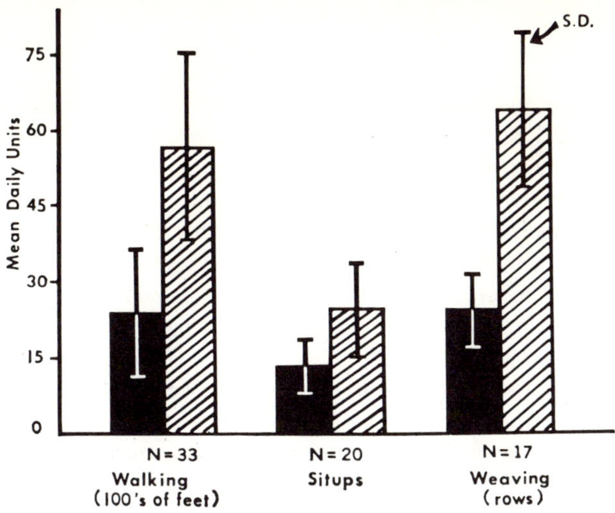

FIGURE 5-3. Changes in performance of most frequently prescribed activities during inpatient treatment. (From "Operant Conditioning in the Treatment of Chronic Pain," by W. E. Fordyce, R. S. Fowler, J. F. Lehmann, B. J. DeLateur, P. L. Sand, and R. B. Trieschmann. *Archives of Physical Medicine and Rehabilitation*, 1973, *54*, 399–408. Reprinted by permission.)

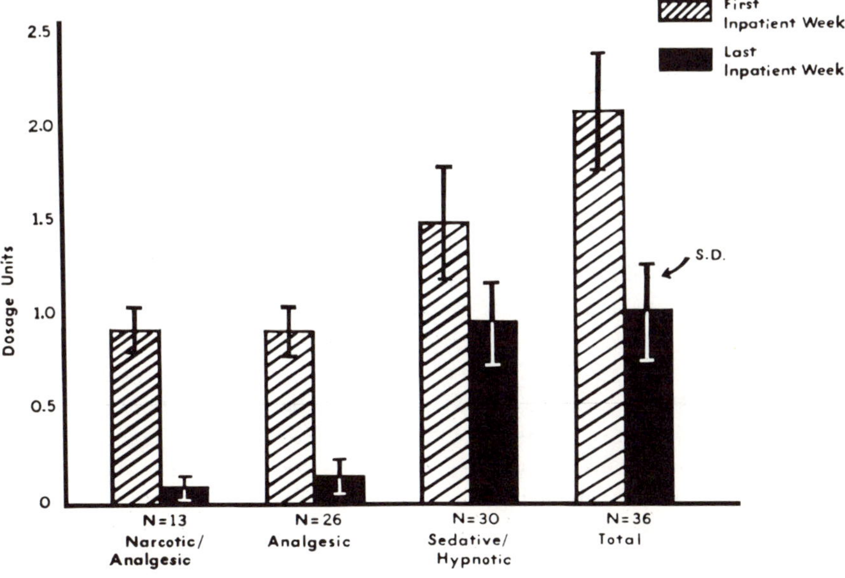

FIGURE 5-4. Changes in medications during inpatient treatment. (From "Operant Conditioning in the Treatment of Chronic Pain," by W. E. Fordyce, R. S. Fowler, J. F. Lehmann, B. J. DeLateur, P. L. Sand and R. B. Trieschmann. In *Archives of Physical Medicine and Rehabilitation*, 1973, *54*, 399–408. Reprinted by permission.)

indicate changes in medication use and physical activity, patients also reported having less pain and being satisfied with changes in their lives.

Perhaps critical to the success of the Fordyce program is the detailed pretreatment assessment in which each potential program participant engages. This includes both physical and psychosocial evaluations. Patients must have failed to respond to other treatment modalities. It is also likely that the cooperative participation of family members or significant others is crucial. Likewise, an acknowledgment that there are *no remaining alternative treatment procedures* may be beneficial. The long-term effectiveness of this approach was recently evaluated at the University of Minnesota Hospitals. Dr. Alan Roberts' program there was instituted shortly after Fordyce's and contains all of the essential elements of Fordyce's program. In an independent follow-up of Roberts' patients, Reinhardt (1979) found that one year or more after completing the program, 77% of the patients were living normal lives for their age and sex. These successful patients were not taking any prescription medications for their pain and were not kept from working by their pain. In contrast, a group of patients who were accepted for Roberts' treatment program, but refused it, reported a markedly different picture. Some 83% were unable to work because of their pain, and they were taking an average of over three different prescription medications for their pain. Roberts (1977) has written a detailed *Pain Clinic and Pain Treatment Program Procedure Manual,* which describes his interdisciplinary behavioral treatment program. Manuals such as this are essential if effective behavioral treatment programs are to be duplicated throughout the country. Dependence upon journal articles and informal communication systems too often jeopardize the success of programs because some critical detail has been omitted.

A cognitive behavioral approach to the treatment of chronic pain has been suggested by Turk (1978). This would involve teaching patients a number of strategies for coping with their pain (for example, relaxation, learning to focus on things other than pain, altering "self-talk," and practicing "self-instructions" aimed toward coping with pain). While such a treatment approach may have considerable potential value, it has not yet been adequately evaluated. Most of the research with cognitive behavior strategies has used subjects whose pain was experimentally induced, rather than subjects who suffered from chronic pain (see Turk, 1977; Genest, 1978). Reports on the use of cognitive behavioral approaches with chronic pain patients (Gottlieb, Strite, Koller, Madorsky, Hockersmith, Kleeman & Wagner, 1977) are difficult to evaluate because these techniques have generally been only a part of a more comprehensive treatment package. For now, we can only say that cognitive behavioral techniques look promising and await further evaluation with a clinical population.

Spinal Cord Injury

Traumatic injury to the spinal cord can have far-reaching effects upon the lives of some patients. With improving health care, rehabilitation, and federal legislation concerning the rights of the handicapped, overall prognosis is much improved over the past few years. During a hospitalization for rehabilitation, many different behaviors need to be worked on, including possible upper and lower extremity functioning, self-care skills, and bowel and bladder care and functioning. Adjustments to disability and altered sexual function may also be problems. An interesting personal account on behavior analysis and the rehabilitation of the spinal cord injured can be found in an article by Goldiamond (1973).

When individuals with spinal cord injuries remain seated for long periods of time, pressure sores or decubitus ulcers may result. If not prevented or properly cared for, these sores may lead to infections, bone inflammation, amputation, and even death. Malament, Dunn, and Davis (1975) reported a unique behavioral procedure that trained individuals to do wheelchair pushups in order to prevent pressure sores. Previous research had indicated that periodic relief of pressure to the buttocks could prevent the occurrence of pressure sores (Kosiak, Kubicek, Olson, Donz, & Kottke, 1958). An avoidance procedure was used to train spinal cord injured individuals to relieve pressure to their buttocks by using their arms to raise their buttocks off the seats of their wheelchairs. When a pushup did not occur in any given ten-minute interval, a 30-second auditory alarm sounded. A pushup of at least four seconds would either terminate or postpone the alarm. This procedure was extremely effective in increasing the frequency of wheelchair pushups (and the number of alarms in any one day likewise decreased). Follow-up of two patients indicated that they continued to do pushups at nearly the same rate without the alarm.

Sand, Fordyce, and Fowler (1973) have described the use of behavioral techniques in increasing the fluid intake of spinal cord injured patients. To minimize the risk of urinary tract infections and kidney stone formation, a daily consumption of approximately 3000 cc of fluid is considered adequate. Sand, Fordyce, and Fowler (1973) posted, at bedside, a daily record of each patient's fluid intake. Social reinforcement during medical and nursing rounds was made contingent upon improved or adequate fluid intake. Data indicated that this procedure was superior to the traditional method of merely providing patients with educational information concerning adequate fluid intake. Other work with the spinal cord injured has included behavioral programs for increasing the consistency of self-care behaviors (Sand, Trieschmann, Fordyce, & Fowler, 1970), decreasing psychiatric complaints (Taylor & Persons, 1970), increasing typing skills (Meyerson, Kerr, & Michael, 1967), and physical therapy (Trotter & Inman, 1968).

In a novel study, Ince, Brucker, and Alba (1977) used classical conditioning to condition bladder responses in patients with spinal cord lesions. A strong electrical stimulation to the lower abdomen functioned as an unconditioned stimulus (UCS), which elicited an unconditioned response (UCR), urination. During conditioning sessions, a mild electrical stimulus (CS) was applied to the inner thigh 0.5 seconds before the onset of the UCS, which lasted 2.5 seconds. Both the CS and UCS terminated simultaneously. With a small number of patients, Ince, Brucker, and Alba (1977) demonstrated that urination could be controlled by the CS, or mild shock to the thigh. This would indicate that it might be possible for such patients to be independent in bladder functioning, eliminating the need for a urinary drainage system or catheterization. Although the results thus far have been encouraging, the work has been merely preliminary and much more needs to be done.

Strokes

Kottke (1974) has estimated that more than 50% of persons who survive strokes have an unnecessary amount of functional disability. In numbers, it is estimated that 75,000 stroke patients in this country each year receive less than adequate rehabilitation, which leads to unsatisfactory lives for victims and families and a vastly increased cost of health maintenance. A number of investigators have examined the utility of behavioral procedures as an adjunct to the rehabilitation of stroke patients. Ince (1969a) has used the reinforcing value of certain therapies to increase attendance at other, less reinforcing, therapies. Goodkin (1966) used verbal reinforcement to increase keypunch machine operating speed and handwriting speed during occupational therapy sessions. Ince (1969b) worked with three patients who were functionally hemiplegic as the result of a stroke. In attempting to increase forearm flexion in the affected extremity, an escape paradigm was used with two patients, whereas the remaining patient received avoidance conditioning. The two subjects in the escape condition received, to the forearm of the nonplegic arm, an electric shock that could be terminated by elbow flexion of the plegic arm. The other patient was delivered a brief auditory signal five seconds before the onset of the shock. The onset of the shock was postponed by ten seconds if a flexion response occurred between the click and the shock. Results of 20 to 25 sessions of these training procedures were: increased elbow flexion responses over baseline, an increase in muscle strength in the plegic extremity, and a generalization of responding to functional activities.

A considerable amount of research has been conducted using EMG biofeedback with stroke patients. The initial work with this population was reported in case-study form by Marinacci and Horande (1960) and was followed by Andrews' (1964) report on work with 20 hemiplegics using visual feedback in an attempt to increase upper extremity functioning. Seventeen of the twenty patients exhibited voluntary control of paretic muscles after a training session of *five minutes or less.* Many others (see Brudny, Korein, Levidow, Grynbaum, Lieberman & Friedmann, 1974) have reported similar findings.

Johnson and Garton (1973) first reported the use of EMG biofeedback in treating foot drop (a paralytic foot condition frequently associated with strokes). This study and the others previously mentioned that involve EMG feedback as an adjunct in neuromuscular rehabilitation have all been uncontrolled outcome studies of either a single case or a group. Basmajian, Kukulka, Narayan, and Takebe (1975) were the first to use a control-group experimental design. Standard physical rehabilitation procedures were compared with these same procedures plus EMG biofeedback with two groups of patients suffering from chronic foot drop. The biofeedback group was significantly superior on a number of different measures and upon follow-up of from 4 to 16 weeks. Fish, Mayer, and Herman (1976) have questioned the validity of this experimentation on the grounds that the patients in the two groups were dissimilar in a number of crucial variables.

As yet, the long-term benefits of EMG biofeedback with stroke patients are open to question (Inglis, Campbell, & Donald, 1976). However, the results thus far have been consistently positive and encouraging. Blanchard and Epstein (1977) have pointed out that it still needs to be demonstrated that the feedback itself is a critical variable. Perhaps the mere presence of the EMG feedback equipment functions as a placebo.

Patients who suffer strokes may have a multiplicity of problems, all of which are potential targets for behavioral intervention. Work thus far indicates that behavior change principles may prove a useful adjunct in the rehabilitation of stroke patients. Areas yet to be explored in any significant way include speech and language problems, memory problems, and difficulties with reasoning and judgment. We have touched on just a few of the major problems within rehabilitation. While the amount of behavior change literature in rehabilitation medicine may seem large, it consists mainly of uncontrolled or poorly controlled studies and case studies, and seldom contains any follow-up data. Only recently has attention been paid to problems of generalization and the transfer of effective treatment procedures to the natural environment. Much work needs to be done to document the comparative effectiveness of behavioral procedures, including EMG biofeedback, before behavioral techniques can have a more significant impact upon rehabilitation medicine. Thus far, the results, particularly those obtained with chronic pain by Fordyce and Roberts and with stroke patients by Basmajian, Brudny, and others, are promising.

FEAR OF MEDICAL PROCEDURES

We all know individuals who avoid medical or dental treatment because they fear a particular procedure. Additionally, the provision of health care services may be much more difficult or complicated for patients who exhibit fear. A number of behavior change techniques have been used to diminish the fear associated with health care procedures.

Turnage and Logan (1974) have reported the successful behavioral treatment of a hypodermic needle phobia. The patient was a 27-year-old woman who lived with this phobia for 22 years. When she was to receive the routine inoculations at the age of five before entering school, she reacted in an extremely violent manner and had to be restrained by her mother and a nurse. With each subsequent injection during her life, she fought violently and had to be physically restrained. After she became pregnant, she even refused to go to the hospital to have her baby until her physician made an oath that he would give her no injections. In anticipation of any scheduled injection, she suffered from diarrhea and loss of sleep and appetite. She would cry for up to a week before a scheduled injection. Treatment for her phobia was sought because she feared she would pass it on to her son, and because she broke two hypodermic needles when she had to go to the hospital emergency room for a blood clot in her ankle. Treatment consisted of the teaching of progressive muscle relaxation, followed by several sessions of imaginal desensitization, culminating in four sessions of *in vivo* desensitization. During *in vivo* sessions, both needle size and time of exposure were systematically manipulated. After a total of ten sessions, the patient's husband actually withdrew blood from her arm. No hint of relapse was noted at six- and ten-month follow-ups.

A combination of *in vivo* systematic desensitization and flooding was used by Nimmer and Kapp (1974) in working with three college students who had long-standing histories of injection phobias. The program consisted of exposure to a graded hierarchy of anxiety-producing events, homework assignments related to hierarchy, exposure to stimuli associated with anxiety (for example, medicinal odors, viewing injections), and finally a scheduled (noncancellable) injection of saline. None of the students resisted receiving the injections, and a six-month follow-up indicated no further problems. One was even donating blood on a periodic basis.

Katz (1974) has described the unique case of a young renal patient who had a phobic reaction to hemodialysis (removing blood from the body via a tube into an artificial kidney machine and then returning it via a tube to the body). This fear began the first time he was dialyzed. He was initially fairly calm; but when the first attempt at vascular catheterization failed, he became very fearful and started to hyperventilate and tremble. This fear continued with subsequent three-times-per-week dialysis treatments. After six weeks, this phobia was referred for treatment. The patient was told that his fear was a learned reaction to this new and painful procedure. Katz then explained the technique of systematic desensitization and that the learned fear could be treated by the application of learning principles. After the patient had been trained in deep muscle relaxation, Katz and the patient constructed a hierarchy of anxiety-eliciting events. These included the following (Katz, 1974):

1. Waking the morning of a scheduled dialysis treatment
2. Being weighed and having blood pressure taken at hospital
3. Being prepared for xylocaine injection
4. Visualizing the catheter for dialysis
5. A trusted technician inserting the catheter
6. A new technician inserting the catheter
7. Withdrawing the catheter immediately after it was inserted
8. Reinserting the catheter

Katz told the patient to imagine each item while he was completely relaxed. The total hierarchy was completed in a single 90-minute session. The patient was told to continue practicing relaxation at home and to think about his success with the hierarchy during his next scheduled visit to the hospital. Katz also made suggestions to the medical staff concerning the patient's management. These included the following (Katz, 1974):

1. Initially using only experienced technicians with whom the patient had not exhibited extreme panic
2. Other technicians should be gradually introduced by having them first only be present, and then start to assist
3. A qualified instructor would explain the procedure in a step-by-step fashion to the patient, including the significance of any irregularities which might occur
4. The patient was to be given encouragement whenever he underwent dialysis without emotional upset

No recurrence of the phobia was observed in the six months following the single desensitization session. New and inexperienced technicians were able to dialyze the patient.

Langer, Janis, and Wolfer (1975) have described the use of two stress-reducing strategies with adult patients about to undergo major surgery. The first was a coping device that involved the cognitive reappraisal of anxiety-evoking events. After the work of Ellis (1962) and Meichenbaum (1971), patients were taught to exercise cognitive control of their thoughts by selective attention so that they were able to distract themselves from aversive aspects of stressful encounters. The second strategy taught consisted of producing an "emotional inoculation" by supplying the patients with information about the forthcoming surgical procedure. Previous work by Janis (1958, 1971) has suggested that such preparatory communications are most effective when they produce a moderate level of anticipatory fear, which leads to a mental rehearsal of the impending feared event and self-delivered reassurances. Experimental applications of these procedures with surgery patients indicated that the coping strategy was effective in reducing both pre- and postoperative stress; however, the preparatory information did not produce this effect. This cognitive behavioral approach is very similar to procedures in the section on chronic pain.

COMPLIANCE WITH MEDICAL REGIMENS

Zifferblatt (1975) has stated that a major portion of medical practice is devoted to encouraging and persuading patients to follow prescribed health-related activities. Gentry (1977) goes so far as to say that the most crucial issue facing modern medicine is adherence or compliance to prescribed medical regimens. Improvement in health is very often related to the degree to which patients are willing to change their health-related behavior and to follow or comply with instructions. If patients refuse to take prescribed medications or will not take them according to a fixed schedule, physicians may be able to do little to improve or to cure disease. If patients will not alter other health-related behaviors (for example, diet, exercise, and rest), the science and technology of modern medicine will be rendered useless in many cases. Much of current experimental literature dealing with patient compliance has been reviewed recently in a book edited by Sackett and Haynes (1976). In general, Sackett and Haynes (1976) and other reviewers (Blackwell, 1973; Marston, 1970; Kasl, 1975) have concluded that the research thus far has provided few guidelines for the practicing health care professional. Conflicting and negative results are not uncommon.

Both Zifferblatt (1975) and Kasl (1975) have characterized noncompliance with medical regimens as a behavior problem. The typical approach to compliance research has been to identify characteristics associated with noncompliance such as age, sex, education, and personality. Knowledge of these factors does little to enable one to alter compliance. Rather, it is more productive to focus on compliance as a behavior (which may be precisely specified or defined) and analyze the ways in which antecedent and consequent events may influence this behavior (Zifferblatt, 1975). Kasl (1975) has agreed when he stated that noncompliance may result from lack of feedback or continuous reinforcement from health professionals, society, and changes in the patient's disease process.

Zifferblatt (1975) has described a framework for physicians to monitor compliance as a behavioral event. First, he recommends that definitions for compliance be extremely precise. In effect, what is done is a task analysis of compliance. What are the exact behaviors that comprise compliance? What motor and verbal behaviors does the patient have to engage in to comply with the medical regimen? Second, the physician must identify events functionally related to compliance. A patient diary of events preceding and following compliance should prove useful here. An example of this may be seen in Table 5-3. Examination of this diary may enable physicians to tailor medical regimens which are more suitable to the patient's

TABLE 5-3. Excerpts from a Functional Analysis Diary.

Date	Time	Antecedents (cues and people)	Consequences	Relevant thoughts
5/16	9:00 AM	Take vitamins, pocket book, orange juice.	Lump in throat and stomach, nausea. Ate breakfast.	A bit grainy, easy to mix.
	12:00 PM	Pocket book, orange juice.	Sipped slowly, lump disappeared, slight nausea.	Glad I remembered. Hope it decreases my appetite!
5/17	2:00 PM	Forgot last evening's medication! Pocket book, orange juice.	Put packets on kitchen counter where I can see them.	
5/18	9:00 AM	Take vitamins, see packets on counter, orange juice.	Slight nausea, put glass and spoon on counter, late breakfast.	Maybe I can make this easier. Ate out. Did not want to take medication along. Too much to explain. Not going to do it!
5/19	9:00 AM	Take vitamins, see packets on counter, orange juice, glass, spoon.	Replace packets, glass and spoon, ate breakfast.	Oops! went out and forgot to take medication. Too sleepy when I came home! That medication is staring at me!
	1:00 AM	Relaxed and nothing to do, reading, alone.	Replace packets, glass and spoon, ate a sandwich.	
5/20	9:00 AM	Take vitamins reminded by Charlie, packets on counter, orange juice, glass, spoon.	Replace packets, glass and spoon, ate breakfast.	
	1:00 AM	Reading, relaxed, alone and hungry.	Replaced packets, glass and spoon, ate a sandwich.	This medication is increasing my appetite!
5/21	9:00 AM	Take vitamins, packets on counter, orange juice, glass, spoon.	Replace packets, glass and spoon, ate breakfast.	Going smoothly! Charlie didn't need to remind me!
	12:30 AM	TV, relaxed, alone and hungry.	Replace packets, glass and spoon, ate some yogurt, went to sleep.	Am I taking the medication to get something to eat? This has got to stop! Evening medication is chaos!

From "Increasing Patient Compliance through the Applied Analysis of Behavior," by S. M. Zifferblatt. In *Preventive Medicine, 1975, 4,* 173–182. Reprinted by permission of the author and Academic Press.

life style. Finally, Zifferblatt presents this framework as a dynamic one rather than static. One should systematically manipulate a variety of variables (events) until compliance is achieved. These might have to do with the saliency of environmental cues, the latency between the cues and compliance behavior, or the degree to which the cues are related to compliance. Table 5-4 outlines some compliance dimensions and their relationship to medication taking.

TABLE 5-4. Comparison of a Number of Similar Medication-Taking Behaviors through a Functional Analysis.

	Antecedents		Behavior	Consequences		
			1. Open packet for bottle 2. Mix powder with liquid or take tablet			Probability of reoc-
	Cue specificity	Event	3. Drink mixture	Event	Latency	currences
(1)	Easily detected and specific to response	Upset stomach	Antiacid	Relief of discomfort	5–10 min	High
(2)	Easily detected and specific to response	Headache	Headache powder	Relief of headache	10–15 min	High
(3)	Ambiguous cues-dis-cernable symptoms	None	Aspirin	Avoidance of arthritic pain	Preventive	Low
(4)	Ambiguous	None	Gelatin (brittle nails)	None	Preventive	Low
(5)	Ambiguous	None	Vitamins	None	Preventive nausea	Low
(6)	Ambiguous	None	Diuretic (hypertension)	None	Preventive	Low
(7)						
(a)	Ambiguous	None	Cholestyramine	None	Preventive	Low
(b)	Explicit time or occasion	Buzzer break-fast sponse cue, table	Cholestyramine	Access to breakfast	1 min	High
(c)	Ambiguous	None	Cholestyramine	$20 bill per ingestion	5 sec	High

From "Increasing Patient Compliance through the Applied Analysis of Behavior," by S. M. Zifferblatt. In *Preventive Medicine*, 1975, *4*, 173–182. Reprinted by permission of the author and Academic Press.

Behavior change professionals have begun to make a number of recommendations useful for promoting compliance with therapeutic regimens. Gentry (1977) has stated that a shaping procedure may prove helpful. Rather than overwhelming patients with a great many changes in health behavior, a step-by-step procedure should be followed. If possible, physicians would be wise to recommend only minimal changes in health-related behaviors at first, and gradually add further recommendations. Gentry further suggests that patients are more likely to be compliant when the prescribed medical regimens are only minimally disruptive to their daily lives. When compliance behaviors compete with or prevent sources of reinforcement, they are likely to be exhibited either minimally or not at all.

Hayes (1977) has suggested several steps to be taken if improvement is to be made in research on compliance with therapeutic regimens. Researchers should: (1) use an inductive approach that results in inductively generated basic principles; (2) use good experimental designs, with single-subject research designs having special merit because of the rapidity with which data can be generated; (3) use settings that allow for a great degree of experimental control; and (4) specify independent and dependent variables precisely and unequivocally.

To date, there has been little behavior analysis research on compliance with therapeutic regimens as such. However, long-term successful treatment of such health-related problems as obesity, smoking, and alcoholism ultimately become problems of compliance (see Chapter 10). Suffice it to say that while behavioral procedures have been extremely successful in changing these behaviors in the short run, long-term follow-up data are either lacking or not very convincing. Researchers and practitioners are now at work on what has become a long-term compliance with therapeutic regimen problems.

The few experiments devoted to applications of behavioral change principles to compliance problems have been relatively successful. Meyer and Henderson (1974), at the Stanford Heart Disease Institute, have reported on a project devoted to changing certain health-related behaviors of individuals with risk of heart disease. The project objectives were to change weight, diet, and smoking habits; to increase physical activity; and to change cholesterol and triglyceride levels as necessary. Subjects were randomly assigned to one of three groups as follows: (1) behavior modification; (2) individual counseling; and (3) single-time physician consultation. The treatment in the behavior modification group involved 2- to 3½-hour weekly group sessions over an 11-week period. Both subjects and their spouses attended. A number of different behavior modification procedures were used, including modeling, reinforcement, monitoring of target behaviors, and education. The individual-counseling-session group consisted of nine 15-minute individual counseling sessions over the course of 11 weeks. The final group of subjects received a 20-minute individual consultation with a physician, in which each subject was informed of his risk of cardiovascular disease. As applicable, weight loss, dietary modification, cessation of smoking, and increase in physical activity were prescribed. Results of this project indicated that the behavior modification and individual counseling groups produced significantly greater changes in diet, weight, physical activity, and smoking than did the single-time physician consultation group. Likewise, the first two treatment groups resulted in significantly greater changes in serum cholesterol and triglyceride levels. Additionally, the behavior modification group maintained these changes in serum cholesterol over a three-month follow-up period significantly better than did the other two groups. Although the behavior modification group was still better than the physician consultation group at the three-month follow-up (for diet, weight loss, smoking, and physical activity), it was not significantly better than the individual counseling group. Unfortunately, it is not clear whether it was the specific "treatment package" that led to the superiority of the first two groups or the total *amount of time* spent on treatment (24 + hours versus 2¼ hours versus 20 minutes) that contributed to obtained differences. Also, variables such as presence of spouse and group versus individual treatment were uncontrolled. If group research designs such as this are to be used, better control of possible independent and extraneous variables is needed. Likewise, longer periods of follow-up are needed, since with subjects such as those with risk of heart disease, lifetime compliance with medical regimens may have to be a goal.

Epstein and Masek (1978) have recently investigated the effects of self-monitoring, pill flavoring, a combination of the two, and a no-treatment control condition upon degree of medication compliance. The self-monitoring conditions proved most effective. The addition of a response-cost procedure improved compliance independent of the past history of noncompliance. This research is also significant because it provides a methodology for evaluating compliance on an out-patient basis without having to use laboratory tests. This was possible because patients were requested to take pills in a prescribed sequence, and certain pills contained ingredients that changed urine color to reddish-orange.

Recent efforts have included Baile and Engel's (1978) work to promote treatment compliance by patients who had recently suffered a myocardial infarction, and Dunbar and Agras' (1978) investigation of methods to promote medication adherence by hypertensives. Common to both were self-monitoring by patients and the use of reinforcement contingent upon compliance. More of this type of research needs to be conducted on compliance with therapeutic regimens. Data are needed on patients with as many different medical problems as possible. It may be that behavior change principles have more potential for benefit in this area than in any other in health care. All health care professionals come in contact with patients who are noncompliant. Systematic application of behavior principles may greatly contribute to the reduction of this problem.

CONCLUSIONS

Major strides must be made in having members of our society assume more responsibility for their own personal health care and well being. Due to the rising cost of health care, this shift in responsibility away from the health professions to the individual can only be cost-effective. To accomplish this shift, a reallocation of resources will be needed, for only 2% to 2.5% of the annual national expenditure on health—$120 billion—is spent on disease prevention and control measures. Health education receives only 0.5% of the $120 billion (Knowles, 1977b). To implement mass personal health education and to teach individuals how to monitor their own health behavior will require not only more money in these directions, but also a massive national shift of effort. Such a shift has taken place in Canada. It is called "Operation Lifestyle" and is a campaign of nationwide health promotion aimed at altering living habits that lead to diseases of lifestyle (Bad lifestyle—Can we tackle it nationally?, 1978) Targets include improved physical fitness, better eating habits, and mass screening for high blood pressure. This effort might be greatly improved by the involvement of behavior change professionals. While much of the past behavior analysis research in health care has dealt with treatment of physical and health-related problems, it is in the area of personal health care and prevention that behavior change principles have the most promise for the future.

Epstein and Martin (1977) have identified several types of prevention. Personal secondary prevention refers to exhibiting behaviors that alter health and prevent chronic disability or disease after the identification of a risk factor (such as high blood pressure or serum cholesterol), while personal primary prevention includes engaging in behaviors that will decrease the probability of risk factor development (such as proper diet and a physical exercise program). Examples of secondary prevention have been presented in this chapter (for example, hypertension). Inroads in personal primary prevention are just beginning and, here, behavior change principles have much to offer.

Benson and his colleagues (Peters, Benson, & Porter, 1977; Peters, Benson, & Peters, 1977) have reported the effects of daily *relaxation* breaks upon 126 volunteers from the corporate offices of a manufacturing firm. Significant changes were recorded in blood pressure, health-related symptoms (for example, headache, nausea, diarrhea), and days recorded as feeling ill. Large-scale intervention programs such as this aimed at primary prevention are extremely exciting. Other examples of this can be seen in major corporations such as Xerox, Phillips Petroleum, and General Foods, which have spent large sums of money on elaborate gymnasiums, swimming pools, and running tracks for their employees. Bonne Bell cosmetics has been a leader in this movement and now claims that 80% of its employees engage in fitness programs (Monkerud, 1978). All employees are given an extra half-hour during lunch break if they participate in a running or exercise program. Employees are also given discounts on jogging equipment, and they are allowed to wear jogging suits the rest of the day whenever they run at noon.

The personal monitoring of health-related parameters is also a potential target for primary prevention through behavior analysis. Hall, Goldstein, and Stein (1977) have outlined a procedure for the teaching of breast self-examination. Other parameters that can be easily monitored include heart rate, blood pressure, weight, and urine testing (by diabetics). Epstein and Cincirpini (1977) have reported that automated blood pressure measurement is now available in some shopping malls. They suggested that behavioral principles could be easily applied to these testing devices (tokens or coupons awarded for participation and for getting a checkup by a doctor if the pressure is elevated over a number of consecutive measurements).

In the area of secondary prevention, Epstein and Cincirpini (1977) have identified behavioral competence and compliance as two major problems. Little effort has been placed on using behavior change techniques to ensure the competence of individuals who engage in behaviors aimed at reducing risk factors. McDonald and Kaufman (1963) provided an early, and potentially useful, approach to the problem when they used teaching machines to teach diabetics the basic elements of treatment and self-care. Unfortunately, few other efforts with teaching machines have been reported. More recently, Renne and Creer (1976) have developed a program for teaching the use of inhalation therapy equipment to asthmatic children. Hopefully, behavior change professionals will have more to offer in the future to the area of behavioral competence and risk factor reduction in both primary and secondary prevention.

The related problem of compliance with medical and therapeutic regimens is equally important to both primary and secondary prevention. Here, behavior analysis has started to have an impact, although it is too soon to come to any firm conclusions. However, the work of Zifferblatt and Wilbur (1977) contained a warning that may apply not only to behavioral applications to compliance, but to all of behavior analysis. They question the premise that a short, concentrated period of influence or treatment is sufficient to help a patient to permanently change his health-related behavior. Instead, Zifferblatt and Wilbur suggest the use of several treatments over a much longer period of time. It may be that the permanent alteration of chronic problems (health-related or otherwise) may require a "chronic" type of treatment that extends throughout a significant portion of a person's life. Certainly, the relatively poor follow-up record obtained to date by behavior change techniques points to the need for a new approach to the maintenance of behavior change.

The large majority of behavior analysis research and treatment within health care has been of the case-study type. Many of the studies have suffered from problems of poor methodology or weak research design. However, more recently the research has definitely improved, and health care will likely be a fruitful area for future behavior analysis work. New methods of data collection have been explored (see Goldstein, Stein, Smolen, & Perlini, 1976; Stein, Goldstein, & Smolen, 1976). Behavior change professionals, with their emphasis on objective measurement and permanent behavior change, have much to offer health care; and with a growing interest in this area, large-scale contributions to the health and well being of our country are likely.

REFERENCES

Adams, K. M. Behavioral treatment of reflex or sensory-evoked seizures. *Journal of Behavior Therapy and Experimental Psychiatry*, 1976, *7*, 123–127.

Alexander, A. B. Asthma. *Behavioral Medicine Newsletter*, 1979, *1*(6), 14–15.

Alexander, A. B., Chai, H., Creer, T. L., Micklich, D. R., Renne, C. M., & Cardoso, R. A. The elimination of cough by response suppression shaping. *Journal of Behavior Therapy and Experimental Psychiatry*, 1973, *4*, 75–80.

Alexander, A. B., & Solanch, L. S. Psychological aspects in understanding and treatment of bronchial asthma. In J. Ferguson & C. B. Taylor (Eds.), *Advances in behavioral medicine*. New York: Spectrum, in press.

Andrews, J. M. Neuromuscular re-education of the hemiplegic with the aid of the electromyograph. *Archives of Physical Medicine and Rehabilitation*, 1964, *45*, 530–532.

Bad lifestyle—Can we tackle it nationally? *Medical News Report*, March 20, 1978, pp. 1, 20.

Baile, W. F., & Engel, B. T. A behavioral strategy for promoting treatment compliance following myocardial infarction. *Psychosomatic Medicine*, 1978, *40*, 413–419.

Basmajian, J. V., Kukulka, C. G., Narayan, M. G., & Takebe, K. Biofeedback treatment of foot-drop after stroke compared with standard rehabilitation techniques: Effects on voluntary control and strength. *Archives of Physical Medicine and Rehabilitation*, 1975, *56*, 231–236.

Belloc, N. B., & Breslow, L. The relation of physical health status and health practices. *Preventive Medicine,* 1972, *1,* 409–421.

Benson, H. B. *The relaxation response.* New York: Morrow, 1975.

Bird, B. L. Behavioral control of seizures. *Behavioral Medicine Newsletter,* 1978, *1*(4), 10–13.

Blackwell, B. Patient compliance. *New England Journal of Medicine,* 1973, *289,* 249–253.

Blanchard, E. B., & Epstein, L. H. The clinical utility of biofeedback. In M. Hersen & P. M. Miller (Eds.), *Progress in behavior modification,* Vol. 3. New York: Academic Press, 1977.

Blanchard, E. B., & Haynes, M. R. Biofeedback treatment of a case of Raynaud's Disease. *Journal of Behavior Therapy and Experimental Psychiatry,* 1975, *6,* 230–234.

Blanchard, E. B., & Young, L. D. Clinical applications of biofeedback training: A review of evidence. *Archives of General Psychiatry,* 1974, *30,* 530–589.

Bootzin, R. Stimulus control treatment for insomnia. *Proceedings of the 80th Annual Convention of the American Psychological Association,* 1972, *7,* 395–396.

Bootzin, R. Stimulus control of insomnia. Unpublished paper, 1973.

Borkovec, T. D. Insomnia. In R. B. Williams & W. D. Gentry (Eds.), *Behavioral approaches to medical treatment.* Cambridge, Mass.: Ballinger, 1977.

Breslow, L. Research in a strategy for health improvement. *International Journal of Health Services,* 1973, 7–16.

Brody, J. E. Help for troubled sleepers. *Family Circle,* June 28, 1977, pp. 2, 69–72, 153.

Brown, B. B. *Stress and the art of biofeedback.* New York: Harper & Row, 1977.

Brudny, J., Korein, J., Levidow, L., Grynbaum, B. B., Lieberman, A., & Friedmann, L. Sensory feedback therapy as a modality of treatment in central nervous system disorders of voluntary movement. *Neurology,* 1974, *24,* 925–932.

Byassee, J. E. Essential hypertension. In R. B. Williams & W. D. Gentry (Eds.), *Behavioral approaches to medical treatment.* Cambridge, Mass.: Ballinger, 1977.

Byassee, J. E., Farr, S., & Meyer, R. Progressive relaxation and autogenic training in the treatment of essential hypertension. Unpublished paper, 1976.

Cerulli, M., Nikoomanesh, P., & Schuster, M. M. Progress in biofeedback treatment of fecal incontinence. *Gastroenterology,* 1976, *70*(5), part 2, A-11/869.

Clark, M., Gosnell, M., & Shapiro, D. The new war on pain. *Newsweek,* April 25, 1977, pp. 48–58.

Cox, D. J., Freundlich, A., & Meyer, R. G. Differential effectiveness of electromyographic feedback, verbal relaxation instructions, and medication placebo without tension headaches. *Journal of Consulting and Clinical Psychology,* 1975, *43,* 892–898.

Creer, T. L. Asthma: Psychological aspects and management. In E. Middleton, C. Reed, & E. Ellis (Eds.), *Allergy: Principles and practice.* St. Louis: Mosby, 1978.

Dunbar, J., & Agras, W. S. A controlled investigation of a behavioral intervention with poor adherers to a medication regimen. Unpublished manuscript, 1978.

Ellis, A. *Reason and emotion in psychotherapy.* New York: Lyle-Stuart, 1962.

Engel, B. T. Operant conditioning of cardiovascular function: A behavioral analysis. In S. Rachman (Ed.), *Contributions to medical psychology,* Vol. 1. Oxford, England: Pergamon Press, 1977.

Engel, B. T., Nikoomanesh, P., & Schuster, M. M. Operant conditioning of rectosphincteric responses in the treatment of fecal incontinence. *New England Journal of Medicine,* 1974, *290,* 646–649.

Engel, G. L. The need for a new medical model: A challenge for biomedicine. *Science,* 1977, *196,* 129–136.

Epstein, L. H., & Cincirpini, P. M. Behavioral medicine III: Health care delivery. *Association for Advancement of Behavior Therapy Newsletter,* 1977, *4*(5), 7–9.

Epstein, L. H., & Martin, J. E. Behavioral medicine. *Association for Advancement of Behavior Therapy Newsletter,* 1977, *4*(3), 5–6.

Epstein, L. H., & Masek, B. J. Behavioral control of medicine compliance. *Journal of Applied Behavior Analysis,* 1978, *11,* 1–9.

Fish, D., Mayer, N., & Herman, R. Letter to the editor: Biofeedback. *Archives of Physical Medicine and Rehabilitation,* 1976, *57,* 152.

Fordyce, W. E. *Behavioral methods for chronic pain and illness.* St. Louis: Mosby, 1976.

Fordyce, W. E., Fowler, R. S., Lehmann, J. F., DeLateur, B. J., Sand, P. L., & Trieschmann, R. B. Operant conditioning in the treatment of chronic pain. *Archives of Physical Medicine and Rehabilitation,* 1973, *54,* 399–408.

Fowler, R. L., & Kimmel, H. D. Operant conditioning of the GSR. *Journal of Experimental Psychology,* 1962, *63,* 563–567.

Friedman, M., & Rosenman, R. *Type A behavior and your heart.* New York: Knopf, 1974.

Furman, S. Intestinal biofeedback in functional diarrhea: A preliminary report. *Journal of Behavior Therapy and Experimental Psychiatry,* 1973, *4,* 317–321.

Genest, M. *A cognitive-behavioral bibliotherapy to ameliorate pain.* Paper presented at the 86th annual convention of the American Psychological Association, Toronto, 1978.

Gentry, W. D. Noncompliance to medical regimen. In R. B. Williams & W. D. Gentry (Eds.), *Behavioral approaches to medical treatment.* Cambridge, Mass.: Ballinger, 1977.

Goldiamond, I. A diary of self-modification. *Psychology Today,* November 1973, pp. 95–102.

Goldstein, M. K., Stein, G. H., Smolen, D. M., & Perlini, W. Bio-behavioral monitoring: A method for remote health measurement. *Archives of Physical Medicine and Rehabilitation,* 1976, *57,* 253–258.

Goodkin, R. Case studies in behavioral research in rehabilitation. *Perceptual and Motor Skills,* 1966, *23,* 171–182.

Gottlieb, H., Strite, L., Koller, R., Madorsky, A., Hockersmith, V., Kleeman, M., & Wagner, J. Comprehensive rehabilitation of patients having chronic low back pain. *Archives of Physical Medicine and Rehabilitation,* 1977, *58,* 101–108.

Guglielmi, R. S. *A double-blind study of the effectiveness of skin temperature self-regulation as a treatment for Raynaud's Disease.* Paper presented at Society for Psychophysiology meeting, Cincinnati, 1979.

Hall, D. C., Goldstein, M. K., & Stein, G. H. Progress in manual breast examination. *Cancer,* 1977, *40,* 364–370.

Hayes, S. C. *Compliance with medical regimens: Methodological problems and one way to begin.* Paper presented at Midwestern Association of Behavior Analysis meeting, Chicago, 1977.

Haynes, S. N., Sides, H., & Lockwood, G. Relaxation instructions and frontalis electromyographic feedback intervention with sleep-onset insomnia. *Behavior Therapy,* 1977, *8,* 644–652.

Health costs: What limit? *Time,* May 28, 1979, pp. 60–68.

Hutchings, D. F., & Reinking, R. H. Tension headaches: What form of therapy is most effective? *Biofeedback and Self-Regulation,* 1976, *1,* 183–190.

Ince, L. P. A behavioral approach to motivation in rehabilitation. *Psychological Record,* 1969, *19,* 105–111. (a)

Ince, L. P. Escape and avoidance conditioning of responses in the plegic arm of stroke patients: A preliminary study. *Psychonomic Science,* 1969, *16,* 49–50. (b)

Ince, L. P., Brucker, B. S., & Alba, A. Conditioning bladder responses in patients with spinal cord lesions. *Archives of Physical Medicine and Rehabilitation,* 1977, *58,* 59–65.

Inglis, J., Campbell, D., & Donald, M. W. Electromyographic biofeedback and neuromuscular rehabilitation. *Canadian Journal of Behavioral Sciences,* 1976, *8,* 299–323.

Jacobson, A. M., Hackett, T. P., Surman, O. S., & Silverberg, E. L. Raynaud phenomenon: Treatment with hypnotic and operant technique. *Journal of American Medical Association,* 1973, *225,* 739–740.

Jacobson, E. *Progressive relaxation.* Chicago: University of Chicago Press, 1938.

Janis, I. L. *Psychological stress: Psychoanalytic and behavioral studies of surgical patients.* New York: Wiley, 1958.

Janis, I. L. *Stress and frustration*. New York: Harcourt Brace Jovanovich, 1971.

Johnson, H. E., & Garton, W. H. Muscle re-education in hemiplegia by use of electromyographic device. *Archives of Physical Medicine and Rehabilitation, 1973, 54,* 320–325.

Kasl, S. V. Issues in patient adherence to health care regimens. *Journal of Human Stress,* 1975, *1,* 5–17.

Katz, R. C. Single session recovery from a hemodialysis phobia: A case study. *Journal of Behavior Therapy and Experimental Psychiatry, 1974, 5,* 205–206.

Keefe, F. J., Surwit, R. S., & Pilon, R. N. Biofeedback, autogenic training, and progressive relaxation in the treatment of Raynaud's Disease: A comparative study. *Journal of Applied Behavior Analysis, 1980, 13,* 3–11.

Kewman, D., & Roberts, A. H. *Skin temperature biofeedback and migraine headaches: A double-blind study.* Paper presented at Biofeedback Research Society meeting, San Diego, 1979.

Knapp, T. J., & Peterson, L. W. Behavior management in medical and nursing practice. In W. E. Craighead, A. E. Kazdin, & M. J. Mahoney (Eds.), *Behavior modification: Principles, issues, and applications.* Boston: Houghton Mifflin, 1976.

Knowles, J. H. Introduction. In J. H. Knowles (Ed.), *Doing better and feeling worse: Health in the United States.* New York: Norton, 1977. (a)

Knowles, J. H. The responsibility of the individual. In J. H. Knowles (Ed.), *Doing better and feeling worse: Health in the United States.* New York: Norton, 1977. (b)

Kosiak, M., Kubicek, W., Olson, M., Donz, J. N., & Kottke, F. J. Evaluation of pressure as a factor in the production of ischial ulcers. *Archives of Physical Medicine and Rehabilitation, 1958, 39,* 623–629.

Kottke, F. J. Historia obscura hemiplegiae. *Archives of Physical Medicine and Rehabilitation,* 1974, *55,* 4–13.

Lake, A., Rainey, J., & Papsdorf, J. D. Biofeedback and rational-emotive therapy in the management of migraine headache. *Journal of Applied Behavior Analysis, 1979, 12,* 127–140.

Langer, E. J., Janis, I. L., & Wolfer, J. A. Reduction of psychological stress in surgical patients. *Journal of Experimental Social Psychology, 1975, 11,* 155–165.

Love, W. A., Montgomery, D. D., & Moeller, T. A. Working paper number 1. Unpublished manuscript, 1974.

Lubar, J. F., & Bahler, W. W. Behavioral management of epileptic seizures following EEG biofeedback training of the sensorimotor rhythm. *Biofeedback and Self-Regulation,* 1976, *1,* 77–104.

Lutker, E. R. Treatment of migraine headache by conditioned relaxation: A case study. *Behavior Therapy, 1971, 2,* 592–593.

Malament, I. B., Dunn, M. E., & Davis, R. Pressure sores: An operant conditioning approach to prevention. *Archives of Physical Medicine and Rehabilitation, 1975, 56,* 161–165.

Marinacci, A. A., & Horande, M. Electromyogram in neuromuscular re-education. *Bulletin of the Los Angeles Neurological Society, 1960, 25,* 57–71.

Marston, M. V. Compliance with medical regimens: A review of the literature. *Nursing Research, 1970, 19,* 312–323.

Matarazzo, J. D. Health psychology: APA's newest division (President's Column). *The Health Psychologist,* 1979, *1*(1), 1.

McDonald, G. W., & Kaufman, M. B. Teaching machines for patients with diabetes. *Journal of American Dietetic Association, 1963, 42,* 209–213.

Meichenbaum, D. H. *Cognitive factors in behavior modification: Modifying what clients say to themselves.* Paper presented at Association for Advancement of Behavior Therapy meeting, Washington, D.C., 1971.

Meyer, A. L., & Henderson, J. B. Multiple risk factor reduction in the prevention of cardiovascular disease. *Preventive Medicine, 1974, 3,* 225–236.

Meyerson, L., Kerr, N., & Michael, J. L. Behavior modification in rehabilitation. In S. W. Bijou & D. M. Baer (Eds.), *Child development: Readings in experimental analysis.* New York: Appleton-Century-Crofts, 1967.

Michael, J. L. Rehabilitation. In C. Neuringer & J. L. Michael (Eds.), *Behavior modification in clinical psychology.* New York: Appleton-Century-Crofts, 1970.

Miller, N. E. Learning of visceral and glandular responses. *Science,* 1969, *163,* 434–445.

Mitchell, K. R. The treatment of migraine: An exploratory application of time-limited behavior therapy. *Technology,* 1969, *14,* 50.

Moeller, T. A., & Love, W. A. A method to reduce arterial hypertension through muscular relaxation. Unpublished paper, 1974.

Monkerud, D. The three-martini lunch is falling prey to the three-mile lunch. *On the Run,* July 6, 1978, pp. 18–19.

Moore, N. Behavioral therapy in bronchial asthma: A controlled study. *Journal of Psychosomatic Research,* 1965, *9,* 257–276.

Morgan, J., & O'Brien, J. S. The counter conditioning of a vomiting habit by sips of ginger ale. *Journal of Behavior Therapy and Experimental Psychiatry,* 1972, *3,* 135–137.

Mostofsky, D. I. Behavior modification and the psychosomatic aspects of epilepsy. In D. Upper & D. S. Goodenough (Eds.), *Behavior modification with the individual patient.* Nutley, N.J.: Roche Laboratories, 1972.

Munford, P. R., Reardon, D., Liberman, R. P., & Allen, L. Behavioral treatment of hysterical coughing and mutism: A case study. *Journal of Consulting and Clinical Psychology,* 1976, *44,* 1008–1014.

Nimmer, W. H., & Kapp, R. A. A multiple impact program for the treatment of injection phobias. *Journal of Behavior Therapy and Experimental Psychiatry,* 1974, *5,* 257–258.

Obrist, P. A. The cardiovascular-behavior interaction—as it appears today. *Psychophysiology,* 1976, *13,* 95–107.

Otis, L. D., & Turner, A. *EMG training and headache reduction: Some methodological issues.* Paper presented at Biofeedback Research Society meeting, Monterey, Calif., 1975.

Parrino, J. J. Reduction of seizures by desensitization. *Journal of Behavior Therapy and Experimental Psychiatry,* 1971, *2,* 215–218.

Patel, C. H. Yoga and biofeedback in the management of hypertension. *The Lancet,* 1973, *2,* 1053–1055.

Patel, C. H. Twelve-month follow-up of yoga and biofeedback in the management of hypertension. *The Lancet,* 1975, *1,* 62–64. (a)

Patel, C. H. Yoga and biofeedback in the management of "stress" in hypertensive patients. *Clinical Science and Molecular Medicine,* 1975, *48,* 171–174. (b)

Patel, C. H., & North, W. R. S. Randomized controlled trial of yoga and biofeedback in management of hypertension. *The Lancet,* 1975, *2,* 93–99.

Peters, R. K., Benson, H., & Peters, J. M. Daily relaxation response breaks in a working population: Effects on blood pressure. *American Journal of Public Health,* 1977, *67,* 954–959.

Peters, R. K., Benson, H., & Porter, D. Daily relaxation response breaks in a working population: Effects on self-reported measure of health, performance and well-being. *American Journal of Public Health,* 1977, *67,* 946–953.

Pomerleau, O. F. On behaviorism in behavioral medicine. *Behavioral Medicine Newsletter,* 1978, *1*(3), 2.

Pomerleau, O. F., & Brady, J. P. Introduction: The scope and promise of behavioral medicine. In O. F. Pomerleau & J. P. Brady (Eds.), *Behavioral medicine: Theory and practice.* Baltimore: Williams & Wilkins, 1979.

Quarti, C., & Renaud, J. A new treatment of constipation by conditioning: A preliminary report. In C. Franks (Ed.), *Conditioning techniques in clinical practice and research.* New York: Springer, 1964.

Rathus, S. A. Motoric, autonomic and cognitive reciprocal inhibition of a case of hysterical bronchial asthma. *Adolescence,* 1973, *8,* 29–32.

Reeves, J. L. EMG-biofeedback reduction of tension headaches: A cognitive skills training approach. *Biofeedback and Self-Regulation,* 1976, *1,* 217–225.

Reinhardt, L. A long-term follow-up study of chronic pain patients treated with a behaviorally oriented inpatient pain treatment program. Unpublished doctoral dissertation, University of Minnesota, 1979.

Renne, C. M., & Creer, T. L. Training children with asthma to use inhalation therapy equipment. *Journal of Applied Behavior Analysis,* 1976, *9,* 1–11.

Roberts, A. R. *The pain clinic and pain treatment program procedure manual.* Minneapolis, Minn.: University of Minnesota, Department of Physical Medicine and Rehabilitation, 1977.

Sackett, D. L., & Haynes, R. B. (Eds.), *Compliance with therapeutic regimens.* Baltimore: Johns Hopkins University Press, 1976.

Sand, P. L., Fordyce, W. E., & Fowler, R. S. Fluid intake behavior in patients with spinal cord injury: Prediction and modification. *Archives of Physical Medicine and Rehabilitation,* 1973, *54,* 254–262.

Sand, P. L., Trieschmann, R. B., Fordyce, W. E., & Fowler, R. S. Behavior modification in the medical rehabilitation setting: Rationale and some applications. *Rehabilitation Research and Practice Review,* 1970, *1,* 11–24.

Schultz, J. H., & Luthe, W. *Autogenic therapy.* New York: Grune & Stratton, 1969.

Schwartz, G. E. Biofeedback as therapy: Some theoretical and practical issues. *American Psychologist,* 1973, *28,* 666–673.

Schwartz, G. E., & Weiss, S. M. Yale conference on behavioral medicine: A proposed definition and statement of goals. *Journal of Behavioral Medicine,* 1978, *1,* 3–12. (a)

Schwartz, G. E., & Weiss, S. M. Behavioral medicine revisited: An amended definition. *Journal of Behavioral Medicine,* 1978, *1,* 249–251. (b)

Seifort, A. R., & Lubar, J. F. Reduction of epileptic seizures through EEG biofeedback training. *Biological Psychology,* 1975, *3,* 157–184.

Sergeant, H. G. S., & Yorkston, N. J. Verbal desensitization in the treatment of bronchial asthma. *The Lancet,* 1969, *7634,* 1321–1323.

Shapiro, D., Crider, A. B., & Tursky, B. Differentiation of an autonomic response through operant reinforcement. *Psychonomic Science,* 1964, *1,* 147–148.

Shapiro, D., & Surwit, R. S. Biofeedback. In O. F. Pomerleau & J. P. Brady (Eds.), *Behavioral medicine: Theory and practice.* Baltimore: Williams & Wilkins, 1979.

Sirota, A. D., & Mahoney, M. J. Relaxing on cue: The self-regulation of asthma. *Journal of Behavior Therapy and Experimental Psychiatry,* 1974, *5,* 65–66.

Somers, A. R. *Promoting health: Consumer education and national policy.* Germantown, Md.: Aspen, 1976.

Stein, G. H., Goldstein, M. K., & Smolen, D. M. Remote medical behavioral monitoring: An alternative for ambulatory health. In J. W. Cullen, B. H. Fox, & R. N. Isom (Eds.), *Cancer: The behavioral dimensions.* New York: Raven Press, 1976.

Sterman, M. B. Neurophysiologic and clinical studies of sensorimotor EEG biofeedback training: Some effects on epilepsy. *Seminars in Psychiatry,* 1973, *5,* 507–525.

Sterman, M. B., & Friar, L. Suppression of seizures in an epileptic following sensorimotor EEG feedback training. *Electroencephalography and Clinical Neurophysiology,* 1972, *33,* 89–95.

Sterman, M. B., LoPresti, R. W., & Fairchild, M. D. Electroencephalographic and behavioral studies of monomethylhydrazine toxicity in the cat. *Technical Report AMRL-TR-69-3,* Wright-Patterson Air Force Base, Ohio, Air Systems Command, 1969.

Sterman, M. B., Macdonald, L. R., Feinstein, B., & Berntsen, I. Analysis of extended narrow-band central cortical EEG biofeedback training. Unpublished manuscript, 1976.

Sterman, M. B., Macdonald, L. R., & Stone, R. K. Biofeedback training of the sensorimotor EEG rhythm in man: Effects on epilepsy. *Epilepsia,* 1974, *15,* 395–416.

Suinn, R. M. The cardiac stress management program for Type A patients. *Cardiac Rehabilitation,* 1975, *5,* 13–15.

Suinn, R. M. Type A behavior pattern. In R. B. Williams & W. D. Gentry (Eds.), *Behavioral approaches to medical treatment.* Cambridge, Mass.: Ballinger, 1977.

Suinn, R. M., & Bloom, L. J. Anxiety management training for Pattern A behavior. *Journal of Behavioral Medicine,* 1978, *1,* 25–35.

Surwit, R. S. Biofeedback: A possible treatment for Raynaud's Disease. *Seminars in Psychiatry,* 1973, *5,* 483–490.

Surwit, R. S. Peripheral vasomotor—Raynaud's Disease. *Behavioral Medicine Newsletter,* 1978, *1*(3), 9–11.

Taylor, G. P., & Persons, R. W. Behavior modification techniques in a physical medicine and rehabilitation center. *Journal of Psychology,* 1970, *74,* 117–124.

Thomas, L. On the science and technology of medicine. In J. H. Knowles (Ed.), *Doing better and feeling worse: Health in the United States.* New York: Norton, 1977.

Trotter, A. B., & Inman, D. A. The use of positive reinforcement in physical therapy. *Physical Therapy,* 1968, *48,* 347–352.

Turk, D. C. *A coping-skills training approach for control of experimentally induced pain.* Unpublished doctoral dissertation, University of Waterloo, 1977.

Turk, D. C. Cognitive-behavioral techniques in the management of pain. In J. P. Foreyt & D. J. Rathjen (Eds.), *Cognitive behavior therapy: Research and applications.* New York: Plenum, 1978.

Turnage, J. R., & Logan, D. L. Treatment of a hypodermic needle phobia by in vivo systematic desensitization. *Journal of Behavior Therapy and Experimental Psychiatry,* 1974, *5,* 67–69.

Turnbull, J. W. Asthma conceived as a learned response. *Journal of Psychosomatic Research,* 1962, *6,* 59–70.

Wallace, R. K., & Benson, H. The physiology of meditation. *Scientific American,* 1972, *226,* 84–90.

Weiss, S. M. News and developments in behavioral medicine. *Journal of Behavioral Medicine,* 1978, *1,* 135–139.

Wickramasekera, I. E. Temperature feedback for the control of migraine. *Journal of Behavior Therapy & Experimental Psychiatry,* 1973, *4,* 343–345.

Wohl, T. H. Behavior modification: Its application to the study and treatment of childhood asthma. *Journal of Asthma Research,* 1971, *9,* 41–45.

Youell, K. J., & McCullough, J. P. Behavioral treatment of mucous colitis. *Journal of Consulting and Clinical Psychology,* 1975, *43,* 740–745.

Zifferblatt, S. M. Increasing patient compliance through the applied analysis of behavior. *Preventive Medicine,* 1975, *4,* 173–182.

Zifferblatt, S. M., & Wilbur, C. S. Maintaining a healthy heart: Guidelines for a feasible goal. *Preventive Medicine,* 1977, *6,* 514–525.

CHAPTER 6

Health Care: Children

A substantial portion of the early behavior change literature was devoted to applications with children. Likewise, there have been within the field of health care a number of applications of behavioral techniques to pediatric health care. The health-related problems of children are somewhat different from those of adults. Acute problems are primarily injuries, infective or parasitic diseases, and respiratory conditions. Chronic conditions most commonly limiting the activity of children are asthma, paralysis, impairments of lower extremities or hips, and bronchitis or sinusitis (Richmond, 1977). An excellent overview of these problems may be found in a recent encyclopedia on pediatric psychology (Wright, Schaefer, & Solomons, 1979). Logan Wright (1976) estimated that between one third and one half of all patients seen at the Children's Hospital of the University of Oklahoma have a behavioral concomitant to their physical illness. It has been estimated that some 35% of children seen by pediatricians in outpatient clinics exhibit behavioral or developmental problems (Duff, Rowe, & Anderson, 1972; Greenwood, 1973). Obviously, these large numbers of children with health-related problems present an enormous burden upon the health care delivery system. As you will see in this chapter, behavior change techniques have been shown to be applicable to a wide variety of children's health problems.

ENCOPRESIS

Pediatricians are frequently faced with children who have problems related to bowel and bladder training and functioning. Behavioral approaches to normal bowel and bladder training and to enuresis are presented in Chapter 7; because frequent fecal soiling by children beyond four years of age (encopresis) can be viewed as maladaptive and a possible target for behavioral intervention, it is properly a subject for the present chapter. A thorough medical assessment by a physician and an attempt at medical management should precede any attempt at control through behavior modification. Treatment of encopresis should preferably be a team effort among the physician, the family, and a psychologist (Nisley, 1976).

An extremely effective treatment program for encopresis was developed by Logan Wright (Wright, 1975; Wright & Walker, 1976). A medical workup was first conducted to rule out the possibility of any organic etiology, and the resulting treatment program carried out in consultation with a physician. Second, the parent and child were interviewed. If necessary, an assessment ruled out the possibility of emotional disturbance or serious psychopathology. (For a child with only moderate personal problems, improvement in general function and emotional stability have been noted as side benefits of the successful treatment of the encopresis.) The third step was to instruct the parents in how to institute the program, since they were responsible for explaining it to the child; occasionally, however, the psychologist explained the program. The treatment program consisted of the following seven components:

1. The child's colon was thoroughly evacuated. This was done with a couple of enemas over the course of a day or two. If this did not work, then it was necessary for the physician to physically clean the colon.

2. Next, the parents required the child to go to the bathroom immediately upon awakening in the morning. (Other times of the day were substituted if preferable.) The parents supervised this and if a reasonable amount of feces was produced, he was praised and given a reward. The day then proceeded as normal.

3. If a reasonable amount of feces was not produced by the child on his own ($\frac{1}{4}$–$\frac{1}{2}$ cup), then the parent inserted a glycerin suppository. The child was directed to dress, eat breakfast, and prepare for school. Usually the suppository would take effect by the time the child had finished breakfast. He was taken back to the bathroom and asked to defecate. If he was successful, a reward was delivered (a smaller reward than would have been delivered had he been successful the first time).

4. If no defecation had yet taken place, and it was near time to leave for school, the child was given an enema by the parent. It was essential that the enema chosen be one that was safe for repeated use and that the parents carefully observed and controlled any side effects. Repeated use of enemas was done only with ongoing consultation with a physician. If an enema was needed to produce defecation, then no reward was given.

5. The child's clothing was examined at the end of every day. A reward was delivered if there was no soiling. Mild punishment was administered if there was soiling.

6. This regime was followed daily with consistency. The program was presented to the parents with a very positive attitude and the explanation that it rarely ever failed. The key elements were to follow the program precisely and consistently. Parents were directed to keep a daily notebook containing precise information about what occurred each day. Weekly reports were mailed to the psychologist. Encouragement and advice were transmitted by weekly phone calls to the family.

7. When no soiling had occurred for two consecutive weeks, the parents began to phase out the program. The use of suppositories and enemas were discontinued during one day of the week; the remainder of the program remained constant. If there was no soiling during this week, then two days off suppositories and enemas were scheduled for the following week. "Off" days were some distance apart. For each successive week in which no soiling occurred, another "off" day (equidistant from those days already off the program) was added. The reward and punishment program was eliminated when the child was completely off suppositories and enemas and free from soiling. Should soiling recur at any time during this phaseout, the parents retreated one step and started again.

Obviously, the use of reinforcers and punishers was crucial to this program. Wright and Walker (1976) suggested that parents allot 20–30 minutes of their time at the end of the day, during which they did anything the child wanted. Typical punishment was loss of privileges such as television viewing time. Wright (1975) has presented 14 cases demonstrating the effectiveness of this program in approximately 15–20 weeks with an average of 16.93 weeks (with ten weeks without soiling). An important element was the rapid decrease in soiling that occurred as the result of the suppository and enema procedures. The child rather immediately achieved success and this success was reinforced. The gradual withdrawal from the program was guided by the child's success. It is no wonder that Wright and Walker (1976) reported that children in their program spontaneously begin to demonstrate improvement in other areas of their lives. Success breeds success.

Christophersen and Rainey (1976) have reported similar results with these procedures with six children at the University of Kansas Medical Center. Additional successes with the treatment of encopresis by behavior modification methods have been reported by Blechman (1979) and others (see Barrett, 1969; Pedrini & Pedrini, 1971; Nilsson, 1976). Most of these professionals have had parents differentially reinforce appropriate passage of feces and ignore or minimally attend to soiling. A somewhat more aversive procedure (requiring the child to clean himself and wash out his soiled clothing with a strong soap) has been used by Ferinden and Handel (1970).

Robert Kohlenberg (1973) has noted that fecal soiling may be produced by a dilated anal sphincter (a muscle that controls the passage of feces from the body), which results in a constant discharge of feces. Working with a 13-year-old male, Kohlenberg reinforced increases in pressure exerted on a balloon filled with fluid and placed into the rectum. The boy was provided with continuous visual feedback by a columnar tube filled with red-tinted water. The height of this water column was a function of pressure exerted in the anal sphincter area. Reinforcers (money) were delivered for maintaining the column of water above a certain criterion level. Considerable success was achieved at surpassing this criterion and, additionally, throughout the experiment his baseline level (resting pressure) tended to increase. One month after discharge from the hospital, the boy's parents reported that there was no soiling for periods of about eight hours. This was in marked contrast to the previous continuous nature of soiling. As the result of this success, physicians postponed a colostomy procedure for the youngster.

Epstein and McCoy (1977) have described an alternative treatment procedure used with a 3-year-old girl with a similar problem. She was neither bowel nor bladder trained and her parents had made no attempts with her because of her frequent and unusual bowel functioning. Initially, a two-week baseline measurement of bowel and bladder accidents was obtained. Next, there were six sequential components to the bladder training program as follows:

1. The girl's pants were checked hourly and, if they were dry, she was praised and given food.
2. If the girl's pants were dry, she was prompted to go to the toilet and to remain seated for two, then gradually three, minutes. If she urinated, she was praised and provided with food reinforcement.
3. If the girl's pants were wet at hourly checks, she was required to change her pants with a minimum of adult attention.
4. Retention training was implemented by having her inform her parents when she had to go. She was asked to retain her urine for 30 seconds at first, and gradually up to two minutes with instructions given to pay attention to how it feels to have to go to the toilet.
5. A star chart replaced primary reinforcers. Initially, she was given one star for each urination and eventually she had to remain dry all day to earn a star.
6. Finally, stars were withdrawn though verbal praise continued.

Only urination resulted in consequences. No program of contingent events was implemented for bowel control. The girl's parents collected data on the number of accidents and successful toilets for both urinations and bowel movements. At the end of five months, no urination accidents were observed until the end of the study, seven weeks later. Surprisingly, the same occurred for bowel movements, despite the fact that no program had been initiated to systematically treat encopresis. Epstein and McCoy noted that a change in number of appropriate bowel movements occurred soon after bladder training was initiated. Additionally, during the initial two-week baseline, there was a high correlation between bowel and urine accidents. In cases such as this, where bowel and bladder functions positively covary, training of one function such as bladder would likely alter the other. Epstein and McCoy believe that the procedure used by Kohlenberg (1973) *might* be extremely anxiety-producing for younger children, for it involves placement of a pressure transducer in the anus to measure changes in sphincter pressure. The procedure outlined above has the advantage that it can be used with younger children and in the home rather than in a hospital or setting with rather sophisticated recording apparatuses. It is a variation of a program developed by Foxx and Azrin (1973), which is discussed more fully in Chapter 7.

CONSTIPATION

Quite the opposite of encopresis, constipation (the retention of feces) can sometimes be a problem in children as well as the elderly. Tomlinson (1970) successfully treated a long-standing problem of bowel retention in a 3-year-old child. From the time toilet training was accomplished at age 2, the frequency of elimination without a laxative averaged only once per week. Extensive medical examinations revealed no physiological dysfunction. Attempts at change through diet proved unsuccessful. It was decided to try to alter the frequency of elimination

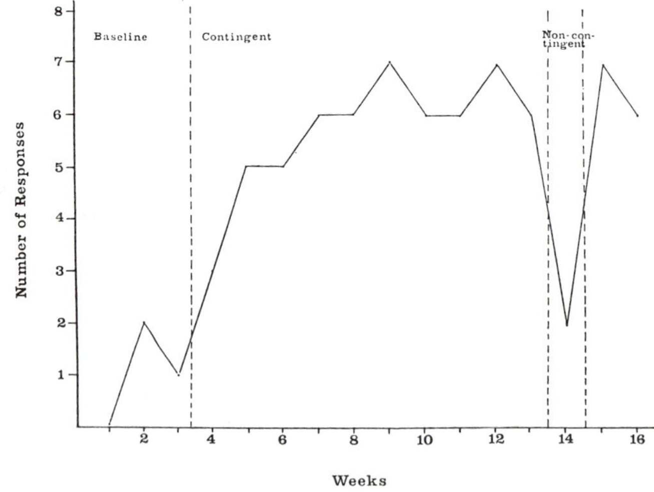

FIGURE 6-1.   Number of voluntary defecations per week. (From "The Treatment of Bowel Retention by Operant Procedures: A Case Study," by J. R. Tomlinson. In *Journal of Behavior Therapy and Experimental Psychiatry*, 1970, *1*, 83–85. Reprinted by permission of Pergamon Press, Ltd.)

through the use of a reinforcer; bubble gum was chosen because the child usually requested it at least once per day. After a base rate had been established, the child was told that after that day, he could obtain bubble gum only by having a bowel movement. Gum was kept in the bathroom to minimize any delay in reinforcement. A mild laxative was administered daily the first week to increase the probability of an appropriate response. Figure 6-1 shows how extremely effective this procedure was. From a base rate of two or fewer voluntary defecations per week, bowel movements increased to a high of seven per week during the contingent delivery of bubble gum.

During the third month of the treatment program, the program was accidentally withdrawn. The boy spent the 14th week at his grandparents' home. Because they had not been informed of the gum contingency, they dispensed gum noncontingently at the child's request. The frequency of bowel movements decreased during this week. The treatment program was reinstated the following week with a rapid increase in the voluntary defecations. The gum reinforcer was replaced by dessert at the end of the evening meal, contingent upon defecation at some time during the day. A follow-up conducted two years after the treatment program had been instituted revealed that the rate remained at six voluntary defecations per week. Similar reinforcement programs using playing in the bathtub (Lal & Lindsley, 1968) and popsicles (Perzan, Boulanger, & Fischer, 1972) have been described.

RUMINATION AND VOMITING

Richmond, Eddy, and Green (1958) have described ruminative vomiting as chronic or habitual vomiting characterized by the regurgitation, chewing, and re-swallowing of food. Death from emaciation or eventual starvation is possible. When a child's life is threatened and all methods of intervention have failed, extreme measures may be necessary. Lang and Melamed (1969) reported the behavioral treatment of such an infant. This baby boy was admitted to the University of Wisconsin Hospital at the age of 9 months. He had had three previous hospitalizations for chronic vomiting and failure to gain weight after the age of 5 months. Extensive medical tests and examinations failed to reveal an organic basis for the infant's frequent regurgitation. Several treatment attempts were unsuccessful. At the time of intervention, the boy weighed 12 lbs, was being fed by a tube through the nose, and *was in critical condition.* Behavioral intervention was viewed as a last effort in view of the persistent life-threatening nature of the vomiting.

After two days of observing the boy during and after meals, it was noted that he reliably regurgitated the large portion of his food within ten minutes of a meal. Thereafter, only small amounts would come up during the remaining day. An aversive conditioning procedure was implemented. This involved a brief one-second shock administered to the child's calf as soon as vomiting occurred (and continued with one-second interpulse intervals until vomiting ceased).[1] Sessions followed feeding and lasted less than one hour. After two sessions, shock was rarely ad-

[1]You will note throughout this book that aversive procedures involving the use of electric shock have been restricted to use with behavior problems that are life-threatening. Additionally, exhaustive attempts at intervention with less intrusive procedures have usually preceded the use of electric shock.

ministered. To provide for generalization and transfer of treatment effects, sessions were subsequently scheduled at different hours of the day. These were done while the boy was playing on the floor, lying in bed, and being held. A progressive decrease in rumination during the rest of the day was reported by the nursing staff. Eventually the boy's mother took over some of the child's caretaking needs and feeding. Five days later, the child was discharged from the hospital, having gained about 4 lbs. At a clinic visit one month later, his weight was 21 lbs; five months later, it was 26 lbs. Vomiting had not recurred since discharge from the hospital. A one-year follow-up revealed that the boy had continued to thrive and that the conditioning treatment had proven permanently successful.

Toister, Condron, Worley, and Arthur (1975) also used contingent electric shock with a 7½-month-old infant hospitalized for vomiting accompanied by a serious weight loss. The investigators were not able to detect any antecedents to the infant's vomiting. Baseline recording revealed that the child vomited 0.48 times per minute. After six days of treatment, the child no longer vomited; and on the eighth day, treatment was terminated with the child's discharge from the hospital (with a 2-lb gain). No vomiting had recurred with follow-up of four and seven months, and the child continued to gain weight. It should be noted that both Toister et al. (1975) and Lang and Melamed (1969) reported dramatic (though anecdotal) side effects of their procedures. The infants began to vocalize more, to smile, to be more alert, and to be generally active. A third replication of these general procedures has been described by Cunningham and Linscheid (1976). Chronic ruminative vomiting by a hospitalized 9½-month-old male was treated by contingent electric shock. Unlike the previous studies, however, from the beginning treatment sessions were conducted at various times, in different locations, and with different observers. These procedures were seen as an aid in facilitating generalization.

An alternative aversive procedure has been reported by Sajwaj, Libet, and Agras (1974). Life-threatening rumination by a hospitalized 6-month-old infant was eliminated by squirting a small amount of lemon juice in her mouth contingent upon the onset of rumination. The child was discharged from the hospital after eight weeks of treatment with a 54% increase in weight from pretreatment weight. No rumination was revealed on a one-year follow-up. Again the authors reported that the infant changed from uninvolved and apathetic to a more normal infant (babbling, smiling, playing, and so on).

Becker, Turner, and Sajwaj (1978) have attempted to document the preceding anecdotal reports more systematically. Lemon juice again was used as an aversive stimulus to treat chronic rumination exhibited by a profoundly retarded 3-year-old girl. Treatment of the rumination proved effective up to a six-month follow-up; however, at nine months rumination had returned. This appeared to be related to a failure in treatment implementation in the home. The most interesting results of the investigation were objectively measured increases in eight behaviors (such as smiles, babbling, spontaneous interactions). Six of these behaviors appeared for the first time in the child's life. Consistent with ethical concerns and the potential side effects of aversive procedures, Ruprecht, Hanson, and Pocrnich (1979) have reported that the repeated use of lemon juice in such a procedure can potentially lead to the erosion of tooth enamel. The point to be learned is that behavior change professionals must pay attention to the costs of using certain behavior change techniques and weigh them against benefits.

SEIZURES

In 1967, Gardner reported the behavioral treatment of seizures exhibited by a 10-year-old girl. Seizures consisted of rhythmical head rolling accompanied by hair pulling. Extensive medical examination during hospitalization resulted in either ambiguous or negative findings. Behavioral assessment revealed that the girl's behavior might be a function of attention received from her parents. Under medical supervision, anticonvulsants were withheld until the possible effects of parental counseling could be assessed. The following intervention plan was implemented at home immediately after the child was discharged from the hospital. The parents were to ignore all seizure-like activity and other highly deviant behaviors such as tantrums. Whenever the girl exhibited appropriate behavior, such as playing with siblings, helping mother, drawing, and the like, parents were to reinforce this behavior with attention. Finally, parents were also asked to ignore possible "substitute" behaviors such as increased somatic complaints. Within two weeks of treatment, the frequency of seizure behavior decreased to zero; tantrums and somatic complaints decreased to about one-half the prehospitalization baseline. After 26 weeks, the parents were instructed to deliberately reinstate their preintervention behavior—attention to the child's somatic complaints and tantrums. Within 24 hours, these behaviors increased to approximately one per hour. The girl also exhibited a seizure. At once the parents, as instructed, returned to the original treatment procedures. There were no additional seizures, and gradually the child's deviant behavior decreased to the level previous to the withdrawal of the program. A one-year follow-up revealed that no further seizures had occurred.

Zlutnick, Mayville, and Moffat (1975) have applied punishment procedures to seizures exhibited by a number of mentally retarded children. They noted that quite frequently epileptics will exhibit a reliable *chain* of behavior before each seizure. They reasoned that if they could interrupt these chains in some way, then they might also prevent or postpone the onset of the seizures. After identifying preseizure behaviors in each child, the general procedure consisted of two steps. First, they shouted "No!" quite loudly; and second, they grasped the child by the shoulders and vigorously shook him once. The use of a single-subject research design demonstrated that this procedure was extremely effective in reducing seizures in two patients and almost eliminating them in two others.

Zlutnick, Mayville, and Moffat (1975) used a different procedure with a 17-year-old mentally retarded female with major motor epilepsy. Her seizures were composed of this chain of behaviors:

1. body becomes tense and rigid;
2. fists are clenched and arms raised to a right angle with trunk;
3. head snaps back and face grimaces; and
4. major motor seizure occurs.

Whenever she engaged in the hand raising, her hands were placed at her side or on her lap, there was a five-second wait, and then a combination of verbal praise and food was administered. The purpose of the five-second delay was to ensure that hand raising would not be contingently reinforced. Figure 6-2 shows the number of seizures this girl had during each phase of the withdrawal-reinstatement single-subject design used.

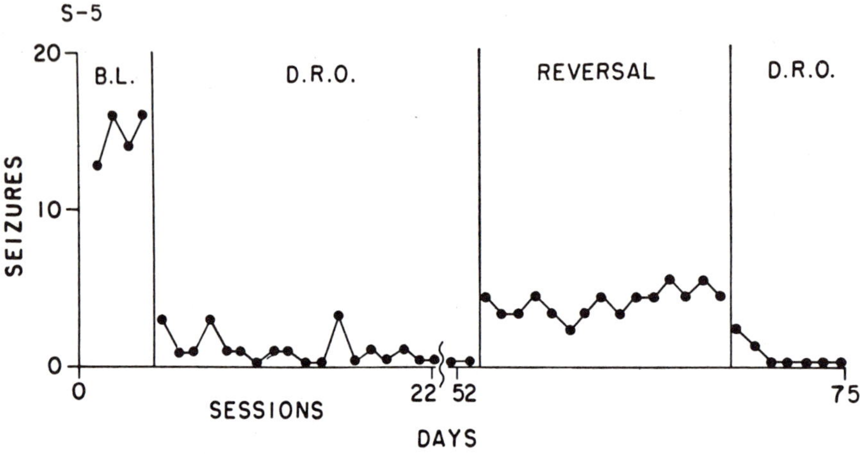

FIGURE 6-2.   Number of minor motor seizures per day. (From "Modification of Seizure Disorders: The Interruption of Behavioral Chains," by S. Zlutnick, W. J. Mayville, and S. Moffat. In *Journal of Applied Behavior Analysis*, 1975, 8, 1–12. Copyright 1975 by the Society for the Experimental Analysis of Behavior, Inc. Reprinted by permission.)

During baseline, seizures averaged about 16 per day. The treatment procedure involved differential reinforcement of other behavior (DRO); reinforcement was delivered contingent upon hands at her side or on her lap. Once implemented, seizures quickly dropped to zero. During the withdrawal phase (reversal), this contingency was removed and there were an average of six seizures per day. Finally, the DRO procedure was reinstated and seizures were rapidly eliminated. A nine-month follow-up revealed that seizures were still at a near-zero level.

The two treatment techniques used by Zlutnick and his colleagues (1975) provide impressive evidence that, with at least some mentally retarded children, seizures can be reduced through environmental manipulation. The follow-up data on these subjects indicate that the procedures can be effective in producing long-term change. While research on such low-rate behavior can be arduous and expensive, nonetheless, paraprofessionals could surely be trained to carry out the treatment program.

ASTHMA

Davis (1972) has estimated that approximately 8.6 million individuals in this country are afflicted with varying degrees of asthma. This condition is characterized by labored breathing, wheezing, and tightness of the chest. Among chronic illnesses, asthma is the leading cause of activity limitation in children (Creer & Christian, 1976). Unfortunately, there is no known cure for asthma (Creer, Renne, & Christian, 1976). Neisworth and Moore (1972) have demonstrated one way in which behavioral intervention may affect asthmatic behavior.

A 7-year-old asthmatic boy displayed repeated and prolonged wheezing and coughing at bedtime. As a result of his severe asthma attacks, he and his parents had to make frequent visits to hospital emergency rooms. Medical treatment did not seem to ameliorate the problem so it was suggested that the parents consult with someone skilled in behavioral techniques. A behavioral assessment of this problem indicated that the child was paid a considerable amount of attention during those attacks. It seemed plausible that asthmatic behavior might have been maintained or amplified by this attention. Likewise, behaviors incompatible with asthma attacks were not being reinforced. A ten-day baseline of bedtime asthmatic behavior collected by the parents showed that these attacks generally lasted from 60 to 80 minutes. Next, the parents were instructed to discontinue all attention to the child during these bedtime episodes. An additional strategy was also employed. Because the child liked to buy his lunch in the school cafeteria, he was told that if, on a given night, he coughed less than the night before, he did not have to take a bag lunch to school the next day. This proved to be a very effective procedure because it permitted reinforcement for even slight improvement and made success highly probable. Initially, asthmatic behavior was more prolonged (up to 95 minutes); but by the 23rd day of treatment and thereafter, it seldom lasted for more than five minutes. Follow-up data were collected for 11 months and the problem remained minimal.

A model treatment program for children with chronic bronchial asthma is that at the Children's Asthma Research Institute and Hospital (CARIH), a division of the National Asthma Center in Denver, Colorado. This residential treatment center has been described by Creer, Renne, and Christian (1976). Five common treatment and rehabilitation goals of CARIH are as follows:

1. Children are taught that asthma should not be the center of their lives.
2. Children are taught self-monitoring and self-control techniques so that they will be able to monitor and control their own behavior.
3. Behavioral excesses exhibited by the children are decreased or eliminated. This is particularly important for any behaviors which might interact with and intensify asthma.
4. Any behavioral deficits, particularly academic ones, are targets for remediation.
5. An all-out effort is made to place the children in the mainstream of family and community activities upon discharge.

Creer, Renne, and Christian (1976) list three common maladaptive behavior patterns related to a child's asthma. At CARIH, individualized programs are often designed for these behaviors. Different types of "panic" behavior are frequently observed as one behavior pattern. These include both a silent or frozen withdrawal at the onset of an asthma attack and a constant demand for attention from parents (concerning medication levels and other matters relating to asthma). At CARIH, children with a "panic" behavior pattern are seen individually and treated by systematic desensitization (see Chapter 5). Children are taught progressive relaxation and then exposed to a number of "panic"-related hierarchies.

A second behavior pattern sometimes exhibited by children is malingering (feigning illness). Although a relatively small number of asthmatic children have this problem, they do represent a larger percentage of hospital days at the National Asthma Center. These children are treated by a variant of timeout from positive reinforcement. Access to all potentially reinforcing stimuli in the hospital (for example, television, peer contact, schoolbooks) is prohibited. No needed medical attention or procedure is eliminated. This procedure has effectively reduced the number and duration of hospitalizations of children suspected of malingering. It teaches the children that the hospital is not a place to avoid unpleasant social relationships, chores, or school. Case studies of this procedure have been described by Creer (1970) and Creer, Weinberg, and Molk (1974).

A third behavior pattern that may create problems involves the proper use of emergency respiratory equipment. Asthma attacks can be prolonged or intensified if children cannot use this equipment in the midst of an attack. Shaping and positive reinforcement are used at CARIH to teach appropriate equipment use (Renne & Creer, 1976).

Perhaps the most important and crucial of the five goals of the CARIH program described by Creer, Renne, and Christian (1976) is to generalize the child's behavior change to his family and community. This generalization requires extremely close contact with parents so they can be taught to use behavioral techniques to manage their child's behavior. Follow-up contacts help to ensure the long-term maintenance of behavior change. CARIH is a model program for rehabilitation of children with chronic illnesses. Although the program is a residential one, the behavioral procedures used are exemplary ones that have implications for the treatment of a wide variety of chronic diseases.

As reported in the last chapter, various attempts at increasing respiratory function in asthmatic patients using a variety of behavior change techniques (for example, relaxation and biofeedback) have failed. A well-controlled study by Alexander, Cropp, and Chai (1979) has shown that, at least in severely asthmatic children, relaxation training cannot produce clinically significant improvements in pulmonary functioning. With asthmatic children, behavior change techniques may most wisely be used to eliminate maladaptive behavior and, perhaps, to counteract fear and anxiety precipitated by an asthma attack (as described in the previous chapter). Since asthma is a medical problem, its treatment should be left to physicians. Behavior change professionals should restrict their activities to correlated nonmedical behaviors (Miklich, 1979).

CEREBRAL PALSY

Cerebral palsy is a developmental disability characterized by defects in motor activity such as weakness, lack of coordination, and paralysis. It is a nonprogressive condition that has resulted from an injury to the brain during the development of the central nervous system. This injury may occur before, during, or after birth. Mental retardation, convulsions, and sensory or perceptual deficits may coexist with motor defects (Cruickshank, 1976; Denhoff & Robinault, 1960; Keats, 1965). The variety and combination of impairments may range from very mild to extremely severe. Martin (1976) has reviewed the literature on behavior modification with the cerebral palsied and noted that the amount of behavioral research with this population is extremely limited when compared with other developmentally disabled groups. Additionally, much of the research is of the case-study type, with little consideration for proper experimental control procedures, generalization data, or follow-up data. The unique problems of this group of handicapped people should prove a challenge for behavior change professionals.

Several recent research studies are worth noting because of their advancement of research design and methodological rigor. Children with spastic type cerebral palsy are prone to sit in many undesirable positions, especially reverse tailor sitting—that is, sitting with one's hips and knees flexed with hips internally rotated and with one's buttocks between one's feet. Bragg, Houser, and Schumaker (1975) noted that although this position provides a wide base of support and free use of both hands, it is destructive to medial knee structures and may result in structural deformities. Additionally, the child who only reverse tailor sits is being deprived of the experience of balance adjustments and sensorimotor feedback afforded by other sitting positions. Bragg and her colleagues (1975) used response priming and contingent reinforcement to alter this sitting pattern in six children with lower limb spasticity (mean age: 3.7 years). As a part of the experimental design, the children were divided into two groups. In sessions conducted in the home, one group received both primes to assume a non-reverse tailor-sitting pattern plus contingent reinforcement (verbal praise plus food), while the second group of three children were not primed, but only reinforced via the same contingency. Figures 6-3 and 6-4 depict the results of this experiment with a multiple baseline design across subjects. Data are presented from both the home and classroom (generalization). Initial increases in non-reverse tailor sitting were greatest for primed children, but over time differences between primed and nonprimed children decreased. Four of the six children demonstrated increased non-reverse tailor sitting in the generalization setting (classroom). Although there are a number of difficulties with this study (such as the relatively small number of subjects for a group comparison and the lack of follow-up data), it is noteworthy for its excellent use of a multiple baseline design and the attempt to assess generalization.

In 30-minute sessions, positive reinforcement was used by Grove and Dalke (1976) to teach three cerebral palsied children to wheel their wheelchairs. Affixed to the children's wheelchairs were counters that precisely recorded the number of wheel revolutions. After an initial baseline recording, the effect of merely instructing the children to look at their counters was assessed. Thereafter, a number of experimental manipulations were introduced, including verbal praise, verbal praise and food, various schedules of reinforcement, and a reversal or withdrawal of reinforcement contingencies. Verbal instructions were found to be ineffective. In order to get the children to look at their counters, reinforcers were necessary. Unfortunately, Grove and Dalke were unable to completely fade out the reinforcer.

This is an issue that many rehabilitation workers find objectionable and further

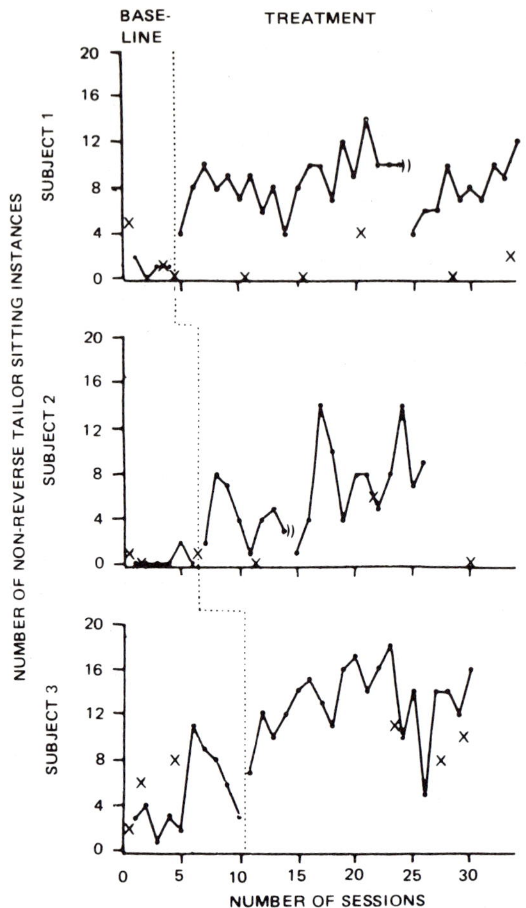

FIGURE 6-3.   Number of non-reverse tailor sitting instances for non-primed group. Dots represent home data, while x's are classroom data. (From "Behavior Modification: Effects on Reverse Tailor Sitting in Children with Cerebral Palsy," by J. H. Bragg, C. Houser, and J. Schumaker. In *Physical Therapy*, 1975, *55*, 860–868. Reprinted with the permission of the American Physical Therapy Association.)

research should demonstrate that there is an effective technology for achieving generalization.

Reducing muscle tone or hypertonia is a frequent goal in the rehabilitation of the cerebral palsied. With more normal muscle tone, success at achieving normal motor patterns is more likely. Methods for promoting more normal muscle tone have included surgery, medication, and therapies involving the use of relaxation. Recently, William Finley and his associates (Finley, Niman, Standley, & Ender, 1976; Finley, Niman, Standley, & Wansley, 1977) have investigated the use of EMG-biofeedback training (electrodes were attached to the forehead) on athetoid and

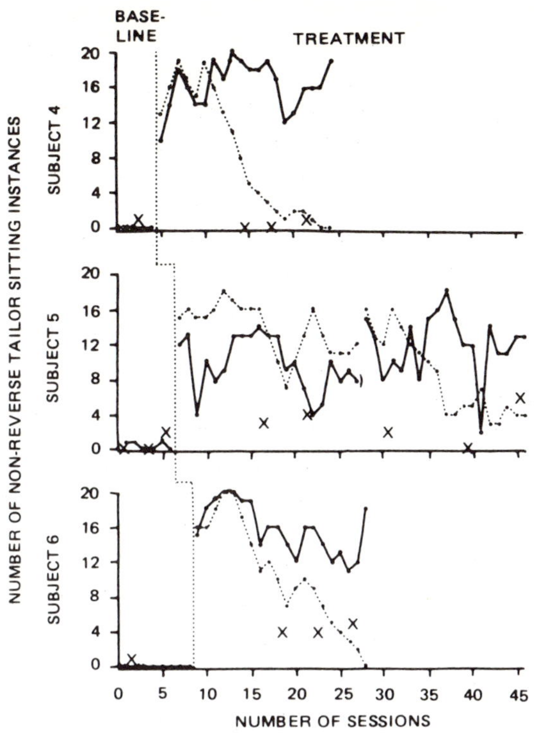

FIGURE 6-4. Number of non-reverse tailor sitting instances for primed group. Dots represent home data, while x's are classroom data. (From "Behavior Modification: Effects on Reverse Tailor Sitting in Children with Cerebral Palsy," by J. H. Bragg, C. Houser, and J. Schumaker. In *Physical Therapy*, 1975, *55*, 860–868. Reprinted with the permission of the American Physical Therapy Association.)

spastic cerebral palsied patients. By using biofeedback, general relaxation might be achieved which would enable rehabilitation therapists to start work on functional, purposeful movement. In the first study (Finley et al., 1976), six athetoid patients, ages 14 to 31, were given twice-weekly EMG-biofeedback sessions for six weeks, with up to 50 minutes' access per session. At the end of the twelve sessions, the six patients averaged slightly over a 50% reduction in mean EMG activity. Measures of speech and motor behavior were also taken pre- and post-biofeedback training. Four patients classified as mildly or moderately impaired improved significantly on speech measures, while two patients classified as severely impaired did not. On motor function tests, all six patients made gains significantly above the chance level.

In a second study (Finley et al., 1977), four spastic cerebral palsied children, ages 6 to 10, participated in a reversal design experiment. During baseline conditions, various speech and motor behaviors were evaluated. Then the children had twice-weekly EMG-biofeedback sessions for six weeks. During these sessions, the children could earn prizes for reducing their frontal EMG activity. A speech and motor reevaluation followed this phase. Next came six weeks of no training with another evaluation at the end. The experiment ended after a four-week period of EMG-biofeedback training was reinstituted. Final speech and motor evaluations were conducted. Frontal EMG activity was significantly reduced by the end of the two phases consisting of EMG-biofeedback and contingent reinforcement. Similarly, changes in speech and motor behavior over baseline and reversal levels were noted. These experiments by Finley and his associates are beginning steps in studying applications of biofeedback to the rehabilitation of the cerebral palsied. Notable is the combination of traditional biofeedback with *more overt* positive reinforcers in the second study (Finley et al., 1977) and the focus on *functional behavior change* in both studies. This is a welcome departure from early biofeedback studies in which other health care problems were studied.

As noted earlier, many other applications of behavioral procedures to the rehabilitation of the cerebral palsied have been published. Most are case studies, and most suffer from methodological deficiencies. Much work needs to be done to determine procedures for promoting generalization and long-term effectiveness. Problems that should lend themselves to intervention that employs behavior change techniques include head control, upper and lower extremity functioning, and drooling. We anticipate significant advances in these areas in the future. An appropriate note of caution has recently been made by Ilmer and Drews (1980). Voluntary motor behavior is very much a function of the development of reflexes in this handicapped population. Before attempting to change the motor behavior of a cerebral palsied individual, a thorough behavioral assessment by health care professionals (for example, physicians, physical therapists, occupational therapists, or speech pathologists) is necessary.

COMPLIANCE WITH MEDICAL PROCEDURES

In the last chapter, we discussed the use of behavior change techniques to increase adult patients' compliance with medical and therapeutic regimens. Children also pose a significant problem for health care workers. Behavior change techniques have been used with noncompliant children in both hospital and home settings.

A frequent problem in pediatric medical practice is refusal to take oral medications. Wright, Woodcock, and Scott (1969) have reported using behavioral techniques on two young children with this problem. The first girl was 24 months old and was suffering from a renal disease. She would either spit out her medication or refuse to open her mouth. When she was given medication by nasogastric tube (tube through the nose), she would vomit the medication as soon as it reached her stomach. The second child was an 18-month-old girl with leukemia. She also refused oral medications and regurgitated them when they were administered by nasogastric tube. The first child was offered oral medication following a period of both social isolation and food deprivation. If the child accepted the medication, reinforcement in the form of attention, praise, hugging, or a piece of candy was delivered. This procedure was extremely successful with the girl. During the course of five weeks, the responsibility for administering the medication was transferred from psychologists to the nurses and dieticians and eventually to the girl's mother. Cooperation from all concerned is an obvious necessity in carrying out a program such as this.

The above procedure proved ineffective with the second girl. She did not take a single pill. An alternative shaping technique was then tried. She was fed only once a day at 6:00 P.M. The psychologists saw her five times a day between 8:00 A.M. and 5:00 P.M. Table 6-1 lists the activities the psychologist carried out with the child each day. Candy and social reinforcement were administered contingent upon the activities. Wright and his associates view these activities as successive approximations of taking a pill.

An attempt was made to mix medicine with the candy during the third session of the fifth day. This proved successful and, several days later, the mother was successfully trained to administer the medication. Although this study was uncontrolled and had no follow-up, it is a model for possible applications of behavior modification to a serious problem frequently confronting the pediatrician. More research on refusal to accept oral medications is needed, for the development of a successful treatment package has the potential of making a significant impact on the health care of children.

Shorkey and Taylor (1973) reported the case of a 17-month-old girl who suffered from second- and third-degree burns over one third of her body. Understandably, she became extremely agitated when nurses approached her for treatment of the burns. Attempts at spraying silver nitrate over her bandages led to crying

TABLE 6-1. Conditioning Successive Approximations of Pill-Taking Behavior

Day	Session Number (10–20 Trials Per Session)	Reinforced Behavior
1	1–5	No success in eliciting acceptance of pill.
2	1, 2	Touch cheek with forefinger.
	3, 4	Touch lip with forefinger.
	5	Touch cheek with forefinger; pill between thumb and middle finger.
3	1	Same as last session.
	2, 3	Touch lip with forefinger; pill between thumb and middle finger.
	4	Touch cheek with pill approximately 1 in. from corner of mouth.
	5	Touch cheek with pill approximately ½ in. from corner of mouth.
4	1	Touch corner of mouth with pill.
	2	Touch lips in center of mouth with pill.
	3, 4	Touch teeth with pill.
	5	Place pill behind teeth; touch tongue with pill.
5	1	Same as last session.
	2–5	Stick tongue out; touch tongue with pill.

and moving her limbs in a distressed manner. The child's behavior gradually became worse, and she eventually refused food and became extremely upset whenever a staff member attempted to approach her. Her general physical condition worsened and skin grafts were discontinued. Shorkey and Taylor speculated that the staff members had become conditioned aversive stimuli as a result of their repeated association with painful treatment. The mere presence of a staff member, therefore, would evoke the undesirable behaviors. A procedure was instituted to teach the child to discriminate between aversive conditions (medical treatment) and non-aversive or social interactions. During treatment times, nurses were instructed to continue wearing green isolation gowns. They were also told not to talk to the child or to handle her any more than necessary. They should not play with her toys or spend any unnecessary time in the room. The regular white room lights were to be left on during these treatment times. On the other hand, during social situations staff members were to wear red sterilized bags with armholes. Upon entering the child's room to play, red flood lights, which had been specially installed, were illuminated. Additionally, during social interaction times, the staff would massage the child's neck and top of her shoulders (which had not been burned) in an attempt to relax her. Similar massages were programmed to precede the child's feeding. On the second day of this discrimination training procedure, changes were seen in the child's behavior. Crying gradually decreased during the social interaction periods. After two weeks, there was no problem at these times. Agitation was limited to the brief treatment periods every two hours. This discrimination procedure continued for 1½ months, after which time the child was in reasonably good physical condition and was eating satisfactorily. The procedure was successfully eliminated for the last two weeks before discharge from the hospital. A two-year follow-up indicated no problems related to physical recovery.

Lowe and Lutzker (1979) have used a multiple baseline design to examine methods for increasing compliance with medical regimen by a 9-year-old female diabetic. She had been hospitalized on numerous occasions because of diabetic acidosis (a toxic condition resulting from the body's inability to utilize sugar). Three health care responsibilities were selected as target behaviors. The first of these was urine testing to determine the concentration of glucose in the urine and to test for acetone (a by-product of the metabolism of fat). This monitoring would indicate the need for dietary alteration and/or insulin administration. Secondly, the girl was to follow a special restricted diet. Adherence to this regimen would promote a more normal blood-sugar level and sugar-free urine. Finally, special care of the foot skin is extremely important because diabetics suffer from decreased circulation in their extremities. Any cuts or bruises are very slow in healing.

To meet the first responsibility, the child was required to collect and test four urine samples each day before each meal and at bedtime. The second responsibility could be met by eating only permitted foods and eating them at prescribed times. Foot care responsibilities were to be met by putting on clean, colorfast socks each day, and each evening washing her feet with mild soap, patting them dry, and inspecting them for cuts and bruises. Baseline data were taken on all of these three responsibilities. These may be seen in Figure 6-5. Initially, a memo condition was introduced serially to each one of the three target responsibilities. The memo

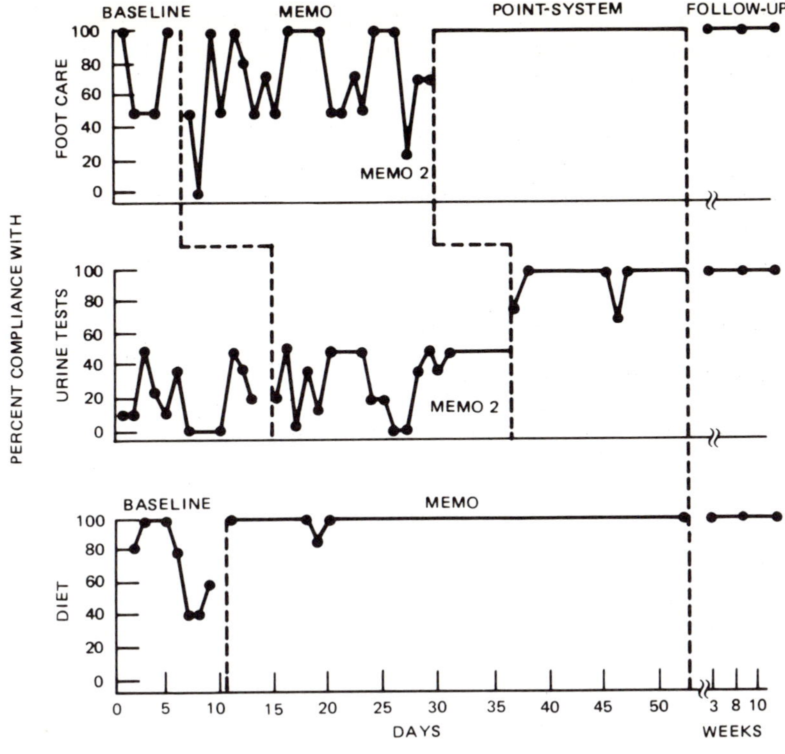

FIGURE 6-5.   Percentage compliance with foot care, urine testing, and diet. (From "Increasing Compliance to a Medical Regimen with a Juvenile Diabetic," by K. Lowe and J. R. Lutzker. In *Behavior Therapy*, 1979, *10*, 57–64. Reprinted by permission of Academic Press and the authors.)

consisted of written instructions (from the experimenters) for completion of one of the three responsibilities. This was similar to the instructions that a physician might give to a patient in a pamphlet. Figure 6-5 shows that the memo was extremely effective in promoting dietary responsibility but had little effect on the other two target responsibilities. Next, a point system was introduced in a staggered manner, first to foot care and then to urine testing. Points were awarded for compliance with these responsibilities. These could be exchanged for tangible reinforcers such as movies, games, and dietary sodas. When this contingency was introduced, increases in compliance were seen immediately. After one month of this program, the frequency of reinforcement was decreased and the experimenters gradually faded out their involvement. A ten-week follow-up indicated that compliance to all three medical responsibilities had been maintained.

The problems associated with compliance with medical regimens are just beginning to draw the attention of behavior change researchers. Recently, Magrab and Papadopoulou (1977) have used a token reinforcement program to increase adherence to dietary restrictions by children on hemodialysis. Undoubtedly, there will soon be applications to a variety of other chronic diseases of childhood.

FEAR OF MEDICAL PROCEDURES

A recent survey (Peterson & Ridley-Johnson, 1980) revealed that 31% of pediatric hospitals had some formal prehospital preparation for children undergoing surgery. Siegel (1976) has noted that the consensus in the literature on hospitalized children is that psychological preparation for surgical or other medical procedures is extremely important. His review of intervention-type research in this area concluded that the results of the studies, unfortunately, are equivocal, have questionable reliability, and suffer from methodological difficulties. The application of behavior change techniques to this problem is just beginning and appears to have much promise.

Barbara Melamed and her associates have conducted a series of studies which have examined the use of filmed modeling. In the first experiment, Melamed and Siegel (1975) had children with impending surgery (for hernias, tonsillectomies, urinary-genital tract difficulties) watch a film called "Ethan Has An Operation." This movie showed 7-year-old Ethan hospitalized for a hernia operation. The movie depicted 15 scenes of various events children most commonly encounter when hospitalized for elective surgery. These included orientation to the hospital and staff, having a blood test, exposure to standard hospital equipment, separation from mother, and operating and recovery room scenes. The child's behavior follows a coping model (Meichenbaum, 1971) whereby he first exhibits some apprehension and anxiety, but then is able to overcome this and finish each event in a successful and nonanxious manner. Throughout the film, explanations of procedures are provided by hospital staff, and the child describes his feelings and concerns. A group of control children saw a film unrelated to their hospitalization. Children who saw the film concerning hospitalization were significantly less fearful on observational, self-report, and physiological measures both pre- and postoperatively than were control group children. Additionally, parents of control group children reported a significant post-hospital increase in frequency of behavior problems, while children who saw the hospitalization film did not demonstrate this increase.

Melamed, Meyer, Gee, and Soule (1976) have attempted to isolate some of the crucial variables in the filmed modeling procedure. This experiment replicated the previous study (Melamed & Siegel, 1975) without the benefit of being combined with an in-hospital preoperative teaching procedure. In addition, the investigators discovered that older children can benefit from seeing the film as much as one week in advance of surgery, while younger children needed a more immediate viewing. It was also determined that the effectiveness of the film was enhanced by similarities in age, sex, and race between one child observer and the child in the film. Finally, Melamed (1976) has reported that children whose parents used modeling, reinforcement, and assurance when their children faced feared situations showed less presurgery anxiety than did children whose families dealt with such reluctance by using punishment.

Cataldo, Bessman, Parker, Pearson, and Rogers (1979) have conducted an extremely interesting study that bears on children's fears of medical procedures and the aversiveness of health care settings. In taking behavioral observation data on children and staff in a pediatric intensive care unit, they found the children to be quite unresponsive to their environment—possibly because the hospital staff provided medical procedures and likely became discriminative for aversive stimuli. To counteract this unresponsive behavior, staff began to engage in play activities with alert children. Consequently, the children became more alert and responsive to their environment. Inappropriate behavior decreased. Rather dramatic changes in behavior occurred as the result of a relatively simple change in staff behavior. We think that future research of this type is warranted in hospital settings; however, we would also like to see some attempt to link behavioral changes to changes in medical status.

DENTISTRY

Applications of behavior modification to dentistry have consisted mainly of attempts to change dental habits and to overcome patient fears. Colquhoun (1973) has argued strongly that periodontists, whose major concerns are changes in patients' diets and dental hygiene, should become familiar with behavior modification techniques. Rosenberg (1974) has outlined behavior methods that might be used in the office practice of pediatric dentistry. They include modeling and positive reinforcement. Attention should be paid to teaching children appropriate behavior while in the dental chair—for example, sitting quietly, keeping hands in lap, keeping mouth wide open. Make the praise descriptive (for example, "Sue, you were really good today because you sat so still. You kept your hands on your lap the whole time. I'm proud of how well you are doing when you come here."). Rosenberg further cautions that it is very important to end children's visits on a positive note. It is tempting to dismiss a screaming, crying child early, but this may only function to reinforce this undesirable behavior.

Martens, Frazier, Hirt, Meskin, and Proshek (1973) conducted a large project that attempted to alter the dental hygiene of second grade school children. An experimental program consisted of three components: (1) behavior modification using tokens exchangeable for prizes; (2) volunteer participation in individual or group projects to learn about dental health; and (3) individual interaction with a dental hygienist (as opposed to the usual group dental health instruction). A control group of children received none of these educational components but received periodic examinations by a dentist. After a baseline screening examination by a dentist, the behavior modification program was explained to the children in the experimental group. They were told that they could earn color-coded plastic chips of different values for merely brushing their teeth and doing a good job. The chips could be exchanged for a variety of prizes such as books, games, puzzles, and small cars. The necessary items for proper dental care (including chewable erythrosin dye tablets for detecting plaque) and a lighted magnifying mirror were placed in the classroom for use at any time. Explicit instructions for brushing teeth were not given.

Children were told that the dental hygienist would make unannounced visits to their classroom to see how well and how consistently they were brushing. Each time the dental hygienist visited, the children's teeth were stained with a dye tablet. If no plaque was observed, a child was given a token worth ten points; if one or two areas of plaque were found, a token worth five points was awarded; a token worth only one point was given if more than two areas of plaque were observed. On Friday afternoons, children were permitted to exchange their tokens for prizes.

Children were given instructions on how to get their teeth cleaner only if they requested it. After two months, a second component, the provision of dental health knowledge, was added. Individual and group projects pertaining to different aspects of dental health were organized according to each child's interest and desire to participate. All completed projects were shared with each class; tokens were awarded contingent upon difficulty of the project and performance.

Results of this total program were highly encouraging. Children in the experimental group showed a 30% reduction in plaque over the school year. A highly significant statistical difference was found between the experimental and control group children. The most exciting finding was that the experimental group of children maintained their level of plaque reduction over the summer *in the absence of any reinforcement program*. Iwata and Becksfort (in press) reported that an oral hygiene education program, which included a reduction in dental fees contingent upon a reduction in dental plaque, produced lower plaque levels than the oral hygiene education program alone. While plaque reduction is a significant goal, ultimately the long-term goal is a reduction or alteration in future dental disease. This outcome remains to be evaluated.

White, Akers, Green, and Yates (1974) have noted that the disruptive behavior of children (which serves to prolong or prevent treatment) is one of the biggest problems of pediatric dentistry today. They had such children view through a one-way mirror a live model undergoing dental treatment. Children were rewarded across six sessions for attending to the treatment. Sessions were five minutes long and were completed during three weeks. During these times, the children observed another child receiving: (1) toothbrushing instructions, (2) an oral examination, (3) prophylaxis, (4) fluoride treatment, (5) an injection, and (6) a restoration procedure. Children who observed these modeling procedures demonstrated significantly more adaptive behavior during dental treatment than did a control group of children.

Melamed and her associates (Melamed, Hawes, Heiby, & Glick, 1975; Melamed, Weinstein, Hawes, & Katin-Borland, 1975) made use of a filmed modeling procedure to reduce children's anxiety and disruptive behavior during the filling of cavities. Children viewed a 13-minute videotape of a child coping with his anxieties during a visit for dental restorative procedures. Melamed (1976) more recently has investigated the filmed modeling treatment in some detail. It appears that a longer modeling film depicting an entire dental restorative procedure is superior to a shorter film or films without children actually receiving the restorative procedures. In contrast to this filmed modeling treatment, Stokes and Kennedy (1980) used a procedure that consisted of *live* observation of another child being treated by a dentist. This process, combined with positive reinforcement, successfully reduced uncooperative behavior during dental treatment. Whether or not such behavior change procedures have had any influence on the day-to-day practice of dentistry is unknown. There has been an increase in the participation of psychologists in the teaching of dental students, but it is doubtful that behavior change techniques have had any appreciable effect on dental practice. We believe that behavior change techniques may prove most valuable in the areas of compliance with suggested dental hygiene procedure and the wearing of orthodontic appliances. A recent study provides an example of this promise.

Claerhout and Lutzker (1977) used a multiple baseline research design to examine the effect of a token economy on a child's flossing and toothbrushing. Figure 6-6 shows that initially toothbrushing and flossing increased when the token economy was introduced. Toothbrushing was exhibited at over 90% compliance while flossing occurred 80% of the time. The program was eventually put in the hands of the child's parents, with only occasional contact from the experimenters by phone in order to collect follow-up data.

If behavior change procedures are to be widely used in dental settings, researchers will have to demonstrate the cost-effectiveness of such procedures. Although a number of experimenters have demonstrated changes in maladaptive and phobic behaviors and in dental hygiene, these changes need to be more clearly related to both time or effort involved and cost as compared to the more typical (or control) procedures generally used. This relationship must be shown not only to convince dental personnel but also to convince administrators and consumers. In this day of accountability and cost-benefit analysis, change is most rapidly

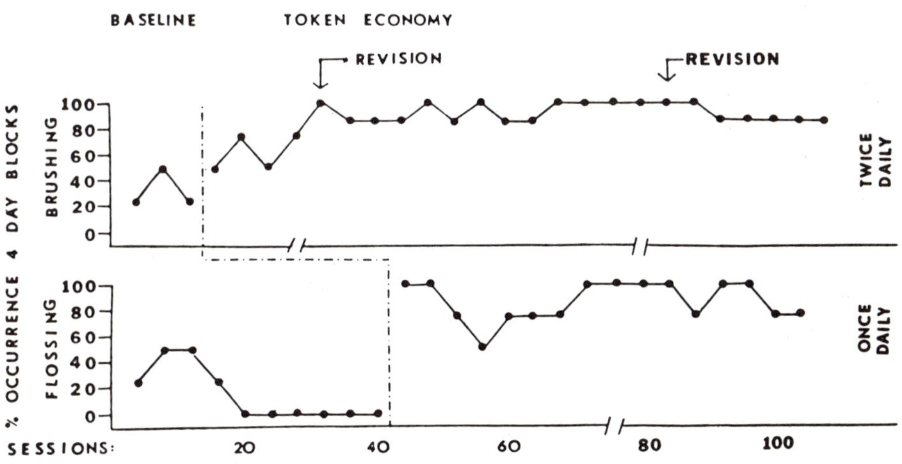

FIGURE 6-6.   Toothbrushing and flossing compliance. (From "Increasing Compliance to a Dental Regimen with a Normal Child," by S. Claerhout and J. R. Lutzker. Paper presented at the American Psychological Association meeting, San Francisco, 1977. Reprinted by permission.)

brought about through solid research programs that can demonstrate that big changes in health-related behavior and savings in health dollars result from relatively low-cost changes in health delivery systems.

CONCLUSIONS

In this chapter, we have seen behavior change procedures applied to a wide variety of children's health care problems. In many ways, the research is just beginning; however, the future is very promising and behavior change applications may have a significant impact on the health of children. Future research will need to pay more attention to the required rigorous methodology of behavior analysis and to long-term follow-up. Undoubtedly, strategies for *maintaining* changes in health-related behavior will have to be explored. Additionally, the cost-effectiveness of behavior change procedures needs to be more carefully documented. Finally, we hope to see research efforts aimed at the prevention of disease, for this area has received little attention from behavior change professionals. Obviously the way to avoid the diseases of lifestyle (for example, heart disease) is to teach children good health habits that will reduce potential risk factors (for example, obesity, stress). In this vein, Boyer (1974) has argued that coronary heart disease is a pediatric problem. We would agree and anticipate future research efforts toward reducing disease in adults via primary prevention during childhood. A variety of public and private "wellness" and "health enhancement" centers have been developed for adults throughout the country (see, for example, Gorney & West, 1980). We hope that similar preventive efforts will be directed toward children, perhaps through the school systems.

REFERENCES

Alexander, A. B., Cropp, G. J. A., & Chai, H. Effects of relaxation training on pulmonary mechanisms in children with asthma. *Journal of Applied Behavior Analysis,* 1979, *12,* 27–35.

Barrett, B. H. Behavior modification in the home: Parents adapt laboratory developed tactics to bowel-train a 5½-year-old. *Psychotherapy: Therapy, Research and Practice,* 1969, *6,* 172–176.

Becker, J. V., Turner, S. M., & Sajwaj, T. E. Multiple behavioral effects of the use of lemon juice with a ruminating toddler-age child. *Behavior Modification,* 1978, *2,* 267–278.

Blechman, E. A. Short- and long-term results of positive home-based treatment of childhood chronic constipation and encopresis. *Child Behavior Therapy,* 1979, *1,* 237–247.

Boyer, J. L. Coronary heart disease as a pediatric problem: Prevention through behavior modification. *American Journal of Cardiology,* 1974, *33,* 784–786.

Bragg, J. H., Houser, C., & Schumaker, J. Behavior modification: Effects on reverse tailor sitting in children with cerebral palsy. *Physical Therapy,* 1975, *55,* 860–868.

Cataldo, M. F., Bessman, C. A., Parker, L. H., Pearson, J. E. R., & Rogers, M. C. Behavioral assessment for pediatric intensive care units. *Journal of Applied Behavior Analysis,* 1979, *12,* 83–97.

Christophersen, E. R., & Rainey, S. Management of encopresis through an outpatient pediatric clinic. *Journal of Pediatric Psychology,* 1976, *1,* 38–41.

Claerhout, S., & Lutzker, J. R. *Increasing compliance to a dental regimen with a normal child.* Paper presented at the American Psychological Association meeting, San Francisco, 1977.

Colquhoun, J. A. Behavior modification in dentistry. *Bulletin of New Zealand Society of Periodontics,* 1973, *35,* 2–8.

Creer, T. L. The use of time-out from positive reinforcement procedure with asthmatic children. *Journal of Psychosomatic Research,* 1970, *14,* 117–120.

Creer, T. L., & Christian, W. P. *Chronically ill and handicapped children.* Champaign, Ill.: Research Press, 1976.

Creer, T. L., Renne, C. M., & Christian, W. P. Behavioral contributions to rehabilitation and childhood asthma. *Rehabilitation Literature,* 1976, *37,* 226–232.

Creer, T. L., Weinberg, E., & Molk, L. Managing a hospital behavior problem: Malingering. *Journal of Behavior Therapy and Experimental Psychiatry,* 1974, *5,* 259–262.

Cruickshank, W. M. The problem and its scope. In W. M. Cruickshank (Ed.), *Cerebral palsy: A developmental disability.* Syracuse: Syracuse University Press, 1976.

Cunningham, C. E., & Linscheid, T. R. Elimination of chronic infant ruminating by electric shock. *Behavior Therapy,* 1976, *7,* 231–234.

Davis, D. J. NIAID initiatives in allergy research. *Journal of Allergy and Clinical Immunology,* 1972, *49,* 323–328.

Denhoff, E., & Robinault, I. P. *Cerebral palsy and related disorders.* New York: McGraw-Hill, 1960.

Duff, R. S., Rowe, D. S., & Anderson, F. P. Patient care and student learning in a pediatric clinic. *Pediatrics,* 1972, *50,* 839–846.

Epstein, L. H., & McCoy, J. F. Bladder and bowel control in Hirschsprung's disease. *Journal of Behavior Therapy and Experimental Psychiatry,* 1977, *8,* 97–99.

Ferinden, W., & Handel, D. V. Elimination of soiling behavior in an elementary school child through the application of aversive techniques. *Journal of School Psychology,* 1970, *8,* 267–269.

Finley, W. W., Niman, C., Standley, J., & Ender, P. Frontal EMG: Biofeedback training of athetoid cerebral palsy patients. *Biofeedback and Self-Regulation,* 1976, *1,* 169–182.

Finley, W. W., Niman, C. A., Standley, J., & Wansley, R. A. Electrophysiologic behavior modification of frontal EMG in cerebral-palsied children. *Biofeedback and Self-Regulation,* 1977, *2,* 59–79.

Foxx, R. M., & Azrin, N. H. Dry pants: A rapid method of toilet training children. *Behaviour Research and Therapy,* 1973, *11,* 435–442.

Gardner, J. Behavior therapy treatment approach to a psychogenic seizure case. *Journal of Counseling Psychology,* 1967, *31,* 209–212.

Gorney, R., & West, L. J. Health enhancement through lifestyle change. *Behavioral Medicine Update,* 1980, *2*(1), 7–8.

Greenwood, R. D. Psychiatry in pediatrics: Emotional guidance in pediatric practice. *Journal of the Kansas Medical Society,* 1973, *74,* 220–223.

Grove, D. N., & Dalke, B. A. Contingent feedback for training children to propel their wheelchairs. *Physical Therapy,* 1976, *56,* 815–820.

Ilmer, S., & Drews, J. Differential analyses of selected prompts and neurological variables in motor assessment of moderately mentally retarded children. *American Journal of Mental Deficiency,* 1980, *84,* 509–517.

Iwata, B. A., & Becksfort, C. M. Behavioral research in preventive dentistry: Compliance with personal hygiene regimens via educational and contingency management techniques. *Journal of Applied Behavior Analysis,* in press.

Keats, S. *Cerebral palsy.* Springfield, Ill.: Thomas, 1965.

Kohlenberg, R. J. Operant conditioning of human anal sphincter pressure. *Journal of Applied Behavior Analysis,* 1973, *6,* 201–208.

Lal, H., & Lindsley, O. Therapy of chronic constipation in the young child by rearranging social contingencies. *Behaviour Research and Therapy,* 1968, *6,* 484–485.

Lang, P. J., & Melamed, B. G. Avoidance conditioning therapy of an infant with chronic ruminative vomiting. *Journal of Abnormal Psychology,* 1969, *74,* 139–142.

Lowe, K., & Lutzker, J. R. Increasing compliance to a medical regimen with a juvenile diabetic. *Behavior Therapy,* 1979, *10,* 57–64.

Magrab, P. R., & Papadopoulou, Z. The effect of a token economy on dietary compliance for children on hemodialysis. *Journal of Applied Behavior Analysis,* 1977, *10,* 573–578.

Martens, L. V., Frazier, P. J., Hirt, K. J., Meskin, L. H., & Proshek, J. Developing brushing performance in second graders through behavior modification. *Health Sciences Report,* 1973, *88,* 818–823.

Martin, J. A. Behavior modification and cerebral palsy. *Journal of Pediatric Psychology,* 1976, *1,* 48–50.

Meichenbaum, D. Examination of model characteristics in reducing avoidance behavior. *Journal of Personality and Social Psychology,* 1971, *17,* 298–307.

Melamed, B. G. *Peer modeled fear behaviors during local anesthesia and its influence on children's dental treatment behavior.* Paper presented at Association for the Advancement of Behavior Therapy meeting, New York, December 1976.

Melamed, B. G., Hawes, R. R., Heiby, E., & Glick, J. The use of filmed modeling to reduce uncooperative behavior of children during dental treatment. *Journal of Dental Research,* 1975, *54,* 797–801.

Melamed, B. G., Meyer, R., Gee, C., & Soule, L. The influence of time and type of preparation on children's adjustment to hospitalization. *Journal of Pediatric Psychology,* 1976, *1,* 31–37.

Melamed, B. G., & Siegel, L. J. Reduction of anxiety in children facing hospitalization and surgery by use of filmed modeling. *Journal of Consulting and Clinical Psychology,* 1975, *43,* 511–521.

Melamed, B. G., Weinstein, D., Hawes, R., & Katin-Borland, M. Reduction of fear-related dental management problems with use of filmed modeling. *Journal of American Dental Association,* 1975, *90,* 822–826.

Miklich, D. R. Health psychology practice with asthmatics. *Professional Psychology,* 1979, *10,* 580–588.

Neisworth, J. T., & Moore, F. Operant treatment of asthmatic responding with the parent as therapist. *Behavior Therapy,* 1972, *3,* 95–99.

Nilsson, D. Treatment of encopresis: A token economy. *Journal of Pediatric Psychology,* 1976, *4,* 42–46.

Nisley, D. D. Medical overview of the management of encopresis. *Journal of Pediatric Psychology,* 1976, *4,* 33–34.

Pedrini, B. C., & Pedrini, D. T. Reinforcement procedures in the control of encopresis: A case study. *Psychological Reports,* 1971, *28,* 937–938.

Perzan, R. S., Boulanger, F., & Fischer, D. G. Complex factors in inhibition of defecation: Review and case study. *Journal of Behavior Therapy and Experimental Psychiatry,* 1972, *3,* 129–133.

Peterson, L., & Ridley-Johnson, R. Pediatric hospital response to survey on prehospital preparation for children. *Journal of Pediatric Psychology,* 1980, *5,* 1–7.

Renne, C. M., & Creer, T. L. Training children with asthma to use inhalation therapy equipment. *Journal of Applied Behavior Analysis,* 1976, *9,* 1–11.

Richmond, J. B., Eddy, E., & Green, M. Rumination: A psychosomatic syndrome of infancy. *Pediatrics,* 1958, *22,* 49–54.

Richmond, J. B. The needs of children. In J. H. Knowles (Ed.), *Doing better and feeling worse: Health in the United States.* New York: Norton, 1977.

Rosenberg, H. M. Behavior modification for the child dental patient. *Journal of Dentistry for Children,* 1974, *41,* 31–34.

Ruprecht, M. J., Hanson, R. H., & Pocrnich, M. A. Some suggested precautions when using lemon juice (citric acid) in behavior modification programs. Unpublished paper, 1979.

Sajwaj, T., Libet, J., & Agras, S. Lemon juice therapy: The control of life-threatening rumination in a 6-month-old infant. *Journal of Applied Behavior Analysis*, 1974, *7*, 557–566.

Shorkey, C. T., & Taylor, J. E. Management of maladaptive behavior of a severely burned child. *Child Welfare*, 1973, *52*, 543–547.

Siegel, L. J. Preparation of children for hospitalization. *Journal of Pediatric Psychology*, 1976, *1*, 26–30.

Stokes, T. F., & Kennedy, S. H. Reducing uncooperative behavior during dental treatment through modeling and reinforcement. *Journal of Applied Behavior Analysis*, 1980, *13*, 41–49.

Toister, R. P., Condron, C. J., Worley, L., & Arthur, D. Faradic therapy of chronic vomiting in infancy: A case study. *Journal of Behavior Therapy and Experimental Psychiatry*, 1975, *6*, 55–59.

Tomlinson, J. R. The treatment of bowel retention by operant procedures: A case study. *Journal of Behavior Therapy and Experimental Psychiatry*, 1970, *1*, 83–85.

White, W. C., Akers, J., Green, J., & Yates, D. Use of imitation in the treatment of dental phobia in early childhood: A preliminary report. *Journal of Dentistry for Children*, 1974, *41*, 106–110.

Wright, L. Outcome of a standardized program for treating psychogenic encopresis. *Professional Psychology*, 1975, *6*, 453–456.

Wright, L. Psychology as a health profession. *The Clinical Psychologist*, 1976, *29*, 16–19.

Wright, L., Schaefer, A. B., & Solomons, G. *Encyclopedia of pediatric psychology*. Baltimore: University Park Press, 1979.

Wright, L., & Walker, C. E. Behavioral treatment of encopresis. *Journal of Pediatric Psychology*, 1976, *4*, 35–37.

Wright, L., Woodcock, J. M., & Scott, R. Conditioning children when refusal of oral medication is life-threatening. *Pediatrics*, 1969, *44*, 969–972.

Zlutnick, S., Mayville, W. J., & Moffat, S. Modification of seizure disorders: The interruption of behavioral chains. *Journal of Applied Behavior Analysis*, 1975, *8*, 1–12.

CHAPTER 7

Children

Ⓜ OST books dealing with behavior modification emphasize the treatment of deviant behavior in children. While the treatment of problem child behavior is, of course, important and interesting, it represents only a fraction of the information we have learned about children in the last few years. Contemporary child development books examine a variety of developmental theories that mostly cite experimental research of a laboratory nature. These books either do not cover problem behavior, or cover it casually at best, and they offer little information that covers child development issues measured behaviorally in natural environments. The purpose of this chapter is to explore several aspects of child development and the treatment of problem child behavior by reviewing articles and research that have approached the investigation of children from a behavioral perspective. In this chapter we look at infant learning, the modification by day-care environments for infants and toddlers, toilet training, the acquisition of skills in preschool children, improving everyday behavior such as shopping and riding in the car, the treatment of problem behavior in the home, and delinquency.

INFANTS AND TODDLERS

One of the earliest behavioral studies with infants using direct measurement procedures was reported in 1958 by Yvonne Brackbill. Dr. Brackbill's study was one of the first with hard data[1] to show the effects of social reinforcement on smiling in infants. Her findings showed how adult social responses affect infant social responses, a landmark result because most discussions about infant learning prior to that time were speculative. The subjects in this pioneering research were eight normal infants (six males and two females) who lived within ten miles of Stanford University. The babies ranged in age from 3½ to 4½ months. In order to qualify as a subject in this study, each baby had to meet the following criteria: (1) old enough to remain awake after feeding; (2) did not respond differentially between mother and another adult; (3) did not cry at especially high rates or intensity; (4) displayed an operant rate of smiling of at least two responses per five-minute interval; and (5) showed an ability to maintain a supine position for five-minute intervals without undue squirming or struggling.

The babies were assigned to one of two experimental groups, a regular reinforcement group (RR) and an intermittently reinforced (IR) group. During experimental conditions, the RR group received social reinforcement for each smiling response throughout that condition. Babies in the IR group began the experimental condition being reinforced for each smiling response, but the reinforcement schedule was gradually thinned to the point where only every fifth smiling response was socially reinforced by the experimenter. For both groups, the study began with a baseline condition where the experimenter presented her emotionless face 15 inches above the baby's face for five-minute intervals. For both groups of babies, the experimental condition involved social reinforcement for smiling on the schedules described above (either RR or IR). The social reinforcement consisted of smiling back at the baby, talking softly to it, picking it up, and jostling, patting, and talking

---

[1]By *hard data* we mean data collected rigorously, as described in Chapter 2.

to it for 30 seconds before putting it back in the crib. The third condition involved extinction whereby the experimenter stopped the social reinforcement procedure for smiling and again remained expressionless with her countenance over the baby's.

The results showed that both groups of babies smiled significantly more frequently during the experimental conditions; in fact, they smiled more than twice as much as during baseline. The extinction condition produced results that were consistent with what would be expected in an operant animal laboratory. The babies in the IR group were more resistant to extinction than the babies in the RR group. That is, it took longer for their frequency of smiling to return to baseline levels than the babies who were on continuous schedules of reinforcement.

The significance of this study by Brackbill lies in the demonstration of the role of social reinforcement of social responses (smiling) in infants and in the demonstration of predictable rates of conditioning and extinction of social responses. Babies are obviously as responsive to social stimuli and the principles of behavior change as older human beings.

Another very important study in infant learning appeared just a year after the Brackbill (1958) study on smiling. In 1959, Rheingold, Gewirtz, and Ross reported on the social conditioning of vocalizations in the infant. The methodology of this study is quite similar to that of the Brackbill (1958) smiling study. In this case, 21

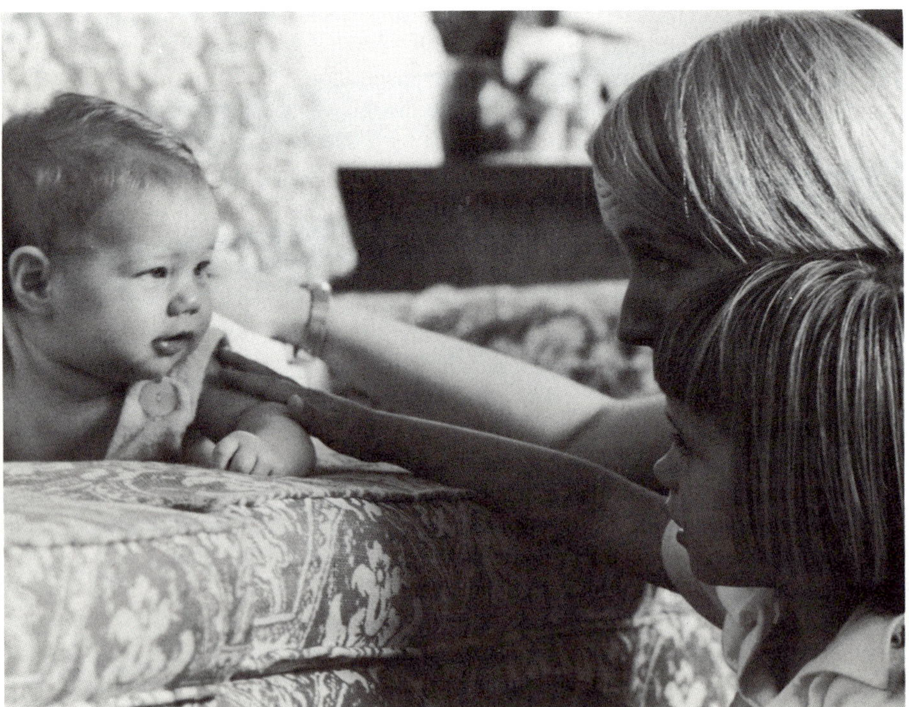

FIGURE 7-1.   Photo courtesy of Sandra Twardosz.

babies who were residents of St. Ann's Infant Asylum in Washington, D.C., served as subjects. The median age was 3 months.

In two similar experiments, each baby was involved in three conditions: baseline, conditioning, and extinction. During each condition, each baby's rate of vocalizations was measured. A vocalization was defined as a discrete sound other than straining sounds, coughs, whistles, squeaks, snorts, noisy breathing, fusses, and cries. As in the Brackbill (1958) study, during baseline the experimenter maintained an emotionless face over the baby during three-minute observation periods, during which vocalizations were recorded. During the conditioning phase, the baby was provided with a social consequence for each vocalization. The consequence took the form of the experimenter grinning at the baby, patting its tummy, and making a "tsking" sound. In both experiments, the rate of vocalizations nearly doubled during the conditioning phase, whereas the rate returned to baseline levels when the consequences were removed during the extinction condition. This study by Rheingold and her colleagues provided more evidence for the role of operant learning in infants.

Several researchers in the last few years have continued to show evidence of the role of behavior change principles in infant learning. We will briefly mention a few of these studies. Bower (1966) showed that the frequency of a head-turning response could be increased by "peekaboo" reinforcement from the experimenter. Watson (1966) taught a 10-week-old baby to swing his arm to strike a hanging object whenever the object stopped swinging. The frequency of a manual response was increased in a 14-week-old infant when that response turned on the light in a darkened room (Friedlander, 1961). And, in a study done in babies' natural home environments, Leuba and Friedlander (1968) found that babies manipulated a knob that produced auditory (chiming) and visual feedback significantly more frequently than they did a knob that provided simple tactile and auditory (clicking) feedback. Thus, a body of information has accrued showing the ability of human infants to learn to control their own environments.

Finally, to conclude our review of infant learning studies, the work of Hursh and Sherman (1973) deserves some attention. In this research, the experimenters looked at the effects of parent-presented models and praise on vocal behavior of their children. That the investigation was conducted in the natural homes of the families who participated is of particular interest.

During the first two phases of the study, two boys and one girl were observed. During those phases, the boys were 15–17 months and 20–24 months old. The girl was 17–19 months old. In the third phase, two other boys, 17 and 24 months old, and another girl, 19 months old, were observed. All observations were made in the living room of each family's home. A tape recorder was used to record the children's vocalizations. The experimenters asked the parents to provide particular consequences for specific sounds made by the children. A multiple baseline design was used, in that "treatment" by the parents was introduced at different points in time with each sound. The results showed that the frequency of a specific vocalization was higher when parents modeled and praised it than when they did not. Modeling and praise when used together were more effective in increasing vocalizations than when they were used separately. In the third phase, the parents were asked to try to increase vocalizations in any way they saw fit. They used modeling almost exclusively and did not produce as effective results as the parents who were instructed to use modeling and praise. Thus, it appears that modeling and praise could be used to facilitate vocalizations and, hence, language acquisition in young children. The Hursh and Sherman (1973) article is an important step in taking the behavioral study of language out of the laboratory and into the home.

These early studies demonstrating the role of behavior change techniques on infant behavior are important because, among other reasons, they help tie together a cohesive theory of behavior change technology. That is, not only are behavior change procedures functional in the treatment of problems, but they play a critical role in normal development.

ENVIRONMENTS FOR YOUNG CHILDREN

One of the most exciting aspects of behavioral research is using the techniques to determine whether existing ways of doing things are as functional as they could be. In the education, care, and training of children, we are discovering that we do some things just because no one has shown us a better way. Many assumptions about the care of children are just that—assumptions that have not been put to any scientific test. Many of the articles described in the next three sections examine some "tried," but, as it turns out, not so "true" procedures in the care and training of children.

There are many theories of how to operate a preschool. Some of them have been researched, some have not; very few have had small components put to experimental, direct investigation. However, in 1972, LeLaurin and Risley looked at the organization of day-care environments in comparing "zone" to "man-to-man" staff assignments. They point out that an overlooked aspect of preschool planning is the way children move from one activity to another. Typical staff assignments are more like "man-to-man" defensive assignments in football or basketball, in that a teacher or care provider is responsible for all the supervision of a group of children. When the last child in the group is finished with an activity, the teacher or care provider then presents the next activity. Gump (1969) has pointed out that moving children from one activity to another in this manner causes behavior divergent from that desired by the teacher because the children in transition are without strong behavioral cues. Another waiting period begins for the children as the teacher prepares the new activity. LeLaurin and Risley (1972) compared the "man-to-man" system to a "zone" system whereby teachers and caretakers are assigned to a particular area. As children complete an activity in a particular area (for example, lunch), they are sent to another area with the waiting adult (for example, bathroom). The "zone" system obviates the need for the child to wait for other children to finish an activity or to wait for the new activity to begin. Observers in the study scanned each area to determine the percentage of children in each area who were engaged in appropriate activities. The "zone" assignment was found to be superior to "man-to-man" in the amount of time children were engaged in planned activity. The implications from these results go beyond their apparent simplicity. What these researchers did was show that by using good behavioral measures, a rearrangement of the "living environment" produced desirable changes in child behavior. Further, this is a good example that not all behavior change techniques involve consequences of behavior; that is, some techniques involve antecedent control to produce desired change. You will see this kind of logic pursued in the next few studies reviewed in this section.

Several components of day-care environments were examined by Doke and Risley (1972). They measured group participation within two different preschool activity schedules. Further, these researchers looked at group versus individual dismissals and teachers working alone or together within each of the two schedules. Finally, Doke and Risley (1972) looked at the effect of gradually impoverishing the environment under the two different schedules. They found that children's participation in activities was high whether they could choose among activities *(Option)* or had them sequenced such that one activity followed another *(No Option)*. This finding was qualified, however, in that participation was impeded under *No Option* if the child was required to wait for other children to finish before being dismissed to the next activity or if there was a reduction in the amount of materials in each required activity. The authors conclude that

> in order to maintain high levels of participation in preschool play activities, it is not necessary to allow children to choose among several alternative activities. High participation may be more efficiently maintained by providing a supply of materials that is adequate to occupy all children in each of a sequence of required activities and staffing by at least two teachers, so that while one teacher is supervising children still finishing one activity another teacher can supervise children who are ready to start the next [p. 405].

They go on to suggest that the *No Option* sequential method of scheduling activities enables each child to have exposure to each activity.

The important utility of the Doke and Risley (1972) research is an empirical validation of a variety of staff and environmental arrangements in the preschool that allow teachers or administrators to make, for the needs and resources of their particular school, plans based on data rather than guesswork—for example, if the school has few materials, the children should probably be allowed to choose among activities; however, if there is a reasonable abundance of materials the *No Option* scheduling might be more practical. Thus, we have here another example of looking at the "living environment" in understanding and changing child behavior.

Still important research in this vein was conducted by Sandra Twardosz and her colleagues (Twardosz, Cataldo, & Risley, 1974). They examined several aspects of care in an infant center and in a toddler care center. In their first of a series of experiments, these researchers determined that the 24 infants (one month old to walking age) could clearly be seen and supervised better in an open as compared to a partitioned environment. Since impaired vision by staff impedes supervision of the children, it would be easy to conclude that an open environment would be more functional; however, these researchers wanted more complete answers. In a second experiment, they determined that the staff were easier to supervise in the open environment. But what effect does an open environment have on the children for important necessities such as sleep? In experiments four and five, Twardosz and her colleagues (1974) examined this issue and found that the babies' sleep in open and partitioned rooms was about the same. (Experiment three, in a partitioned room, showed little differences in sleep whether the room was quiet and dark or noisy and light.) Finally, the researchers examined whether an open environment was conducive to training preacademic activities (puzzles, bead stringing, and so on). It was thought that this kind of activity might produce more attention and learning if toddlers were in an area partitioned from the distractions of the other children and staff. The results, however, showed that the toddlers paid as much attention and performed the tasks just as well in the open environment as in a more secluded environment. The overall results of these studies led to conclusions that, if properly managed (a point not to be taken lightly), open environments are probably more functional than partitioned environments in the day care of infants and toddlers.

Once again, we see examples of the utility of direct behavioral measures in answering questions about producing productive behavior change in children's environments. The work of the Living Environment Group at Kansas has resulted in a book on how to set up an infant center (Herbert-Jackson, O'Brien, Porterfield, & Risley, 1977).

More answers in child care were provided by Todd Risley's Living Environment Group in a study reported in 1977 (Herbert-Jackson & Risley). They examined "Behavioral Nutrition: Consumption of Foods of the Future by Toddlers." In this study at the toddler day-care center, behavioral measures of food consumption and tasting were combined with nutrient analysis of foods to determine whether children would accept TVP (textured vegetable protein) and nonfat dry milk as well as more common sources of protein and calcium. It was found that the children ate approximately the same amounts of TVP foods as "regular" foods. Their protein intake remained about the same whatever kind of food they ate, and their calcium intake increased with the nonfat dry milk supplements. Since TVP may ultimately prove to be healthier and less wasteful worldwide in the drain of resources, these results are not only encouraging, but may prove to be very crucial.

Following a logic similar to that of evaluating children's preference for foods by measuring how much they eat, Quilitch, Christophersen, and Risley (1977) evaluated children's play materials by measuring which materials were checked out and played with the most under a variety of conditions. Observers recorded which toys children checked out in a recreation facility and with which ones they played. At the end of each day a supervisor completed a questionnaire on toy management, safety, and durability. Most toys were used by children both individually and in groups. There were differences across sexes and age groups. Overall toy use and appeal correlated highly. Prolonged forced sampling of little-used toys did not add to their attractiveness. The utility of these studies lies in the demonstration of a system for evaluating children's play materials, the results of which could benefit manufacturers, recreation authorities, educators, care providers, and parents.

TOILET TRAINING AND BEDWETTING

Probably no other area of child behavior and development sparks as much controversy as toilet training. Many traditional psychologists have suggested that parental preoccupation with toilet training their toddlers could result in irreparable harm. Spock (1976) suggests a very permissive attitude to toilet training. Ilg and Ames (1955) have recommended waiting until the child is at least around 3 years old before embarking on the toilet-training task. An area of agreement between more traditional professionals and behaviorists is that highly punitive procedures in training should be avoided. Prior to 1969, little scientific data existed on techniques for toilet training. In 1969, Madsen, Hoffman, Thomas, Koropsak, and Madsen described research that compared reinforcement procedures, and reinforcement plus a buzzer-signal device, to two control groups: (1) requesting parents to try whatever they thought would work in training their child, and (2) a no-contact control group. Using contingent social and edible rewards, the parents in the reinforcement group were told to gradually increase the amount of time the child spent on the potty and to profusely reward correct performance. The parents in the reinforcement-plus-buzzer-pants group were given identical instructions, but were also provided with buzzer pants to aid in the toilet-training process. The pants had sensing devices that triggered a low-intensity buzzing sound on a cigarette-case-sized unit worn by the child. When the buzzer sounded, the mother rushed the child to the potty where the correct response could be performed and reinforced. In a buzzer-pants-only group, parents were provided with pants for the children, but no reinforcement instructions. In the parents' method control group, mothers were told "we will ask you for the next four weeks to do exactly as you had planned to do before you heard of our project" (p. 127). Parents of the no-contact controls simply reported on successes and accidents at the beginning and end of the four-week period. The results showed that there were significant differences in successes for the reinforcement group and the reinforcement plus buzzer-pants group over the other three groups. The two reinforcement groups were not significantly different from each other. In looking at rates of accidents, all three experimental groups showed significant decreases over the two control groups. The findings further showed that older children (16–24 months and older) had more successes than younger children (12–16 months); however, successes were noted in these younger children contrary to what might be predicted by child development professionals.

Obviously, buzzer pants have never become the rage for aiding parents in the toilet-training process. They probably are not practical (in terms of convenience) and thus not marketable. Nonetheless, the Madsen et al. work was an important step in research in the toilet training of children in that it showed the value of reinforcement procedures in the training process and further showed that at least some children could be toilet trained as young as 12 months of age.

Probably one of the most important studies in behavioral child development was reported in 1973 by Drs. Richard Foxx and Nathan Azrin (Foxx & Azrin, 1973). This study paved the way for Azrin and Foxx's national bestselling book, *Toilet Training in Less Than a Day* (1974). The work of these two researchers at Anna Mental Health Center and Southern Illinois University demonstrated that normal children of the ages of 20–36 months could become completely responsible for their own toilet habits after four hours or less of intensive behavioral training. Almost every behavioral principle and procedure is used in what came to be known as "rapid toilet training." After a child passes a readiness test that demonstrates instructional, motor, and bladder readiness, some preliminary effort is made by the trainer (parent, paraprofessional, or professional). This effort involves purchasing a potty chair with a bowl easily removable from the top, a doll that wets, training pants for the doll, several pairs of oversized training pants for the child, and a large supply of the child's favorite snacks (candy, pretzels, and so on) and liquids. The trainer also prepares a "friends who care" list of friends, relatives, pets, and fictional characters who will be proud of the child's new toileting prowess. Training itself involves "loading" the child with at least 32 ounces of liquid (which ensures the occurrence of the target response). This is done by using the liquid as contingent reinforcement throughout training. Modeling and role-rehearsal are major components in training in that the child puts the doll through all the training procedures the child goes through. The child's (and doll's) pants are checked every five minutes and the child is put on the potty every 15 minutes (the doll is also "pottied" frequently). Correct toilet responses are heartily reinforced with praise and liquid and edible reinforcement. Toilet accidents are handled by a positive practice procedure that involves telling the child in a stern way the inappropriateness of his or her behavior and in rapid succession making several trips from the point of the accident to the potty to demonstrate appropriate protocol (which includes the child emptying and cleaning the potty, pulling up and down his or her own pants, and flushing the toilet). Although no component analysis research has been done with rapid toilet-training procedures, it would seem that positive practice is a very critical part of the training process. Azrin and Foxx (1974) report that, using rapid toilet training, their *trained technicians* were successful with over 200 children. This finding and the distribution of the book for mass public consumption has both excited and concerned other researchers.

In 1976, Lutzker and Drake (1976) compared four groups of mother-child pairs in variations of the rapid toilet-training methodology. One group of mothers was given the Azrin and Foxx book, told to read it and to try the procedures with their children. This simulated the parent's buying the book on their own and trying the procedures. Another group of mothers was provided with the book and was given a classroom lecture and review on the procedures. This was done to see if a lecture would facilitate rapid toilet training. A third group of mothers was provided with a 1½-hour direct training demonstration of rapid toilet training, a two-page summary of the procedures, and no book. Finally, John Drake went into the homes of the fourth group and trained the children himself, which method was analogous to the training of the children on whom Azrin and Foxx validated training procedures for their book. The results showed that all groups were able to significantly reduce the number of accidents from pre- to posttraining, but only the children trained by the paraprofessional (John Drake) showed complete toilet independence as suggested by the book. The results, thus, force us to mixed conclusions. While parents can seemingly get their children well "on the road" to being toilet trained by the Azrin and Foxx procedures, it would seem that one-day independence suggested by the book might be more difficult to achieve when the parents try to "go it alone." Further on the positive side, the children trained by the paraprofessional were trained in about two hours rather than the four hours suggested by the book. On the other hand, some mothers who were originally assigned to the book-only group dropped out of the research either prior to training after reading the book and feeling that they could not do the procedures, or after they began training, having severe problems with the child, feeling frustrated, and quitting.

Two other studies further examined the utility of the rapid toilet-training book. Butler (1976) found that 39 of 49 children were successfully toilet trained by their mothers who were given the Azrin and Foxx book to read, but were also exposed to a series of lectures and role-playing sessions. Matson and Ollendick (1977) studied ten mother-child pairs. Five mothers were provided simply with the book; the other five mothers were given the book plus pretraining and assistance during training. The second group of mothers were far more successful in producing independent toileting with their children than the mothers whose only resource was the book. These authors further report negative emotional side effects by mothers and children who did not benefit from supervised training. The results of these three studies (Lutzker & Drake, 1976; Butler, 1976; Matson & Ollendick, 1977) suggest that some reservations are in order in the wide dissemination of child training advice, specifically rapid toilet training.

Nocturnal enuresis (bedwetting) is a fairly common problem in children. A behavioral treatment methodology was developed as early as 1938 by Mowrer and Mowrer, who used a moisture-sensitive pad device that signaled micturation of the sleeping child. When parents heard the signal, they rushed to the child's room and whisked the child off to the bathroom, where the disrupted elimination response was allowed to be completed. While this conditioning procedure has had some notable success, Yates (1969) reported only a 53% success rate and Lovibond (1964) suggested as high as a 35–40% relapse rate after two years. Thus, while the Mowrer and Mowrer (1938) conditioning procedures may be effective for some children, the search for other fruitful procedures has continued. A fascinating case study was reported by Nordquist (1971) in which bedwetting was eliminated when the parents were taught to modify the pre-bedtime noncompliance of their 5½-year-old boy. No direct treatment of bedwetting was ever implemented. A brief reversal condition followed by retraining showed a functional relationship between noncompliance and bedwetting with this child. Unfortunately, these exciting results have never been successfully replicated. Moore (1977) tried to replicate the Nordquist (1971) results with three noncompliant children and was unsuccessful with all three children.

Once again, we see Dr. Nathan Azrin in the forefront of developing functional treatment and training procedures. In 1974, Azrin, Sneed, and Foxx reported the successful use of a procedure they have called dry-bed training. This involves one night of very intensive training (and a very sleepy trainer), followed by a posttraining supervision period. During intensive training, the child is awakened every hour, reinforced for correct toileting, required to engage in positive practice for accidents (which are signalled by a buzzer pad device), and required to do cleanliness training. During posttraining, the child is aroused for positive practice and cleanliness training contingent upon accidents. Of the 24 children Azrin, Sneed, and Foxx (1974) originally studied, 17 stopped wetting completely while seven others required some retraining.

Dry-bed training was compared to retention control training by Doleys, Ciminero, Tollison, Williams, and Wells (1977). Nineteen children served as subjects in the study. Some of the children received dry-bed training while others received retention control training. These latter children received their training in the daytime by being reinforced for longer and longer periods of urine retention. The logic was that this daytime training would generalize to nighttime with the children thus retaining their urine while they slept. The results showed dry-bed training was effective, whereas retention training was basically ineffective for those children exposed to it.

In an attempt to make dry-bed a more convenient and even more effective technique, Azrin and Thienes (1978) revised the procedure and subsequently produced highly successful results. Fifty children were successfully trained using "enuresis training" whereas a control group of children who merely used the buzzer pad had few successes. Of the children who were given enuresis training, accidents were reduced to 25% on the first night, 10% after the first month, and 2% after one year. Table 7-1 shows the exhaustive procedures used in enuresis training. The focus of the procedures is on positive reinforcement and positive practice rather than on the negative aspects of bedwetting. The authors further report that subsequent to the study, some parents were provided with 1½ hours of in-office training by a counselor and successfully carried out enuresis training with their own children. With the replication of these results, another significant step has thus been achieved; for, despite the efficacy of enuresis training, it takes a tremendous whole-day effort by a trainer, a not particularly cost-effective prospect. Furthermore, a high "burnout" rate of trainers might be predicted if parents cannot be taught to do the procedures on their own. The replication has been provided by Wyckoff (1978), who found that spending 48 minutes going over an outline of dry-bed procedures was sufficient to produce a 100% success rate with parents who, after learning what was expected of them, went through with it.

As can be seen by the studies reviewed in this section, behavior change procedures that lead to a system of child rearing practices are constantly being developed and perfected. Of concern in any such system is ethics (to be dealt with

TABLE 7-1. Dry-Bed Procedures

I. Training day
  A. Afternoon
    1. Parents and child are informed of the entire procedure
    2. Child is encouraged to drink his favorite beverage to increase urination
    3. Child is requested to attempt initiation of urination every .5 hr
      a. If child feels the need to urinate, he is asked to hold for increasingly longer periods of time
      b. If child *has* to urinate, he is asked to lie in bed as if he were asleep then jump up and go to the bathroom, role-playing what he should do at night. He then is rewarded with a beverage and praise
    4. Child is motivated to work at dry beds
      a. Parents and child review inconveniences caused by bedwetting
      b. Parents contract with the child for rewards to be given after first dry night and after a specified series of dry nights
      c. Child specifies persons he'd like to tell when he can keep dry
      d. Child is given a chart to mark to show his progress posting this in a prominent spot

B. One hour before bedtime with parents watching
  1. Child is informed of all phases of maintenance procedures
  2. Child role-plays cleanliness training
      a. Child is required to put on own pajamas
      b. Child is required to remove sheets and put them back on
  3. Child role-plays positive practice in toileting
      a. Child lies down in bed as if asleep (lights out)
      b. Child counts to 50
      c. Child arises and hurries to bathroom where he attempts urination
      d. Child returns to bed
      e. Steps a–d repeated 20 times with parent counting trials
C. At bedtime
  1. Child repeats instructions on accident correction and nighttime awakenings to trainer
  2. Child continues to drink fluids
  3. Parents talk to child about rewards and their confidence in child
  4. Comments on dryness of sheets
  5. Child retires for the night
D. Hourly awakenings till 1 AM
  1. If child is dry
      a. Minimal prompt is used to awaken
      b. Child is asked what he should do
          1. If can wait another hour
              i. Trainer praises his urinary control
              ii. Child returns to bed
          2. If must urinate
              i. Child goes to bathroom
              ii. Trainer praises him for correct toileting
              iii. Child returns to bed
      3. Child feels bed sheets and comments on their dryness
      4. Trainer praises child for having dry bed
      5. Child is given fluids (after 11 PM discontinue beverages)
      6. Child returns to sleep
  2. When an accident has occurred
      a. Parent awakens child and reprimands him for wetting
      b. Parent directs child to bathroom to finish urinating
      c. Child is given cleanliness training
          1. Child changes night clothes
          2. Child removes wet sheets and places them in dirty laundry
          3. Child obtains clean sheets and remakes bed
      d. Positive practice in correct toileting (20 trials) is performed immediately after cleanliness training
      e. Child is reminded that positive practice is necessary before bed the following evening
E. Parents check the child .5 hr early the next morning
II. Post-training parental supervision
A. If dry in the morning
  1. Point out to child .5 hr before his usual bedtime that he may stay up that extra .5 hr because he needn't practice and would be awakened .5 hr earlier that night
  2. Point out his chart to show his progress toward rewards
  3. Tell visitors to the home how he is keeping his bed dry
  4. Bring his success up at least three times a day
B. If wet in the morning
  1. Wake him .5 hr early asking him what he should do and to feel his sheets
  2. Child is required to change his bed and pajamas
  3. Child does positive practice in correct toileting (20 trials)
  4. Child does positive practice (20 trials) .5 hr before bed that night
  5. Child marks chart and is told we will try again tomorrow
  6. Tell visitors to the home that the child is learning to keep his bed dry

---

in Chapter 13). You can see the added concern of behavior change practitioners who, while engaged in a search for effective procedures, are also concerned with validation (Lutzker & Drake, 1976; Matson & Ollendick, 1977; Doleys et al., 1977). A study by Martin (1977) deserves brief mention here. He looked at the effects of positive and negative adult-child interactions on children's task performance and task preferences. In individual sessions, an adult directed three boys to work on each of three tasks (chip sorting, pegboard, and bead stringing). Within any given session the on-task behavior for one task was praised, the off-task behavior for one task was reprimanded, and performance on a third task was ignored. The manner in which the adult interacted with each boy on a particular task varied from day to day. After each session, the boys were given a choice of which of three tasks they would like to play with while the adult left the room for a minute. Reprimand for off-task produced the highest rates of performance, *but* when the adult left the room, the boys *never* chose a task to play with on which they had been reprimanded that day. Thus, the Martin (1977) study serves as a good reminder to us that punitive or aversive procedures, although effective when the child is under adult control, may, indeed, produce some unwanted side effects. This is a point to keep in mind in examining any behavior change procedure.

EVERYDAY BEHAVIOR

How often have you noticed (or have you been bothered by) unpleasant family interactions on a shopping trip? Perhaps at the grocery store you merrily push your cart down the aisle, and a 7-year-old boy whooshes by and bumps your cart. With his arm extended, he knocks over six cans of cling peaches (one can of which "clings" to your foot), and is followed by Mom yelling "Get your - - - back here or I'll smack the daylights out of you." These scenes are, of course, not only discomforting for you, the shopper, they are unpleasant for the storekeeper and the family involved. Barnard, Christophersen, and Wolf (1977) were the first behavior change professionals to formally examine family interactions in the supermarket. Three boys (two 6-year-olds and a 5-year-old) and their mothers participated in the study. Three of the primary measures of the study during shopping trips were product disturbances, proximity to the parent, and mother-child verbal interactions. The experimental design was a multiple baseline treatment across responses with each child—that is, after baseline data rates of product disturbance and proximity to parents stabilized, the same treatment was introduced for product disturbances. Treatment involved the extension of a simple point system that was already in effect in the boys' homes. At periodic intervals during the shopping the mother provided descriptive praise and a point for what the child was doing right (for example, "Here's a point for being so close to me"). Points were lost for inappropriate behavior. At home, the points were exchangeable for a variety of goodies and privileges. The boys showed considerable improvement in those two problem areas during shopping trips. Further, the mothers rated their satisfaction with shopping with the boys as greatly improved.

In another study concerned with family shopping trips, Clark, Greene, Macrae, McNees, Davis, and Risley (1977) developed and evaluated a parent advice package. Several families participated in the research. In their first experiment, these authors eliminated the distracting behavior of four children (two in each of two families). Specifically, the parents allotted a predetermined amount of money available to each child at the beginning of the shopping trip. A response-cost procedure was initiated whenever the children violated the stated decorum for the trip. The response cost was the loss of a nickel for each infraction. The procedure was quite effective in modifying the disruptive behavior of the children in both families; however, because of foresight by the researchers in terms of collecting other important data, they noticed some negative side effects. That is, the response-cost procedures reduced the occurrence of social and educational comments made between children and their parents. Thus, even though the children became better behaved, the shopping trips were still not a vehicle for pleasant family interactions. This result, left untreated, would be fuel aplenty for the detractors of behavior change procedures who argue (to some degree with appropriate concern) that the behavioral professional is not concerned with the "whole person," family dynamics, or the relationship between behavior change of one person and the effects of that change on the overall environment. Fortunately, Clark et al. further developed procedures that both improved behavior and increased the children's social and educational comments while shopping. The procedures involved the same response-cost procedures as did the first experiment, with an additional four days of coaching the parents in the avoidance of coercive remarks and in talking to the children about shopping. In a final experiment, the validity of the advice package was tested with six mothers and their children. The results showed that the written advice package

FIGURE 7-2. Poorly behaved children on a shopping trip are a problem for all concerned. (From *Shopping with Children: Advice for Parents*, by B. F. Greene, H. B. Clark, and T. R. Risley. Copyright 1977 by Academic Therapy Publications. Reprinted by permission.)

FIGURE 7-3.   With proper efforts, a shopping trip can be a pleasant educational experience for the entire family. (From *Shopping with Children: Advice for Parents,* by B. F. Greene, H. B. Clark, and T. R. Risley. Copyright 1977 by Academic Therapy Publications. Reprinted by permission.)

without other professional intervention was functional in greatly improving behavior and overall family enjoyment during shopping trips. The results of this work stimulated a book, *Shopping with Children* by Greene, Clark, and Risley (1977), which is intended for public consumption. The development, evaluation, and dissemination of a variety of training packages covering a variety of normal family interactions can be expected to be a prolific area for research in the next ten years.

Another area of normal family interaction is conversation at the dinner table. By observing mealtime conversation in the home, Jewett and Clark (1979) found that most talk in middle-class families seems to be predominantly adult and disciplinary. In order to develop mutually interesting family conversations, these researchers developed an in-school program that taught four preschoolers to initiate interesting conversation with their family during meals. The program involved role playing and reinforcement for the children's reiterating the interesting topics they had initiated during the previous night's dinner. A multiple baseline design across topics showed that training at school in a particular topic for conversation would generalize to the dinner table whenever the training was introduced. The topics the children were taught to discuss were the parents' work, siblings, school, and statements of appreciation directed toward parents or siblings. While further research will show whether this kind of training could be widely disseminated, the results of this Jewett and Clark (1979) study are highly encouraging. Many family advice books (Ginott, 1965; Gordon, 1975) stress the need for family, parent-child communication, but these books have a tendency to be vague at best in procedural descriptions of how to achieve that communication. Again, we can look to behavior change professionals to pave the way in family communication.

As we saw in Chapter 3, propaganda, mass public advertising for the public good, seems to produce mixed results. We have been constantly reminded over the past several years to use seat belts in our automobiles. The data (just like data on the hazards of cigarette smoking) are abundantly clear that seat belts do save lives. The use of restraint devices for children in cars is important not only for the child's safety in the event of an accident, but also because an unrestrained child poses a danger to the safe operation of the vehicle. Nonetheless, despite advertising efforts, many families do not restrain their children in the car. Dr. Edward Christophersen of the University of Kansas Medical Center conducted an important study that examined the behavior of children riding in automobiles (Christophersen, 1977). An observer rode with the mother on repeated 15-minute test rides and collected data on the child's behavior. Children who were in car seats displayed high rates of appropriate safe behaviors whereas unrestrained children did not. When car seats were introduced to children who had not previously been using them, their appropriate behavior increased dramatically. Further research should concentrate on children's behavior during longer trips.

Other efforts in the area of the safety of children have shown up in the work of Yeaton and Bailey (1978), who developed a program for training crossing guards to teach functional street-crossing skills to grade school children. The training was provided to several guards in the Tallahassee, Florida, community. Elimination of the disruptive bus-riding behavior of a 10-year-old retarded male was produced by a token reinforcement program developed by Chiang, Iwata, and Dorsey (1979). They taught a bus driver to administer the program by utilizing a hand counter on the dashboard and dividing the bus route into intervals based on geographic landmarks. Substantial reduction in disruptive behavior occurred. Dr. Brandon Greene and his colleagues studied over 80 children (Greene, Barber, & Bailey, in press) in efforts to reduce disruptive behavior on two school buses. Greene created a device that monitored noise levels on the buses. As long as the children kept the noise below the criterion level, rock music played from four speakers on the bus. However, if the noise level went above criterion in the front of the bus, one of a series of eight lights, which were visible to all of the children, lighted. If enough lights on the panel went on in any one trip (indicating the noise threshold was too high), music was not played the following day. Disruptive noise was greatly reduced using this system. Especially practical about Greene's technique was its automation, which did not depend on the driver or the observers' interventions. Whether bus systems will be willing to utilize similar devices on a large scale is another question.

CHANGING PROBLEM BEHAVIOR

In changing problem behavior of children at home and school, it is almost always necessary to have parents and teachers act as primary change agents, somehow under the watchful eye of the behavioral professional. If the professional acts as the primary change agent, there is little hope for any maintenance of behavior change. In an early study in the behavior modification of children, Wahler (1969) looked at the behavior of two boys from different families in their homes and at school. After baseline, both sets of parents were instructed on how to provide social and physical reinforcement for cooperative behavior. One boy's parents were instructed to ignore inappropriate behavior, while the other boy's parents were instructed to use the child's bedroom as timeout for inappropriate behavior. This treatment produced considerable improvement in the cooperative behavior of the boys in both homes. A brief reversal condition demonstrated that, indeed, the treatment procedures were the responsible variables for change; however, a disappointing result was that no functional change generalized to the school. Thus, Wahler then trained both boys' teachers, one in differential attention, one in differential attention plus timeout. The procedures were reintroduced at home concurrent with their introduction at school. Cooperative and appropriate behavior was then observed in both settings. The results of this study confirmed other early data that productive behavior change could be produced using parents and teachers as the change agents. It was also an early demonstration that generalization of behavior across settings cannot be expected; it needs to be programmed (Baer, Wolf, & Risley, 1968; Stokes & Baer, 1977).

Wahler has most recently found that socioeconomic factors and what he calls "insular vs. noninsular" family factors are critical in predicting the success of a behavior modification intervention (Wahler, Afton, & Fox, 1979; Wahler & Fox, 1980). High-risk families consisting of lower-class, nonworking single mothers who have few outside social contacts other than "kinfolk" and helping agency personnel are not good candidates for any therapeutic intervention. The best "treatment" for these families would seem to be a vocational/educational intervention.

Much of the early studies in the treatment of deviant family interactions came from the work of Gerald Patterson and his colleagues at Oregon Research Institute.[2] For example, Arnold, Levine, and Patterson (1975) found that untreated siblings' behavior improved without direct treatment when the parents were taught behavior change procedures with a different target child in the family. These researchers further found that there appears to be a certain amount of capriciousness in families who label a particular child in the family aggressive, or noncompliant, or in some way deviant. They found that aggressive *families* produce aggressive children and that children labeled aggressive were no more so than the other members of the family.

Another relatively early demonstration of behavior change in homes was provided by Hall, Axelrod, Tyler, Grief, Jones, and Robertson (1972). Four parents who were enrolled in a Responsive Teaching class carried out the experiments with their own children. The parents variously used reinforcement, extinction, and punishment. One child's wearing of an orthodontic device was increased by the use of time checks backed up by contingent monetary payoffs for wearing the device. Household task performance was increased by the mother of a Campfire Girl by using a simple point system with a variety of monetary and other tangible backup reinforcers. Extinction for whining, crying, and complaining was used by the parents of a 4-year-old boy with considerable success in reducing those behaviors.

---

[2]Dr. Gerald Patterson has been one of the most active behavior change researchers. The entire focus of his work has been in family behavior change. Coverage of all of his research efforts would take an entire chapter. The interested reader is referred to two books: *Living with Children* by Patterson and Gullion (1968) and *Families* by Patterson (1971).

Finally, a mother reduced the time it took for her 5-year-old daughter to get dressed in the morning by making television watching contingent upon getting dressed within 30 minutes of awakening. These four simple experiments further confirmed the practicality of teaching parents to change their children's problem behavior.

A home point system was used to modify the behavior of five children between the ages of 5 and 10 in two homes (Christophersen, Arnold, Hill, & Quilitch, 1972). Chores, bickering, and inappropriate verbal behavior toward the parents were chronic problems with these children. Points and response cost fines were introduced sequentially across problem behaviors (multiple baseline). Earned points were exchanged for a variety of privileges, such as bike riding, and special events, such as drive-in movies and picnics. The token reinforcement program proved to be effective in changing 15 problem behaviors in one family and six chronic problem behaviors in the other family. The parents in both families rated all 21 behavior changes as significant improvements.

Sometimes the simplest of contingencies can be effective, yet it often takes the advice of a professional to bring them to light for parents. Knight and McKenzie (1974) eliminated thumbsucking in three girls, ages 3, 6, and 8. The experimenters read the children's favorite stories to them just before naptime contingent upon no thumbsucking. The stories were interrupted by the experimenters each time the child put her thumb in her mouth. The mothers were instructed in maintenance procedures following the clear demonstration of the utility of the procedures in reducing thumbsucking. It is never made clear by these authors why the mothers were not made the primary change agents in the first place.

One of the most controversial studies within the area of behavior modification with children was reported in 1974 by Rekers and Lovaas. Their study demonstrated reinforcement control of pronounced feminine behaviors in a boy almost 5 years old whose psychological evaluation referred to him as showing "childhood cross-gender identity." The child engaged in frequent dressing in female clothes, use of cosmetics, showed female mannerisms, preferred female playmates and "feminine activities,"[3] "preference for the female role," female voice inflection, and an expressed desire to be a girl. Training across behaviors was accomplished by training the mother in the clinic and the home to act as the primary change agent. The mother was instructed to use social and token reinforcement for "masculine behavior" and to place "feminine behavior" on extinction. After intensive treatment, the child's sex-role behavior changed and follow-up measures showed the change to be durable in that the boy behaved in a male sex-role manner. The authors suggested that they had demonstrated prevention of adult transsexualism by changing behaviors in the child that adults with gender-identity problems (transsexuals) retrospectively report to be similar to their childhood behavior. This study showed how seemingly complex and persistent behavior (in essence, the child's personality) could be changed through intensive parent training and behavior change procedures. This study, however, sparked a lively exchange among behavioral child specialists as to the ethics of intervening in sex-role behavior of young children.

Hyperactive behavior in children has been observed by teachers, parents, and professionals. Despite many treatment strategies, few careful behavioral studies

[3]These are Rekers' and Lovaas' terms.

have been done which evaluate treatment modalities. Stimulant medication (Ritalin, or methylphenidate) has been a common medical treatment prescribed by pediatricians and psychiatrists in an attempt to correct hyperactive behavior in children (O'Leary, 1980). In one of very few direct behavioral studies, Ayllon and Roberts (1974) compared the effects of Ritalin with those of behavior modification in the classroom. They found that while both Ritalin and behavior modification suppressed hyperactive behavior, the drug seemed to impede academic performance while behavior modification enhanced it. (This study is reviewed in more detail in Chapter 8, "Classrooms").

Shafto and Sulzbacher (1977) compared reinforcement procedures with Ritalin in examining a preschool child's activities, social, verbal, and academic behaviors. These researchers found that the child engaged in fewer free-play activity changes (in part the frequent changing of activities is what got him labeled hyperactive) during behavior modification whereas the Ritalin produced more variable effects. At higher doses, the Ritalin increased attention to tasks, but seemed to make the child's speech less intelligible, and he was less responsive to instructions from teachers that required him to do something. Thus, with this child, it would seem that drugs produced variable effects on his behavior whereas behavior modification produced more predictable behavior. The utility of studies such as this lies in the demonstration that any treatment procedure can and should be evaluated on as many dimensions of the child's behavior as is practical and feasible. That is, instead of merely looking at the effects of treatment on his hyperactive behavior, the authors studied several aspects of the child's behavior. The further utility of this study is that directly observed behavior was recorded and that treatment success or failure was based on those measures rather than more subjective measures such as clinical observation by a professional, rating scales, or projective tests.

A nearly 9-year-old boy named Arnold was the subject of a study by Wulbert and Dries (1977). Arnold had been referred to a mental health center because of hyperactive behavior and poor school achievement. He had been given Ritalin for two years. In this study, Ritalin was compared with placebo (no drugs) and with reinforcement contingencies. The child was observed both at home and at the clinic. Medication and contingency management affected some behaviors but not others, but generalization to the home was not observed where contingency management procedures were never introduced. When Ritalin was compared with placebo, no differences were noted in the frequency of Arnold's repetitive hand movements and distractible behavior at the clinic. A multiple baseline design with reversals was used to examine the role of contingency management procedures. These examinations showed that reinforcement contingencies, not medication, were responsible for behavior change in the clinic. On the other hand, in the home where reinforcement contingencies were not employed, but Ritalin was, the drug reduced aggressive behavior, but repetitive hand movements increased. This study provides another example of the need to evaluate children's behavior on several dimensions and suggests, again, that children's reactions to treatments are idiosyncratic.

One of the important areas of the behavior modification of children is investigating to what extent parents can act as primary change agents and how much training parents require to become effective change agents. Reisinger and Ora

(1977) found that parents were able to generalize their training from the clinic to the home whether observations were obtrusive in the home (live observers) or unobtrusive (tape recordings). These are important results in light of the next few studies we review here because a contention of a careful analysis of studies showing generalization from clinic to home could be that observers act as discriminative stimuli for the parents. Thus, in the observer's presence parents show the skills they were taught in the clinic, but when the observers are not in the home the parents may revert to their old, ineffective ways of interacting with their problem children. The Reisinger and Ora (1977) study allays this concern, however.

The effectiveness of a standardized parent training program was evaluated by Peed, Roberts, and Forehand (1977). They examined the behaviors of mothers and their noncompliant children both in the clinic and at home. Some of the mother-child pairs were assigned to a treatment group and were exposed to the standardized treatment program. Other mother-child pairs formed a waiting list control group. In the clinic, measures were taken on the mother and child during "the child's game" and "the parent's game" while at home the pairs were examined for child compliance to alpha commands, compliance to total commands, parental attends, rewards, and the percentage of contingent attention, parental questions, parent-beta commands, and parent criticisms. In the child's game, mothers in the clinic were instructed to engage in any activity that the child chose and to allow the child to determine the nature and rules of the interaction. In the parent's game, the mothers were told to engage in activities whose rules and nature were determined by her. In the home, the mother was instructed to remain in two adjoining rooms with the child, ignore the observer, avoid having visitors, telephone calls, or the television on during the observations. (It might be noted that it was never discussed whether or not the mothers had any difficulty in arranging this somewhat "artificial" home environment. The "artificial" environment might cause some question as to the representativeness of the home data.)

Some definitions are in order at this point. *Alpha commands* are orders, rules, suggestions, or questions to which a motor response by the child is appropriate and feasible (for example, "Please set the table."). *Beta commands* are those statements to which the child has no opportunity to comply (for example, "You had better wise up."). *Rewards* involved verbal and physical signs of approval; *attends* were descriptive comments concerning the child's behavior, and questions where verbal responses to interrogatives were required. *Criticisms* were negative or disapproving statements, *warnings* described aversive consequences for failure to comply, and *timeout* was the clear use of a removal contingency for inappropriate behavior. *Compliance* was scored as occurring within five seconds of an alpha command.

The treatment phase followed baseline measurements in the clinic and home and consisted of two phases. The first phase taught the mother to be a more effective reinforcing agent by increasing the frequency and range of social consequences and eliminating nonfunctional commands and criticisms. She practiced these skills with the therapist and was given direct instruction on the procedures. One of the most important and unique features of this treatment was that the mother had to demonstrate a specified performance criterion in the first phase of treatment before going on to the second phase. Quite often parent training is considered accomplished on a much more subjective basis. The second phase involved teaching the mothers the use of timeout procedures and concise commands. The results of the direct observations showed that both parents and children in the treatment group demonstrated considerable behavior change in the clinic and the home. The control group did not change during the waiting period. A fascinating finding was that *both* the treatment and control group mothers reported positive changes indicating that *any* involvement with the clinic may cause the mothers to rate change in their children positively. The most important finding was that the standardized treatment program implemented by clinical graduate students did effect change. Thus, the development of "packaged" programs may be a breakthrough in the treatment of problem children. Of major concern with these programs is that they be validated in as many dimensions as possible with as large and varied groups as possible (Azrin, 1978).

Considerably more research has come out of the University of Georgia examining several aspects of parent-child training. Twenty-seven mother-child pairs were studied by Roberts, Forehand, McMahon, and Roberts (in press). They looked at the effects of parental instruction-giving on child compliance. Three groups were used in this examination: (1) command training wherein mothers were simply taught to issue specific, single instructions followed by a five-second interval in which the mother was not to physically or verbally interfere with the child; (2) command plus timeout training wherein mothers learned the same commands as the other group, but were also taught the use of a simple timeout procedure; and (3) a placebo control wherein mothers met with therapists who used active listening (Gordon, 1975) about their child behavior problems. Mothers who were exposed to command training plus timeout produced the greatest amount of compliance in their children and the most significant within-group differences pre- and posttraining. The mothers who received command training only also showed significant within-group pre-post changes in compliance in their children. Maternal perception of child change as measured by a three-point scale was more greatly affected by the two training procedure groups as compared to the placebo group.

There are problems with home-based studies, which can be overcome by continued attempts to improve research. Eyberg and Johnson (1974) found that parents have a tendency to say their children's behavior has improved even when direct observational data show the contrary. This kind of reactivity or demand characteristic is well known from clinical literature and must be considered in any "social validation" of home-based research.

Results somewhat discrepant from other studies we have examined investigating the role of didactic material in producing behavior change (Lutzker & Drake, 1976; Butler, 1976; Matson & Ollendick, 1977) were obtained by McMahon, Griest, Forehand, and Ogden (1979). They showed from 50% to 80% reductions in inappropriate mealtime behavior by exposing parents to a brochure on modifying mealtime behavior. These results are similar to those of Jewett and Clark (1979) in that didactic materials appear to be functional training tools when they are applied to a specific behavior problem. One problem with the study by McMahon et al., however, is that the mothers were well educated. Research in the use of written training materials with mothers with broader educational and socioeconomic backgrounds is in order.

Another encouraging result from the Georgia group comes from a study by Humphreys, Forehand, McMahon and Roberts (in press) in which they examined the effects of parent training on untreated siblings. Mothers who had been taught to modify the behavior of one child in the family who had been labeled deviant then generalized the training by treating other children in the family. Thus, the mothers showed their newly learned behavioral skills with all of the children in the family. Relatively short and obtrusive observation periods were used to glean these results. If longer and less obtrusive recording periods show similar success in parent generalization, considerable progress in child behavior modification will be demonstrated. Not surprisingly, generalization from home to school (where behaviorally untrained teachers rather than the newly trained parents hold the contingencies) was not shown in a study of 11 mother-child pairs (Forehand, Sturgis, McMahon, Aguar, Green, Wells, & Breiner, in press).

DELINQUENCY

Crime and delinquency have presented some of the most difficult problems for mental health professionals. Once a youth starts making contacts with the law, chances are great that he or she will spend a lifetime in a revolving door with the justice system. Not only have treatment programs failed to change alarming recidivism rates, but at least one study, Teuber and Powers (1953), suggested that a youth's chances of avoiding a life of crime are greater if he or she avoids mental health professionals! On the other hand, one of the most hopeful and successful treatment programs for delinquent and predelinquent youth has been developed by Montrose Wolf, Dean Fixsen, Lonnie and Elaine Phillips, and their many colleagues at the Achievement Place Research Project. The first report of this project appeared in the behavioral literature in 1968 (Phillips, 1968). In this study, Lonnie Phillips provided evidence that a token reinforcement program could be effective in changing the behavior of predelinquent youth who lived in a family-style, community-based behavioral teaching program, Achievement Place in Lawrence, Kansas. Phillips provided evidence that token reinforcement backed up by allowance, bicycle privileges, TV, games, tools, snacks, "freedom," staying up late, and coming home late from school, along with fines (response cost) for inappropriate behavior, were effective in reducing aggressive statements made by the boys, increasing bathroom cleanliness, punctuality, and homework, and decreasing the use of the word *ain't*. A reversal design showed that threats with no fines were ineffective; thus, tokens with backups and fines were the critical variables in changing the boys' behavior.

Achievement Place model homes thus incorporate several important components for a treatment approach to the modification of delinquent behaviors. First, the homes are community-based; that is, the boys or girls learn to change their behavior in the environment in which they have gotten into trouble. Perhaps this feature increases the likelihood of generalized treatment results from the home to the adolescents' natural environments. Also, members of the community take an active role in the development, implementation, and governing of an Achievement Place project.

Second, the behavior change environment is a family-style situation rather than an institutional setting. Most professionals agree that "normalized" behavior change can best be accomplished in environments that deviate as little as possible from natural home settings. This is in strong contrast to the institutional/correctional-setting environment.

Further, the Achievement Place program is based on an applied behavior analysis model, combining behavior change procedures with applied research on several components of the program.

Finally, the behavior change approach is considered an educational model delivered by professionally trained "teaching-parents" rather than paraprofessional correctional officers as might be found in a juvenile detention facility.

These ingredients are combined to promote a day-to-day life for the residents of Achievement Place that might resemble much of the routine of almost any family; however, more rigorous contingencies are applied to these youths than in the "average" family. The boys or girls have responsibilities that are clearly defined. Points are awarded for fulfilling responsibilities such as chores, homework, participation in self-improvement programs (in the home), helping other residents, and so on. Points are lost for rule violations and behavior not conducive to the youths' rehabilitation. The youths go to school each day, engage in family outings, family responsibilities, shopping, and so on.

One remarkable feature of the Achievement Place Project is that while most treatments come and go, Achievement Place has thrived and grown since 1966. In fact, there are many replications all over the country today. Undoubtedly, one of the major factors in this success is the constant and consistent behavioral research effort in evaluating Achievement Place. In the remainder of this section we briefly review some of those efforts.

In 1970, Bailey, Wolf, and Phillips looked at home-based reinforcement and the modification of classroom behavior. In their first experiment, these authors showed that when the boys were scored by their special summer school teacher with *yeses* and *nos* for studying all period and obeying class rules, their behavior in school improved markedly when *yeses* earned them privileges at Achievement Place. Experiments II and III demonstrated similar success with two Achievement Place boys in regular public school classrooms. Experiment III showed that fading from daily feedback and reinforcement was possible without diluting the success of the program.

Four aspects of self-reporting on the behavior of Achievement Place boys were studied by Fixsen, Phillips, and Wolf (1972). They found that: (1) the boys were not "naturally" reliable observers; (2) reliability of peer reporting was improved by providing training on behavioral definitions and making points contingent on agreement between each boy's peer report and an adult observer's report; (3) the reliability of self-recording was improved by adding a point contingency for agreements between self-reports and peer reports; and (4) giving self-reports and peer reports did not change the boy's room cleaning behavior.

One aspect of the Achievement Place Program is a limited self-government. To an extent, the youth are allowed to govern themselves including the making and changing of some rules and contingencies. Two experiments conducted by Fixsen, Phillips, and Wolf (1973) examined the role of some of the procedures in the boys' participation in the self-government system. One experiment showed that more boys participated in the discussion of consequences for a rule violation when they had complete responsibility for setting the consequences during "trials" than when teaching-parents set the consequences before the trial. The second experiment showed that more trials were called by the teaching-parents on peer-reported infractions than when the boys were also responsible for calling the trials.

The social validation and training of conversational skills in an Achievement Place for girls was accomplished by Minkin, Braukmann, Minkin, Timbers, Timbers, Fixsen, Phillips, and Wolf (1976). In the addition of training an important social skill (conversation) that helps the girls on the road to behavioral rehabilitation, the authors importantly validated the training by having independent outside observers rate the quality of the girls' conversational skills before and after training. Again, in a continuing search to improve an already successful program, Willner

FIGURE 7-4. Photo courtesy of Sandra Twardosz.

et al. (1977) trained and validated the youth-preferred social behaviors of teaching-parents. Further, it was demonstrated that these characteristics—such as calm and pleasant voice, offering to help, joking, positive feedback, and fairness (and several others)—could be trained. This study has added greatly to the training of teaching-parents and continued success of the program.

In many ways the Achievement Place Project research is symbolic of the whole field of applied behavior analysis. It deals with socially relevant behavior, has objectified it, turned treatment into a technology, has socially validated several treatment procedures and outcomes, has been shown to be cost-effective, and continues to be self-analytic and self-critical in attempts at ongoing improvement. While follow-up data (Wolf, 1977) have not been as strong as had been hoped for, this continual "self-analysis" will undoubtedly continue to improve the Achievement Place Project, until long-term data are as impressive as the short-term data.

CONCLUSIONS

In this chapter we have gone from looking at the arrangement of environments and behavior of infants and toddlers to the training of conversational skills in delinquent youth. Within that range we have also examined the training of skills to children, the modification of "everyday" behavior such as shopping, and the treatment of deviant behavior in the home. The application and refinement of behavior change technology with children offers the opportunity to provide children with enriched potential in their development which, in turn, provides them with increased freedom in the control of their own environments. The applications of behavior change principles with children might be the most important application of all.

REFERENCES

Arnold, J. E., Levine, A. G., & Patterson, G. R. Changes in sibling behavior following family intervention. *Journal of Consulting and Clinical Psychology,* 1975, *43,* 683–688.

Ayllon, T., Layman, D., & Kandel, H. J. A behavioral-educational alternative to drug control of hyperactive children. *Journal of Applied Behavior Analysis,* 1975, *8,* 137–146.

Ayllon, T., & Roberts, M. D. Eliminating discipline problems by strengthening academic performance. *Journal of Applied Behavior Analysis,* 1974, *7,* 71–76.

Azrin, N. *Behavioral methodology: Research design versus field testing.* Symposium paper presented at the 86th annual convention of the American Psychological Association, Toronto, 1978.

Azrin, N. H., & Foxx, R. M. *Toilet training in less than a day.* New York: Simon & Schuster, 1974.

Azrin, N. H., Sneed, T. J., & Foxx, R. M. Dry-bed training: Rapid elimination of childhood enuresis. *Behaviour Research and Therapy,* 1974, *12,* 147–156.

Azrin, N. H., & Thienes, P. M. Rapid elimination of enuresis by intensive learning without a conditioning apparatus. *Behavior Therapy,* 1978, *9,* 342–354.

Baer, D. M., Wolf, M. M., & Risley, T. R. Some current dimensions of applied behavior analysis. *Journal of Applied Behavior Analysis,* 1968, *1,* 91–97.

Bailey, J. S., Wolf, M. M., & Phillips, E. L. Home-based reinforcement and the modification of pre-delinquents' classroom behavior. *Journal of Applied Behavior Analysis,* 1970, *3,* 223–233.

Barnard, J. D., Christophersen, E. R., & Wolf, M. M. Teaching children appropriate shopping behavior through parent training in the supermarket setting. *Journal of Applied Behavior Analysis,* 1977, *10,* 49–59.

Bower, T. G. R. The visual world of infants. *Scientific American,* 1966, *215,* 80–92.

Brackbill, Y. Extinction of the smiling response in infants as a function of reinforcement schedule. *Child Development,* 1958, *29,* 115–124.

Butler, J. F. The toilet training success of parents after reading *Toilet training in less than a day. Behavior Therapy,* 1976, *7,* 185–191.

Chiang, S. J., Iwata, B. A., & Dorsey, M. F. Elimination of disruptive bus riding behavior via token reinforcement on a "distance-based" schedule. *Education and Treatment of Children,* 1979, *2,* 101–109.

Christophersen, E. R. Children's behavior during automobile rides: Do car seats make a difference? *Pediatrics,* 1977, *60,* 69–74.

Christophersen, E. R., Arnold, C. M., Hill, D. W., & Quilitch, H. R. The home point system: Token reinforcement procedures for application by parents of children with behavior problems. *Journal of Applied Behavior Analysis,* 1972, *5,* 485–497.

Clark, H. B., Greene, B. F., Macrae, J. W., McNees, M. P., Davis, J. L., & Risley, T. R. A parent advice package for family shopping trips: Development and evaluation. *Journal of Applied Behavior Analysis,* 1977, *10,* 605–624.

Doke, L. A., & Risley, T. R. The organization of day-care environments: Required vs. optional activities. *Journal of Applied Behavior Analysis,* 1972, *5,* 405–420.

Doleys, D. M., Ciminero, A. R., Tollison, J. W., Williams, C. L., & Wells, K. C. Dry bed training and retention control training: A comparison. *Behavior Therapy,* 1977, *8,* 541–548.

Eyberg, S. M., & Johnson, S. M. Multiple assessment of behavior modification with families: Effects of contingency contracting and order of treated problems. *Journal of Consulting and Clinical Psychology,* 1974, *42,* 594–606.

Fixsen, D. L., Phillips, E. L., & Wolf, M. M. Achievement Place: The reliability of self-reporting and peer-reporting and their effects on behavior. *Journal of Applied Behavior Analysis,* 1972, *5,* 19–30.

Fixsen, D. L., Phillips, E. L., & Wolf, M. M. Achievement Place: Experiments in self-government with pre-delinquents. *Journal of Applied Behavior Analysis,* 1973, *6,* 31–47.

Forehand, R., Sturgis, E. T., McMahon, R. J., Aguar, D., Green, K., Wells, K. G., & Breiner, J. Parent behavioral training to modify child noncompliance: Treatment generalization across time and from home to school. *Behavior Modification,* in press.

Foxx, R. H., & Azrin, N. H. Dry pants: A rapid method of toilet training children. *Behaviour Research and Therapy,* 1973, *11,* 435–442.

Friedlander, B. Z. Automated measurement of differential operant performance in human infants. *American Psychologist,* 1961, *16,* 350.

Ginott, H. G. *Between parent and child.* New York: Macmillan, 1965.

Gordon, T. *Parent effectiveness training.* New York: Peter H. Wyden, 1975.

Greene, B. F., Barber, F. H., & Bailey, J. B. An analysis and education of disruptive behavior on school buses. *Journal of Applied Behavior Analysis,* in press.

Greene, B. F., Clark, H. B., & Risley, T. R. *Shopping with children: Advice for parents.* San Rafael, Calif.: Academic Therapy Publications, 1977.

Gump, P. V. Intra setting analysis: The third grade classroom as a special but instructive case. In E. P. Willems & H. L. Rausch (Eds.), *Naturalistic viewpoints in psychological research.* New York: Holt, Rinehart & Winston, 1969.

Hall, R. V., Axelrod, S., Tyler, L., Grief, E., Jones, F. C., & Robertson, R. Modification of behavior problems in the home with a parent as observer and experimenter. *Journal of Applied Behavior Analysis*, 1972, *5*, 53–64.

Herbert-Jackson, E., O'Brien, M., Porterfield, J., & Risley, T. *The infant center: A complete guide to organizing and managing infant daycare*. Baltimore: University Park Press, 1977.

Herbert-Jackson, E., & Risley, T. R. Behavioral nutrition: Consumption of foods of the future by toddlers. *Journal of Applied Behavior Analysis*, 1977, *10*, 407–413.

Humphreys, L., Forehand, R., McMahon, R., & Roberts, M. Parental behavioral training to modify child noncompliance: Effects on untreated siblings. *Journal of Behavior Therapy and Experimental Psychology*, in press.

Hursh, D. E., & Sherman, J. A. The effects of parent-presented models and praise on the vocal behavior of their children. *Journal of Experimental Child Psychology*, 1973, *15*, 328–339.

Ilg, F., & Ames, L. B. *Child behavior from birth to ten*. New York: Harper & Row, 1955.

Jewett, J., & Clark, H. B. Teaching preschoolers to use appropriate dinnertime conversation: An analysis from school to home. *Behavior Therapy*, 1979, *10*, 589–605.

Knight, M. E., & McKenzie, H. S. Elimination of bedtime thumbsucking in home settings through contingent reading. *Journal of Applied Behavior Analysis*, 1974, *7*, 33–38.

LeLaurin, K., & Risley, T. R. The organization of daycare environments: "Zone" versus "man-to-man" staff assignments. *Journal of Applied Behavior Analysis*, 1972, *5*, 225–232.

Leuba, C., & Friedlander, B. Z. Effects of controlled audio-visual reinforcement on infants' manipulative play in the home. *Journal of Experimental Child Psychology*, 1968, *6*, 87–89.

Lovibond, S. H. *Conditioning and enuresis*. New York: Macmillan, 1964.

Lutzker, J. R., & Drake, J. A. *A comparison of trainer-training techniques to produce rapid toilet training in children*. Paper presented at the 84th Annual Convention of the American Psychological Association, Washington, D.C., 1976.

Madsen, C. H., Hoffman, M., Thomas, D. R., Koropsak, E., & Madsen, C. K. Comparisons of toilet training techniques. In D. M. Gelfand (Ed.), *Social learning in childhood*. Belmont, Calif.: Brooks/Cole, 1969.

Maloney, K. B., & Hopkins, B. L. The modification of sentence structure and its relationship to subjective judgments of creativity in writing. *Journal of Applied Behavior Analysis*, 1973, *6*, 425–433.

Martin, J. A. Effects of positive and negative adult-child interactions on children's task performance and task preferences. *Journal of Experimental Child Psychology*, 1977, *23*, 493–502.

Matson, J. L., & Ollendick, T. H. Issues in toilet training normal children. *Behavior Therapy*, 1977, *8*, 549–553.

McMahon, R. S., Griest, D. L., Forehand, R., & Odgen, J. K. *Effects of knowledge of social learning principles on enhancing treatment outcome and generalization in a parent training program*. Paper presented as a part of a symposium, "Deviant Family Systems," at the 13th Annual Convention of the Association for the Advancement of Behavior Therapy. San Francisco, December 13–16, 1979.

Minkin, N., Braukmann, C. J., Minkin, B. L., Timbers, G. D., Timbers, B. J., Fixsen, D. L., Phillips, E. L., & Wolf, M. M. The social validation and training of conversational skills. *Journal of Applied Behavior Analysis*, 1976, *9*, 127–139.

Moore, M. C. *An examination of the response-response relationship between nocturnal enuresis and oppositional behavior: An extension and replication of Nordquist*. Unpublished thesis, University of the Pacific, 1977.

Mowrer, O. H., & Mowrer, W. M. Enuresis—A method for its study and treatment. *American Journal of Orthopsychiatry*, 1938, *8*, 436–459.

Nordquist, V. M. The modification of a child's enuresis: Some response-response relationships. *Journal of Applied Behavior Analysis*, 1971, *4*, 241–247.

O'Leary, K. D. Pills or skills for hyperactive children. *Journal of Applied Behavior Analysis,* 1980, *13,* 191–204.

Patterson, G. R. *Families: Applications of social learning to family life.* Champaign, Ill.: Research Press, 1971.

Patterson, G. R., & Gullion, M. E. *Living with children: New methods for parents and teachers.* Champaign, Ill.: Research Press, 1968.

Peed, S., Roberts, M., & Forehand, R. Evaluation of the effectiveness of a standardized parent training program in altering the interaction of mothers and their noncompliant children. *Behavior Modification,* 1977, *1,* 323–350.

Phillips, E. L. Achievement Place: Token reinforcement procedures in a home-style rehabilitation setting for "pre-delinquent" boys. *Journal of Applied Behavior Analysis,* 1968, *1,* 213–223.

Quilitch, H. R., Christophersen, E. R., & Risley, T. R. The evaluation of children's play materials. *Journal of Applied Behavior Analysis,* 1977, *10,* 501–502.

Reisinger, J. J., & Ora, J. P. Parent-child clinic and home interaction during toddler management training. *Behavior Therapy,* 1977, *8,* 771–786.

Rekers, G. A., & Lovaas, O. I. Behavioral treatment of deviant sex-role behaviors in a male child. *Journal of Applied Behavior Analysis,* 1974, *7,* 173–190.

Rheingold, H. L., Gewirtz, J. L., & Ross, H. W. Social conditioning of vocalizations in the infant. *Journal of Comparative and Physiological Psychology,* 1959, *52,* 68–73.

Roberts, M. W., Forehand, R., McMahon, R., & Roberts, M. The effect of parental instruction-giving on child compliance. *Behavior Therapy,* in press.

Sajwaj, T., Libet, J., & Agras, S. Lemon-juice therapy: The control of life-threatening rumination in a six-month-old infant. *Journal of Applied Behavior Analysis,* 1974, *7,* 557–563.

Shafto, F., & Sulzbacher, S. Comparing treatment tactics with a hyperactive preschool child: Stimulant medication and programmed teacher intervention. *Journal of Applied Behavior Analysis,* 1977, *10,* 13–20.

Spock, B. *Baby and child care.* New York: Pocket Books, 1976.

Stokes, T. F., & Baer, D. M. An implicit technology of generalization. *Journal of Applied Behavior Analysis,* 1977, *10,* 349–367.

Teuber, H. L., & Powers, E. Evaluating therapy in a delinquency prevention program. *Psychiatric Treatment,* 1953, *21,* 138–147.

Twardosz, S., Cataldo, M. F., & Risley, T. R. An open environment design for infant and toddler care. *Journal of Applied Behavior Analysis,* 1974, *7,* 529–546.

Wahler, R. G. Setting generality: Some specific and general effects on child behavior therapy. *Journal of Applied Behavior Analysis,* 1969, *2,* 239–246.

Wahler, R. G., Afton, A. D., & Fox, J. J. The multiply entrapped parent: Some new problems in parent training. *Education and Treatment of Children,* 1979, *2,* 279–286.

Wahler, R. G., Berland, R. M., & Coe, T. D. Generalization process in child behavior change. In B. B. Lahey & A. E. Kazdin (Eds.), *Advances in clinical child psychology* (Vol. 2). New York: Plenum Press, 1979.

Wahler, R. G., & Fox, J. J. Solitary toy play and time out: A family treatment package for children with aggressive and oppositional behavior. *Journal of Applied Behavior Analysis,* 1980, *13,* 23–29.

Watson, J. S. The development and generalization of "contingency awareness" in early infancy: Some hypotheses. *Merrill Palmer Quarterly,* 1966, *12,* 123–136.

Willner, A. G., Braukmann, C. J., Kirigin, K. A., Fixsen, D. L., Phillips, E. L., & Wolf, M. M. The training and validation of youth-preferred social behaviors of child-care personnel. *Journal of Applied Behavior Analysis,* 1977, *10,* 219–230.

Wolf, M. M. *Achievement Place: Treatment of delinquents and predelinquents in a community-based group home program.* Presented at California Behavior Analysis Conference: Training and the developmentally disabled, 1977.

Wulbert, M., & Dries, R. The relative efficacy of methylphenidate (Ritalin) and behavior-modification techniques in the treatment of hyperactive child. *Journal of Applied Behavior Analysis,* 1977, *10,* 21–31.

Wyckoff, J. L. *A clinical replication of the dry bed enuresis procedure with parents as trainers.* Paper presented at the 86th annual convention of the American Psychological Association, Toronto, 1978.

Yates, A. J. *Behavior therapy.* New York: Wiley, 1969.

Yeaton, W. H., & Bailey, J. B. Teaching pedestrian skills to young children: An analysis and one-year follow-up. *Journal of Applied Behavior Analysis,* 1978, *11,* 315–330.

CHAPTER 8

Classrooms

In the last chapter we saw how behavior change principles have been applied with children in care facilities, homes, grocery stores, and automobiles. In this chapter we examine the applications of behavior change principles in classrooms from preschools to college—applications that have included behavior control, academic performance, creativity, and more—and we analyze such traditional tools as homework, lecturing, and tutoring. Finally, we see how a behavioral approach to college teaching has produced some big changes in many halls of higher education.

In an address before the American Psychological Association in 1968, Dr. Sidney Bijou outlined "What Psychology Has to Offer Education—Now" (Bijou, 1970). In his remarks, Dr. Bijou detailed what a behavioral approach to education should include, and in doing so, predicted what actually did happen in the following decade. Among his remarks, he noted,

> We can offer a set of concepts and principles derived exclusively from experimental research; we can offer a methodology for applying these concepts and principles directly to teaching practices; we can offer a research design which deals with changes in the individual child (rather than inferring them from group averages); and we can offer a philosophy of science which insists on observable accounts of the relationships between individual behavior and its determining conditions [p. 66].[1]

He described the analysis of functional relationships among variables including the pupil's behavior, the teacher's behavior, the instructional materials, reinforcement contingencies, and other conditions of the setting. He notes that in his book on *The Technology of Teaching,* Skinner (1968) describes teaching as a situation in which the teacher arranges the contingencies of reinforcement to expedite learning by the child.

Bijou addressed another issue of interest to many people concerned about behavioral approaches to education: whether edible and other tangible reinforcers were to be the major tools of behavior change in the classroom. Bijou argued, however, that contrived reinforcers—such as indications of progress, approval, and privilege—are not always meaningful to a child. Bijou recommended the following behavior analysis process for classrooms (compare the process outlined in Chapter 2):

1. state in objective terms the desired or terminal goal behavior;
2. assess the child's behavioral repertoire relevant to the task;
3. arrange in sequence the stimulus material or behavioral criteria for reinforcement;
4. start the child on that unit in the sequence to which he can respond correctly about 90% of the time;
5. manage the contingencies of reinforcement with the aid of teaching machines and other devices to strengthen successive approximations to terminal behavior and to build conditioned reinforcers that are intrinsic to the task;
6. keep records of the child's responses as a basis for modifying the materials and teaching procedures.

[1]From "What Psychology Has to Offer Education—Now," by S. W. Bijou. In *Journal of Applied Behavior Analysis,* 1970, *3,* 65–71. Copyright 1970 by the Society for the Experimental Analysis of Behavior, Inc. This and all other quotations from this source are reprinted by permission.

We should note that, although most of Bijou's recommendations have come to pass, teaching machines have never become as widely used as Skinner had proposed. Bijou's final recommendation was that educators themselves learn behavior change principles.

PRESCHOOL

As the studies examined in Chapter 7 have shown, some cherished concepts about children may not withstand the test of scientific scrutiny. Several of the studies in this section challenge either traditionally held concepts or practices with preschool children.

As parents and teachers, we often find ourselves giving elaborate instructions to children (and college students and our friends!) in attempts to instruct them or establish what we call instructional control. After casual preschool observations, Miller and LeBlanc (1973) were concerned that preschool children may, in fact, tune out instructions and thus perform less well if those instructions are too lengthy or detailed. They therefore conducted a study that compared the acquisition of the skill of matching a letter symbol to its sound during minimal instruction and during detailed instruction. The results showed minimal instruction to be superior to detailed instruction for acquiring preacademic skills. Further, it appeared that, if anything, detailed instructions impeded performance by confusing the children. Here we see another very important lesson provided to us by research utilizing behavioral procedures with children.

Have you ever tried to teach a young child to tie his or her own shoes? It can become a tiresome experience for the adult and the child. Without any other exposure to training procedures, teaching shoe tying is usually quite haphazard. Most often the adult gets his or her big hands in the way, which, among other things, makes it difficult for the child to see the model attempted by the adult. Margaret Cooper, Judith LeBlanc, and Barbara Etzel, at the University of Kansas, developed, refined, and tested a set of procedures that make for rapid, painless, nearly errorless learning of shoe tying by young children (Cooper, LeBlanc, & Etzel, 1968; Cooper & Etzel, 1969). The procedures make use of many behavior change procedures (stimulus control, shaping, fading, chaining, modeling, and token and social reinforcement). The training starts out, not on the child's own shoe, but with a shoe nailed to a board with a black and a white square painted in opposite corners. In addition, the shoe has one extra-long black shoelace and one extra-long white shoelace. Each lace also has a piece of tape on it. Each step of the program is modeled for the child by the adult; then the child is asked to imitate. The first step involves taking the black lace and having it "fly" (crossing it over) to the black square at the top, opposite side of the board. The white lace "flies" to the opposite white box and the child has learned, without effort, to cross the laces. Many similar tricks are used in the program. The adult's hands never get in the child's way. Research on the program showed rapid skill acquisition (with quick generalization to their own shoes) by most of the children tested.[2] Teaching preschool children to tie their own

[2]For a detailed description of the program, write to: Dr. Barbara Etzel, Department of Human Development, University of Kansas, Lawrence, KS 66045.

shoes is a safety measure, a convenience, and a boost to their self-esteem. Again in the Kansas preschool, we see "old ways" challenged and replaced by a functional behavioral technology.

Many detractors of behavior analysis have argued that while behavior change specialists might be able to demonstrate proficiency in the development of such concrete skills as toilet training and shoe tying, they have no mechanisms for dealing with the more ethereal aspects of human development such as creativity. Given the comparatively short history of behavior analysis, it really did not take very long for behavior analysts to start studying—as they did other areas of human development—the development of creativity in children. Dr. Elizabeth Goetz and her colleagues at the University of Kansas have been the primary researchers involved in the behavior analysis of creativity. In addition, Maloney and Hopkins (1973) were among the first to study creativity by looking at the composition skills of fourth, fifth, and sixth graders. In their study, Maloney and Hopkins (1973) reinforced particular grammatical forms in the children's compositions and found generality in the children's writing; that is, the children started showing new forms without being directly reinforced for them. Perhaps, most importantly, independent raters scored the children's essays as being, in fact, more creative.

Goetz and her associates have examined a variety of creative responses in preschool children. They have looked at blockbuilding, easel painting, felt-pen drawing, Lego building, and dancing. They have analyzed the effects of descriptive social praise on creative blockbuilding with three preschool girls (Goetz & Baer, 1973). After baseline measures of form diversity with the blocks had been established, "treatment" with each successive child involved descriptive social praise by the teacher for form diversity within a single construction. As this occurred, the children started generating all kinds of new forms. A DRO reversal condition showed that the occurrence of this generalized creativity was clearly a function of the reinforcement procedures. In 1972, Goetz and Salmonson applied similar procedures with three preschoolers in examining form diversity in easel painting. Fallon and Goetz (1975) did the same with felt-pen drawings; their study included 6–10-week follow-ups. The two children who had received the most reinforcement during their initial training showed considerable form diversity during follow-up (even though the reinforcement contingencies had been removed). The third child, who had received less reinforcement during training, did not do as well during the follow-up, but showed more form diversity than she had during baseline. Thus, using discrete measures, applied behavioral experimental designs, and a little creativity of their own, these researchers have begun to explore areas of child development previously not thought to be the domain of the behaviorist. It appears from these studies that if we conceive of creativity as the exhibiting of novel (and initially unreinforced) responses, we can show that our traditional behavior change concepts apply to the development and production of creative responses. Much exciting work in this area lies ahead.

Sharing is something most adults feel is important for young children to learn. The operators of many preschools like to promote the notion that sharing is something that the preschool environment fosters. Casual observation at a preschool might lead you to a different conclusion. If you watch children and their

FIGURE 8-1.   Photo courtesy of Shirley O'Brien.

teachers at preschool you will notice that although considerable efforts are made to get the children to share, the efforts are often not fruitful. Barton and Osborne (1978) have reported on the development of classroom sharing by a teacher who used positive practice procedures. Three girls and two boys in a kindergarten at the Utah School for the Deaf served as the subjects in this study. Baseline data showed low rates of sharing by the children. The positive practice procedure involved having the teacher sequentially check the students for nonsharing. When he discovered a nonsharing child, the child was put through "verbal" positive practice sharing. The child took the role of either initiator or acceptor. The initiator role required an invitation to share; the acceptor role involved an agreement to share. When the child was found not to be sharing, he or she was required to go through the positive practice three times. The procedures brought a considerable increase in sharing by all the children. Critically, the procedures produced no apparent emotional side effects for the children and were easily implemented by, and without considerable disruption for, the teacher. Thus, if sharing can also be considered a skill, we have yet another example of behavior change procedures being used to facilitate the development of functional, highly adaptive social behavior of young children.

In another study, Barton and Ascione (1979) investigated three approaches to facilitating verbal and physical sharing in children enrolled in a university preschool. The generality and durability of the trained behaviors were also examined. After a free play period, the children were taught to share physically and verbally.

The training included a rationale on the importance of sharing verbal instructions, modeling by a trained child, rehearsal by the child in training, and prompting and praise from the experimenter when the child practiced sharing. A second group of children was not trained. After each free play observation session, the children were observed in a different setting. Follow-up observations were conducted four weeks after training had terminated. Generality of the training showed up in children who had been taught to share verbally. Weak generalization occurred for children who had been taught to share verbally and physically, and no generality was shown in children who were taught only physical sharing. These results suggest that a considerable training effort is necessary to get preschool children to demonstrate good sharing skills.

Three Head Start children (each 4 years old) were the subjects of a study reported by Bornstein and Quevillon (1976), who examined the effects of a self-instructional package on these "overactive" boys. The self-instructional package consisted of a two-hour training session during which the experimenter: (1) modelled a task while talking aloud to himself; (2) had the boy perform the task under the verbal instructions of the experimenter; (3) had the boy engage in the task while talking aloud to himself with the experimenter whispering instructions; (4) had the boy whisper while the experimenter made lip movements, but no sound; (5) had the boy perform the task while moving his lips, but making no sound; (6) had the subject perform the task with covert self-instruction (thought to himself). The self instructions were items such as, "What does the teacher want me to do? I'm supposed to copy the picture. First I draw a line, then I . . . . I did really well on that one." The dependent measures were the percentage of on-task behaviors in class. The multiple baseline design across subjects showed that the self-instructional package increased on-task behavior almost fourfold with good follow-up results 90 days later.

If self-instructional approaches were regularly so effective, they would have certain advantages over teacher-implemented techniques because they do not involve teacher training and a subsequent modification of teacher behavior. Some disappointing results were reported by Friedling and O'Leary (1979), who tried to replicate the Bornstein and Quevillon (1976) self-instructional training procedures with four hyperactive second and third graders. On-task behavior and academic performance in reading and arithmetic served as the dependent measures of this study. The results were compared to the performance of a group of hyperactive children who received attention and irrelevant practice. Basically, there was a complete failure to replicate Bornstein and Quevillon's results. The self-instructional program did not facilitate on-task or academic performance, and the results with the experimental children were no better than with the attention-practice group of children. However, when both groups of children were given tokens for on-task behavior, it improved dramatically. Friedling and O'Leary are cautious in interpreting their results; they point out that perhaps the older children in their study had longer histories of academic and behavior problems in the classroom than the preschool children studied by Bornstein and Quevillon. We (the authors) tend to be skeptical of "cognitive" behavior change procedures and feel that their value, at best, is in supplementing more direct techniques.

BEHAVIOR CONTROL

An advantage in teaching children appropriate behavior in the classroom relates to the changes they make throughout their school careers. If a child gets labeled as a chronic problem, every year he risks each new teacher's behaving differently toward him—something that undoubtedly furthers the problem. In 1970, Broden, Bruce, Mitchell, Carter, and Hall studied the behavior of two highly disruptive second grade boys in a school in an economically deprived neighborhood. They examined the effects of teacher attention, a variable that had been clearly shown to be a powerful reinforcer with younger children, on the attending behavior of the two boys. After baseline, in the first experimental phase, the teacher increased the amount of attention one of the boys, Edwin, received contingent upon attending to his tasks. Not only did this differential attention procedure affect Edwin's attending, it also—to a lesser but not insignificant way—positively affected Greg's (the boy who sat next to Edwin). In the next phase of the study, differential attention was provided to Greg and not to Edwin. This caused Greg's behavior to continue to improve, but decreased Edwin's improvements. When both boys received the teacher's attention for their attending behavior, both displayed high rates. Thus, this study showed that a teacher's attention can be a powerful reinforcer for second grade boys, and that there can be a positive "spillover" effect whereby reinforcing one child produces positive behavior change in a second child.

Three different reinforcement procedures were effective in reducing inappropriate behavior in a classroom of trainable mentally retarded children (Deitz & Repp, 1973). In one study, the talking-out behavior of an 11-year-old boy was decreased by allowing him five minutes of free time for a talk-out rate of 0.06 per minute. Thus, the challenge of being well behaved in the classroom was positively reinforced with an easily arranged, available contingency, free time. In a second study, talking-out by the entire class was reduced by a DRL schedule of reinforcement that provided two pieces of candy at the end of the day for rates of talking less than 0.10 per minute. In a third study, inappropriate verbalizations of an entire high school business class were eliminated by a DRL contingency that gradually reduced the limits to zero. When the contingency was met, the class was allowed to use Friday as a free day. Although these free-time contingencies might seem to detract from overall study time in class, it should be remembered that teachers typically spend inordinate amounts of time attending to deviant classroom behavior—so a little free time is well worth it, for both teachers and students, for it produces a more functional classroom environment. Of considerable importance in these three studies is that the teachers reported ease in using the procedures.

How do grade school students regard their disruptive peers? This question was examined by using sociometric measures in addition to direct behavioral observations of children in a first grade classroom (Drabman, Spitalnik, & Spitalnik, 1974). The class was divided into four groups. Baseline data were gathered on a disruptive child and a well-behaved child in each group. Four different types of token reinforcement programs were introduced to each of the four groups after baseline. Every ten days the token programs were switched among the four groups of children so that eventually each group of children was exposed to each of the following four programs: (1) each child received points redeemable for free time individually dependent on his or her behavior; (2) 15 minutes of free time was allotted to the whole group depending on the behavior (improvement) of the most disruptive child; (3) the number of minutes of free time allotted to the whole group was calculated as a function of the behavior of the highest scoring child (for example, 12 points = 12 minutes, 13 = 13, and so on, up to 15 minutes maximum); (4) free time was allotted to the group on the basis of points earned by a randomly chosen child. The sociometric measures examined responsibility, friendship, and funniness. All the systems were effective in reducing disruption, including, perhaps surprisingly, program four. In fact, in terms of ease of use and preference, the group in which free time was allotted according to the behavior of a randomly chosen child was the most functional. The sociometric data showed that disruptive children were rated by their peers as more responsible when reinforcement was determined by the behavior of the most disruptive child. The authors point out the value not only of producing favorable behavior change through simple, cost-effective procedures, but also of producing the positive side effect of improving problem children's sociometric status.

One of the earliest studies using group contingencies in the classroom was reported by Schmidt and Ulrich (1969). The subjects were 29 fourth-graders in a free-study period. As often is the case in study hall, the noise level was excessive, which made it difficult for any children to concentrate. During baseline, a sound-level meter was used in the classroom. As the informal observations had noted, the sound meter showed noise levels to be quite high during baseline. A simple contingency was implemented whereby reinforcement consisted of a two-minute addition to the gym period and a two-minute break immediately contingent upon a ten-minute period of unbroken quiet. If the sound level went higher than 42 decibels, the timer was set for a full ten minutes, thus delaying breaks. The procedure was immediately and durably effective in quieting the children. Similar procedures were used to modify out-of-seat behavior. Although there was, unfortunately, no report from the authors, it might be assumed that the children accomplished more studying when the study hall was quieter and the children were in their seats. Further, the children undoubtedly enjoyed experiencing the procedures, for in addition to the challenge of trying to beat the timer, they were able to earn more breaks and longer gym periods.

An innovative, and historically early, behavioral classroom study was reported in 1969 by Barrish, Saunders, and Wolf. They developed and evaluated an easy-to-use, effective package involving individual contingencies for group consequences, which they called the Good Behavior Game. Using a combined multiple baseline (across time and settings) and reversal design, the dramatic effects of the game were demonstrated. As can be seen in Figure 8-2, the rates of talking-out and out-of-seat of the fourth graders in their math and reading periods were dramatically reduced. The Good Behavior Game involves dividing the class into two teams and posting the class rules. Whenever a child violates one of the classroom rules, a mark is tallied against his or her team. At the end of the day, the team with the lowest number of points (as in golf) wins, or, if both teams score below a gradually

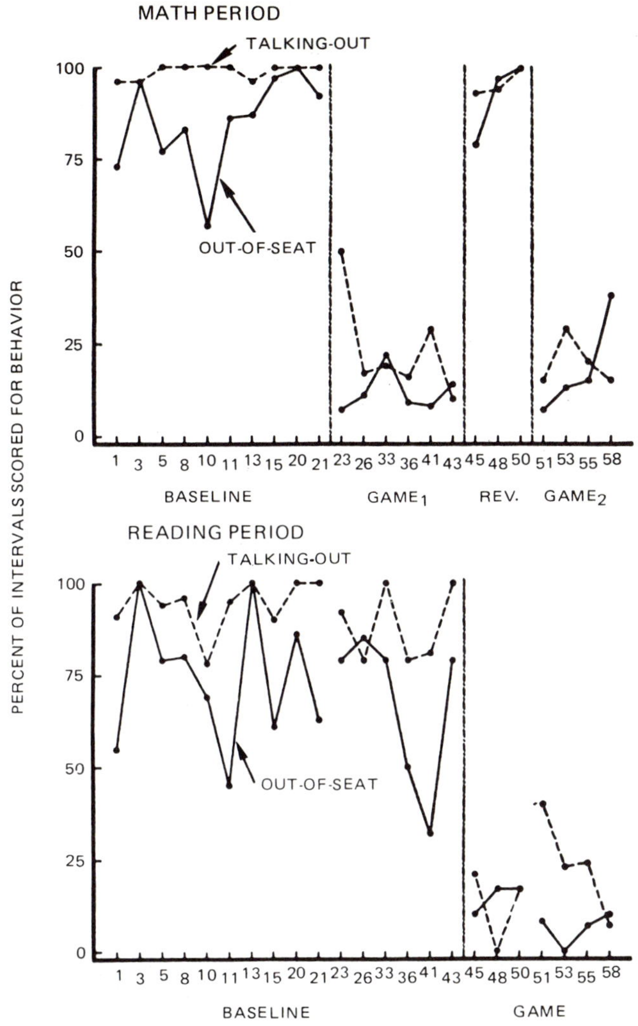

FIGURE 8-2.   Percent of 1-minute intervals scored by an observer as containing talking-out and out-of-seat behaviors occurring in a classroom of 24 fourth-grade school children during math and reading periods. In the baseline conditions the teacher attempted to manage the disruptive classroom behavior in her usual manner. During the game conditions, out-of-seat and talking-out responses by a student resulted in a possible loss of privileges for the student and the team. (From "Good Behavior Game: Effects of Individual Contingencies for Group Consequences on Disruptive Behavior in a Classroom," by H. H. Barrish, M. Saunders, and M. M. Wolf. In *Journal of Applied Behavior Analysis*, 1969, *2*, 119–124. Copyright 1969 by the Society for the Experimental Analysis of Behavior, Inc. Reprinted by permission.)

faded criterion, both teams win. Winners receive easily available privileges such as extra recess, lining up privileges at lunch, badges, and so on. In this first study, and in some of the replications we will review, it turned out that no team ever lost. Both the children and teacher were satisfied with playing the Good Behavior Game and with its effect on behavior. Perhaps a minor drawback to the Good Behavior Game is that it focuses on "bad" rather than "good" behavior, although the results do produce "good" behavior, and, importantly, children like it.

A replication and systematic analysis of the Good Behavior Game was done by Medland and Stachnik (1972). Two groups of children in a fifth grade reading class were exposed to: baseline, the game including red lights for inappropriate behavior and green lights for appropriate behavior, a condition of "rules" only, rules plus lights alone, and a return to the game plus lights. The two game conditions reduced disruptive behavior by 97% and 99%. After being associated with the game, rules and lights without backup game privileges were also effective in reducing out-of-seat and disruptive behavior and increasing hand-raising.

Concerned that children could become bored with the Good Behavior Game, White and Lutzker (1974) examined the ways in which the game could be modified without disrupting its overall positive effects. After baseline data showed a 60% rate of disruptive behavior, the Good Behavior Game was played in a manner almost identical to the original game as described by Barrish, Saunders, and Wolf (1969). The first game condition produced a dramatic reduction of the highly disruptive behavior of a seventh/eighth grade music appreciation class (during baseline conditions casual observation noted little appreciation of music!). A brief return to baseline conditions without the game saw disruptive behavior return to over 60%. The next three conditions involved changing characteristics of the game to see how those changes affected behavior. Condition "C" was identical to the original game, except the teacher assigned new teams. Some of the students had complained about being required to sit on the same side of the room with their teammates rather than anywhere they wanted, so the next condition ("D") was run to see what differences in behavior, if any, there would be with teacher-determined teams, but no required seating. The final condition ("E") involved the students choosing their own teams and the teacher assigning the seating. The results were that all three new conditions significantly reduced problem behavior. It appears that teacher-assigned teams along with assigned seating was the most effective, but the design of the study does not allow for a firm conclusion to that effect. (That is, only a counterbalanced design with the same conditions run in a different sequence in another classroom could confirm this suggestion.) The teacher, principal, and students were delighted with the results and the teacher continued to use variations of the Good Behavior Game with success for the remainder of the entire school year. She did remark, however, that discussions with the class about daily and weekly reinforcers sometimes became too lengthy at the beginning of class and that sometimes she had to strain to come up with ideas for novel and desired reinforcers. Nonetheless, she had chosen some creative and relevant ones, such as playing folk music on her guitar, awarding pennants denoting winners of the game, and running out to a far corner of the yard to scream for five minutes (the students, not the teacher!).

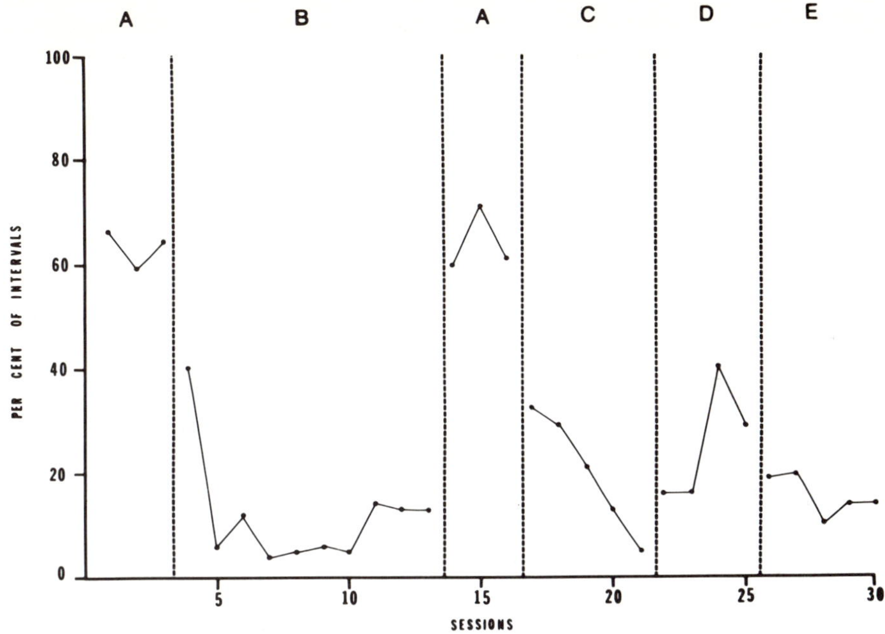

FIGURE 8-3.   A = baseline; B = Good Behavior Game; A = Baseline; C = Good Behavior Game with new team; D = Good Behavior Game, no seating assignment; E = Good Behavior Game with student-selected team and teacher-selected seating. (From *Good Behavior Game: A further component analysis,* by S. A. White & J. R. Lutzker. Paper presented at the 82nd Annual Convention of the American Psychological Association, New Orleans, August 1974.)

Before we move on, one more replication of the Good Behavior Game deserves mention. Harris and Sherman (1973a) reported the game to be effective in reducing talking-out and out-of-seat in two classrooms. A component analysis showed the effective aspects of the game to be the division of the class into teams, consequences for the winning team(s), and established criteria for winning. Perhaps slightly discouraging was that despite the dramatic reduction of disruptive behavior, academic performance (math and English) showed only modest improvement.

Several other contingencies affecting classroom behavior have also been studied. O'Leary, Kaufman, Kass, and Drabman (1970) looked at loud versus soft reprimands by the teacher and the way they affected children in five different classrooms. Soft reprimands delivered personally to the disruptive students were considerably more effective than loud reprimands that could be heard by all of the class members. (The loud reprimands seemed to *increase* disruptive behavior!)

Martin (1977) found that children worked harder (on task) under reprimand conditions over ignoring and praise, but whenever given a choice of tasks, they *never* chose the task on which they had been reprimanded. This is an important finding to consider when choosing among classroom behavior control strategies.

A timeout room (a quiet place) was used by Lahey, McNees, and McNees (1973) to reduce the frequent occurrences of an "obscene verbal tic" made by a 10-year-old "educable mentally retarded" student. The timeout procedure was used only after a treatment of attempted satiation (having the boy rapidly repeat the obscene word over and over again) reduced, but did not eliminate the problem behavior.

In a study which sought to determine the controls of disruptive classroom behavior, Solomon and Wahler (1973) found that peer reinforcement (laughing, smiling, and so on) was more frequently directed at, and responsible for maintaining more, disruptive behavior than was teacher attention. These researchers were then able to teach children to modify their peers' disruptive behavior by rearranging the social contingencies in the same manner as has been suggested for parents and teachers, attending to appropriate behavior and ignoring inappropriate behavior.

ETHICAL CONCERNS

As in many other areas of application, the use of behavior change procedures in classrooms has not been without controversy. Concerned that behavior modification in the classroom was just another attempt to stifle grade school children, Winett and Winkler (1972) fired charges at the field that our goal was to have children "be still, be quiet, be docile." In reaching their conclusion, these authors reviewed several journal articles on behavior modification in the classroom which focused on behavior control. They contended that the behavioral professional was in danger of becoming a "hired gun" for traditional education. They called for behavior change professionals to focus their powerful and practical technology on the development of open classrooms and behavioral self-management programs for grade school children.

In a rejoinder to Winett and Winkler (1972), O'Leary (1972) presented a cogent argument that while every behavior change professional should always be concerned with the ethics of the behavior he or she is being asked to change, little evidence was presented that open classrooms were necessarily functional for all children or that the demonstration of appropriate classroom behavior was necessarily bad for children. In fact, O'Leary suggested that teaching children classroom decorum may be providing them with an important skill that would be useful to them now and later in other settings. In addition, Winett and Winkler had seriously omitted from their discussion many articles that dealt with other than mere behavioral control. One of the major areas of investigation by the behavioral classroom researcher has been using the technology to challenge many traditional educational concepts. Thus, O'Leary accuses Winett and Winkler of producing a straw-man model child in their argument.

Perhaps this issue has no real answer. As you will see in several of the following studies reviewed in this chapter, many issues other than behavior control have been investigated since Winett and Winkler presented their argument. On one hand we need to thank them for calling our attention to the issue, and on the other hand, O'Leary might be correct in saying that it is a straw-man issue. Perhaps you will form your own opinion after reading this chapter.

TEACHER BEHAVIOR

Token economies—the use of points, chips, or other "bridging the gap" reinforcers backed up by privileges and tangible reinforcers—have been demonstrated to be effective in classrooms representing a broad range of ages of the students and a broad range of educational achievements (Broden, Hall, Dunlap, & Clark, 1970; McLaughlin & Malaby, 1972). In a slightly different "twist," researchers at the University of Connecticut took advantage of a token economy in a transitional classroom of "would-be" second graders to analyze the effect of the system on the teacher's behavior toward the children (Breyer & Allen, 1975). While the on-task behavior of the students improved, it was also found that the token economy produced higher rates of positive and negative teacher comments than did baseline conditions. These results suggest that in trying to modify teacher behavior in order to produce changes in student behavior, the researcher should not expect dramatic global changes in the teacher's repertoire. There is little question that teachers can be taught to modify the behavior of their students; Thomas, Becker, and Armstrong (1968) were among the first to demonstrate this by systematically varying a teacher's behavior in order to reduce disruptive behavior in a middle primary school. Hopes for broad, sweeping changes in the teacher's behavior are, however, clearly unrealistic, a conclusion supported by data from the following two studies.

In a study in which attempts to change classroom behavior were not the goals, Mary Alice White (1975) utilized direct behavioral observation procedures to record the natural rates of teacher approval and disapproval exhibited in classrooms for grades 1–12. The results were quite discouraging. First, there was an inverse relationship between grade level and amount of teacher approval; that is, as children advance through the grades, the rates of teacher approval go down. Further, after the second grade, rates of teacher disapproval greatly exceed rates of approval. These results should be kept in mind by any naive behavior modifier who may go into a classroom with a goal of making a teacher a high-rate "praiser"! These data are a further testimony for the necessity to continue to develop procedures such as the Good Behavior Game and token economies in the modification of classroom behavior. Some cross-cultural support for White's (1975) data were provided more recently by Thomas, Presland, Grant, and Glynn (1978), who studied ten seventh grade classrooms in New Zealand with more than 50% Polynesian students. Their data were found to be very similar to White's (1975) in showing natural rates of teacher disapproval exceeding rates of approval. They conclude their study by saying "finally, it is possible that some teachers clearly feel that appropriate behavior deserves little recognition" (p. 94). We address this issue again later in this chapter, when we discuss teacher training.

A unique approach to classroom behavior change was employed by Graubard, Rosenberg, and Miller (1974). They report several studies in which children were taught to modify teacher behavior. In the first study, special education students whose ages ranged from 12–15 years were taught to make eye contact with the teacher while asking for help and making comments such as, "It makes me feel good when you praise me." This effort made for a dramatic increase in positive teacher behavior and a decrease in negative teacher behavior. In another study, emotionally handicapped students were taught to make use of behavior change procedures with "normal" children, thus increasing the number of positive contacts between the handicapped and normal students. While procedures such as these sound promising, replications have not been evident.

ACADEMIC PERFORMANCE

In the Good Behavior Game replication by Harris and Sherman (1973a) we saw that improved behavior did not lead to greater improved academic performance in the two classrooms those researchers studied. A different tack was taken by Ayllon and Roberts (1974). They placed contingencies directly on academic performance and examined the correlated changes in classroom behavior. Five fifth grade, highly disruptive boys from a class of 38 middle-class urban children were observed. During reading class the teacher conducted 15-minute "performance sessions" during which both academic performance and rates of disruptive behavior were recorded. During baseline, the boys' disruptive behavior averaged 34% and academic performance hovered just below 50%. An ABAB reversal design was used to evaluate the role of a point system for improved academic performance and its effect on disruptive behavior. Not surprisingly, disruptive behavior was found to be incompatible with working at a high rate in order to try to increase academic output. During the two treatment ("B") conditions, disruptive behavior dropped to very low rates (near zero during the last several days of the experiment) and academic performance rose to an average of 85%. The points that the boys earned were backed up by daily reinforcers, which cost from 1–20 points or were "bidded" for in an auction and included access to game room, extra recess time, buying a Ditto master, having copies run off, reviewing grades in the teacher's book, reducing detention, changing the assigned cafeteria table, having the lowest test score removed, and becoming an "assistant teacher." The backup weekly reinforcers' cost range was from 6–15 points with several items "up for bid at auction" and included such items as seeing a movie, having a "good work letter" sent home to parents, becoming the classroom helper for a whole week, becoming the ball captain for a week, and doing a bulletin board. While the results of the Ayllon and Roberts (1974) study are certainly encouraging and the approach in trying to manage disruptive behavior indirectly by manipulating academic behavior is unique, conclusions about the overall utility of these procedures deserves caution. First, remember that the observation and treatment procedures were only 15 minutes of a much longer classroom day. The authors provide no discussion as to how these boys behaved at other times during the day or in nonclassroom, but related situations, such as the playground, cafeteria, and lining up. Future research in this vein is surely needed.

Taking the logic of the Ayllon and Roberts (1974) study a step further, Marholin and Steinman (1977) compared two different procedures in the same classroom with the four most disruptive boys and the four least disruptive (age range 10–12 years) in a class of 19 special education children. In this case, 30-minute observation periods were used to observe the children under the following conditions: baseline, baseline with teacher absent, on-task behavior reinforced, on-task behavior reinforced with teacher absent, accuracy/rate reinforced, accuracy/rate reinforced with teacher absent, on-task reinforced, on-task reinforced with teacher absent, accuracy/rate reinforced, accuracy/rate reinforced with teacher absent. Thus, they were able to compare reinforcement for academic rate performance and its effect on behavior to reinforcement for behavior and its effect on academic rate and accuracy. Within both of those conditions, the effect of the teacher's presence or absence was also analyzed. The reinforcers in this study were points backed up by free time. The results showed that regardless of which "treatment" condition was in effect, on-task behavior declined and disruptive behavior increased considerably when the primary teacher was not in the room (aides dispensed the reinforcers), but more so with on-task as opposed to rate-accuracy reinforcement. Further, when the teacher was gone, rate (problems attempted) and accuracy of math performance declined. On-task behavior, rate, and accuracy, however, were greatly enhanced when the teacher was present and points were made contingent upon rate and accuracy. When on-task behavior alone was reinforced, it increased, but with no correlated change in rate or accuracy. The authors suggest that the implications of the results are that reinforcing academic rate and accuracy brings the children under greater stimulus control of the materials, rather than the less generalized control of the teacher when only behavior (decorum) is reinforced. Again, these results are quite encouraging. Future research with longer treatment conditions will determine the durability of this logic of stimulus control.

OTHER CLASSROOM ISSUES

The purpose of this section of the chapter is to review the variety of age ranges and skills to which behavior change procedures in a variety of different kinds of classrooms have been applied, and to review studies that have sought to determine the utility of traditional educational concepts such as homework or length of teacher contacts. Finally, there is a review of studies that have examined other questions such as the role of psychotropic medication, the potential development of race relations, and more.

Quite often when a presentation or workshop is done for a group of teachers, the utility of applications to grade school classrooms is the first to become apparent to teachers. Several will often ask, "But how could these procedures be adapted to secondary education? My students won't be motivated by badges, teacher attention, or being ball captain." Well, as far back as 1969, a demonstration was made showing the application of behavior change procedures in a high school English class (McAllister, Stachowiak, Baer, and Conderman, 1969). Somewhat surprisingly, teacher attention was shown to be a potent reinforcer for the 25 students in the class at Lawrence, Kansas, High School. The treatment variable was praise, such as "Thank you for not talking," by the teacher for quiet and still behavior directed at the whole class and stern personal reprimands, such as "Jane, stop talking," for turning around or talking out. The results showed strong and durable change over time in the rates of talking out and turning around by the students. The procedures were easily implemented by the teacher. Unfortunately, no formal information was solicited from the students regarding how they felt about the procedures or results.

Music played on a popular radio station was used by Wilson and Hopkins (1973) to reduce noise intensity in four junior high school home economics classes. While on-task, in-seat behavior is not a requirement of a home economics class and thus there is greater mobility for the students, excessive noise levels still do not represent proper decorum for a classroom. In addition to the novelty of using the radio as a contingent reinforcer, Wilson and Hopkins (1973) made it so that the teachers did not have to collect data or deliver the contingencies. Instead, a microphone was hung 8 feet above the floor in the classroom. The microphone led to a voice-operated relay which was set to operate whenever the noise level in classroom "A" exceeded 76 decibels. Teachers in the other three classrooms ("B," "C," and "D") requested 70 decibels as the criterion level. Whenever the relay was triggered, the radio, which was on, then went off. A multiple baseline design across three of the classrooms and a reversal design were used to demonstrate that the contingency of playing the radio depending on reduced levels of noise was responsible for keeping the students' noise at a quite acceptable level. In this study we see another example of trying to make behavior change procedures easy on everyone concerned. The students were allowed a usually infrequent treat (radio) in the classroom as a daily and fairly continuous reinforcer, and the teachers had a reduced level of noise in which to teach, and did not have to change their own routines in order to implement the program.

As we briefly mentioned in the last chapter, creative writing was put to an experimental analysis by Maloney and Hopkins (1973). A variety of compositional variables were objectified and scored. After several baseline compositions were scored, the fourth, fifth, and sixth grade students were divided into teams and played "the good writing" game, which involved points that were later exchangeable for candy and extra recess. The points were made contingent upon the use of different adjectives, different action verbs, and different sentence beginnings. The use of these parts of speech increased dramatically whenever points were added to them. Further, independent raters (a graduate student in English and a graduate student in German) scored the stories written under the good writing game as more creative than those written during baseline. The only fault that we can find here is that there has not been enough of this kind of research since this important study.

Can reinforcement procedures produce improved race relations? In a small way, and to some extent, it has been shown that reinforcement can promote racial integration in first grade children (Hauserman, Walen, and Behling, 1973). Sitting with and being seated by a new friend in the school cafeteria was modified by teacher directions combined with reinforcement and by positive reinforcement alone. Generalization measures were also taken within the cafeteria and during free play in the classroom. The first data collected were on who sat with whom at lunch. All children who "sat with a new friend today" received reinforcement so as not to single out the seven Black children who represented the racial minority of the class. In the first treatment condition, a prompt was used whereby the children were assigned to sit with a "new friend" in the lunchroom. Further, the teacher praised that behavior as it occurred. During the next phase of the study (nine days), the teacher encouraged and reinforced, but did not directly prompt, interracial sitting in the lunchroom. This condition was followed by a return to baseline procedures. During the prompt plus reinforcement phase of the study, there was virtually no generalization of interracial free play, but there were some increased interactions in the lunchroom. During the "experimental phase" there was a considerable increase in generalized interracial play in the free play situation in the classroom, with a moderate increase over baseline (reflecting a slight decrease from the prompt condition) in interracial interactions in the lunchroom. During the brief (five days) reversal condition, the rates of interracial interactions in the classroom and the lunchroom returned to baseline levels. While the authors of the study propose a consideration of the lack of programmed generalization as an explanation for the disappointing results of the final condition, one of the major considerations should be the relatively short (nine-day) length of the experimental condition. With the promising results of that condition, it might be assumed that these first grade children were "just getting to know each other." Socialization at ages 6–7 certainly takes the form of children taking longer than nine school days to become friends with several other children. It would also have been useful to glean information from the children themselves through direct interviews or sociograms on how they *felt* about their "new" friends, or on the teacher's obvious efforts to promote new friendships. Nonetheless, the potential utility of the procedures in this study should not be overlooked. In a decade where nearly full integration of the schools will be accomplished, behavior change procedures should be in the forefront of attempts to promote harmony and understanding.

How do behavior change procedures affect the behavior of "untreated" peers in the classroom? This question has been addressed in two different ways in two studies. In a combined reversal and multiple baseline design, two pairs of moderately retarded school children were exposed sequentially to three contingent social reinforcement conditions for attentive behavior (Kazdin, 1973). Nontarget children who sat near the target subjects received no specially directed social reinforcement for their attentive behavior, but that behavior was observed and recorded nonetheless. The results predictably showed considerable improvements in the attentive behavior of the target children, but the attentive behavior of the adjacent children also improved significantly. This "bonus" result can be called "vicarious reinforcement" (Bandura & Walters, 1963). Even more surprising was that during a brief reversal condition when target children were reinforced for inattentive behavior and thus showed predictable decreases in attentive behavior, the newly acquired attentive behavior of the nontarget children remained high. Kazdin (1973) attributes these results to the discriminative stimulus (S^D) properties of the social reinforcement itself, which, once developed, served as a cue for attentiveness in the nontarget subjects independent of the contingencies in effect for the target subject.

A similar study (Christy, 1975) addressed a similar issue. Often when educators first hear of behavior change applications in classrooms, they react with reticence in part attributable to a concern that setting up treatment programs for target problem children might negatively affect nontarget children who, for whatever reasons (jealousy presumably being one) might perform less well when they see other children reap the rewards of a treatment program. Of particular concern to critics seems to be the use of tangible rewards. Concerned by this issue, Pauline Christy experimentally addressed the question. The subjects of her study were two classes of children whose ages ranged from 3.5 years to 6 years. Using a multiple baseline design, three consecutive children who showed particularly low baseline rates of in-seat behavior received verbal praise and food rewards for in-seat behavior. Peers who displayed both low and high rates of in-seat during baseline were also observed to see how the reinforcement procedures for the target children affected their in-seat, aggressive, nonagressive, disruptive, and complaint behavior. Contrary to predictions that might be made by detractors of behavior change applications in the classroom, not only did problems not increase in peer observers of treatment, but several improvements in the behavior of nontarget children occurred. That is, in-seat behavior increased and complaints decreased throughout the course of the study. Thus, both the results of the Kazdin (1973) and the Christy (1975) studies would suggest not only that behavior change procedures in the classroom do not produce negative side effects in untreated peers, but also that the procedures seem to produce unprogrammed positive side effects.

Another potential problem area in behavior change applications in classrooms is that many teachers report that even procedures that have been demonstrated to be effective are difficult for them to implement. If this is so, and those of us who have consulted to educational systems have found it to be, then a continual search for easily implemented and cost-efficient procedures for teachers' use becomes our charge. Lahey, Gendrich, Gendrich, Schnelle, Gant, and McNees (1977) evaluated the use of daily report cards that were sent home to the parents of disruptive kindergarten children. The system required minimal teacher involvement. The teacher merely sent home a "brag sheet" that indicated whether the child had behaved appropriately that day. The cover letter to parents prompted them to praise their children for good "brag sheets." Whatever the parents did at home was apparently effective, as the disruptive behavior in the classroom of two groups of children decreased markedly. It is, of course, possible that the "brag sheets" themselves served as reinforcers and some parents may have done very little to encourage improved school behavior, but in any case, the procedures *were* effective and cost-efficient in that the teachers found them easy to use and willingly did so.

It has been estimated that as many as 200,000 children in the United States receive daily doses of amphetamines in an attempt to control their hyperactivity (Krippner, Silverman, Cavallo, & Healy, 1973). There are some reasonably respectable data to suggest that methylphenidate (Ritalin) and chlorpromazine (Thorazine) control hyperactivity in laboratory and applied settings (Hollis & St. Omer, 1972; Comly, 1971), although Sulzbacher (1973) has questioned the validity of the assessment devices in these studies. Until recently, however, there were no studies that sought directly to assess hyperactivity through in-classroom and in-home repeated measurement of observable hyperactive behavior. A study reported in 1975 by Ayllon, Layman, and Kandel looked at academic performance and classroom behavior with three school children in regimens of both on and off medication and on and off behavior modification. Hyperactive behavior was observed independently and separately in the three children, ages 8, 9, and 10, in their math and reading classes. The first baselines were recorded with the children on their prescribed medication regimens. The second baseline was recorded with the children off their medication regimens. A multiple baseline design across math and reading was used to assess the effects of the behavioral intervention on their academic and hyperactive behavior. The behavior intervention took the form of token reinforcement contingent upon correct academic responses, similar in logic to the Ayllon and Roberts (1974) study that showed that when accuracy rate was reinforced, overall behavior improved. When medication was discontinued, hyperactive behavior increased from 20% to 80%, but math and reading performance also increased. When the behavioral intervention was then introduced while the children were off medication, hyperactive behavior decreased to its 20% level, while math and reading performance jumped from 12% accuracy to 85% accuracy. Thus, a few tentative conclusions are in order. With these three children, Ritalin controlled hyperactive behavior, but seemed to impede academic performance. On the other hand, reinforcing academic performance greatly enhanced that performance and produced a correlated control of hyperactive behavior. A major drawback in the discussion of this fine, pioneering piece of research is that there is no report of how the children behaved in school outside of math or reading class or how they behaved at home when they were off medication. Further, there was no extensive follow-up to this study. Therefore, whereas a behavioral approach to the treatment of hyperactive behavior looks promising, more intra- and intersubject data (as would surely be suggested by the ecological psychologist, Willems, 1977) are in order before a strong conclusion is justified.

Further support for a behavioral approach has been provided by Shafto and Sulzbacher (1977). They used two treatment tactics, food and contingent praise, and varying doses of Ritalin in an evaluation of the effects on a preschool child's activity changes. Most critically, other behaviors were observed and recorded; these were social, verbal, and academic. During contingent praise conditions, fewer hyperactive responses (as measured by free-play activity changes) occurred. During medication regimens, hyperactivity was variable. The drug seemed to help the child stay on task, but at higher doses it seemed to decrease the intelligibility of speech and responsiveness to teacher statements that needed a response (mands). This study serves several useful purposes: first, it provides observational data on the effects of Ritalin versus behavior modification; second, it provides a model for such evaluative research; and, finally, it is a good example for the need to collect as many data on as many relevant behaviors as possible.

An all-day classroom analysis of the behavioral treatment of hyperactivity was provided by O'Leary, Pelham, Rosenbaum, and Price (1977). They used the Conners' Teacher Rating Scale (TRS) and the Problem Behavior Rating (PBR) to measure pre- and posttreatment effects on nine children (grades 3–5) in a treatment group and eight hyperactive children in a control group. Neither group of children differed significantly on the pretreatment assessment devices, but there were significant differences between the treatment group and the control group posttreatment with a considerable improvement (statistically significant) also shown pre-post for the treatment group. This study lends support for the advocates of a behavioral approach as an alternative (and medically safer) approach to medication in the treatment of hyperactive behavior. Two cautions are again in order, however. Once again, no data are presented nor is a discussion point addressed as to any formal or subjective report of the generality of the children's improved behavior across settings (the playground, lunchroom, home, on shopping trips, and so on). Furthermore, as "hard-nosed" applied behavior analysts, we have to look especially askance at a study that relies solely on rating-scale measures without a "backup" or primary system of direct behavioral observation.

Despite the flaws we have noted in the studies dealing with hyperactive behavior, more and improved behavioral studies can be expected to appear over the next several years (O'Leary, 1980), especially those dealing with an objective analysis of the role of sugar and additives in the diets of hyperactive children.

As we have mentioned before, often we do things as parents and teachers that have never been evaluated in a scientific way. For example, a heated debate between or among educators, parents, college students, high school students, and grade school children could easily be generated by bringing up the topic of . . . homework! In an especially creative study, V. William Harris (Southwest Indian Youth Center) and James A. Sherman (University of Kansas) (1974) conducted two experiments that addressed three questions of the effect of homework in social studies and math in three sixth grade classrooms. The first question addressed was "What effect does assigning homework have on students' subsequent classroom performance?" The second question addressed was "Could a method be developed that increased the number of students who completed their homework assignments with accuracy?" And finally, "What effect would the accurate completion of homework assignments have on the student's subsequent classroom performance?" In other words, despite the uproar and otherwise weak literature on homework, Harris and Sherman (1974) were the first to assess directly whether and in what way homework has any utility. To those who champion homework for homework's sake as some sort of self-disciplinary device, the results must be disappointing. When no contingencies were provided for the completion of homework, very little got done. Also, whether homework without consequences gets assigned seemed to have no effect on subsequent classroom performance. Increasing homework completion by providing early-to-recess and early dismissal consequences increased homework completion but not classroom performance. However, classroom performance was greatly enhanced when students provided consequences for the *accurate* completion of their homework. The utility of this kind of strategy for research goes far beyond the issue of homework. As we will see in looking at the other studies in the remainder of this section of this chapter, and in so many studies in this book, when a question arises it can almost always be answered by utilizing the observational, design (and sometimes treatment) logic of our behavior change technology.

In another attempt to experimentally assess an educational issue, these same two researchers, Harris and Sherman (1973b) examined "the effects of peer tutoring and consequences on the math performance of elementary classroom students," specifically the effects of unstructured peer tutoring on the math performance of fourth and fifth grade students. Students worked on math during two sessions each day. The problems in each session were of comparable type and difficulty. When students tutored each other over the same math problems on which they would be tested later in the daily sessions, higher rates and accuracy were produced than under conditions without peer tutoring. Early recess consequences for accuracy further enhanced performance subsequent to tutoring. A question of whether it was exposure to the appropriate study material itself or the tutoring *per se* that produced the improved performance was addressed by exposing the students to an independent study condition during which they received the same study material as during the tutoring phase, but were not allowed to tutor each other over it. The results implied that it was the tutoring that facilitated performance. The generalized effects of tutoring were examined by providing the students with similar, but not identical material to study in preparation for testing. This also produced high rates and accuracy of performance. Thus, the results suggest that the combined use of peer tutoring plus consequences for accurate performance on subsequent tests greatly enhance both the rate and accuracy of that subsequent performance, at least with math. Further evidence with data from other subject disciplines (for example, reading, spelling, social studies) would be more convincing.

The length of teacher contacts when responding to the hand-raising of a child seeking help during study time in the classroom was manipulated and assessed by Scott and Bushell (1974). Contact was defined as the amount of time the teacher spent personally tutoring sixth graders in a small instructional group in math. The target behavior recorded was the amount of off-task behavior shown by the students. Baseline data showed that the average teacher contact was 38 seconds. During a second condition (after baseline), the teacher was asked to maintain contact with a student for at least 50 seconds. In the final condition, contact time was reduced to 20 seconds. The results showed a significant increase in *off-task* behavior when teacher contact was 50 seconds. The best on-task performance occurred when teacher contact was held to 20 seconds. Thus, it appears that lengthy teacher contact serves to reinforce off-task behavior. This is another piece of valuable information gained from classroom studies. If these results are replicated, the information should be imparted to teachers.

Safety is an area in which schools often try to provide training. Children 5–9 years of age have a relatively high probability of being involved in a pedestrian accident (Biehl, Older, & Griep, 1969). Despite attempted training efforts by schools and institutions such as Boy Scouts and Girl Scouts, casual observation would note that one of the reasons for this high accident rate is that many grade school children have poor pedestrian skills. In Chapter 7 we briefly mentioned a unique study by William H. Yeaton and Jon S. Bailey (1978), in which the effects of a pedestrian skill training package were analyzed. In addition, data and some remedial instruction were provided one year after the termination of the original study. Twelve children in each of two elementary schools participated in the study. Six components of correct street crossing were observed: (1) wait at curb, (2) look both ways, (3) watch vehicle distance, (4) walk, (5) continue to look, and (6) stay i crosswalk. Four phases used in the training package were: (1) telling children the correct steps involved, (2) modeling the correct steps, (3) asking the children to verbalize the correct steps, and (4) allowing the children to practice with a crossing guard providing them with direct feedback. The multiple baseline design across two groups of children showed the training procedures to be effective both at the training site and at a generalization setting where no guard was present. The one-year follow-up showed that pedestrian safety skill was maintained by some of the children, and others recovered the skill after very brief remedial training. We see in this study by Yeaton and Bailey (1978) the development, assessment, and refinement of an important set of skills too often "sloppily" taught by schools and parents. The next ten years will see a considerable proliferation of this kind of research.

We have already addressed the problem of the cost benefit or willingness of teachers to implement behavior change procedures in their classrooms. One possible partial solution is teaching children to modify their own behavior or nurture the development of what many call "self-control" procedures. Several studies in this area have been reported. Children have been taught to set their own standards of performance (Bandura & Perloff, 1967; Drabman, 1973; Felixbrod & O'Leary, 1973) and to self-dispense reinforcers (Bolstad & Johnson, 1972). Several problems, however, have surfaced and may explain why these procedures have not become a panacea for education. One practical problem is that someone *still* has to teach these "self-control" procedures to children; the children still require frequent scrutiny, for they adopt lenient standards for themselves (Felixbrod & O'Leary, 1973). Finally, there has been a paucity of follow-up data in the classroom self-control procedures; nonetheless, the procedures offer some promise in the bag of change tools of the behavioral researcher.

Before moving on to our discussion of behavioral approaches in higher education, we need to mention the issue of teacher training. You might ask, given these studies on behavior change applications in classrooms, whether teachers are now being trained to use these procedures. Our reluctant answer would probably be to direct you to ask a recently graduated teacher what he or she knows about behavioral *studies* on tutoring, homework, self-control procedures, comparisons of behavior modification to drugs in the control of hyperactivity, and so on, and the likely response from that teacher will be one of limited information. By and large, teachers are not taught to teach. They are exposed to a variety of developmental and educational theories, but other than a questionably supervised student teaching experience, have little "hands-on" training. If they are exposed to behavior modification, it is likely from a theoretical base in part of a class. There are, of course, exceptions to this pessimistic picture we are painting, and as we have made predictions about other areas of applications for the next decade, we can safely predict that teacher training will become more behavioral in the years ahead. But progress may be slower than in other application areas. Throughout the United States there probably are fewer behaviorally oriented teacher training programs than behaviorally oriented psychology, rehabilitation, social work, and human development programs. Changes will occur, however, because the technology of behavior change works well and the consumers of education programs (educational students, grade school students, and parents) will ultimately demand and receive functional teacher training.

HIGHER EDUCATION

In the beginning of this chapter, we alluded to "big changes" in higher education. We do not mean students protesting impersonalization as they did in the 1960s; we do not mean students challenging political educational dogma as they did in the 1970s. What we do mean is that educators and students alike are becoming aware of, and using in greater numbers, a behavioral technology for higher education that for many has produced more learning in a more pleasant way than the traditional lecture-midterm-final method of college teaching. Three labels are associated with this approach. They are: (1) the Keller Plan; (2) PSI (Personalized System of Instruction or its variation, Contingency Managed Lecture); (3) Mastery Learning. Whatever you choose to call it, its roots go back to Dr. Fred S. Keller, a graduate school roommate of B. F. Skinner. In an Invited Address before the American Psychological Association in 1967 entitled "Good-Bye Teacher," Professor Keller articulated a plan for college teaching that was based on behavioral principles rather than Socratic tradition (Keller, 1968). Very importantly, he also presented data to show that his model for teaching was superior to traditional college classroom approaches. Some of the components that he stressed were: a high degree of individualization, thus allowing even large numbers of students to progress at their own pace; "terminal skills for each course, together with the carefully graded steps leading toward this end" (p. 79); a high predetermined criterion (mastery) level for each student; the use of other college students as teachers; immediate feedback on performance; frequent testing; and the minimization of the role of lecture. Keller, himself, compared this model to a more traditional one and found his model to be more effective. Since 1968, PSI has been put to nearly microscopic research. Probably no other area of behavior change applications has been so carefully and systematically researched. Countless questions have been asked and answered. The questions came from both within and outside the field. Within the field there were questions such as, "Is self-pacing an important component of the model?" Semb, Conyers, Spencer, and Sanchez Sosa (1975) basically concluded that an instructor-paced procedure that placed contingencies such that students avoided falling behind, but allowed them to get ahead, was superior to self-pace by reducing the bothersome number of dropouts in self-pace. Thus, a modication of the Keller Plan has been recommended and adopted within the field because of research on the model. Criticisms from outside the field included such arguments as, "Well, on a short-term basis because of frequent testing, PSI may show to be superior to traditional lecture technique, but what about long-time results?" Corey, McMichael, and Tremont (1970) answered this question with a five-month follow-up to a group comparison study. While both groups showed a significant decrease in scores compared to the original final examination, the students who had been taught by PSI still showed greater mastery over the course content than the lecture-group students. Born, Davis, Whelan, and Jackson (1972) found that study time for students under the two formats was about the same, but that performance under PSI was clearly superior. But how do students *like* PSI? Typically, as measured by comparative ratings, they like it better than traditional methods (Becker & Shimway, 1972; Roop, 1973; Friedman, 1972). Let us admit, however, from considerable personal experience in using the model that the few students who do not like PSI seem to sincerely detest it!

We could literally devote the rest of the book to reviewing all of the components of PSI that have been studied along with several fine replications of those studies, but instead we will mention just a few more and then draw some conclusions. Discussion groups have been used as ancillary tools in both traditional and PSI formats. Blackburn, White-Blackburn, and Lutzker (1977) conducted four studies to examine the role of varying discussion groups in a large Abnormal Psychology class taught by PSI. They found that academic performance is not differentially affected by having or not having discussion groups nor by having or not having contingencies on attendance or performance during discussion groups. Thus, what we see is what might be called a threshold effect in that PSI *works* and varying other components does not dilute the overall effectiveness of the model. In that same vein, White-Blackburn, Blackburn, and Lutzker (in press) compared objective versus subjective weekly quizzes on subsequent performance on unit and final examinations. No differences were found in the overall high performance. All students experienced both kinds of quizzes and, naturally, some preferred one format over another even though their performance was not differentially affected by either. The results of these two studies led White-Blackburn, Blackburn, and Lutzker (in press) to conclude that as long as the PSI format is adhered to, other variations can be offered and manipulated in order to satisfy student preference. For example, a "cafeteria" selection could be available to any student whose mastery is assured by the instructor holding to the basic PSI components, by allowing a student to attend lecture or not, have objective or subjective quiz items, go to discussion groups or not, and so on.

Another important question addressed by the PSI literature is that dealing with generalization or concept formation—that is, critics have argued that students might be able to recall material for which they have provided study guides and frequent quizzes, but they might not be able to generalize or assimilate that material to novel, but related, concepts. In careful studies that included outside ratings, Miller and Weaver (1972), Semb (1974), and Miller and Weaver (1976) showed that concept formation and generalization not only occurs, but is facilitated by PSI.

Research in PSI has proliferated and expanded into several disciplines such as mathematics (Rash & Grimm, 1976), nonacademic fields on the job (McMichael, Brock, & Delong, 1976), food and nutrition (Boren & Foree, 1977), astronomy (Hodge, 1977), English (Guillermo, 1977), engineering (Fivaz, 1977), and across grade levels and cultures. This is a testimony to the foresight of Professor Keller and a harbinger of the explosion of PSI technology for the teaching of almost every conceivable human endeavor in the decade ahead.

CONCLUSIONS

Research on behavior change techniques in classrooms has ranged from preschool to college, has included academic issues, behavior control, and other issues such as racial integration and safety. In the future we look toward more applications in teacher training, and other nontraditional academic issues such as, perhaps, conservationism. And in higher education we expect to see PSI used in a variety of disciplines in almost every college and university.

REFERENCES

Ayllon, T., Layman, D., & Kandel, H. J. A behavioral-educational alternative to drug control of hyperactive children. *Journal of Applied Behavior Analysis*, 1975, *8*, 137–146.

Ayllon, T., & Roberts, M. D. Eliminating discipline problems by strengthening academic performance. *Journal of Applied Behavior Analysis*, 1974, *7*, 71–76.

Bandura, A., & Perloff, B. Relative efficacy of self-monitored and externally imposed reinforcement systems. *Journal of Personality and Social Psychology*, 1967, *7*, 111–116.

Bandura, A., & Walters, R. H. *Social learning and personality development*. New York: Holt, Rinehart & Winston, 1963.

Barrish, H. H., Saunders, M., & Wolf, M. M. Good behavior game: Effects of individual contingencies for group consequences on disruptive behavior in a classroom. *Journal of Applied Behavior Analysis*, 1969, *2*, 119–124.

Barton, E. J., & Ascione, F. R. Sharing in preschool children: Facilitation, stimulus generalization, response generalization, and maintenance. *Journal of Applied Behavior Analysis*, 1979, *12*, 417–430.

Barton, E. J., & Osborne, J. G. The development of classroom sharing by a teacher using positive practice. *Behavior Modification*, 1978, *2*, 231–250.

Becker, W. A., & Shimway, L. K. Innovative methods of learning in a general genetics course. *Journal of Heredity*, 1972, *63*, 122–128.

Biehl, B. M., Older, S. J., & Griep, D. J. Pedestrian safety: A report by an Organization for Economic Co-operation and Development research group. Washington, D.C.: O.E.C.D. Publications Center, October 1969.

Bijou, S. W. What psychology has to offer education—now. *Journal of Applied Behavior Analysis*, 1970, *3*, 65–71.

Blackburn, T. C., White-Blackburn, G., & Lutzker, J. R. *The effects of different discussion formats in a PSI course*. Paper presented at the 85th Annual Convention of the American Psychological Association, San Francisco, 1977.

Bolstad, O. D., & Johnson, S. M. Self-regulation in the modification of disruptive behavior. *Journal of Applied Behavior Analysis*, 1972, *5*, 443–454.

Boren, A. R., & Foree, S. B. Personalized instruction applied to food and nutrition in higher education. *Journal of Personalized Instruction*, 1977, *2*, 39–42.

Born, D. G., Davis, M., Whelan, P., & Jackson, D. College student study behavior in a personalized instruction course and in a lecture course. In G. Semb (Ed.), *Behavior analysis and education—1972*. Lawrence, Kansas: Follow Through Project, 1972.

Bornstein, P. H., & Quevillon, R. P. The effects of a self-instructional package on overactive preschool boys. *Journal of Applied Behavior Analysis*, 1976, *9*, 179–188.

Breyer, N. L., & Allen, G. J. Effects of implementing a token economy on teacher attending behavior. *Journal of Applied Behavior Analysis*, 1975, *8*, 373–380.

Broden, M., Bruce, C., Mitchell, M. A., Carter, V., & Hall, R. V. Effects of teacher attention on attending behavior of two boys at adjacent desks. *Journal of Applied Behavior Analysis,* 1970, *3,* 199–203.

Broden, M., Hall, R. V., Dunlap, A., & Clark, R. Effects of teacher attention and a token reinforcement system in a junior high school special education class. *Exceptional Children,* 1970, *36,* 341–349.

Christy, P. R. Does use of tangible rewards with individual children affect peer observers? *Journal of Applied Behavior Analysis,* 1975, *8,* 187–196.

Comly, H. Cerebral stimulants for children with learning disorders. *Journal of Learning Disabilities,* 1971, *4,* 484–490.

Cooper, M. L., & Etzel, B. C. *The programming and development of preacademic skills.* Presented at Society for Research in Child Development, Santa Monica, 1969.

Cooper, M. L., LeBlanc, J. M., & Etzel, B. C. (Producers). *A shoe is to tie.* Edna A. Hill Child Development Laboratories, Dept. of Human Development, University of Kansas, January 1968 (10 min. film).

Corey, J. R., McMichael, J. S., & Tremont, P. J. *Long-term effects of personalized instruction in an introductory psychology course.* Paper presented at the meeting of the Eastern Psychological Association, Atlantic City, N.J., 1970.

Deitz, S. M., & Repp, A. C. Decreasing classroom misbehavior through the use of DRL schedules of reinforcement. *Journal of Applied Behavior Analysis,* 1973, *6,* 457–463.

Drabman, R. S. Child versus teacher administered token programs in a psychiatric hospital school. *Journal of Abnormal Psychology,* 1973, *1,* 68–87.

Drabman, R., Spitalnik, R., & Spitalnik, K. Sociometric and disruptive behavior as a function of four types of token reinforcement programs. *Journal of Applied Behavior Analysis,* 1974, *7,* 93–101.

Fallon, M. P., & Goetz, E. M. The creative teacher: The effects of descriptive social reinforcement upon the drawing behavior of three preschool children. *School Applications of Learning Theory,* 1975, *7,* 27–45.

Felixbrod, J. J., & O'Leary, K. D. Effects of reinforcement on children's academic behavior as a function of self-determined and externally imposed contingencies. *Journal of Applied Behavior Analysis,* 1973, *6,* 241–250.

Fivaz, R. Physics for engineers: A European attempt at PSI. *Journal of Personalized Instruction,* 1977, *2,* 156–161.

Friedling, C., & O'Leary, S. G. Effects of self-instructional training on second and third grade hyperactive children: A failure to replicate. *Journal of Applied Behavior Analysis,* 1979, *12,* 211–219.

Friedman, C. P. A model for improving "advanced" courses in physics. *American Journal of Physics,* 1972, *40,* 1602–1606.

Goetz, E. M., & Baer, D. M. Social control of form diversity and the emergence of new forms in children's blockbuilding. *Journal of Applied Behavior Analysis,* 1973, *6,* 209–217.

Goetz, E. M., & Salmonson, M. M. The effect of general and descriptive reinforcement on "creativity" in easel painting. In G. B. Semb (Ed.), *Behavior Analysis in Education.* Lawrence: University of Kansas Printing Service, 1972. Pp. 53–61.

Graubard, P. S., Rosenberg, H., & Miller, M. B. Student applications of behavior modification to teachers and environments or ecological approaches to social deviancy. In R. Ulrich, T. Stachnik, & J. Mabry (Eds.), *Control of human behavior: Behavior modification in education* (Vol. 3). Dallas: Scott, Foresman, 1974.

Guillermo, A. R. Teaching news writing by the PSI method. *Journal of Personalized Instruction,* 1977, *2,* 111–113.

Harris, V. W., & Sherman, J. A. Use and analysis of the "Good Behavior Game" to reduce disruptive classroom behavior. *Journal of Applied Behavior Analysis,* 1973, *6,* 405–417. (a)

Harris, V. W., & Sherman, J. A. Effects of peer tutoring and consequences on the math performance of elementary classroom students. *Journal of Applied Behavior Analysis,* 1973, *6,* 587–597. (b)

Harris, V. W., & Sherman, J. A. Homework assignments, consequences, and classroom performance in social studies and mathematics. *Journal of Applied Behavior Analysis,* 1974, *7,* 505–519.

Hauserman, N., Walen, S. R., & Behling, M. Reinforced racial integration in the first grade: A study in generalization. *Journal of Applied Behavior Analysis,* 1973, *6,* 193–200.

Hodge, P. W. Student exploration in a PI course on the planets. *Journal of Personalized Instruction,* 1977, *2,* 51–52.

Hollis, J., & St. Omer, V. Direct measurement of psychopharmacologic response: Effects of chlorpromazine on motor behavior of retarded children. *American Journal of Mental Deficiency,* 1972, *76,* 397–407.

Johnston, J. M., & Johnston, G. T. Modification of consonant speech-sound articulation in young children. *Journal of Applied Behavior Analysis,* 1972, *5,* 233–246.

Kazdin, A. E. The effect of vicarious reinforcement on attentive behavior in the classroom. *Journal of Applied Behavior Analysis,* 1973, *6,* 71–78.

Keller, F. S. "Good-bye teacher . . . ." *Journal of Applied Behavior Analysis,* 1968, *1,* 79–89.

Krippner, S., Silverman, R., Cavallo, M., & Healy, M. A study of hyperkinetic children receiving stimulant drugs. *Academic Therapy,* 1973, *8,* 261–269.

Lahey, B. B., Gendrich, J. C., Gendrich, S. I., Schnelle, J. F., Gant, D. S., & McNees, M. P. An evaluation of daily report cards with minimal teacher and parent contacts as an efficient method of classroom intervention. *Behavior Modification,* 1977, *1,* 381–394.

Lahey, B. B., McNees, M. P., & McNees, M. C. Control of an obscene "verbal tic" through timeout in an elementary school classroom. *Journal of Applied Behavior Analysis,* 1973, *6,* 101–104.

Maloney, K. B., & Hopkins, B. L. The modification of sentence structure and its relationship to subjective judgments of creativity in writing. *Journal of Applied Behavior Analysis,* 1973, *6,* 425–433.

Marholin, D., II, & Steinman, W. M. Stimulus control in the classroom as a function of the behavior reinforced. *Journal of Applied Behavior Analysis,* 1977, *10,* 465–478.

Martin, J. A. Effects of positive and negative adult-child interactions on children's task performance and task preferences. *Journal of Experimental Child Psychology,* 1977, *23,* 493–502.

McAllister, L. W., Stachowiak, J. G., Baer, D. M., & Conderman, L. The application of operant conditioning techniques in a secondary school classroom. *Journal of Applied Behavior Analysis,* 1969, *2,* 277–285.

McLaughlin, T. F., & Malaby, J. Intrinsic reinforcers in a classroom token economy. *Journal of Applied Behavior Analysis,* 1972, *5,* 263–270.

McMichael, J. S., Brock, J. F., & Delong, J. Job-relevant navy training and Keller's personalized system of instruction: Reduced attrition. *Journal of Personalized Instruction,* 1976, *1,* 41–44.

Medland, M. B., & Stachnik, T. J. Good behavior game: A replication and systematic analysis. *Journal of Applied Behavior Analysis,* 1972, *5,* 45–51.

Miller, L. K., & Weaver, F. H. A multiple baseline achievement test. In G. Semb (Ed.), *Behavioral analysis and education—1972.* Lawrence, Kansas: University of Kansas, 1972.

Miller, L. K., & Weaver, F. H. A behavioral technology for producing concept formation in university students. *Journal of Applied Behavior Analysis,* 1976, *9,* 289–300.

Miller, R. M., & LeBlanc, J. M. *Experimental analysis of the effect of detailed and minimal instructions upon the acquisition of preacademic skills.* Paper presented at the 81st Annual Convention of the American Psychological Association, Montreal, 1973.

O'Leary, K. D. Behavior modification in the classroom: A rejoinder to Winett and Winkler. *Journal of Applied Behavior Analysis,* 1972, *5,* 505–511.

O'Leary, K. D. Pills or skills for hyperactive children. *Journal of Applied Behavior Analysis,* 1980, *13,* 191–204.

O'Leary, K. D., Kauffman, K. D., Kass, R. E., & Drabman, R. S. The effects of loud and soft reprimands on the behavior of disruptive students. *Exceptional Children,* 1970, *37,* 145–155.

O'Leary, K. D., Pelham, W. E., Rosenbaum, A. R., & Price, G. H. Behavioral treatment of hyperkinetic children: An experimental evaluation of its usefulness. In K. D. O'Leary & S. G. O'Leary (Eds.), *Classroom management: The successful use of behavior modification.* New York: Pergamon Press, 1977.

Rash, A. M., & Grimm, R. L. Individualized instruction in mathematics in an open junior high school. *Journal of Personalized Instruction,* 1976, *1,* 23–27.

Roop, J. M. Contingency management in the teaching of economics: Some results from an intermediate microeconomics course. *Intermountain Economic Review,* 1973, *4,* 53–71.

Schmidt, G. W., & Ulrich, R. E. Effects of group contingent events upon classroom noise. *Journal of Applied Behavior Analysis,* 1969, *2,* 171–179.

Scott, J. W., & Bushell, D., Jr. The length of teacher contacts and student's off-task behavior. *Journal of Applied Behavior Analysis,* 1974, *7,* 39–44.

Semb, G. The effects of mastery criteria and assignment length on college student test performance. *Journal of Applied Behavior Analysis,* 1974, *7,* 61–69.

Semb, G., Conyers, D., Spencer, R., & Sanchez Sosa, J. J. An experimental comparison of four pacing contingencies in a personalized instruction course. In J. Johnston (Ed.), *Behavior research and technology in higher education.* Springfield, Ill.: Charles C Thomas, 1975.

Shafto, F., & Sulzbacher, S. Comparing treatment tactics with a hyperactive preschool child: Stimulant medication and programmed teacher intervention. *Journal of Applied Behavior Analysis,* 1977, *10,* 13–20.

Skinner, B. F. *The technology of teaching.* New York: Appleton-Century-Crofts, 1968.

Solomon, R. W., & Wahler, R. G. Peer reinforcement control of classroom problem behavior. *Journal of Applied Behavior Analysis,* 1973, *6,* 49–56.

Stokes, T. F., & Baer, D. M. An implicit technology of generalization. *Journal of Applied Behavior Analysis,* 1977, *10,* 349–367.

Sulzbacher, S. I. Psychotropic medication with children: An evaluation of procedural biases in results of reported studies. *Pediatrics,* 1973, *51,* 513–517.

Thomas, D. A., Becker, W. C., & Armstrong, M. Production and elimination of disruptive classroom behavior by systematically varying teacher's behavior. *Journal of Applied Behavior Analysis,* 1968, *1,* 35–45.

Thomas, J. D., Presland, I. E., Grant, M. D., & Glynn, T. L. Natural rates of teacher approval and disapproval in grade 7 classrooms. *Journal of Applied Behavior Analysis,* 1978, *11,* 91–94.

White, M. A. Natural rates of teacher approval and disapproval in the classroom. *Journal of Applied Behavior Analysis,* 1975, *8,* 367–372.

White, S. A., & Lutzker, J. R. *Reducing disruptive behavior in a seventh grade music class by using the "good behavior game": A further component analysis.* Paper presented at the 82nd Annual Convention of the American Psychological Association, New Orleans, 1974.

White-Blackburn, G. W., Blackburn, T. L., & Lutzker, J. R. Effects of objective versus subjective quizzes in a PSI course. *Teaching of Psychology,* in press.

Willems, E. P. Steps toward an ecobehavioral technology. In A. Rogers-Warren & S. F. Warren (Eds.), *Ecological perspectives in behavior analysis.* Baltimore: University Park Press, 1977.

Wilson, C. W., & Hopkins, B. L. The effects of contingent music on the intensity of noise in junior high home economics classes. *Journal of Applied Behavior Analysis,* 1973, *6,* 269–275.

Winett, R., & Winkler, R. Current behavior modification in the classroom: Be still, quiet, and docile. *Journal of Applied Behavior Analysis,* 1972, *5,* 499–504.

Yeaton, W. H., & Bailey, J. S. Teaching pedestrian safety skills to young children: An analysis and one-year followup. *Journal of Applied Behavior Analysis,* 1978, *11,* 315–339.

Severe Problems: Institution and Community Intervention

ONE of the major social movements of the 1960s and 1970s has been the transition from institutionalization to community-based treatment and education for the mentally ill and mentally retarded. The reasons for this movement are numerous and complex. They involve a growing expansion in civil rights for all citizens through legislation, court cases, and social conscience. The principle of normalization (Wolfensberger, 1972) is certainly central. Individuals who are segregated from society in institutions behave differently as the result of the different treatment they receive. Such individuals, if placed in normal society, will behave "more normally" as a function of the normal society around them. Also, continued concern about the rising costs of institutionalization probably contributed significantly to the deinstitutionalization movement. The development of medications useful in the management of psychotic and maladaptive behavior was another important factor. Finally, the belief that individuals would receive a superior educational and treatment program and more services in the community was certainly important.

The role of behavior change techniques in the deinstitutionalization process, over time, may prove to be a critical variable. Great strides, particularly in the community treatment and education of the mentally retarded, have been made by using behavior change techniques with these populations. In this chapter, we will first examine the historical development of the application of behavior change techniques to the mentally ill and then, in the second half of the chapter, do likewise for the mentally retarded. By necessity, we will look at both institutional and community applications.

MENTAL ILLNESS

Table 9-1 briefly describes some of the earliest applications of behavior change techniques to the mentally ill, primarily those with a diagnosis of psychosis. These studies, with a few exceptions, are characterized by the absence of acceptable research designs (see Chapter 2), the lack of information about generalization, and the failure to obtain follow-up data. They are important, however, because they "broke ground" and were the first attempts to change the behavior of the mentally ill through direct environmental manipulation rather than through more traditional

TABLE 9-1. Early Applications of Behavior Change Techniques to the Mentally Ill

Investigator(s)	Date	Behavior
Lindsley and Skinner	1954	lever pulling
Peters and Jenkins	1954	problem solving
Lindsley	1956, 1960	lever pulling
Ayllon and Michael	1959	self-feeding
King, Armitage, and Tilton	1960	complex motor behavior
Rickard, Dignam, and Horner	1960	delusional speech
Isaacs, Thomas, and Goldiamond	1960	mutism
Ayllon and Haughton	1962	mealtime behavior

psychotherapy or medical management. They led to the development of token economy wards in institutions that more systematically attempted to evaluate the use of behavior change techniques with the mentally ill. We will now look at several of these token economy wards.

Anna State Hospital

The earliest and perhaps most frequently described and cited ward-wide token economy program was developed at Anna State Hospital in Anna, Illinois, by Drs. Teodoro Ayllon and Nathan H. Azrin (Ayllon & Azrin, 1964, 1965, 1968a, 1968b). Work on the design of this total ward-wide program was begun in 1961 (Kazdin, 1978). Patients were able to earn tokens for a wide variety of self-care behaviors (brushing teeth, combing hair, and so on), jobs (meal server, clerical helper, and so on), and assorted activities such as bed-making and participating in an exercise group (Ayllon & Azrin, 1968b). As may be seen in Table 9-2, a wide variety of reinforcers was available. Behaviors that were reinforced by tokens were individualized for each patient. Ayllon and Azrin (1968b) make much of what they call the *relevance of behavior rule*. In essence, only those behaviors that are likely to continue to be reinforced after training (in the token economy program) should be targeted for change—that is, behaviors selected should be those that are important for, and likely to be reinforced in, the natural community environment in which the patient is eventually placed. (Thus, their heavy emphasis is on work-related behaviors.) The use of a token system obviously permits the individualization of reinforcers also.

TABLE 9-2. List of Reinforcers Available for Tokens

	No. of Tokens Daily
I. Privacy	
Selection of Room 1	0
Selection of Room 2	4
Selection of Room 3	8
Selection of Room 4	15
Selection of Room 5	30
Personal Chair	1
Choice of Eating Group	1
Screen (Room Divider)	1
Choice of Bedspreads	1
Coat Rack	1
Personal Cabinet	2
Placebo	1–2
	Tokens
II. Leave from the Ward	
20-min walk on hospital grounds (with escort)	2
30-min grounds pass (3 tokens for each additional 30 min)	10
Trip to town (with escort)	100
III. Social Interaction with Staff	
Private audience with chaplain, nurse	5 min free
Private audience with ward staff, ward physician (for additional time— 1 token per min)	5 min free

TABLE 9-2 (cont.)

Private audience with ward psychologist	20
Private audience with social worker	100
IV. Devotional Opportunities	
Extra religious services on ward	1
Extra religious services off ward	10
V. Recreational Opportunities	
Movie on ward	1
Opportunity to listen to a live band	1
Exclusive use of radio	1
Television (choice of program)	3
VI. Commissary Items	
Consumable items such as candy, milk, cigarettes, coffee, and sandwich	1–5
Toilet articles such as Kleenex, toothpaste, comb, lipstick, and talcum powder	1–10
Clothing and accessories such as gloves, headscarf, house slippers, handbag, and skirt	12–400
Reading and writing materials such as stationery, pen, greeting card, newspaper, and magazine	2–5
Miscellaneous items such as ashtray, throw rug, potted plant, picture holder, and stuffed animal	1–50

From "The Measurement and Reinforcement of Behavior of Psychotics," by T. Ayllon and N. H. Azrin. In *Journal of the Experimental Analysis of Behavior*, 1965, *8*, 357–383. Copyright 1965 by the Society for the Experimental Analysis of Behavior, Inc. Reprinted by permission.

The effectiveness of Ayllon and Azrin's program can best be shown by looking at some data from one of their many experiments (1965). Table 9-3 provides some information about the patients who participated in this experiment. Figure 9-1 shows the data obtained in an attempt to evaluate whether delivery of tokens contingent upon targeted behavior (on-the-ward jobs) was necessary to maintain the targeted behavior. This is a BAB design (contingent reinforcement, then noncontingent reinforcement, then return to contingent reinforcement). Because these data points are for groups of patients rather than individuals, one should inquire as to the effect of this manipulation upon individual patients. Wisely, Ayllon and Azrin (1965) have provided these data, which can be seen in Table 9-4. Only eight of the 44 patients failed to earn tokens for jobs on the ward during the contingent reinforcement phase.

Ayllon and Azrin (1965) attributed the eight failures to their inability to find effective reinforcers. Perhaps to combat this problem, they developed a procedure called *reinforcer sampling* (Ayllon & Azrin, 1968a), which involved requiring patients to participate in activities that they did not find reinforcing (had a low probability of participating in). These included outdoor walks, listening to music, and attending movies. After a brief forced reinforcer sampling period of several days, patients continued to participate in these activities even though they *now had to pay tokens to participate*.

It should be noted that while the Anna State Hospital program was extremely innovative and gave rise to numerous replications, it was not without criticism. Stahl and Leitenberg (1976) have stated that the data presented in Figure 9-1 are open to a different interpretation because patients were told, in effect, that they

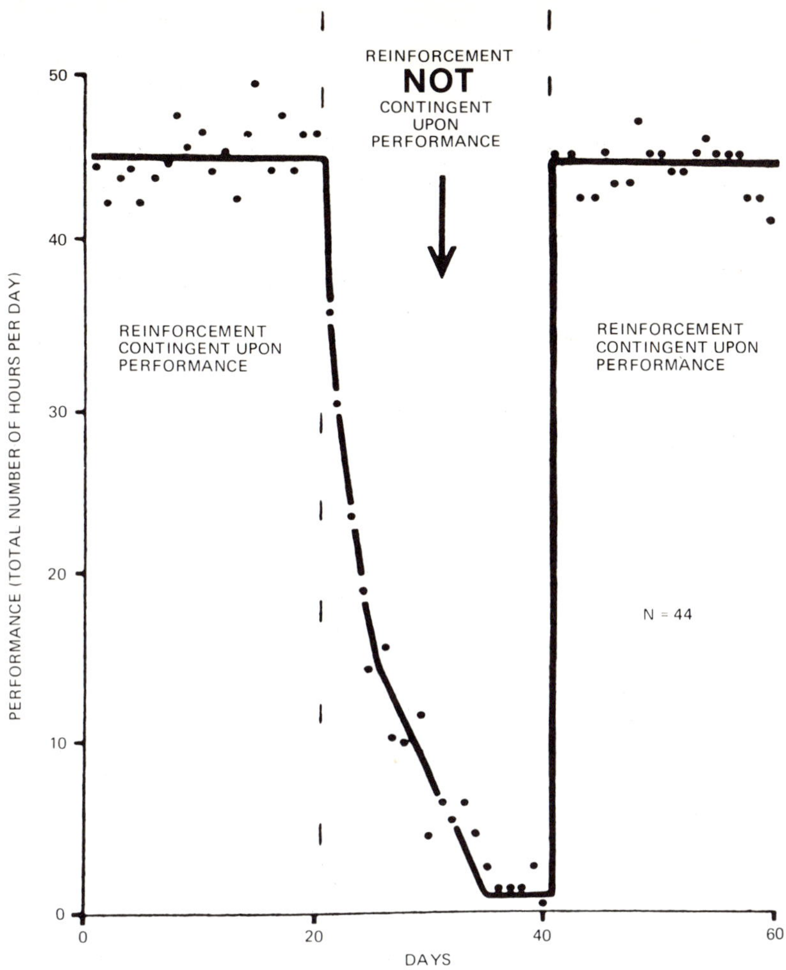

FIGURE 9-1.   The total number of hours of the on-ward performance by a group of 44 patients. (From "The Measurement and Reinforcement of Behavior of Psychotics," by T. Ayllon and N. H. Azrin. In *Journal of the Experimental Analysis of Behavior*, 1965, 8, 357–383. Copyright 1965 by the Society for the Experimental Analysis of Behavior, Inc. Reprinted by permission. Additional experiments are found in *The Token Economy*, by T. Ayllon and N. H. Azrin, Appleton-Century-Crofts, 1968.)

were getting a paid vacation during the noncontingent reinforcement phase. It is possible that this instructional set played a functional role in the patient's behavior instead of, or in addition to, the noncontingent reinforcement. Additional criticisms include the lack of data on psychotic behavior or symptoms and the need for follow-up information on the patients (Stahl & Leitenberg, 1976).

TABLE 9-3. Age, Years of Hospitalization, Diagnosis, and Drugs for 44 Patients Studied

Subject	Age	Years of Hospital-ization	Diagnosis	Tranquilizing Drugs
S-1	60	5	schizophrenic reaction, hebephrenic type	none
S-2	33	6	mental defective, moderate	phenothiazine derivative
S-3	42	2	mental defective, moderate	none
S-4	37	6	schizophrenic reaction, chronic undifferentiated type	phenothiazine derivative
S-5	72	8	schizophrenic reaction, paranoid type	phenothiazine derivative
S-6	37	8	schizophrenic reaction, chronic undifferentiated type	none
S-7	44	12	mental defective, moderate	none
S-8	55	29	schizophrenic reaction, hebephrenic type	none
S-9	65	22	schizophrenic reaction, paranoid type	none
S-10	48	27	schizophrenic reaction, catatonic type	phenothiazine derivative
S-11	71	18	schizophrenic reaction, paranoid type	none
S-12	36	13	manic depressive psychosis, mixed type	phenothiazine derivative
S-13	56	1	schizophrenic reaction, paranoid type	none
S-14	58	7	schizophrenic reaction, mixed type	none
S-15	71	27	schizophrenic reaction, hebephrenic type	none
S-16	35	11	schizophrenic reaction, chronic undifferentiated type	none
S-17	45	10	mental defective, severe with psychotic reaction	none
S-18	55	25	schizophrenic reaction, paranoid type	none
S-19	50	13	schizophrenic reaction, paranoid type	none
S-20	74	37	schizophrenic reaction, chronic undifferentiated type	none
S-21	31	9	schizophrenic reaction, chronic undifferentiated type	phenothiazine derivative
S-22	59	4	schizophrenic reaction, chronic undifferentiated type	none
S-23	41	22	schizophrenic reaction, hebephrenic type	phenothiazine derivative
S-24	24	10	schizophrenic reaction, chronic undifferentiated type	phenothiazine derivative
S-25	37	19	schizophrenic reaction, hebephrenic type	phenothiazine derivative
S-26	61	13	schizophrenic reaction, paranoid type	none
S-27	44	8	schizophrenic reaction, chronic undifferentiated type	phenothiazine derivative
S-28	58	12	schizophrenic reaction, paranoid type	phenothiazine derivative
S-29	59	19	psychosis with syphilitic meningo encephalitis	none
S-30	42	15	schizophrenic reaction, mixed type	phenothiazine derivative
S-31	35	13	schizophrenic reaction, chronic undifferentiated type	phenothiazine derivative
S-32	46	16	schizophrenic reaction, paranoid type	phenothiazine derivative

S-33	39	20	schizophrenic reaction, hebephrenic type	phenothiazine derivative
S-34	47	8	schizophrenic reaction, paranoid type	phenothiazine derivative
S-35	62	29	schizophrenic reaction, catatonic type	none
S-36	61	27	schizophrenic reaction, mixed type	none
S-37	72	11	psychosis with cerebral arteriosclerosis	none
S-38	61	11	mental defective, severe	none
S-39	45	22	schizophrenic reaction, catatonic type	none
S-40	58	33	schizophrenic reaction, hebephrenic type	none
S-41	49	23	schizophrenic reaction, hebephrenic type	none
S-42	55	13	mental defective with psychotic reaction	none
S-43	47	22	schizophrenic reaction, hebephrenic type	phenothiazine derivative
S-44	64	30	schizophrenic reaction, catatonic type	none

Mean age: 51   Range: 24–74 years   Mean years of hospitalization: 16   Range: 1–37 years
From "The Measurement and Reinforcement of Behavior of Psychotics," by T. Ayllon and N. H. Azrin. In *Journal of the Experimental Analysis of Behavior*, 1965, 8, 357–383. Copyright 1965 by the Society for the Experimental Analysis of Behavior, Inc. Reprinted by permission.

Palo Alto Veterans Administration Hospital

Drs. John Atthowe and Leonard Krasner (1968) reported the use of a token economy program with 60 chronic psychiatric patients at a Veterans Hospital. Much like the Ayllon and Azrin token economy, they sought to improve self-care, social skills, and work habits. The tokens patients earned were exchangeable for canteen items and different activities (for example, watching TV). Patients earned more and more privileges as their behavior improved. Ultimately, patients were able to "buy themselves" out of the token economy. A comparison or AB experimental design was used with a baseline of approximately six months. Considerable improvement was seen, during the token economy comparison phase, on a variety of social and interpersonal measures. Additionally, hospital discharges *doubled* as compared to the preceding 11-month period. Unfortunately, almost half of those discharged returned within nine months. Again, there have been some criticisms of this pioneer program. Obviously, the readmission data indicate a need to attend to problems of generalization and the transition to community living. Davison (1969) has noted that other behavior change techniques (for example, systematic desensitization, aversion therapy) were being used which could have had some unevaluated effect upon the program outcome. Stahl and Leitenberg (1976) have pointed out that the variability among the patients in the program cannot be assessed since Atthowe and Krasner presented their data in terms of group means and percentages.

Patton State Hospital

Reports of early efforts with a token economy at Patton State Hospital come from many sources (see Gericke, 1965; Bruco, 1966; Schaefer, 1966; Schaefer & Martin, 1966). The token economy and psychiatric patients were very similar to those described earlier. Programs were individualized and included a response-cost component (loss of tokens) for inappropriate behaviors, as well as administration

TABLE 9-4. Number of Tokens Earned and Spent by the 44 Patients

Subject	Tokens earned for: Off-ward jobs	On-ward jobs	Self-care	Total tokens earned	Tokens spent
S-7	1015	789	90	1894	1873
S-2	805	730	84	1619	2351
S-5	910	369	117	1396	999
S-3	1190	44	39	1273	1794
S-8	980	120	92	1192	2127
S-1	910	191	81	1182	1424
S-9	00	1032	142	1174	1189
S-6	1050	00	66	1116	938
S-22	00	954	88	1042	753
S-4	875	00	95	970	1165
S-34	00	763	89	852	741
S-35	00	770	73	843	325
S-26	455	269	93	817	995
S-32	00	577	63	640	553
S-14	00	409	113	522	227
S-21	00	392	24	416	269
S-30	00	196	123	319	221
S-19	00	231	83	314	310
S-13	00	263	9	272	166
S-33	00	232	19	251	118
S-36	00	167	74	241	170
S-40	00	126	90	216	673
S-17	00	108	96	204	237
S-39	00	141	43	184	221
S-38	00	68	115	183	82
S-27	00	91	90	181	337
S-44	00	29	143	172	205
S-20	00	162	7	169	70
S-15	00	71	91	162	39
S-24	00	38	111	149	176
S-18	00	30	115	145	152
S-12	00	91	49	140	86
S-16	00	40	67	107	74
S-11	00	00	89	89	87
S-43	00	48	39	87	121
S-31	00	00	85	85	1
S-37	00	00	85	85	47
S-25	00	4	69	73	37
S-10	00	00	44	44	3
S-42	00	15	23	38	32
S-29	00	00	36	36	5
S-23	00	00	30	30	23
S-28	00	00	28	28	2
S-41	00	00	15	15	1
Total	8,190	9,560	3,217	20,967	21,419
Mean	186.14	217.36	73.11	476.61	486.79
Range:	0-1,190	0-1,032	7-143	15-1,894	1-2,351

Note:—Based on the first period of 20 days of contingent reinforcement.

From "The Measurement and Reinforcement of Behavior of Psychotics," by T. Ayllon and N. H. Azrin. In *Journal of the Experimental Analysis of Behavior*, 1965, 8, 357–383. Copyright 1965 by the Society for the Experimental Analysis of Behavior, Inc. Reprinted by permission.)

of tokens contingent upon appropriate target behaviors. The overall program involved progressing through three living units with an ultimate graduation to the community. Much of the information on the Patton Project is descriptive and anecdotal; however, Schaefer and Martin (1966) presented encouraging data on 20 chronic patients as compared to a non-token-economy control group. During a three-month period of intervention, token economy patients improved on a variety of activity and responsibility measures as compared to the control group.

Other Token Economies and Some Comments

These token economies were just the beginning of an extremely important advance in the treatment of the institutionalized psychiatric patients. Soon, a number of others were reporting on their programs (Steffy, Hart, Craw, Torney, & Marlett, 1968; Lloyd & Garlington, 1968; Ellsworth, 1969; Heap, Boblitt, Moore, & Hord, 1970). While it is possible to criticize most of these programs for some aspect of experimental methodology, they are important nevertheless, for they led to the wide application of behavior change techniques to hospitalized psychiatric patients. It is also likely that some programs may have erred on the side of focusing on developing *more manageable patients* rather than toward increasing the functional living skills needed for community living. Additionally, as previously mentioned, in most cases few data were presented on the change in psychotic behavior as such, group data were common, and long-term effectiveness was not assessed. An additional problem (which developed more recently) has to do with the legal and ethical implications of token economies (Wexler, 1973). Because of increasing concern for the civil liberties of individuals in institutions, most of the early token economies could not be exactly duplicated today because patients had to exchange tokens for meals, beds, and other necessities.

Paul's Psychosocial Treatment Project

Natural outgrowths of these early token economy programs in psychiatric institutions have been attempts at comparative outcome studies (comparing token economies with other approaches and routine treatment control groups). Examples of such studies include Gripp and Magaro (1971); Shean and Zeidberg (1971); Birky, Chambliss, and Wasden (1971); and Maley, Feldman, and Ruskin (1973). While in general, most outcome studies have favored token economy programs, most of these studies have been subject to question on a variety of methodological grounds (Paul & Lentz, 1977; Stahl & Leitenberg, 1976). The most recent and certainly best designed outcome study has been described in Gordon Paul and Robert Lentz's *Psychosocial Treatment of Chronic Mental Patients* (1977). We present next the critical elements, outcomes, and conclusions of this massive effort (which, despite this review, can be fully appreciated and understood only by a thorough reading of their book).

Patients for the study were drawn from four state hospitals in central Illinois. They were divided into three groups of 28 (14 males and 14 females) matched on numerous variables. The two treatment groups were housed at a new regional mental health center and were in identical adjacent facilities of 12,000 square feet each. The project began in the fall of 1968 and continued for 4½ years. Professional and nonprofessional staffing patterns in the two treatment groups were comparable to the state hospital group over this time period. Additionally, in order to control a number of variables, the treatment staff rotated *daily* between the milieu and social-learning programs. Thus, staff had to be trained and manuals written on both approaches. Although there were a number of differences between the two treatment units, there were also a number of commonalities, particularly the ten basic rules of conduct in effect for both units (see Table 9-5).

TABLE 9-5. Ten Basic Rules of Conduct

1. Take care of yourself—always present a desirable appearance.
2. Complete your own housekeeping jobs and participate with others in other jobs.
3. Act, talk, and think straight.
4. Demonstrate ladylike or gentlemanly behavior.
5. Demonstrate respect for yourself and for the rights and property of others.
6. Interact in a cooperative and active manner with staff, residents, and others.
7. All scheduled activities should be attended and participated in.
8. Skills and work habits which can provide an income after discharge should be acquired and demonstrated.
9. Progress through each of the four step levels of the program and permanently return to community living.
10. Do not act "crazy."

Adapted from G. L. Paul and R. J. Lentz, *Psychosocial Treatment of Chronic Mental Patients.* Cambridge, Mass.: Harvard University Press, 1977.

The social learning treatment program was based on earlier work by Ayllon and Azrin and others. Program content consisted of self-help skills, jobs, classes in community living skills, small group training in individual and interpersonal problems, and the like. The token economy procedural rules for staff may be seen in Table 9-6.

TABLE 9-6. Token Economy Procedural Rules

1. Always reinforce appropriate behavior at once.
2. Undesirable behavior should never be reinforced.
3. Social reinforcement should be paired with a description of the desirable behavior exhibited when delivering reinforcement.
4. Prompts and instructions should be used to shape desirable behavior.
5. Token exchanges, chips, behavior, and relevant criteria should always be recorded.

Adapted from G. L. Paul and R. J. Lentz, *Psychosocial Treatment of Chronic Mental Patients.* Cambridge, Mass.: Harvard University Press, 1977.

The milieu unit program consisted of classes and activities, informal social interaction times, large community meetings where decisions about the unit could be made, and so on. The milieu unit procedural rules for staff may be seen in Table 9-7. Some interesting data concerning the amount of time spent in different activities in the three settings can be seen in Table 9-8.

TABLE 9-7. Milieu Unit Procedural Rules

1. Positive statements and feedback should always be used.
2. Undesirable behavior should never be ignored (provide negative feedback).
3. Resident responsibility, decision-making, and problem-solving should be maximized.
4. Cohesiveness within the living groups should be maximized.
5. The occurrence of positive statements, negative feedback, and resident's behavior should always be recorded.

Adapted from G. L. Paul and R. J. Lentz, *Psychosocial Treatment of Chronic Mental Patients.* Cambridge, Mass.: Harvard University Press, 1977.

TABLE 9-8. Percentage of Time Spent per Week in Activity

Activity	Hospital	Milieu and Token Economy
Drug administration	6.3%	3.1%
Unstructured	63.8%	11.6%
Meals	18.8%	14.7%
Morning and evening routines	6.3%	11.6%
Meetings, classes, structured activities	4.9%	58.9%

Adapted from G. L. Paul and R. J. Lentz, *Psychosocial Treatment of Chronic Mental Patients.* Cambridge, Mass.: Harvard University Press, 1977. Reprinted by permission.

The amount of data collected on the two treatment programs and the hospital unit throughout the 4½ years is mind boggling. These include rating scales, frequency data, and time sampling data. Data were also collected serially on the staff's attitude toward mental illness. Obviously, we can only share some of the data here, but the interested student is encouraged to consult Paul and Lentz (1977) for a wealth of information. Also of considerable interest are anecdotes concerning numerous uncontrollable events that impinged upon the project (including deaths, kidnappings, bomb threats, and verbal attacks by state legislators and newspapers). Truly, this is a book to be read by anyone considering conducting a major treatment evaluation within a state institutional system.

What about the outcomes of the project? Throughout the book, comparative data are presented on each six months of the project. The social learning approach proved more effective on numerous measures than the milieu approach at every six-month interval. Figure 9-2 provides a summary of the behavioral rating data for all patients treated in the study (additional patients were added to groups to replace those who made community transitions, deaths, and so on). Other data are presented to show that more patients from the social learning program returned to the community and that the two treatment programs were much more cost-effective than the traditional hospital treatment group.

Despite these and other remarkable outcomes in this well-controlled study, it has been subjected to some criticism (and there will probably be more in the future). For example, Loucks (1978) has questioned the experimental design, specifically the rotation of the staff between the social learning and milieu units (perhaps this rotation did not provide the optimal milieu program). Further, only a small percentage (less than 10%) of those patients treated were able to remain in the community. While this may be a telling statistic when evaluating the success or failure of the project, we would rather view this statistic in relation to the type of patient included in the project (probably the most severely impaired and chronic patients), and speculate about what this outcome may say about establishing realistic treatment goals for this population. While a return to "normal" community living is certainly an ideal goal for those in institutions, with our present technology this may be impossible for a percentage of chronic psychiatric patients. We believe that probably more desirable outcomes for this group will be found someplace between the institution and "normal" community living (at least until our technology improves significantly).

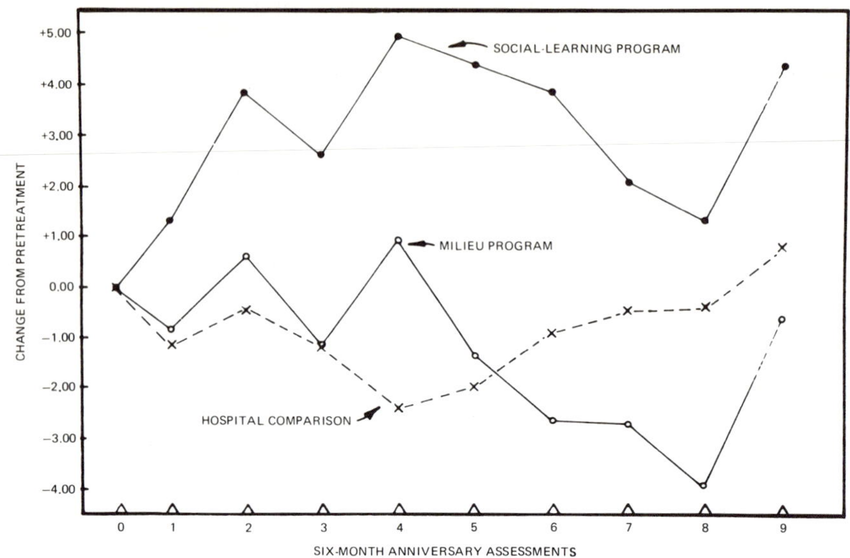

FIGURE 9-2.   Changes in overall functioning from the inpatient assessment battery. (From *Psychosocial Treatment of Chronic Mental Patients,* by G. L. Paul and R. J. Lentz. Copyright 1977 by Harvard University Press. Reprinted by permission.)

Redd, Porterfield, and Anderson (1979) expressed reservations about some of the treatment procedures of the project (for example, "timeout" periods of up to three days). While we would support their criticism, based on the information contained in the book, we wish we had more information about the manner in which decisions were made concerning timeout lengths, why it was necessary to equate them in both treatment units when the target behavior (aggression) was a major problem only in the milieu unit, and the exact procedure that was followed in securing approval for the use of these extended timeouts (what were the appropriate review committees and who were the members of these committees?). When such extreme treatment measures are employed, considerable information and data are needed before any firm conclusions can be made concerning ethical and legal issues.

Community Treatment

In the remainder of the portion of the chapter devoted to mental health problems, we would like to focus briefly on some of the applications of behavior change techniques as treatment has moved from institutions into the community. Social skills training has been one of the major areas of endeavor. Social skills are behaviors that enable one to interact favorably with other individuals in social settings. They are behaviors that produce positive and negative reinforcers and that enable one to escape or avoid aversive stimuli (Libet & Lewinsohn, 1973). We have known for some time that social skills are lacking in institutionalized mental patients (Zigler & Phillips, 1961; Phillips & Zigler, 1964) and have concluded that these skills may be necessary for successful community living. A comprehensive social skills training program has recently been developed by Goldstein, Sprafkin, and Gershaw (1976). This package consists of audio tapes, a text for therapists, notebooks for clients, and other aids. The program is based on modeling by a therapist, role playing, social reinforcement, and transfer training so as to generalize new social skills. Table 9-9 contains a sample of the social skill areas covered by this excellent program.

TABLE 9-9. Sample Social Skill Areas

Expressing a compliment: Telling someone that you like something about him or about his actions.

Expressing appreciation: Letting another person know that you are grateful for something he has done for you.

Expressing encouragement. Telling someone that he should try to do something which he is not sure that he can do.

Asking for help: Requesting that someone who is qualified help you in handling a difficult situation which you have not been able to manage by yourself.

Giving instructions: Clearly explaining to someone how you would like a specific task done.

Expressing affection: Letting someone know that you care about him or her.

Expressing a complaint: Telling someone that he is responsible for creating a particular problem for you and attempting to find a solution for the problem.

Persuading others: Attempting to convince another person that your ideas are better and will be more useful than his.

Expressing anger: Presenting your angry feelings in a direct and honest manner.

Responding to praise: Letting a person know that you are pleased with his praise and that you appreciate it.

Responding to the feelings of others: Trying to understand what the other person is feeling and communicating your understanding to him.

Apologizing: Telling someone sincerely that you are sorry for something you have done to cause him discomfort.

Following instructions: Carrying out directions in a competent manner and giving your reactions.

From *Skill Training for Community Living: Applying Structured Learning Therapy,* by A. P. Goldstein, R. P. Sprafkin, and N. J. Gershaw. Copyright 1976 by Pergamon Press, Ltd. Reprinted by permission.

Programmatically, somewhere between the state institution and community living is the short-term treatment psychiatric ward in a general hospital. Agras (1976) has reviewed the limited amount of behavior change research in this setting. At least in the scientific literature there appear to be only a small number of places around the country where behavior change techniques are being used in any systematic, research-oriented way. The reasons for this are probably varied and related mainly to administrative issues. Perhaps in the future, general hospitals will be more likely to run psychiatric units based on behavior change techniques. An interesting comparative study has been conducted by Gershone, Errickson, Mitchell, and Paulson (1977) at the University of Minnesota Hospital. They compared patients' behavior on two wards—a general psychiatric ward and a token economy ward—in their hospital. Patients in the token economy spent less time in bed, attended more activities, were better groomed, and made fewer comments related to mental status (for example, "I'm crazy, sick, anxious, depressed," and so on).

Treatment of psychiatric patients in state hospitals was to be decreased and replaced by a whole range of services centered around community mental health centers as a result of the Community Mental Health Centers Act of 1963. Liberman, King, and DeRisi (1976) have reviewed the application of behavior change techniques in these settings. Major research projects have been undertaken in mental health centers in Huntsville, Alabama, and by Dr. Robert Liberman, in Oxnard, California. Both centers have developed a variety of community-based services (for example, marriage counseling, psychiatric day treatment, parent training, and so on) which are based almost entirely on behavior change techniques. Because these projects were heavily funded by federal grants, accountability was a major component. Both centers have contributed a variety of research studies (particularly the Oxnard project, which has been quite prolific) that have demonstrated the effectiveness of behavior change techniques in community settings. While there has not been anything close to a nationwide movement to change all community mental health centers to carbon copies of Huntsville and Oxnard, behavior change techniques are finding their way into more and more mental health centers. In certain states, progress toward using these techniques has been rapid; again, this is and will be a matter of administrative decisions more than anything else. We are quite optimistic, however, that behavior change techniques hold much promise as one means of helping those with psychiatric problems live in the community.

MENTAL RETARDATION

There has probably been more behavior change research published in the area of mental retardation than in any other clinical problem. Table 9-10 briefly outlines some of the earliest behavioral research with this population. The earliest studies were directed more toward basic research on operant conditioning with the aim of demonstrating that retarded individuals could learn by the application of operant techniques. Thereafter, the first studies on teaching adaptive behavior occurred and a proliferation of work began.

TABLE 9-10. Early Applications of Behavior Change Techniques to the Mentally Retarded

Investigator(s)	Date	Purposes
Fuller	1949	To teach arm raising
Orlando and Bijou	1960	To study simple and complex schedules of reinforcement
Bijou and Orlando	1961	To study complex schedules of reinforcement
Barrett and Lindsley	1962	To study discrimination learning
Ellis	1963	Toilet training
Spradlin	1964	Self-feeding

It will be impossible to describe or even mention the hundreds of published behavior change studies with the mentally retarded. The interested student is encouraged to read one or more of the excellent reviews published elsewhere (Birnbrauer, 1976; Barrett, 1977). We believe that this research is extremely significant and has contributed greatly in improving the education, treatment, and care of the mentally retarded. Furthermore, these "breakthroughs" with retarded persons, in part, have led to the expansion of behavior change techniques to the multiple areas of human development seen throughout this book. While we cannot deny the importance of legislation, court decrees, and the normalization principle, we would assert that behavior change technology has allowed for the smooth implementation of many of the changes brought about by them. After a brief discussion and conceptualization of mental retardation, we will briefly describe several early behavior change applications within state institutions and then turn to specific techniques used with adaptive and maladaptive behaviors.

Individuals from many different disciplines have struggled through the years in attempts to come up with a suitable definition of mental retardation. Indeed, the term itself has evolved from such distasteful names as idiots, imbeciles, feebleminded, subnormal, and mentally defective. Definitions and classifications have, at times, been based on severity of symptoms, causes, and clinical symptoms (Robinson & Robinson, 1965). We have come to the realization that a score on an intelligence test is insufficient information by which to classify someone as mentally retarded. We have focused more on evaluating the skills or adaptive behaviors an individual possesses before making our diagnosis. Because of this history of ever-changing definitions, we are so uncomfortable with current definitions that we would prefer to avoid including one. We would, rather, like to describe Dr. Sidney Bijou's concept of mental retardation (Bijou, 1963, 1966, 1968a, 1968b), for it most reflects our own attitude. While Bijou does not call it that, *behavioral retardation* might be a better way of describing mental retardation as he views it. The development of retarded behavior does not require any special theory; rather, it occurs as a function of the same behavioral principles (as described in Chapter 1 of this book) as normal behavior does. Development, in general, is a result of interactions between the behavior of the individual (as a biologically functioning system) and environmental events. Retardation will occur when conditions prevent, delay, or reduce the development of effective ways of interacting with the environment (Bijou, 1968b). Behavioral retardation can occur as the result of a number of different events including: (1) alteration of the anatomical structure or physiological functioning of a child, which may restrict the response potentiality of a child and also the number of stimuli that a child can process; (2) restricted reinforcement, noncontingent reinforcement, or inconsistent reinforcement; (3) restriction of normal environmental stimuli/activities, which prevents the learning of normal skills; and (4) experience with strong aversive stimuli, such as strong punishment or an injury from accident (Bijou, 1968a). You can see that mental retardation or behavioral retardation can be a complex problem resulting from many factors. Bijou's analysis logically leads to remediation of retarded behavior through the behavior change techniques described throughout this book. Retarded people have difficulty learning in normal environments; our task is to reconstruct or program the environment so as to maximize their learning potential. We must, as Ogden Lindsley (1964) has said, create a prosthetic learning environment.

Early Programs in Institutions

One of the first institutions for the mentally retarded where extensive investigations of behavior change techniques were conducted was Rainier School in Washington. Here, Drs. Sidney Bijou, Jay Birnbrauer, and Montrose Wolf implemented a token economy system for classroom performance. Tokens could be exchanged for a variety of reinforcers (Birnbrauer & Lawler, 1964; Birnbrauer, Wolf, Kidder, & Tague, 1965; Bijou, Birnbrauer, Kidder, & Tague, 1966). An interesting follow-up of some of the residents who participated in this program has been conducted by Sulzbacher and Kidder (1975), and Table 9-11 compares students from the token economy program (Program Learning Center or PLC) with matched cohorts. It is obvious that, in the long run, this behavior change program was very effective.

TABLE 9-11. Comparisons of PLC Students with Matched Cohorts on Selected Indices of Subsequent Success

	PLC *(n = 52)*	*Cohort* *(n = 30)*
Percentage who are currently productively engaged (working or in school)	91.5	76.6
Percentage living in community	68.5	66.7
Percentage who live independently and are fully employed	13	10
Percentage who failed on placement and were returned to institution	1.8	13.3
Percentage who have committed legal offenses	0	6.6

From Stephen I. Sulzbacher and John D. Kidder, "Following Up on the Behavior Analysis Model." In *Behavior Analysis,* Eugene Ramp and George Semb, Eds., © 1975, p. 67. Reprinted by permission of Prentice-Hall, Inc., Englewood Cliffs, New Jersey.

A similar program was developed at Parsons Training Center in Kansas by Frederic Girardeau, Joseph Spradlin, and James Lent. Again, a token economy was established; however, behavior targets were not limited to classroom performance. Self-care behaviors, talking, and social behaviors were reinforced (Girardeau & Spradlin, 1964; Spradlin & Girardeau, 1966; Lent, 1966).

Gerald Bensberg, Cecil Colwell, and Robert Cassell (1965) developed a cottage-based behavior change program for teaching self-help skills at Pinecrest School in Louisiana. Shaping procedures and food reinforcers were used to teach such things as self-feeding, dressing, and toileting. As the result of the successes from these and several other behavior change programs, treatment of the retarded in most institutions gradually became based more and more on behavior change techniques. Today, there is probably not a public institution in the entire country where behavior change techniques are not the major treatment approach.

Behavioral Assessment and Task Analysis

One of the areas of recent advancement in the area of mental retardation has been the proliferation of instruments that assess the adaptive behavior in a variety of functional domains. As noted in Chapter 2, Walls, Werner, Bacon, and Zane (1977) have written a comprehensive evaluation of the checklist type of behavioral assessment. Most of the checklists contain items arranged by domain, such as gross motor skills, fine motor skills, receptive language, self-help skills, and so on. Within each domain, items are arranged in sequential order from easiest to most difficult. Tables 9-12 and 9-13 show examples of receptive language and dressing domains from the Minnesota Developmental Programming System checklist. In most settings, use of various behavioral checklists form the basis for program planning (and subsequent evaluation) for the mentally retarded. A more comprehensive discussion of assessment of the mentally retarded and other handicapped groups may be found in a book edited by Sabatino and Miller (1979).

TABLE 9-12. Receptive Language Scale

1. Turn head toward the source of a sound
2. Responds by eye contact or verbal acknowledgement when name is called
3. Responds to the instruction, "Look at me," with 2 seconds of eye contact
4. Obeys a simple instruction such as, "Come here."
5. Performs the appropriate action when the word "me" is used [as in] "Give *me* the ball."
6. Stops an activity upon request such as, "No," or "Stop."
7. Listens to a story for 3 minutes
8. Understands prepositions by following instructions such as "Put the ball *in* the box," or "Put the broom *behind the door.*
9. Responds to nonverbal communications from others such as frowning, crying, smiling, etc., by returning the gesture or giving an appropriate verbal response
10. Points to pictured objects in a book upon request
11. Points to many common objects such as a ball, spoon, etc., upon request
12. Points to 10 body parts such as nose, eyes, mouth, etc., upon request
13. Follows two-step directions in order such as, "Get the ball and close the door."
14. Points to a large object and a small object upon request
15. Identifies 3 colors out of a group of colors when asked, "Which color is blue? Red? (etc.)"
16. Follows three-step directions such as, "Stand up, open the book, and move the chair."
17. Follows verbal directions to get from building to building in a familiar setting
18. Listens to a one-page story and answers, "Yes" or "No," to specific questions about it
19. Listens to a one-page story and answers questions about it such as, "What happened first to Tom?"
20. Summarizes a TV program in own words

From *Minnesota Developmental Programming System: Behavioral Scales,* by W. H. Bock and R. F. Weatherman. Copyright 1976 by the University of Minnesota. Reprinted by permission of the Regents of the University of Minnesota and the authors.

A second recent major advancement in the area of mental retardation has been in the area of program development and task analyses of adaptive behaviors. In the early 1970s, we recall sitting at our desks in our offices and writing programs for institutional staff to use in teaching specific skills such as toileting, eating with utensils, and so on. We came to realize that there were probably hundreds of professionals sitting at their desks in public institutions doing *exactly the same*

TABLE 9-13. Dressing Scale

1. Offers little or no resistance while being dressed and undressed
2. Extends and withdraws arms and legs while being dressed and undressed
3. Removes slip-over shirt
4. Removes socks, underpants, unzipped outer pants and unbuttoned shirt or dress
5. Undresses self completely (may need help with belt or bra)
6. Puts on underpants, slip-over shirt or dress, outer pants, and socks
7. Puts on coat or jacket (need not fasten)
8. Unzips clothing with front zippers
9. Dresses self completely except for fastenings such as buttons, zippers, ties, or hooks
10. Puts on and takes off outer clothing including coat, hat, gloves and boots without assistance on fastenings
11. Puts shoes on correct feet
12. Buttons clothing
13. Starts and closes a front zipper
14. Ties a bow knot in shoelaces
15. Laces shoes with a lace in each eyelet
16. Puts on and takes off ties, scarves, belts, watches, or jewelry
17. Puts on outer wear without reminder in response to cold or rain
18. Changes dirty clothing without reminder
19. Selects clothing for seasonal and weather conditions and different occasions
20. Selects correct size, type, and style of clothing at a store

From *Minnesota Developmental Programming System: Behavioral Scales,* by W. H. Bock and R. F. Weatherman. Copyright 1976 by the University of Minnesota. Reprinted by permission of the Regents of the University of Minnesota and the authors.

thing! This waste of effort has been rectified through better communication networks (such as the newsletter of The Association for the Severely Handicapped), the publication of large collections of task-analyzed skills (Wheeler, Miller, Dukes, Salisbury, Merritt, & Horton, 1977), and the publication of manuals aimed at teaching specific behaviors such as those developed by Project More (hairwashing, toothbrushing, eating, and so on), toilet training (Foxx & Azrin, 1973b), language (Lovaas, 1977; Guess, Sailor & Baer, 1977), and imitation (Striefel, 1974). Tables 9-14 and 9-15 show examples of the type of task analysis now available. Also noteworthy are a number of books and manuals designed to help parents teach specific skills to their handicapped children, such as the *Steps to Independence* series developed by Bruce Baker and his associates (1977–78) and Martin Kozloff's *Educating Children with Learning and Behavior Problems* (1974).

Adaptive Behavior

Obviously, it will be impossible to extensively review all of the research on the use of behavior change techniques in teaching adaptive behavior. We would like to make a few observations, however, about this work and then examine one particular program in detail. Finally, we will make some comments about future directions. There are certain commonalities that one can find in most of the research on teaching adaptive behavior to the mentally retarded. The first of these is a *task analysis* approach taken to teaching (Anderson & Faust, 1973). A specific skill, such as toothbrushing, is broken down into very minute steps and these steps are then taught or chained together in a sequential manner. Frequently within steps it

TABLE 9-14. Task Analysis: Undressing—Pullover Shirt

Specific Target Behavior: When given the command, "———, take off your shirt," student removes pullover shirt.

General Instructions: Method I—Backward Chaining Procedure. Conduct training sessions in bedroom or bathroom. Use this program for polo shirts, undershirts, and pullover sweaters.

Prereq.:

Materials: Complete the program using a shirt which is a size or two larger than the student's own size; then practice whole sequence with proper size shirt.

Goal or Step (Student Behavior)	*Method (Trainer Behavior)*
9. Pulls hem above stomach.	9. Give command, "———, take off your shirt." Have student grasp both sides of bottom hem of shirt and pull shirt up above stomach. (Standing either in front or back of student is easiest position for trainer.)
8. Bunches shirt under arms.	8. Have student pull shirt up under arms.
7. Pulls collar to back of head.	7. Have student reach behind head and grasp back of collar with preferred hand and pull collar to back of head.
6. Pulls collar to top of head.	6. Have student pull collar to top of head.
5. Pulls shirt over head.	5. Have student pull collar off head and continue pulling until body of shirt comes completely over head (at this point shirt is on both arms and stretches across front of student under his chin). Student may need to be encouraged to use other hand to aid in bringing shirt over head during this step.
4. Pulls shirt sleeve of preferred arm to below elbow.	4. Have student pull sleeve of *preferred arm* to below elbow.
3. Pulls shirt sleeve off preferred arm.	3. Have student pull sleeve of shirt off *preferred arm*.
2. Pulls shirt sleeve of non-preferred arm to below elbow.	2. Have student pull sleeve of *non-preferred arm* to below elbow.
1. Pulls shirt sleeve off non-preferred arm.	1. Have student pull sleeve of shirt off *non-preferred arm*.

From *Murdoch Center C & Y Program Library: A Collection of Step-by-Step Programs for the Developmentally Disabled,* by A. J. Wheeler, R. A. Miller, J. Dukes, E. W. Salisbury, V. Merritt, and B. Horton. Copyright 1977 by Murdoch Center. Reprinted by permission.

is necessary to reinforce successive approximations or to shape behavior. Sometimes it may also be necessary to use prompts (physical, verbal, modeling, and so on) and then to fade them out. In teaching some tasks, a discrete trial approach is taken, whereby a series of successive trials are given with a specific task, and are presented with feedback for correct responses and perhaps some corrective feedback for incorrect responses. The final element common to almost all uses of behavior change techniques in the teaching of adaptive behaviors is the use of positive reinforcement. We are pleased to see in the literature that reinforcement is frequently individualized or that token reinforcement systems are being used. Another trend is the exploration of novel types of reinforcers such as vibration (Murphy, Nunes, & Hutchings-Ruprecht, 1977; Johnson, Firth, & Davey, 1978). These, then, are the critical elements of most adaptive behavior change programs: task analysis, chaining, successive approximation, prompting, discrete trial presentation, and positive reinforcement.

TABLE 9-15. Task Analysis: Knife—Spreading

Specific Target Behavior: Student uses knife to spread when appropriate foods are presented.

General Instructions: Method I—Backward Chaining Procedure. Begin program using very soft spreads, then gradually introduce spreads which are more difficult to spread.

Prereq.: Choosing Proper Utensil (SH-Ea-11)

Materials:

Goal or Step (Student Behavior)	*Method (Trainer Behavior)*
7. *Optional:* Holds food with nonpreferred hand.	7. If necessary, have student hold food in palm of nonpreferred hand (e.g., bread), on fingertips (e.g., roll), or on plate with fingertips.
6. Picks up knife.	6. Have student pick up knife with preferred hand and hold with sharp edge of blade downward.
5. Scoops spread onto knife blade.	5. Have student lower blade straight downward and scoop spread onto flat side of knife blade.
4. Moves knife to food.	4. Have student carry knife with flat side of blade upward holding spread (to avoid spilling) to food.
3. Places knife blade on edge of food.	3. Have student lower knife with flat side of blade (holding spread) upward then turn flat side of blade (holding spread) downward to come in contact with food.
2. Spreads spread.	2. Have student move flat side of blade across food until spread is spread as desired.
1. Places knife on edge of plate.	1. Have student place knife on edge of plate or in appropriate place if no plate was used.

From *Murdoch Center C & Y Program Library: A Collection of Step-by-Step Programs for the Developmentally Disabled,* by A. J. Wheeler, R. A. Miller, J. Dukes, E. W. Salisbury, V. Merritt, and B. Horton, Copyright 1977 by Murdoch Center. Reprinted by permission.

Exemplary of adaptive behavior programs is the toilet training program developed by Azrin and Foxx (1971). Based on research with profoundly retarded in a state institution, they have written a manual, *Toilet Training the Retarded* (Foxx & Azrin, 1973b), which is being used in settings all over the country. Table 9-16 outlines the major steps in this program. It is quite similar to the procedure they developed for normal children described in Chapter 7. The major differences are that it may take longer (Figure 9-3 shows the training data for the nine adults in the original study), the use of more prompts may be necessary (or physical prompts as opposed to verbal instructions), and additional skills, such as dressing and undressing and initiating approaches to the toilet, may need to be taught. In addition to the training procedure seen in Table 9-16, there is also a maintenance procedure to be used (see Table 9-17). Another difference is the use of what is called Full Cleanliness Training, which is instituted after the client first self-initiates an approach to the toilet. This is an overcorrection or restitution procedure that involves requiring the person to mop up the floor, change pants, and wash out the wet pants. While Azrin and Foxx's toilet training program is initially time consuming (they recommend as long as possible each day and *no less than four hours*) the success achieved after relatively few days (as seen in Figure 9-3) is astounding. This means that those who work with the mentally retarded will have to spend much less time in the long run on the process of taking the retarded to the toilet and changing their wet clothing. The time they have gained as a result of training can then be spent on teaching other necessary adaptive skills.

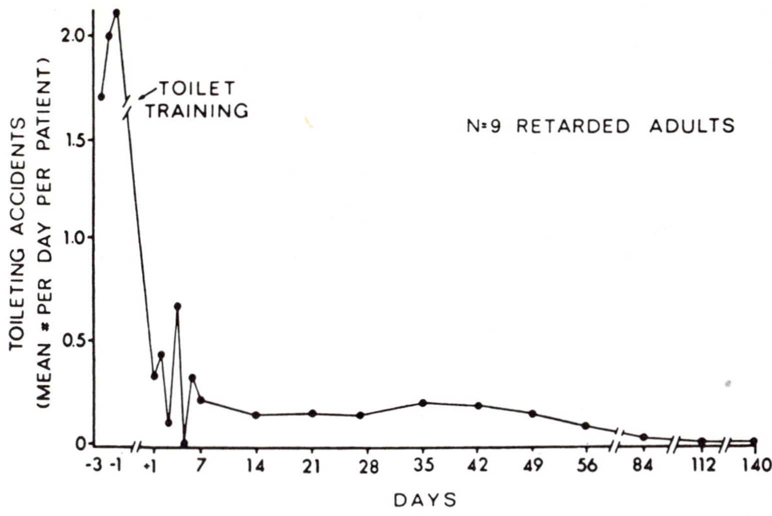

FIGURE 9-3.   The effect of toilet training on the frequency of accidents. (From "A Rapid Method of Toilet Training the Institutionalized Retarded," by N. H. Azrin and R. M. Foxx. In *Journal of Applied Behavior Analysis*, 1971, *4*, 89–99. Copyright 1971 by the Society for the Experimental Analysis of Behavior, Inc. Reprinted by permission.)

TABLE 9-16. Outline of Toilet Training Procedure

I. When No Accidents Occur
1) Resident seated in chair when not seated on toilet bowl
2) Resident drinks fluids every half-hour
3) Scheduled toileting of resident every half-hour
4) Resident given edible and social reinforcer every 5 min while dry
5) Shaping of undressing and dressing during toileting
6) Resident given edible and social reinforcer following elimination in toilet bowl and returned to chair.

II. When Accidents Occur
1) Trainer disconnects pants alarm
2) Trainer obtains resident's attention
3) Resident walks to laundry area to obtain fresh clothing
4) Resident undresses himself
5) Resident walks to nearby shower, receives shower, and dresses himself
6) Resident obtains mop or cloth and cleans soiled area on chair or floor
7) Resident handwashes soiled pants, wrings pants out, and hangs pants up to dry
8) Trainer removes resident's chair from use
9) 1-hour timeout procedures:
   a) no edibles or social reinforcers every 5 min;
   b) no fluids every 30 min;
   c) chair not available;
   d) continue 30-min scheduled toilet periods.

From "A Rapid Method of Toilet Training the Institutionalized Retarded," by N. H. Azrin and R. M. Foxx. In *Journal of Applied Behavior Analysis*, 1971, *4*, 89–99. Copyright 1971 by the Society for the Experimental Analysis of Behavior, Inc. Reprinted by permission.

TABLE 9-17. Post-Training Ward Maintenance Procedure

I. General Procedure
1) Advance assignment of one attendant for Toilet Responsibility each shift
2) Snack period between breakfast and lunch and between lunch and dinner
3) Residents pants inspected at mealtime, snacktime and bedtime (6 times daily)
4) Attendant initials record sheet when residents checked; record sheet sent directly to supervisor
5) Discontinued use of both apparatuses for detecting eliminations.

II. When Accidents Occur
1) Cleanliness training whenever an accident was detected:
   a) Resident walks to laundry area to obtain fresh clothing
   b) Resident undresses himself
   c) Resident walks to nearby shower, receives shower and dresses himself
   d) Resident obtains mop or cloth and cleans soiled area on chair or floor
   e) Resident handwashes soiled pants, wrings pants out, and hangs pants up to dry
2) Delay of meal for 1 hr if accident prior to meal
3) Omission of snacks if accident prior to snack
4) Attendant initials and records each accident

Minimal Maintenance — Starts Eight Weeks after Training
1) Inspections only at mealtime and bedtime
2) Cleanliness training given for accidents

Termination of Maintenance Procedure — When resident is continent for at least one month.
1) No regular inspections for that patient
2) Cleanliness training given for accidents when detected

From "A Rapid Method of Toilet Training the Institutionalized Retarded," by N. H. Azrin and R. M. Foxx. In *Journal of Applied Behavior Analysis*, 1971, *4*, 89–99. Copyright 1971 by the Society for the Experimental Analysis of Behavior, Inc. Reprinted by permission.

Before leaving the area of adaptive behavior, we would like to comment on some recent trends. Language has been an area of considerable deficit for many of the mentally retarded. Stemming from early work on imitation and the formation of response classes (Baer, Peterson, & Sherman, 1967; Wheeler & Sulzer, 1970;

Martin, 1971; Lutzker & Sherman, 1974), a number of language training programs based on behavior change principles have been developed (Lovaas, 1977; Guess, Sailor, & Baer, 1977). Simultaneously, we have seen the application of nonverbal communication systems, such as sign language and Bliss Symbolics, to the mentally retarded. We would like to see the use of more behavior change techniques in teaching them nonverbal communication systems. A step in this direction was taken by Reid and Hurlbut (1977) who taught a picture-board communication system to nonvocal retarded adults using verbal instructions, manual guidance, and verbal praise.

Finally, although we spoke about using behavioral assessment to set adaptive behavior goals for the mentally retarded, we are not certain if we yet have a complete understanding of the skills necessary for a mentally retarded person to function in the community. Certainly, social skills are essential and more efforts are needed here. Some investigators have thought seriously about the problem of community living and have attacked deficit areas as they are uncovered. Notable is Dr. Anthony J. Cuvo who, with his colleagues, has used the task-analysis procedures described earlier to teach the mentally retarded change computation, mending skills, and how to make emergency phone calls, as well as working on teaching specific jobs such as janitorial skills (Cuvo, Veitch, Trace, & Konke, in press; Cronin & Cuvo, 1979; Risley & Cuvo, in press; Cuvo, Leaf, & Borakove, 1978). Another one of the critical elements of Cuvo and his colleagues' research is that the task analyses are validated by experts such as sewing teachers, janitors, and home economists. We need many more efforts such as these to produce independent and semi-independent living skill programs; hopefully, more critical survival skill training programs will be developed. Social skills training for the mentally retarded has been overlooked until recently (Bornstein, Bach, McFall, Friman, & Lyons, 1980). There is a need for investigations of how to disseminate these programs and train trainers to use them, and for long-term follow-up of the mentally retarded in community placements.

Maladaptive Behavior—Autism

We begin this section on the use of behavior change techniques to reduce maladaptive behavior in the retarded with a discussion of Ivar Lovaas' treatment program for autistic children at the Neuropsychiatric Institute at the University of California at Los Angeles. Lovaas pioneered efforts to manage major behavior problems in a severely handicapped population. While autism may be different from mental retardation, many of the problems presented (especially in the area of maladaptive behavior) and behavior change techniques used are similar. Additionally, infantile autism is now regarded by most as an organic disease, despite the presence of psychiatric-like symptoms (Coleman, 1978).

Ritvo and Freeman (1977) have characterized autism as a behaviorally defined syndrome with the essential features usually being exhibited before 30 months of age. These features are: (1) disturbances of developmental rates and sequences of motor, cognitive, and social-adaptive skills; (2) hyper- or hyporeactivity to sensory stimuli; (3) disturbances of speech, language cognition, and nonverbal communication; and (4) disturbances of the capacity to appropriately relate to people, objects, and events. While some may have thought at one time that the use of behavior change techniques would cure autism, there are probably few, if any, people working with this population who would say this now. Behavior change techniques have been used to suppress the symptoms (for example, language deficits, self-stimulating behavior, ritualistic or compulsive behaviors, avoidance of people, and so on) of autism, but they have not eliminated autism. Work with this population is extremely tedious and necessarily long-lasting. It requires patience and expertise. Even with optimal programs and the alteration of some problems, autism still exists.

Lovaas' program focused on the use of behavior change techniques to teach social behaviors, develop language skills and eliminate self-stimulatory behaviors. Undoubtedly, he pioneered the way toward the use of the discrete trial method, shaping, chaining, prompting, and contingent positive reinforcement with the severely handicapped. Numerous well-controlled research investigations have documented the effectiveness of these techniques (Lovaas, Berberich, Perloff, & Schaeffer, 1966; Lovaas, Freitag, Kinder, Rubenstein, Schaeffer, & Simmons, 1966; Lovaas, Freitas, Nelson, & Whalen, 1967; Lovaas & Simmons, 1969). In 1973, Lovaas, Koegel, Simmons, and Long published a summary of their treatment of

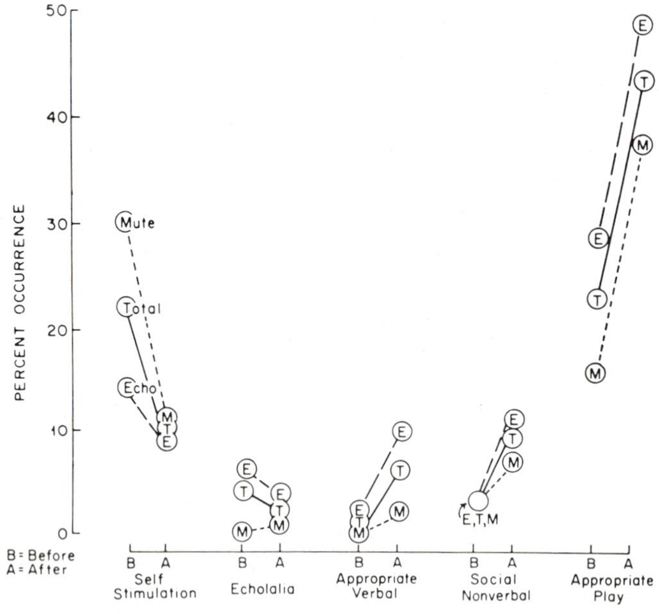

FIGURE 9-4. Multiple response measures for autistic children. (From "Some Generalization and Follow-Up Measures on Autistic Children in Behavior Therapy," by O. I. Lovaas, R. Koegel, J. Q. Simmons, and J. S. Long. In *Journal of Applied Behavior Analysis*, 1973, 6, 131–166. Copyright 1973 by the Society for the Experimental Analysis of Behavior, Inc. Reprinted by permission.)

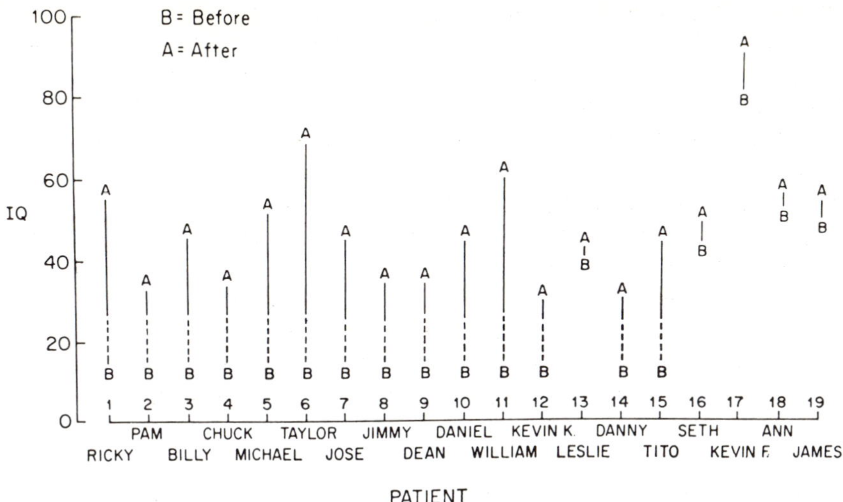

FIGURE 9-5.   IQ scores before and after treatment. Dotted lines indicate the patient was untestable before treatment. (From "Some Generalization and Follow-Up Measures on Autistic Children in Behavior Therapy," by O. I. Lovaas, R. Koegel, J. Q. Simmons, and J. S. Long. In *Journal of Applied Behavior Analysis*, 1973, 6, 131–166. Copyright 1973 by the Society for the Experimental Analysis of Behavior, Inc. Reprinted by permission.)

20 autistic children and some follow-up data. Figure 9-4 presents data on multiple response measures on these children. Improvement can be seen in the form of increased adaptive behavior and decreased maladaptive behavior. Figure 9-5 shows changes in IQ scores for the children as the result of treatment. The changes are impressive, although it is significant that almost all of these children remained functionally mentally retarded. Finally, Figure 9-6 presents follow-up data on a number of the children. The ultimate outcome for these children was highly dependent on the environment to which they returned. Children of parents who were "good" at using behavior change techniques did better than parents who were not.

Recent efforts toward working with autistic children have focused on parent training and stimulus overselectivity. A series of studies (Lovaas, Schreibman, Koegel, & Rehm, 1971; Lovaas & Schreibman, 1971; Koegel & Wilhelm, 1973; Schreibman & Lovaas, 1973; Reynolds, Newsom, & Lovaas, 1974; Rincover & Koegel, 1975) has shown that autistic (and to some extent retarded) children attend to very specific stimuli in their environment (for example, their behavior comes under the control of a much more restricted stimulus than does the behavior of normal children). This has led to extremely important research on the effect of stimulus overselectivity upon training and upon generalization. Research on parent training has shown that a very comprehensive training package is needed for parents to improve their autistic children's behavior (Koegel, Glahn, & Nieminen, 1978).

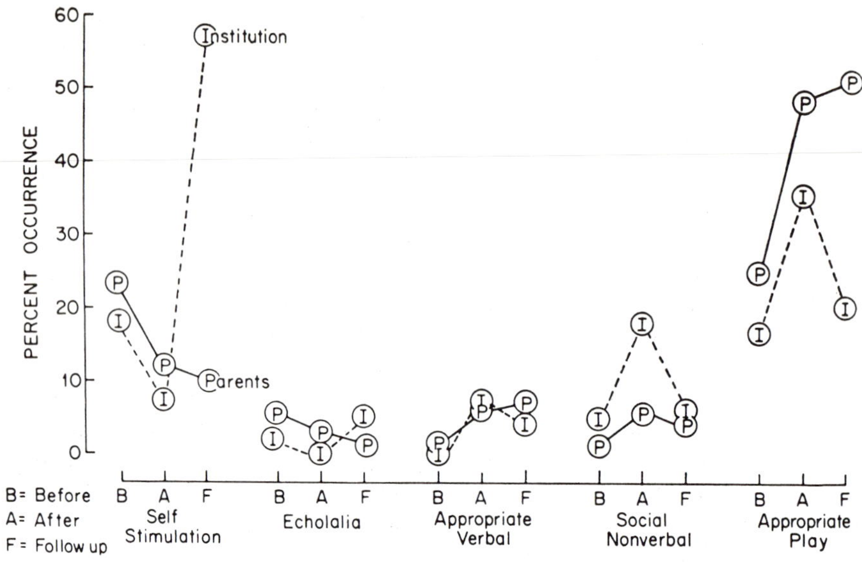

FIGURE 9-6.   Multiple response follow-up measures. Percent occurrence of the various behaviors is plotted on the ordinate before (B) and after (A) treatment and for the latest follow-up (F) measures. "I" refers to the average results for four children who were institutionalized, and "P" refers to average results for nine children who were discharged to their parents' care. (From "Some Generalization and Follow-Up Measures on Autistic Children in Behavior Therapy," by O. I. Lovaas, R. Koegel, J. Q. Simmons, and J. S. Long. In *Journal of Applied Behavior Analysis*, 1973, 6, 131–166. Copyright 1973 by the Society for the Experimental Analysis of Behavior, Inc. Reprinted by permission.)

While Lovaas and his associates found that many maladaptive behaviors (particularly the self-stimulating ones) decreased as adaptive behaviors were taught (Lovaas & Newsom, 1976), they were also confronted with certain maladaptive behaviors, which, they found, they had to try actively to eliminate. In one of the first examples of this (Lovaas, Schaeffer, & Simmons, 1965), they decreased the self-stimulatory and aggressive behaviors of two autistic children and increased physical contact with adults. This was accomplished through a procedure that involved escape from, and later, avoidance of electric shock.

Both extinction (Bucher & Lovaas, 1968; Lovaas & Simmons, 1969) and contingent electric shock (Lovaas, Schaeffer, & Simmons, 1965; Lovaas & Simmons, 1969; Lovaas, Litrownik, & Mann, 1971) have been systematically examined as treatments for self-injurious behavior and self-stimulating behavior. Figure 9-7 represents the use of extinction or ignoring the self-destructive behavior of two children (Lovaas & Simmons, 1969). Data on the use of contingent electric shock for the same problem in another child can be seen in Figure 9-8.

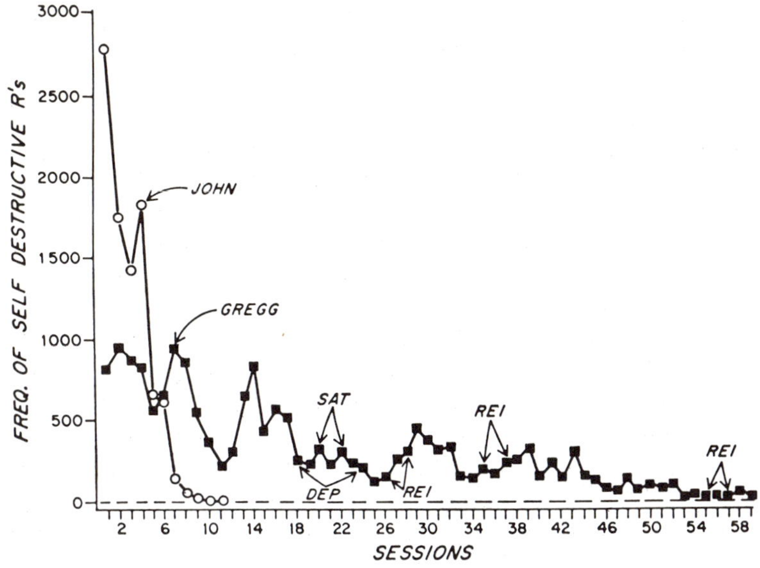

FIGURE 9-7.   Self-destructive behavior of two children over successive days of extinction treatment, during 90-minute sessions. SAT stands for satiation, DEP for deprivation, and REI for reinforcement. (From "Manipulation of Self-Destruction in Three Retarded Children," by O. I. Lovaas and J. Q. Simmons. In *Journal of Applied Behavior Analysis*, 1969, 2, 143–157. Copyright 1969 by the Society for the Experimental Analysis of Behavior, Inc. Reprinted by permission.)

The obvious question that such data present concerns choosing between a "less restrictive" procedure such as extinction and a "more restrictive" procedure such as electric shock. This is an extremely difficult decision and must be based on an examination of the severity and topography of the behavior. The use of extinction may be obviated in certain situations, as it could lead to a less immediate result and could, in a sense, be more restrictive (Budd & Baer, 1976). Throughout this book, whenever electric shock has been used, it has been restricted to situations where the problem behavior was life-threatening (for example, rumination or severe self-injurious behavior) or severely aggressive toward others (for example, biting, eye gouging). We believe that this is as it should be and that severe forms of punishment, such as electric shock, should be restricted to a limited group of problem behaviors and then only when attempts at less restrictive alternatives have failed.

Maladaptive Behavior—Reduction Techniques

Luckily, there are between these two extremes numerous other procedures that can be used to eliminate maladaptive behaviors. Bates and Wehman (1977) have recently surveyed the literature on the application of behavior change tech-

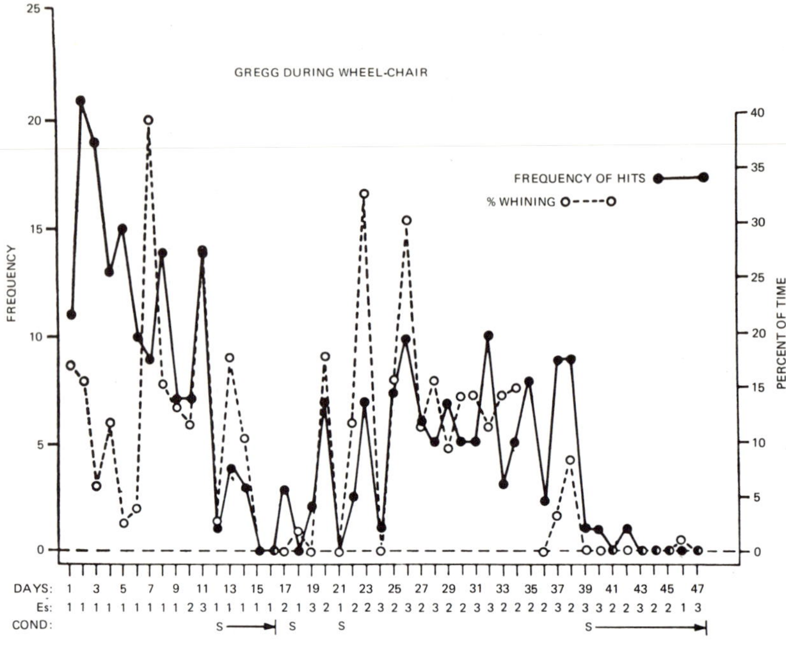

FIGURE 9-8.   Self-destructive behavior during wheelchair sessions as a function of shock (S) and the attending adult (E) who delivered shock. Each session lasted 2.5 minutes. (From "Manipulation of Self-Destruction in Three Retarded Children," by O. I. Lovaas and J. Q. Simmons. In *Journal of Applied Behavior Analysis*, 1969, 2, 143–157. Copyright 1969 by the Society for the Experimental Analysis of Behavior, Inc. Reprinted by permission.)

niques to the maladaptive behavior of the mentally retarded, and a summary of the findings can be seen in Table 9-18.

According to Table 9-18, the three behavior change treatments used most often are differential reinforcement of other behavior (DRO), timeout, and over-correction. We would like to describe briefly some examples of these procedures. Peterson and Peterson (1968) reported treating the self-injuring behavior (SIB) of an 8-year-old boy with differential reinforcement of other behavior (DRO). He was seen in 15-minute treatment sessions during one or more meals per day. After an initial baseline phase, ¼ teaspoonful of his meal was fed to him contingent upon a 3–5-second interval without any SIB. A third phase was added during which the boy had to walk across the treatment room (12 feet) and sit in a chair. He was given food contingent upon no SIB during this time. Following a reversal phase, this third phase was reintroduced. The results of this experiment demonstrated the effectiveness of the delivery of food contingent upon the absence of SIB (see Johnson & Baumeister, 1978, for a review of the treatment of SIB).

TABLE 9-18. Percentage of Behavior Problems Treated by Different Methods

	Aggressive Behavior	Self Injurious Behavior	Stereo-typical Behavior	Classroom Disruptions Behavior	Non-compliant Behavior	Inappropriate Social Behavior	Totals
DRO		1.8%	5.4%	5.4%	1.8%	5.4%	23.2%
DRO & Punishment	1.8%	5.4%				1.8%	12.5%
Time Out	7.1%		1.8%	3.6%	1.8%	1.8%	16.1%
Response Cost and Time Out	3.6%						3.6%
Response Cost			1.8%	3.6%	1.8%		7.1%
Overcorrection	3.6%		5.4%			10.7%	19.6%
Restraint and Instruction					5.4%		5.4%
Electric Shock		3.6%					3.6%
Extinction				3.6%			3.6%
Satiation						1.8%	1.8%
Nonspecific Environmental Changes	1.8%	1.8%					3.6%
	17.9%	16.1%	14.3%	19.6%	10.7%	21.4%	

From "Behavior Management with the Mentally Retarded: An Empirical Analysis of the Research," by P. Bates and P. Wehman. In *Mental Retardation*, 1977, *15*, 9–12. Reprinted by permission of the American Association on Mental Deficiency.

While there were no follow-up data on this program, it does point the way to a possible effective positive method for eliminating maladaptive behavior. For example, Lutzker (1974) used a DRO procedure (social reinforcement) to reduce the frequency with which a mentally retarded adult exhibited himself. It is difficult to find studies, however, that have used DRO to the exclusion of other techniques. Most often it is combined with some other procedure (Polvinale & Lutzker, 1980). We believe that this is unfortunate, for some systematic research on the efficacy of DRO as a technique to eliminate maladaptive behavior would prove of great potential benefit to settings which might prohibit more restrictive procedures. Also worthy of study would be DRL (differential reinforcement of low rates of behavior) schedules as a possible behavior change technique for behaviors that are not too intolerable.

Timeout from positive reinforcement has been somewhat better examined as a technique for eliminating maladaptive behavior in the mentally retarded. For example, White, Nielsen, and Johnson (1972) have studied the length of timeout as a variable with 20 institutionalized retardates. One-minute, 15-minute, and 30-minute timeouts were compared as a part of programs to reduce such behaviors as aggression, tantrums, and self-destruction. The two longer time lengths were more effective in reducing target behaviors, but there was *no difference* between them. Since baselines and different timeout lengths were alternated serially across time, a second important finding of this study is that brief timeouts are more effective when used *first* rather than *after* target subjects have been exposed to longer timeout durations. Favell, McGimsey, and Jones (1978) have found that physical restraint (usually a method of timeout) can function as a reinforcer and actually increase non-SIB behavior. Other investigators have combined timeout with other procedures such as DRO in the treatment of aggression and SIB (Bostow & Bailey, 1969; Repp & Deitz, 1974). Comparisons have also been made (in the reduction of antisocial behavior) between timeout and response cost, with the finding that longer timeouts (30 minutes) were equivalent to loss of a large number of tokens (30), while both were more effective than shorter timeouts (5 minutes) and loss of a small number of tokens (5) (Burchard & Barrera, 1972). Finally, Calhoun and Matherne (1975) have found that continuous schedules of timeout were better than intermittent schedules of timeout (FR 5, FR 2) in decreasing aggressive behavior in a retarded child; however, Clark, Rowbury, Baer, and Baer (1973) demonstrated that intermittent schedules of timeout may effectively control behavior once it has been reduced to a low frequency by a continuous schedule of timeout. In summary, timeouts have been found to be a very effective procedure for use in reducing the maladaptive behavior of the mentally retarded. Continuous (rather than intermittent) applications of longer timeouts (rather than brief ones) appear to be most effective. More research, however, is certainly needed on the duration question, for we are aware of many unpublished studies that have demonstrated the effectiveness of very brief timeouts. Hobbs and Forehand (1977) have written an excellent review of the use of timeout.

Ollendick and Matson (1978) have recently reviewed the use of overcorrection as a technique to eliminate maladaptive behaviors. You will recall that Azrin and Foxx (1971) first described this technique in their description of their toilet training

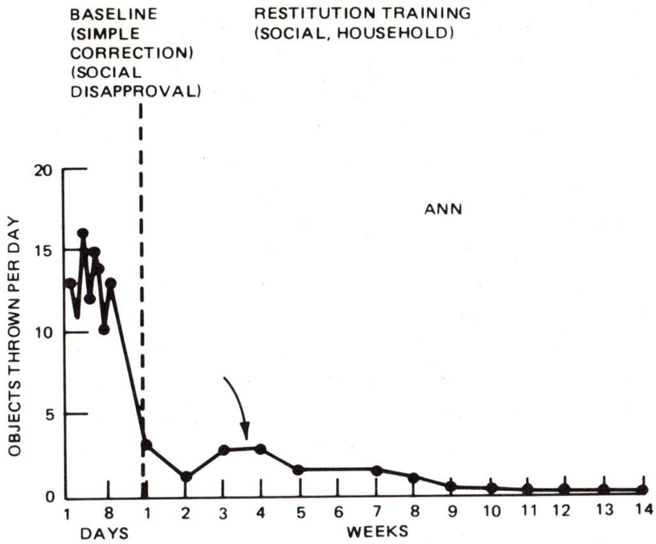

FIGURE 9-9.   The effect of restitution training on the number of objects thrown. (From "Restitution: A Method of Eliminating Aggressive-Disruptive Behavior of Mentally Retarded and Brain Damaged Patients," by R. M. Foxx and N. H. Azrin. In *Behaviour Research and Therapy*, 1972, *10*, 15–27. Reprinted by permission of Pergamon Press, Ltd.)

program for the retarded. Overcorrection involves restitution (correcting the consequences of maladaptive behavior, including at times to excess) and positive practice (requiring that a related appropriate behavior be practiced, at times to excess). The effectiveness of overcorrection is dependent upon: (1) relating the restitution directly to the maladaptive behavior; (2) implementing the restitution immediately; (3) prolonging the time period of the restitution; and (4) requiring the restitution to be performed continuously without resting (Foxx & Azrin, 1972). Figures 9-9 and 9-10 show data from two aggressive-disruptive female mentally retarded residents of an institution who were treated by overcorrection (Foxx & Azrin, 1972). Very evident is the immediate effectiveness of the procedures. The person whose behavior is graphed in Figure 9-9 overturned and threw furniture. After an initial baseline, with each incidence she was required to spend at least 30 minutes remaking the bed or straightening up the furniture, then either smoothing out all other beds on the ward or cleaning all furniture on the ward or sweeping and mopping the entire floor. In addition, she was required to apologize to all individuals on the ward or reassure them that she was sorry. A similar procedure was used on the woman whose behavior is depicted in Figure 9-10. She bit residents and staff frequently. After an initial baseline, she was required to spend 10 minutes cleaning her mouth with a toothbrush soaked in an oral antiseptic. If she broke skin tissue when biting anyone, she was required to wash the area, apply antiseptic, and

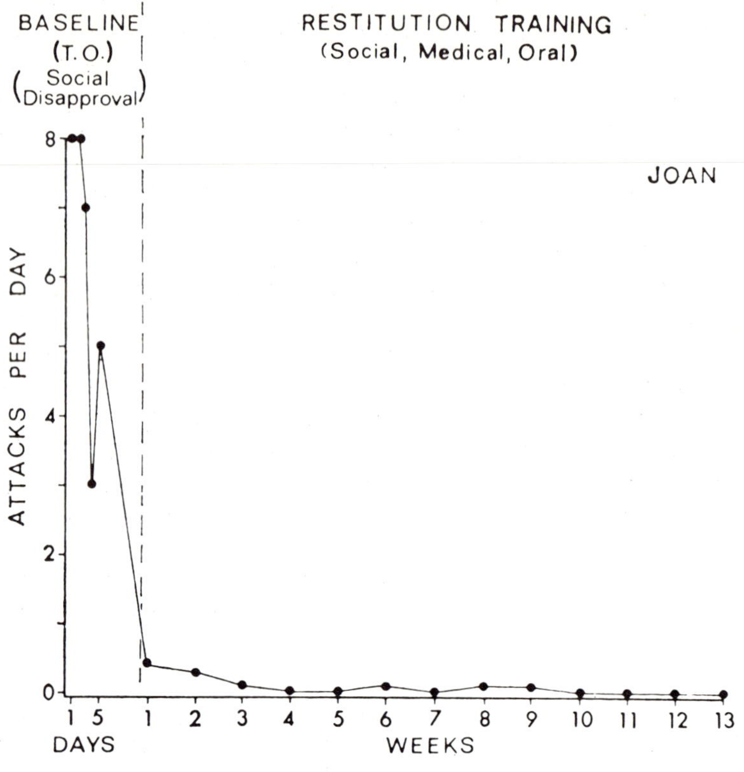

FIGURE 9-10.   The effect of restitution training on the number of attacks. (From "Restitution: A Method of Eliminating Aggressive-Disruptive Behavior of Mentally Retarded and Brain Damaged Patients," by R. M. Foxx and N. H. Azrin. In *Behaviour Research and Therapy*, 1972, *10*, 15–27. Reprinted by permission of Pergamon Press, Ltd.)

bandage it. Next, she was required to reassure the victim that the incident would not recur. The data from both of these women are truly impressive, as is a series of studies using similar techniques to treat aggression (Webster & Azrin, 1973), self-stimulatory behavior (Foxx & Azrin, 1973a), vomiting (Azrin & Wesolowski, 1975a), and floor sprawling (Azrin & Wesolowski, 1975b). While it is difficult to deny the demonstrated effectiveness of overcorrection, we would caution that it is not an easy technique to use, that it requires training and supervision, and that less restrictive alternatives should be tried first.

A variety of other procedures have been used in single case studies to eliminate maladaptive behavior in the retarded. These include lemon juice squirted into the mouth (Becker, Turner, & Sajwaj, 1978; Mayhew & Harris, 1979), forced arm exercise, which is similar to an overcorrection procedure for SIB (DeCatanzaro & Baldwin, 1978; Davidson-Gooch, 1980), and facial screening or covering the face of a retarded person with a terry cloth bib contingent upon SIB (Zeigob,

Becker, Jenkins, & Bristow, 1976; Lutzker, 1978). Replications of these and other procedures with more subjects are needed before their effectiveness can be adequately evaluated.

Some of the legal issues and trends relating to the mentally retarded have been extensively reviewed elsewhere (Thompson & Grabowski, 1977; Katz-Garris, 1978). We will only briefly discuss the most important here (and how they relate to the application of behavior change techniques). The major legal impetus for improving the care of the mentally retarded involves the so-called *Right to Treatment*. The court case of *Wyatt vs. Stickney* (1972) in Alabama was the landmark case for the retarded. It established that the retarded in institutions have the right to an individualized treatment plan that includes a statement of the needs and problems of the resident, written short- and long-term goals, the use of the least restrictive treatment techniques to achieve these goals, and a method for monitoring and altering the treatment plan as needed. This sounds remarkably similar to the behavior analysis process described in Chapter 2. Because of their emphasis on accountability, behavior change techniques are ideal for implementing the *Wyatt* and subsequent court decisions. The next most important court decision was *Pennsylvania Association for Retarded Children vs. Commonwealth of Pennsylvania* (1971, 1972), which determined that retarded children had the right to a free public education (no matter how severely retarded). Eventually, Congress got into the act and Public Law 94–142 (1975), or the "Education for the Handicapped Children Act of 1975," was promulgated. This act not only specifies a free, appropriate education for all handicapped children designed to meet each one's unique needs; it also provides their parents with rights and protections.

Aside from these events, there are probably three basic principles or protections that have strongly influenced the behavioral treatment of the retarded. As described by Thompson and Grabowski (1977), these are: (1) the least restrictive alternatives doctrine; (2) the cruel and unusual punishment provision of the Eighth Amendment to the U.S. Constitution; and (3) the doctrine of informed consent. In planning treatment programs for the retarded, particularly when trying to decrease maladaptive behavior, one must produce evidence that less restrictive treatment alternatives have failed before a more restrictive procedure can be used (for example, it must be shown that positive procedures such as DRO have failed before a procedure such as timeout could be used). The cruel and unusual punishment provision can be interpreted to restrict the use of aversive procedures that would be obviously inhumane (Thompson & Grabowski, 1977); however, there is certainly a lack of specificity here. What is considered humane in one setting might not be so in others. We would advocate use of a multidisciplinary review committee to screen use of all moderate or severe aversive and deprivation procedures (Thompson & Grabowski, 1977, Appendix). Finally, the doctrine of informed consent compels behavior change professionals to obtain consent whenever possible from mentally retarded clients if moderate or severe aversive and deprivation procedures are to be used. When the retarded person is judged not competent to give consent, then consent should be sought from parents or nearest relatives.

We welcome the new legal and legislative advances made with regard to the mentally retarded for we believe that, if anything, they encourage the use of behavior change techniques. Likewise, we strongly support the protections given the retarded that we have just described. We must admit that the potential for abuse certainly exists within behavior change techniques. Abuses can be avoided and prevented by observing the basic rights and protection of the retarded.

The question of less restrictive alternatives is extremely pertinent to our discussion of methods for decreasing maladaptive behaviors. The trend in many treatment settings has been to establish review committees to evaluate proposed intervention programs that involve aversive and deprivation procedures (timeout, overcorrection, electric shock, and so on). A function of these committees should be to look at these programs in terms of least restrictive alternatives. We certainly applaud such efforts and will be discussing such issues in the final chapter of this book.

CONCLUSIONS

In this chapter we have reviewed the use of behavior change applications with both the mentally ill and mentally retarded. It should be obvious that great strides have been made with the mentally retarded. In the future, we would hope to see a continuing emphasis on the task analysis of adaptive behaviors (along with validation studies). Certainly there is a need to pursue new techniques and methods for decreasing problematic behaviors such as SIB. The long-term success of our procedures with severe maladaptive behaviors and with autism needs to be evaluated. It is likely that additional effort will need to be put into methods for moving from "more restrictive" to "less restrictive" methods of controlling severe maladaptive behaviors. Along with the deinstitutionalization movement has come a need for training school and day-program staff, group home staff, and parents in the use of behavior change techniques. Certainly we will have to find ways of doing this effectively (see Chapter 13). Progress with the mentally ill has been more limited for they have not received the same attention from behavior change professionals as have the mentally retarded. We believe that this is unfortunate and are encouraged by the success of the behaviorally oriented community mental health centers in Oxnard and Huntsville. In the future, other community-based programs may begin to pattern their services after these two centers. We are certain that behavior change techniques have the potential to benefit the lives of the mentally ill in much the same way that they have already benefited the mentally retarded.

REFERENCES

Agras, W. S. Behavior modification in the general hospital psychiatric unit. In H. Leitenberg (Ed.), *Handbook of behavior modification and behavior therapy.* Englewood Cliffs, N.J.: Prentice-Hall, 1976.

Anderson, R. C., & Faust, G. W. *Educational psychology: The science of instruction and learning.* New York: Dodd, Mead, 1973.

Atthowe, J. M., Jr., & Krasner, L. Preliminary report on the application of contingent reinforcement procedures (token economy) on a "chronic" psychiatric ward. *Journal of Abnormal Psychology,* 1968, *73,* 37–43.

Ayllon, T., & Azrin, N. H. Reinforcement and instructions with mental patients. *Journal of the Experimental Analysis of Behavior,* 1964, *7,* 327–331.

Ayllon, T., & Azrin, N. H. The measurement and reinforcement of behavior of psychotics. *Journal of the Experimental Analysis of Behavior,* 1965, *8,* 357–383.

Ayllon, T., & Azrin, N. H. Reinforcer sampling: A technique for increasing the behavior of mental patients. *Journal of Applied Behavior Analysis,* 1968, *1,* 13–20. (a)

Ayllon, T., & Azrin, N. H. *The token economy: A motivational system for therapy and rehabilitation.* New York: Appleton-Century-Crofts, 1968. (b)

Ayllon, T., & Haughton, E. Control of the behavior of schizophrenic patients by food. *Journal of the Experimental Analysis of Behavior,* 1962, *5,* 343–352.

Ayllon, T., & Michael, J. The psychiatric nurse as a behavioral engineer. *Journal of the Experimental Analysis of Behavior,* 1959, *2,* 323–334.

Azrin, N. H., & Foxx, R. M. A rapid method of toilet training the institutionalized retarded. *Journal of Applied Behavior Analysis,* 1971, *4,* 89–99.

Azrin, N. H., & Wesolowski, M. D. Eliminating habitual vomiting in a retarded adult by positive practice and self-correction. *Journal of Behavior Therapy and Experimental Psychiatry,* 1975, *6,* 145–148. (a)

Azrin, N. H., & Wesolowski, M. D. The use of positive practice to eliminate persistent floor sprawling by profoundly retarded persons. *Behavior Therapy,* 1975, *6,* 627–631. (b)

Baer, D. M., Peterson, R. F., & Sherman, J. A. The development of imitation by reinforcing behavioral similarity to a model. *Journal of the Experimental Analysis of Behavior,* 1967, *10,* 405–416.

Baker, B. L., Brightman, A. J., Heifetz, L. J., Murphey, D. M., Carroll, N. B., Heifetz, B. B., & Hinshaw, S. P. *Steps to independence: A skills training series for children with special needs.* Champaign, Ill.: Research Press, 1977–78.

Barrett, B. H. Behavior analysis. In J. Wortis (Ed.), *Mental retardation and developmental disabilities* (Vol. 9). New York: Brunner/Mazel, 1977.

Barrett, B., & Lindsley, O. R. Deficits in acquisition of operant discrimination and differentiation shown by institutionalized retarded children. *American Journal of Mental Deficiency,* 1962, *67,* 424–436.

Bates, P., & Wehman, P. Behavior management with the mentally retarded: An empirical analysis of the research. *Mental Retardation,* 1977, *15,* 9–12.

Becker, J. V., Turner, S. M., & Sajwaj, T. E. Multiple behavioral effects of the use of lemon juice with a ruminating toddler-age child. *Behavior Modification,* 1978, *2,* 267–278.

Bensberg, G. J., Colwell, C. N., & Cassell, R. H. Teaching the profoundly retarded self-help activities by behavior shaping techniques. *American Journal of Mental Deficiency,* 1965, *69,* 674–679.

Bijou, S. W. Theory and research in mental (developmental) retardation. *Psychological Record,* 1963, *13,* 95–110.

Bijou, S. W. A functional analysis of retarded development. In N. R. Ellis (Ed.), *International review of research in mental retardation* (Vol. 1). New York: Academic Press, 1966.

Bijou, S. W. Behavior modification in the mentally retarded. *Pediatric Clinics of North America,* 1968, *15,* 969–987. (a)

Bijou, S. W. The mentally retarded child. *Psychology Today,* 1968 (June), *2,* 47–51. (b)

Bijou, S. W., Birnbrauer, J. S., Kidder, J. D., & Tague, C. Programmed instruction as an approach to teaching of reading, writing, and arithmetic to retarded children. *The Psychological Record,* 1966, *16,* 505–522.

Bijou, S. W., & Orlando, R. Rapid development of multiple-schedule performances with retarded children. *Journal of the Experimental Analysis of Behavior,* 1961, *4,* 7–16.

Birky, H. J., Chambliss, J. E., & Wasden, R. A comparison of residents discharged from a token economy and two traditional psychiatric programs. *Behavior Therapy,* 1971, *2,* 46–51.

Birnbrauer, J. S. Mental retardation. In H. Leitenberg (Ed.), *Handbook of behavior modification and behavior therapy.* Englewood Cliffs, N.J.: Prentice-Hall, 1976.

Birnbrauer, J. S., & Lawler, J. Token reinforcement for learning. *Mental Retardation,* 1964, *2,* 275–279.

Birnbrauer, J. S., Wolf, M. M., Kidder, J. D., & Tague, C. Classroom behavior of retarded pupils with token reinforcement. *Journal of Experimental Child Psychology,* 1965, *2,* 219–235.

Bornstein, P. H., Bach, P. J., McFall, M. E., Friman, P. C., & Lyons, P. D. Application of a social skills training program in the modification of interpersonal deficits among retarded adults: A clinical replication. *Journal of Applied Behavior Analysis,* 1980, *13,* 171–176.

Bostow, D. E., & Bailey, J. Modification of severe disruptive and aggressive behavior using brief timeout and reinforcement procedures. *Journal of Applied Behavior Analysis,* 1969, *2,* 31–37.

Bruco, M. Tokens for recovery. *American Journal of Nursing,* 1966, *66,* 1799–1802.

Bucher, B., & Lovaas, O. I. Use of aversive stimulation in behavior modification. In M. R. Jones (Ed.), *Miami symposium on the prediction of behavior, 1967: Aversive stimulation.* Coral Gables: University of Miami Press, 1968.

Budd, K., & Baer, D. M. Behavior modification and the law: Implications of recent judicial decisions. *The Journal of Psychiatry and Law,* a special reprint, Summer 1976, 171–244.

Burchard, J. D., & Barrera, F. An analysis of timeout and response cost in a programmed environment. *Journal of Applied Behavior Analysis,* 1972, *5,* 271–282.

Calhoun, K. S., & Matherne, P. The effects of varying schedules of timeout on aggressive behavior of a retarded girl. *Journal of Behavior Therapy and Experimental Psychiatry,* 1975, *6,* 139–143.

Clark, H. B., Rowbury, T., Baer, A. M., & Baer, D. M. Timeout as a punishing stimulus in continuous and intermittent schedules. *Journal of Applied Behavior Analysis,* 1973, *6,* 443–455.

Coleman, M. The autistic syndromes. In J. Wortis (Ed.), *Mental retardation and developmental disabilities* (Vol. 10). New York: Brunner/Mazel, 1978.

Cronin, K. A., & Cuvo, A. J. Teaching mending skills to mentally retarded adolescents. *Journal of Applied Behavior Analysis,* 1979, *12,* 104–109.

Cuvo, A. J., Leaf, R. B., & Borakove, L. S. Teaching janitorial skills to the mentally retarded: Acquisition, generalization, and maintenance. *Journal of Applied Behavior Analysis,* 1978, *11,* 345–355.

Cuvo, A. J., Veitch, V., Trace, M. W., & Konke, J. Teaching change computation to the mentally retarded. *Behavior Modification,* in press.

Davidson-Gooch, L. Autism reversal: A method for reducing aggressive-disruptive behavior. *The Behavior Therapist,* 1980, *3,* 21–23.

Davison, G. C. Appraisal of behavior modification techniques with adults in institutional settings. In C. M. Franks (Ed.), *Behavior therapy: Appraisal and status.* New York: McGraw-Hill, 1969.

DeCatanzaro, D. A., & Baldwin, G. Effective treatment of self-injurious behavior through a forced arm exercise. *American Journal of Mental Deficiency,* 1978, *82,* 433–439.

Ellis, N. R. Toilet training the severely defective patient: An S-R reinforcement analysis. *American Journal of Mental Deficiency,* 1963, *68,* 98–103.

Ellsworth, J. R. Reinforcement therapy with chronic patients. *Hospital & Community Psychiatry,* 1969, *20,* 36–38.

Favell, J. E., McGimsey, J. F., & Jones, M. L. The use of physical restraint in the treatment of self-injury and as positive reinforcement. *Journal of Applied Behavior Analysis,* 1978, *11,* 225–241.

Foxx, R. M., & Azrin, N. H. Restitution: A method of eliminating aggressive-disruptive behavior of mentally retarded and brain damaged patients. *Behaviour Research and Therapy,* 1972, *10,* 15–27.

Foxx, R. M., & Azrin, N. H. The elimination of autistic self-stimulatory behavior by overcorrection. *Journal of Applied Behavior Analysis*, 1973, *6*, 1–14. (a)

Foxx, R. M., & Azrin, N. H. *Toilet training the retarded: A rapid program for day and nighttime independent training*. Champaign, Ill.: Research Press, 1973. (b)

Fuller, P. R. Operant conditioning of a vegetative human organism. *American Journal of Psychology*, 1949, *62*, 587–590.

Gericke, O. L. Practical use of operant conditioning procedures in a mental hospital. *Psychiatric Studies & Projects*, 1965, *3*, 2–10.

Gershone, J. R., Errickson, E., Mitchell, J. E., & Paulson, D. A. Behavioral comparison of a token economy ward and a standard psychiatric treatment ward. *Journal of Behavior Therapy and Experimental Psychiatry*, 1977, *8*, 381–385.

Girardeau, F. L., & Spradlin, J. E. Token rewards in a cottage program. *Mental Retardation*, 1964, *2*, 345–351.

Goldstein, A. P., Sprafkin, R. P., & Gershaw, N. J. *Skill training for community living: Applying structured learning therapy*. New York: Pergamon Press, 1976.

Gripp, R. F., & Magaro, P. A. A token economy program evaluation with untreated control ward comparisons. *Behaviour Research and Therapy*, 1971, *9*, 137–149.

Guess, D., Sailor, W., & Baer, D. M. *Functional speech and language training for the severely handicapped*, Parts I and II. Lawrence, Kansas: H. & H. Enterprises, 1977.

Heap, R. F., Boblitt, W. E., Moore, C. H., & Hord, J. E. Behavior-milieu therapy with chronic neuropsychiatric patients. *Journal of Abnormal Psychology*, 1970, *76*, 349, 354.

Hobbs, S. A., & Forehand, R. Important parameters in the use of timeout with children: A reexamination. *Journal of Behavior Therapy and Experimental Psychiatry*, 1977, *8*, 365–370.

Isaacs, W., Thomas, J., & Goldiamond, I. Application of operant conditioning to reinstate verbal behavior in psychotics. *Journal of Speech and Hearing Disorders*, 1960, *25*, 8–12.

Johnson, D., Firth, H., & Davey, G. C. L. Vibration and praise as reinforcers for mentally handicapped people. *Mental Retardation*, 1978, *16*, 339–342.

Johnson, W. L., & Baumeister, A. A. Self-injurious behavior: A review and analysis of methodological details of published studies. *Behavior Modification*, 1978, *2*, 465–487.

Katz-Garris, L. The right to education. In J. Wortis (Ed.), *Mental retardation and developmental disabilities*. New York: Brunner/Mazel, 1978.

Kazdin, A. E. *History of behavior modification*. Baltimore: University Park Press, 1978.

King, G. F., Armitage, S. G., & Tilton, J. R. A therapeutic approach to schizophrenics of extreme pathology: An operant-interpersonal method. *Journal of Abnormal and Social Psychology*, 1960, *61*, 276–286.

Koegel, R. L., Glahn, R., & Nieminen, G. S. Generalization of parent training results. *Journal of Applied Behavior Analysis*, 1978, *11*, 95–109.

Koegel, R. L., & Wilhelm, H. Selective responding to the components of multiple visual cues by autistic children. *Journal of Experimental Child Psychology*, 1973, *15*, 442–453.

Kozloff, M. A. *Educating children with learning and behavior problems*. New York: Wiley, 1974.

Lent, J. R. A demonstration program for intensive training of institutionalized mentally retarded girls. *Project News of Parsons State Hospital and Training Center*, 1966, *2*, 8–19.

Liberman, R. P., King, L. W., & DeRisi, W. J. Behavior analysis and therapy in community mental health. In H. Leitenberg (Ed.), *Handbook of behavior modification and behavior therapy*. Englewood Cliffs, N.J.: Prentice-Hall, 1976.

Libet, J., & Lewinsohn, P. M. The concept of social skill with special references to the behavior of depressed persons. *Journal of Consulting and Clinical Psychology*, 1973, *40*, 304–312.

Lindsley, O. R. Operant conditioning methods applied to research in chronic schizophrenia. *Psychiatric Research Reports,* 1956, *5,* 118–139.

Lindsley, O. R. Characteristics of the behavior of chronic psychotics as revealed by free-operant conditioning methods. *Diseases of the Nervous System,* 1960, *21,* 66–78.

Lindsley, O. R. Geriatric prosthetics. In R. Kastenbaum (Ed.), *New thoughts on old age.* New York: Springer, 1964.

Lindsley, O. R., & Skinner, B. F. A method for the experimental analysis of behavior of psychotic patients. *American Psychologist,* 1954, *9,* 419–420.

Lloyd, K. E., & Garlington, W. K. Weekly variations in performance on a token economy psychiatric ward. *Behaviour Research and Therapy,* 1968, *6,* 407–410.

Loucks, S. Token research. *Contemporary Psychology,* 1978, *23,* 642–644.

Lovaas, O. I. *The autistic child: Language development through behavior modification.* New York: Irvington, 1977.

Lovaas, O. I., Berberich, J. P., Perloff, B. F., & Schaeffer, B. Acquisition of imitative speech by schizophrenic children. *Science,* 1966, *151,* 705–707.

Lovaas, O. I., Freitag, G., Kinder, M. I., Rubenstein, B. D., Schaeffer, B., & Simmons, J. Q. Establishment of social reinforcers in two schizophrenic children on the basis of food. *Journal of Experimental Child Psychology,* 1966, *4,* 109–125.

Lovaas, O. I., Freitas, L., Nelson, K., & Whalen, C. The establishment of imitation and its use for the development of complex behavior in schizophrenic children. *Behaviour Research and Therapy,* 1967, *5,* 171–181.

Lovaas, O. I., Koegel, R., Simmons, J. Q., & Long, J. S. Some generalization and follow-up measures on autistic children in behavior therapy. *Journal of Applied Behavior Analysis,* 1973, *6,* 131–166.

Lovaas, O. I., Litrownik, A., & Mann, R. Response latencies to auditory stimuli in autistic children engaged in self-stimulatory behavior. *Behaviour Research and Therapy,* 1971, *9,* 34–49.

Lovaas, O. I., & Newsom, C. D. Behavior modification with psychotic children. In H. Leitenberg (Ed.), *Handbook of behavior modification and behavior therapy.* Englewood Cliffs, N.J.: Prentice-Hall, 1976.

Lovaas, O. I., Schaeffer, B., & Simmons, J. Q. Building social behavior in autistic children by use of electric shock. *Journal of Experimental Research in Personality,* 1965, *1,* 99–109.

Lovaas, O. I., & Schreibman, L. Stimulus overselectivity of autistic children in a two-stimulus situation. *Behaviour Research and Therapy,* 1971, *9,* 305–310.

Lovaas, O. I., Schreibman, L., Koegel, R., & Rehm, R. Selective responding by autistic children to multiple sensory input. *Journal of Abnormal Psychology,* 1971, *77,* 211–222.

Lovaas, O. I., & Simmons, J. Q. Manipulation of self-destruction in three retarded children. *Journal of Applied Behavior Analysis,* 1969, *2,* 143–157.

Lutzker, J. R. Social reinforcement control of exhibitionism in a profoundly retarded adult. *Mental Retardation,* 1974, *12,* 46–47.

Lutzker, J. R. Reducing self-injurious behavior by facial screening. *American Journal of Mental Deficiency,* 1978, *82,* 510–513.

Lutzker, J. R., & Sherman, J. Producing generative sentence usage by imitation and reinforcement procedures. *Journal of Applied Behavior Analysis,* 1974, *7,* 447–460.

Maley, R. F., Feldman, G. L., & Ruskin, R. E. Evaluation of patient improvement in a token economy treatment program. *Journal of Abnormal Psychology,* 1973, *82,* 141–144.

Martin, J. A. The control of imitative and non-imitative behaviors in severely retarded children through "generalized instruction following." *Journal of Experimental Child Psychology,* 1971, *11,* 390–400.

Mayhew, G., & Harris, F. Decreasing self-injurious behavior: Punishment with citric acid and reinforcement of alternative behavior. *Behavior Modification,* 1979, *3,* 322–336.

Murphy, R. J., Nunes, D. L., & Hutchings-Ruprecht, M. Reduction of stereotyped behavior in profoundly retarded individuals. *American Journal of Mental Deficiency,* 1977, *82,* 238–245.

Ollendick, T. H., & Matson, J. L. Overcorrection: An overview. *Behavior Therapy,* 1978, *9,* 830–842.

Orlando, R., & Bijou, S. W. Single and multiple schedules of reinforcement in developmentally retarded children. *Journal of the Experimental Analysis of Behavior,* 1960, *3,* 339–348.

Paul, G. L., & Lentz, R. J. *Psychosocial treatment of chronic mental patients.* Cambridge, Mass.: Harvard University Press, 1977.

Pennsylvania Association for Retarded Children v *Commonwealth of Pennsylvania,* 344 F. Supp. 1257 (E.D. Pa. 1971).

Pennsylvania Association for Retarded Children v *Commonwealth of Pennsylvania,* 343 F. Supp. 279 (E.D. Pa. 1972).

Peters, H. N., & Jenkins, R. L. Improvement of chronic schizophrenic patients with guided problem-solving, motivated by hunger. *Psychiatric Quarterly Supplement,* 1954, *28,* 84–101.

Peterson, R. F., & Peterson, L. R. The use of positive reinforcement in the control of self-destructive behavior in a retarded boy. *Journal of Experimental Child Psychology,* 1968, *6,* 351–360.

Phillips, L., & Zigler, E. Role orientation, the action-thought dimension and outcome in psychiatric disorder. *Journal of Abnormal and Social Psychology,* 1964, *68,* 381–389.

Polvinale, R. A., & Lutzker, J. R. Elimination of assaultive and inappropriate sexual behavior by reinforcement and social restitution. *Mental Retardation,* 1980, *18,* 27–30.

Public Law 94–142 *(Education for All Handicapped Children Act of 1975).*

Redd, W. H., Porterfield, A. L., & Anderson, B. L. *Behavior modification: Behavioral approaches to human problems.* New York: Random House, 1979.

Reid, D. H., & Hurlbut, B. Teaching nonvocal communication skills to multihandicapped retarded adults. *Journal of Applied Behavior Analysis,* 1977, *10,* 591–603.

Repp, A. C., & Deitz, S. M. Reducing aggressive and self-injurious behavior of institutionalized retarded children through reinforcement of other behaviors. *Journal of Applied Behavior Analysis,* 1974, *7,* 313–324.

Reynolds, B. S., Newsom, C. D., & Lovaas, O. I. Auditory overselectivity in autistic children. *Journal of Abnormal Child Psychology,* 1974, *2,* 253–263.

Rickard, H. C., Dignam, P. J., & Horner, R. F. Verbal manipulation in a psychotherapeutic relationship. *Journal of Clinical Psychology,* 1960, *16,* 364–367.

Rincover, A., & Koegel, R. L. Setting generality and stimulus control in autistic children. *Journal of Applied Behavior Analysis,* 1975, *8,* 235–246.

Risley, R., & Cuvo, A. J. Training mentally retarded adults to make emergency telephone calls. *Behavior Modification,* in press.

Ritvo, E. R., & Freeman, B. J. Current status of biochemical research in autism. *Journal of Pediatric Psychology,* 1977, *2,* 149–152.

Robinson, H. B., & Robinson, N. M. *The mentally retarded child: A psychological approach.* New York: McGraw-Hill, 1965.

Sabatino, D. A., & Miller, T. L. (Eds.), *Describing learner characteristics of handicapped children and youth.* New York: Grune & Stratton, 1979.

Schaefer, H. H. Investigations on operant conditioning procedures in a mental hospital. In J. Fisher & R. E. Harris (Eds.), *Reinforcement theory in psychological treatment: A symposium.* California Mental Health Research Monographs, No. 8, 1966.

Schaefer, H. H., & Martin, P. L. Behavioral therapy for "apathy" of hospital schizophrenics. *Psychological Reports,* 1966, *19,* 1147–1158.

Schreibman, L., & Lovaas, O. I. Overselective response to social stimuli by autistic children. *Journal of Abnormal Child Psychology,* 1973, *1,* 152–168.

Shean, J. D., & Zeidberg, A. Token reinforcement therapy: A comparison of matched groups. *Journal of Behavior Therapy and Experimental Psychiatry,* 1971, *2,* 95–105.

Spradlin, J. E. The Premack hypothesis and self-feeding by profoundly retarded children: A case report. *Parsons Project Working Paper #79,* Parsons State Hospital and Training Center, Parsons, Kansas, 1964.

Spradlin, J. E., & Girardeau, F. L. The behavior of moderately and severely retarded persons. In N. R. Ellis (Ed.), *International review of research in mental retardation,* Vol. 1. New York: Academic Press, 1966.

Stahl, J. R., & Leitenberg, H. Behavioral treatment of the chronic mental hospital patient. In H. Leitenberg (Ed.), *Handbook of behavior modification and behavior therapy.* Englewood Cliffs, N.J.: Prentice-Hall, 1976.

Steffy, R. A., Hart, J., Craw, M., Torney, D., & Marlett, N. Operant behavior modification techniques applied to severely regressed and aggressive patients. *Canadian Psychiatric Association Journal,* 1968, *14,* 59–67.

Striefel, S. *Teaching a child to imitate: A manual for developing motor skills in retarded children.* Lawrence, Kansas: H. & H. Enterprises, 1974.

Sulzbacher, S. I., & Kidder, J. D. Following up on the behavior analysis model: Results after ten years of early intervention with institutionalized mentally retarded children. In E. Ramp & G. Semb (Eds.), *Behavior analysis: Areas of research and application.* Englewood Cliffs, N.J.: Prentice-Hall, 1975.

Thompson, T., & Grabowski, J. (Eds.). *Behavior modification of the mentally retarded* (Appendix). New York: Oxford University Press, 1977.

Thompson, T., & Grabowski, J. Ethical and legal guidelines for behavior modification. In T. Thompson & J. Grabowski (Eds.), *Behavior modification of the mentally retarded.* New York: Oxford University Press, 1977.

Walls, R. T., Werner, T. J., Bacon, A., & Zane, T. Behavior checklists. In J. D. Cone & R. P. Hawkins (Eds.), *Behavioral assessment: New directions in clinical psychology.* New York: Brunner/Mazel, 1977.

Webster, D. R., & Azrin, N. H. Required relaxation: A method of inhibiting agitative-disruptive behavior of retardates. *Behaviour Research and Therapy,* 1973, *11,* 67–78.

Wexler, D. B. Token and taboo: Behavior modification, token economies and the law. *California Law Review,* 1973, *61,* 81–109.

Wheeler, A. J., Miller, R. A., Dukes, J., Salisbury, E. W., Merritt, V., & Horton, B. *Murdoch Center C & Y Program Library: A collection of step-by-step programs for the developmentally disabled.* Butner, N.C.: Murdoch Center, 1977.

Wheeler, A. J., & Sulzer, B. Operant training and generalization of a verbal response form in a speech-deficient child. *Journal of Applied Behavior Analysis,* 1970, *3,* 139–147.

White, G. D., Nielsen, G., & Johnson, S. M. Timeout duration and suppression of deviant behavior in children. *Journal of Applied Behavior Analysis,* 1972, *5,* 111–120.

Wolfensberger, W. *Normalization.* Toronto: National Institute on Mental Retardation, 1972.

Wyatt v *Stickney,* 344 F. Supp. 373, 344 F. Supp. 387 (M.D. Ala. 1972).

Zeigob, L., Becker, J., Jenkins, J., & Bristow, A. Facial screening: An analysis of clinical applicability. *Journal of Behavior Therapy and Experimental Psychiatry,* 1976, *7,* 355–357.

Zigler, E., & Phillips, L. Psychiatric diagnosis and symptomology. *Journal of Abnormal and Social Psychology,* 1961, *63,* 69–75.

CHAPTER 10

Personal Problems: Obesity, Smoking, Chemical Dependency

IN this chapter and the next chapter, we discuss some of the many and varied personal problems that trouble people in their daily living. This chapter is devoted to habits and personal problems that very directly affect one's health. These problems have been called addictive behaviors because often a psychological and/or physical dependence exists. Although obesity, smoking, alcoholism, and drug abuse might have been discussed in previous chapters on health care, we believe that these problems are of such importance that they deserve separate treatment. In the next chapter, we discuss anxiety and depression. These, too, are personal problems that trouble a great number of people in their daily living.

OBESITY

It has been estimated that 80 million Americans (40% of the total population) are at least 20 lbs above the ideal weight for their age, sex, and height (Knowles, 1977). With older Americans the problem is even worse, because 35% of men and 40% of women over 40 years of age are at least 20% overweight (Stuart & Davis, 1972). That obesity creates added health risks cannot be denied. Ball (1973) has outlined seven major hazards for obese patients as follows: increased incidence of (1) heart disease, (2) hypertension, (3) postsurgical complications, (4) hypoventilation (shallow breathing), (5) insulin antagonism, (6) gynecological irregularities, and (7) toxemia. It is obvious, from the large number of self-help books available (Mahoney & Mahoney, 1976; Jeffrey & Katz, 1977; Stuart, 1978) and from the number of clinics and clubs (for example, Weight Watchers International, TOPS, Counterweight), that a sizable segment of our society is concerned about losing weight.

In 1958, Stunkard summarized the obesity treatment literature and concluded that large numbers do not remain in treatment, and those who do probably do not lose a significant amount of weight. Those who lose weight regain most of it. This problem was echoed by Wyden (1965), who stated that between ages 21 and 50, the obese go on 1.5 diets each year and undertake at least 15 significant diets that usually fail. What has been the impact of the behavior change technology upon this problem? Is the outlook for the obese still so gloomy? For one thing, it is certain that obesity has been one of the major targets of behavior change professionals. Loro (1978) has compiled a bibliography of 182 references of behavioral treatments of obesity published between 1962 and 1976. With this much research on the problem, one would think that we might be close to eliminating obesity as a problem in our society. Obviously, that is not the case. To understand why, we will review the pertinent literature since the early 1960s and then try to come to some conclusions as to why obesity remains a problem.

The first behaviorally based approach to the treatment of obesity was proposed by Ferster, Nurnberger, & Levitt (1962). Their treatment program was based on teaching individuals self-control techniques (manipulation of environmental contingencies and the utilization of stimulus control principles). Stuart (1967) capitalized on these proposed procedures and developed an extremely effective treatment program for eight obese subjects. Stuart's data are presented in Figure 10-1. Treatment consisted of 30-minute sessions three times per week for four to five weeks.

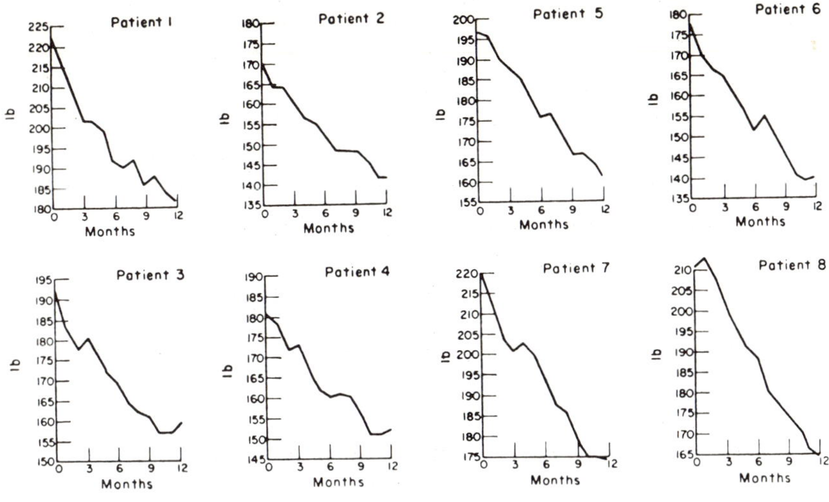

FIGURE 10-1.   Weight profile of eight women undergoing behavior therapy for overeating. (From "Behavioral Control of Overeating," by R. B. Stuart, *Behaviour Research and Therapy*, 1967, 5, 357–365. Reprinted by permission of Pergamon Press, Ltd.)

The important elements of the program included: (1) recording of time and quantity of all food consumption; (2) weighing in before each meal and before bedtime; (3) removal of food from all places in the house except the kitchen; (4) pairing eating with no other activity (such as TV watching); (5) setting a weight-loss goal of 1–2 pounds per week; (6) slowing down the pace of eating; and (7) substituting other activities for between-meal eating. It is obvious from Figure 10-1 that Stuart's program was extremely successful and to this date remains perhaps the best demonstration of the effectiveness of behavior change techniques. It was soon replicated by others (Harris, 1969; Penick, Filion, Fox, & Stunkard, 1971), demonstrated to be superior to control groups (Wollersheim, 1970; Stuart, 1971), and shown to be effective with a written manual and no therapist (Hagen, 1974). All of this led Stunkard (1972) to conclude that behavior modification was superior to any previous method for the treatment of obesity. Unfortunately, few studies have produced weight loss amounts as sizable as Stuart (1967).

The next most important development in the behavioral treatment of obesity came with the publication of a book by Stuart and Davis, *Slim Chance In a Fat World* (1972). This well-written treatment manual provided a wealth of information about their three-pronged attack on obesity: (1) management of the eating and exercise environment, (2) nutritional management, and (3) management of energy expenditure through increasing exercise. A major focus was on the situational management of overeating. Many of the important elements were developed in Stuart's (1967) earlier study. Table 10-1 lists the elements of the Stuart and Davis (1972) program.

TABLE 10-1. Stuart and Davis (1972) Program

Eat in only one place in one room and do not engage in other activities simultaneously
Do not purchase foods which contribute to overeating
Do not include high calorie condiments in meals; have other family members serve their own sweets; clean off plates directly into the garbage
Make overeating as difficult as you can
Positively reinforce acceptable eating
Engage others to monitor your eating
Avoid contact with excessive food by serving small portions and leaving the table when finished
Use small plates or spread out the food so that portion will look larger
Plan meals for regular hours and do not skip meals
Have a reasonable array of acceptable foods to choose from, along with acceptable amounts
Uneaten allowable food from meals may be used as a snack
Foods should be served as attractively as possible
The pace of eating should be slowed
Be neutral to undesirable deviations to your diet plan
Try to remember both the ultimate and immediate aversive consequences of problematic eating
Graphs and charts for eating, exercise, and weight should be updated daily
External reinforcement should be provided for compliance with exercising and eating requirements and/ or weight loss
Efforts to change weight-related behaviors should be socially reinforced

Adapted from R. B. Stuart and B. Davis, *Slim Chance in a Fat World: Behavioral Control of Obesity.* Copyright 1972 by Research Press.

Stuart and Davis' (1972) program was based on situational and self-control aspects of eating and exercising. From Table 10-1, it is obvious that efforts are made to manipulate antecedent, consequence, and response variables. The tone of their book was directed toward a long-term plan for losing weight, with the caution that it may be necessary to occasionally reintroduce specific aspects of the program, long after one's weight goal has been attained. With much foresight, Stuart and Davis (1972) warned that if maintenance is overlooked there may be a gradual dissipation of some or all constructive changes.

Since the publication of the Stuart and Davis (1972) book, much effort has gone into determining the necessary and sufficient elements for the successful behavioral weight-loss program. Stunkard and Mahoney (1976) have reviewed much of the research in this component analysis. Based on this review and on more current research, we will try to summarize for you the current state of the art.

From Stuart's (1967) initial research on, most behavioral weight-loss programs have had subjects self-monitor their eating (and, frequently, exercise) behavior. A number of studies have shown that self-monitoring alone is not sufficient to maintain weight loss (Stuart, 1971; Mahoney, 1974). Nonetheless, most researchers do agree that it is an important component which should be included in a total treatment package. Indeed, Bellack, Schwartz, and Rozensky (1974) have provided some evidence that it is better to write down everything to be eaten immediately prior to eating rather than wait until after the food is consumed.

Little specific attention has been paid to the role of setting weight-loss goals in behaviorally oriented obesity programs. While it is an implicit part of most programs, there are some data to indicate that setting goals alone does not contribute significantly to weight loss (Mahoney, 1974). It has been the experience of investigators that individuals in obesity treatment programs usually set unrealistically high goals. Some considerable amount of effort must be spent to alter this. It may be that a focus on a weekly weight-loss goal might lead to more effective treatment than an overall weight-loss goal. This has yet to be investigated, however.

Most treatment programs have included information about nutrition, exercise, and calories. Many obese individuals are simply ignorant as to the number of calories contained in the food they consume. In addition, they may have many false beliefs (for example, that avocados are low in calories) about the calorie content of foods. Different systems have been used, such as total calories or the exchange system presented by Stuart and Davis (1972). Research thus far has demonstrated that information about nutrition and exercise is insufficient to produce maintenance of weight loss (Stuart, 1971; Levitz & Stunkard, 1974). More recently, however, there is some evidence that strenuous, aerobic exercising (particularly running) may at times be sufficient to maintain a significant weight loss (Zuti & Golding, 1976).

The delivery of reinforcers and/or punishers, contingent upon success or failure in weight-loss programs, has been frequently used. Typical procedures include refunding of portions of a deposit or fee (Harris & Bruner, 1971; Harris & Hallbauer, 1973) and return or loss of prewritten checks (perhaps sent to a disliked political or social organization) or valuables (Mann, 1972). While such contingencies have proven extremely effective, there may be difficulty in moving from the weight-loss to the maintenance phase (generalization), due to dependence upon material reinforcers or punishers. One solution to this, obviously, is to gradually shift to more natural reinforcers before maintenance. Another one would be to continue material reinforcers and punishers during maintenance. A third solution would be to train patients' family members in contingency contracting to be used both during treatment and maintenance (Lutzker & Lutzker, 1977). It should be noted that more weight loss and better maintenance are achieved by reinforcing habit change than by concentrating on weight loss *per se* (Mahoney, 1974); this was pointed out by Mann (1972).

Although an abundance of behavioral programs have made use of social support (reinforcement) from a group and/or a therapist, the contribution of this component has been relatively unevaluated. Mixed results have been obtained (Wollersheim, 1970; Hagen, 1974; Mahoney, Moura, & Wade, 1973). These may be a function of the type of social support used; and, further, social reinforcement from a group or therapist may lead to problems in maintenance of weight loss, as previously mentioned. If this should prove to be a problem, the solution would be to train subjects' families to deliver social reinforcement during both treatment and maintenance. Fremouw and Zitter (1980) have recently found that "couples" groups, where the spouse of the overweight person attended, produced and maintained more weight loss than "individual" groups, where the spouse of the overweight person did not attend group meetings.

Jeffrey (1974) has found that self-reinforcement and self-punishment are superior to a therapist-administered contingency program in promoting *maintenance* of weight loss (no differences were found in the amount of weight lost during treatment). Another study found self-reinforcement to be superior to self-punishment (Mahoney, Moura, & Wade, 1973). More research is needed to further document the importance of self-administered contingencies, for this component may prove to be extremely critical in promoting maintenance of weight loss.

Many of the original program components suggested by Ferster, Nurnberger, and Levitt (1962) and Stuart (1967) were stimulus control procedures. As Stunkard and Mahoney (1976) have stated, the function of stimulus control techniques is to gradually and progressively restrict both the frequency and the range of cues associated with the act of eating. Thus far, most of the research documenting the superiority of stimulus control procedures (Wollersheim, 1970; Abrahms & Allen, 1974; Hagen, 1974) has involved other components (Bellack, 1975). In addition, in the Mahoney, Moura, and Wade (1973) study, stimulus control information did not produce weight loss unless accompanied by other treatment components.

Two final treatment components discussed by Stunkard and Mahoney (1976) are aversion therapy and cognitive restructuring strategies. Little research has been conducted using aversive techniques. Of major concern is the attrition rate. Mahoney and his colleagues (Mahoney, Moura, & Wade, 1973; Mahoney & Mahoney, 1976) have been leaders in studying the importance of cognitive strategies for promoting weight loss. Most promising is their work toward cleaning up food-related thoughts ("cognitive ecology"). Efforts were made to alter weight-related self-verbalizations such as "I just don't have the will power," "I'm too busy," "This will never work" (Mahoney, Moura, & Wade, 1973). The importance of altering these cognitive self-statements is more fully discussed in Mahoney's recent book for the public market, *Permanent Weight Control* (Mahoney & Mahoney, 1976). As yet, however, the role of self-statements and cognitive restructuring is unevaluated.

For more details concerning individual research studies examining the behavioral treatment of obesity, the reader might consult one or more of the excellent reviews, including Abramson (1973, 1977), Hall and Hall (1974), Bellack (1975), Leon (1976), Abrams (1979), and Wooley, Wooley, and Dyrenforth (1979). The previously mentioned bibliography of work from 1962 through 1976 (Loro, 1978) might also be useful. Uniformly, these reviewers have been impressed with the efficacy of behavioral approaches to the treatment of obesity. However, they have also been cautious and critical of the shortcomings of previous research, for behavior change techniques have obviously not eliminated the problem of obesity. Some of their typical comments follow:

> It has been demonstrated that several behavioral procedures are effective in treating obesity, at least on a short-term basis. . . . Future research . . . should attempt to assess the long-term effects of treatment and predict which treatment will be effective for a given individual. (Abramson, 1973, p. 554)

> Long-term evaluations (six months or more) are needed. (Hall & Hall, 1974, p. 362)

> The results of most studies indicate that weight loss rarely continues after treatment and when it does, it occurs at a reduced rate. (Bellack, 1975, p. 80)

> A more appropriate criterion for the effectiveness of various treatment methods would appear to be weight maintenance rather than initial weight reduction. (Leon, 1976, p. 574)

> While promising, behavior therapy has not, as yet, been clearly demonstrated to be an effective, permanent, and practical treatment for obesity. (Brightwell & Sloan, 1977, p. 898)

If these comments are not serious enough, Azrin (1978) has recently stated that most behavioral programs for obesity have resulted in an average weight loss of ten pounds. He has suggested that we ought to tell clients (subjects) that they should expect to lose only about ten pounds as the result of our behavioral treatment program. Finally, Zifferblatt and Wilbur (1977) have concluded that behavioral researchers have failed to demonstrate that their techniques are useful for producing long-term change. "Initial changes in health behavior are usually achieved, but these changes are rarely translated into lasting change" (Zifferblatt & Wilbur, 1977, p. 516).

The search for solutions to problems associated with behavioral treatment of obesity should point the way to future research needs. Central is the need to produce a methodology for promoting lasting weight loss. Stunkard and Mahoney (1976) have suggested that weight-loss maintenance could be increased by providing intermittent contacts, after the end of formal treatment, emphasizing the learning of long-term eating habits, training patients in self-monitoring and reinforcement and in problem solving, and focusing on family support. The critical element in promoting long-term, gradual weight loss and maintenance may be *continuous* monitoring and follow-up by treatment staff, over an extremely protracted period of time (Zifferblatt & Wilbur, 1977). Surely, it is folly to expect to change long-established habits in the short period of time encompassed by the typical number of treatment sessions in most behavior change programs (especially since food is a powerful positive reinforcer for most people). Chronic problems, such as obesity, probably need "chronic" treatment programs. Behavior change professionals have been surprised by the lack of weight-loss maintenance. This might not have occurred had they not ignored the caution of Stuart and Davis (1972): "Maintenance is the stepchild of most behavior programs which, if overlooked, can lead to the gradual dissipation of any and all constructive changes" (p. 96).

Research is also needed into behavioral assessment for obesity treatment programs. It may be that we will be able to predict which patients are most likely to profit from a behavioral treatment approach with the use of more refined assessment (Cooke & Meyers, 1980; Abramson, 1973; Jeffrey, 1972). On the other hand, we may also be able to predict which patients are most likely to drop out of treatment and to revise our program with that in mind. Recently, there has been a movement among behavior change professionals to produce "treatment packages" that can be used with large numbers of individuals. This approach is contrary to the individual assessment, functional analysis of behavior roots of behavior analysis. Too many individuals are likely to be treatment failures if we neglect our individual analysis approach. A rereading of the original Ferster, Nurnberger, and Levitt (1962) paper, on the behavioral treatment of obesity, should remind us that we are trying to change the behavior of individuals and not groups. Pertinent to this are recent discussions (Stunkard & Mahoney, 1976; Leon & Roth, 1977; Wooley, Wooley, & Dryenforth, 1979) as to the causes of obesity. It should be obvious to everyone that they are extremely complex and, perhaps, more individualized than we normally think. Stunkard and Mahoney (1976) go so far as to say that at times our programs "may have helped a person who biologically *should be* obese to maintain a statistically normal, but biologically abnormally low, body weight" (p. 54). Obesity is a function of many factors (for example, developmental, genetic, metabolic) and not merely the learning of bad eating habits.

Other future research directions include devising effective treatment programs for children (since it is really more efficient and easier to change behavior before it has become a long-term problem) and special populations (Aragona, Cassady, & Drabman, 1975; Wheeler & Hess, 1976; Kingsley & Shapiro, 1977; Bjorgaard, Capell, & Martin, 1977). Jeffrey (1976b) has proposed research toward a macroanalysis in the prevention and treatment of obesity. This would include attempts to alter eating behavior through improved nutritional education and food labeling and examining the role of advertising and vending machines. Macroenvironmental methods of increasing exercise include improved mass media and other educational attempts, national standards for sports and recreation facilities, and employer-sponsored recreational facilities.

Finally, there are now a number of behaviorally oriented books available in bookstores for aiding the obese in self-treating their problem. The vast majority of these have been written by researchers and clinicians who have had much experience with the overweight (*Permanent Weight Control,* Mahoney & Mahoney, 1976; *Take It Off and Keep It Off,* Jeffrey & Katz, 1977; *Act Thin, Stay Thin,* Stuart, 1978). While it may be that some people will be able to alter their eating behavior and lose weight by reading one or more of these books, none of them have been experimentally validated—that is, there is no evidence that one can read one of the books and lose weight. The efficacy or utility of such self-help books or nonprescriptive therapies has been heatedly debated (Glasgow & Rosen, 1978; Rosen, 1976, 1977; Goldiamond, 1976) and we are of the opinion that either self-help books (of all types, not just behavioral) should be experimentally validated or a warning should be included in the book indicating that it has not been validated. Unfortunately, validating any complex behavior change program in written form is difficult and seldom done. Therefore, at this time most self-help books, such as the obesity examples, are best used in conjunction with a trained therapist.

SMOKING

In 1964, the Surgeon General's Advisory Committee on Smoking and Health issued a report that concluded that cigarette smoking was a significant health hazard in our country. A further indictment against smoking was issued by the Surgeon General in a 1971 report to Congress (Smolensky, 1977). In addition to lung cancer, smoking has been found to be associated with emphysema, chronic bronchitis, and coronary artery disease (Mausner & Platt, 1971). While there are approximately 30 million ex-smokers in the United States, one-third of all adults smoke (Terry, 1977). Over 60% of these Americans have tried to stop smoking, at least once, and failed (USPHS, 1976). While many smokers certainly wish to give up their habit, there are many who do not. You will see that consideration of these statistics may be important in any massive attempt to apply behavior change techniques to the problem of smoking.

Solutions to the health hazard of smoking have proceeded along four different fronts (Smolensky, 1977). The first has been to try to reduce the number of young smokers (those in the 12–18-year-old group). This has been attempted primarily through anti-smoking education attempts in public schools. While behavior change principles would seem to have promise with this age group, there has been, as yet, no systematic research. A second major effort has been in attempts to help people to stop smoking. There are anti-smoking clinics in most major cities, and behavior change principles have been used in trying to eliminate smoking in some of these clinics and in other settings. We review the results later in this chapter. A third development has been the tobacco industry's work on finding a "safe cigarette." While the tar and nicotine content have been altered, much more research needs to be done. Finally, if a large proportion of smokers are unable to give up cigarettes, it may be that some measure of improved health could be obtained by altering the topography of their smoking (the number of cigarettes, the type of cigarettes, the number of puffs, and so on). Behavior change research is just beginning in this area, and as you will see, it holds much promise.

Yates (1975) has identified a number of behavior change techniques that have proven relatively successful in producing a reduction in the number of cigarettes smoked. The major techniques include: (1) aversive conditioning through administering an electric shock while the subject is smoking (Berecz, 1972a, 1972b; Whitman, 1972); (2) satiation through rapid smoking (Lichtenstein, Harris, Birchler, Wahl, & Schmahl, 1973; Marston & McFall, 1971); (3) pairing of hot, stale, smoky air with smoking (Grimaldi & Lichtenstein, 1969; Schmahl, Lichtenstein, & Harris, 1972); (4) consumption of a pill which produces nausea when combined with smoking (Marston & McFall, 1971; Whitman, 1972); (5) contingency contracting (Bernstein, 1970; Winett, 1973); and (6) training in self-monitoring and self-control (Ober, 1968; Sachs, Bean, & Morrow, 1970).

Despite the generally positive results of most of these procedures, Yates (1975) laments the fact that frequently control group procedures produce equivalent reductions in smoking behavior. A second major problem is that, whenever follow-up of four or more months are conducted, most of the reduction in smoking behavior is wiped out (Yates, 1975). As Zifferblatt and Wilbur (1977) have said, the critical problem is helping people remain nonsmokers, rather than getting people to quit smoking. Many people say, "Quitting is *easy;* I do it several times a week!" This relapse is depicted quite well in Figure 10-2, which is a compilation of data from 87 studies with varying samples and types of treatment (for comparison purposes, similar data are also presented for heroin and alcohol). The conclusion is obvious and all too similar to that found with treatment of obesity: maintenance of behavior change is a challenging problem. This has resulted in a shift to much more complex and comprehensive treatment approaches, to an emphasis on the posttreatment maintenance phase, and to establishing treatment goals somewhat short of abstinence. More recent reviewers (Bernstein & McAlister, 1976; Lichtenstein & Danaher, 1976; Frederiksen & Simon, 1978; Pechacek & Danaher, 1979; Pechacek, 1980) reflect a new optimism not found in earlier reviews (Hunt & Matarazzo, 1973; Bernstein, 1969).

Before leaving the problem of smoking, we will look briefly at some of the more recent research that is representative of this renewed optimism. One of the most researched and most effective methods for helping people to stop smoking

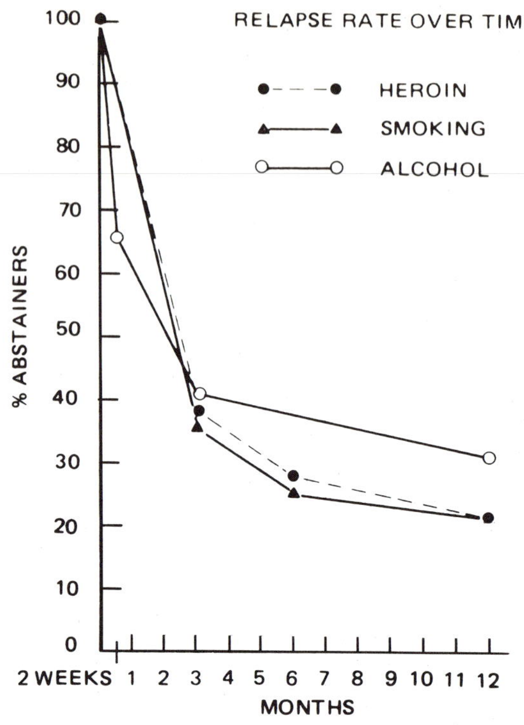

FIGURE 10-2.   Relapse curves based on 84 smoking modification studies (results of three heroin and one alcohol study are included for comparison). (From "Relapse Rates in Addiction Programs," by W. A. Hunt, L. W. Barnett, and L. G. Branch. Copyright 1971 by the *Journal of Clinical Psychology.* Reprinted by permission.)

is rapid smoking (Lichtenstein, Harris, Birchler, Wahl, & Schmahl, 1973). This procedure is outlined in Table 10-2. Danaher (1977) has reviewed many of the recent investigations of rapid smoking. Although a long term follow-up (two to six years) by Lichtenstein and Penner (1977) revealed that rapid smoking produced abstinence in 36–47% of those treated, others (Curtis, Simpson, & Cole, 1976; Danaher, 1977; Glasgow, 1977) have obtained less impressive results of 30% abstinence after six months. It may be that the reduced level of success is due to a lack of emphasis on client-therapist relationships and/or inflexibility in the number of treatment sessions (Bernstein & Glasgow, 1979). It should be noted that despite the fact that this is a relatively easy-to-use method of treatment, there are some risks. Since there is likely to be stress to the cardiovascular system, the procedure should not be used with individuals over 40, pregnant women, or people who have a history of heart disease, diabetes, or chronic obstructive pulmonary disease (Danaher & Lichtenstein, 1978). Lichtenstein and Glasgow (1977) also recommend that those wishing to undergo rapid smoking treatment should obtain approval from their personal physician.

TABLE 10-2. Rapid Smoking Procedure

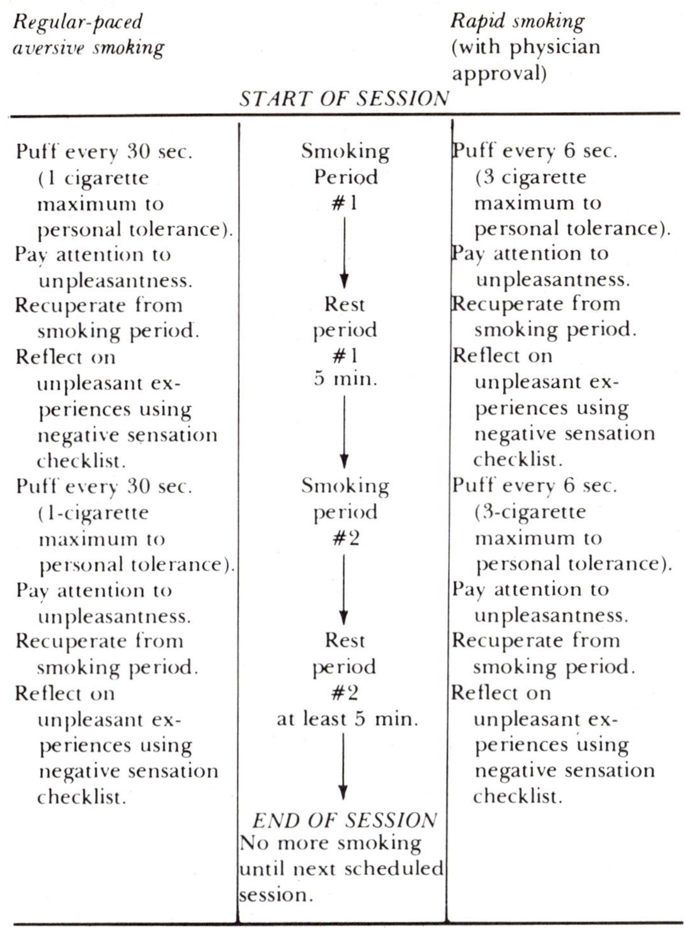

Regular-paced aversive smoking		*Rapid smoking (with physician approval)*
	START OF SESSION	
Puff every 30 sec. (1 cigarette maximum to personal tolerance). Pay attention to unpleasantness. Recuperate from smoking period. Reflect on unpleasant experiences using negative sensation checklist.	Smoking Period #1 ↓ Rest period #1 5 min. ↓	Puff every 6 sec. (3 cigarette maximum to personal tolerance). Pay attention to unpleasantness. Recuperate from smoking period. Reflect on unpleasant experiences using negative sensation checklist.
Puff every 30 sec. (1-cigarette maximum to personal tolerance). Pay attention to unpleasantness. Recuperate from smoking period. Reflect on unpleasant experiences using negative sensation checklist.	Smoking period #2 ↓ Rest period #2 at least 5 min. ↓	Puff every 6 sec. (3-cigarette maximum to personal tolerance). Pay attention to unpleasantness. Recuperate from smoking period. Reflect on unpleasant experiences using negative sensation checklist.
	END OF SESSION No more smoking until next scheduled session.	

From Brian G. Danaher and Edward Lichtenstein, *Become an Ex-Smoker*, © 1978, p. 60. Reprinted by permission of Prentice-Hall, Inc., Englewood Cliffs, New Jersey.

Flaxman (1976, 1978) has described a comprehensive package consisting of self-control techniques, aversive conditioning through warm and smoky air, and rapid smoking until satiation. She also demonstrated that abrupt smoking cessation was more effective than gradual cessation. Further, the treatment package was enhanced for women (but not men) who delayed the quitting date as opposed to quitting smoking immediately. Successful cessation of smoking at a six-month follow-up ranged up to 62%.

Dericco, Brigham, and Garlington (1977) have used a multiple baseline, component-analysis design to examine satiation, cognitive control, and aversive conditioning techniques for the suppression of smoking behavior. Satiation consisted of rapid smoking. Cognitive control employed covert sensitization (Cautela, 1967). Aversive conditioning was programmed through variable, unexpected electric shocks

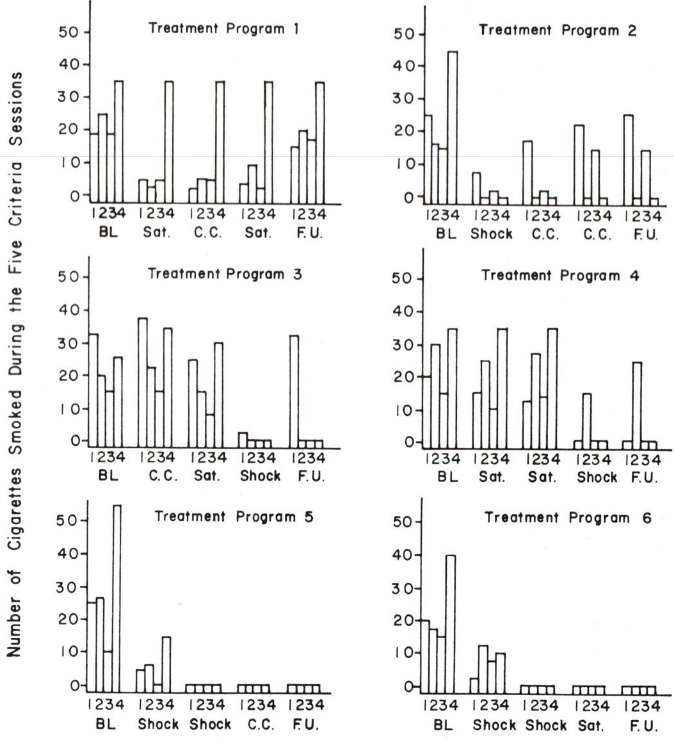

FIGURE 10-3.   Four subjects in each of six treatment program sequences including satiation (SAT), cognitive control (CC), contingent shock (Shock), and six-month follow-up (F.U.). (From "Development and Evaluation of Treatment Paradigms for the Suppression of Smoking Behavior," by D. A. Derrico, T. A. Brigham, and W. K. Garlington, *Journal of Applied Behavior Analysis*, 1977, *10*, 173–181. Copyright 1977 by the Society for the Experimental Analysis of Behavior, Inc. Reprinted by permission.)

administered while smoking. The satiation and cognitive control procedures proved ineffective in producing decreased smoking with follow-ups of six months. On the other hand, contingent shock produced lasting suppression at a six-month follow-up. Figure 10-3 shows that subjects who had two series of contingent shock were not smoking on follow-up. To date, this has proven to be one of the most dramatic demonstrations of the effect of contingent shock procedures. The major differences between this and previous aversive conditioning studies were that more sessions were conducted, increased shock levels were used, and additional shock sessions were programmed after subjects stopped smoking. Certainly, further research is needed to determine the critical components of this highly successful treatment package.

The work of Frederiksen and his associates (Frederiksen & Peterson, 1976a; Frederikson & Peterson, 1976b; Frederiksen, 1977; Frederiksen & Simon, 1978) has offered an alternative to abstinence from smoking. This approach has focused on the topography of smoking in addition to the rate of smoking. *What* a person smokes (the brand) and *how* he or she smokes it are both extremely important and are potential targets for change (Frederiksen, Miller, & Peterson, 1977). Support for a goal of a reduction in smoking rate (rather than abstinence) comes from several quarters and is supported by the contention that low rate smoking (less than 20 cigarettes each day) considerably reduces health risks (McAlister, 1975). A reduction in smoking rate as a goal, or controlled smoking, should be an extremely attractive alternative to the large number of Americans who, as yet, do not wish to give up the habit entirely. Controlled smoking has been borrowed from controlled approaches to alcohol. It consists of three major components as follows: (1) a switch in cigarette brand to one less dangerous (Wald, 1976) or to a pipe; (2) an alteration in smoking topography including number of puffs, length of puffs, and frequency of inhalation; and (3) a decrease in the number of cigarettes smoked (Frederiksen, 1977; Frederiksen and Simon, 1978). Figure 10-4 is a flow chart of the basic program devised by Frederiksen (1977).

The data obtained from controlled smoking studies (Frederiksen & Peterson, 1976a; Frederiksen, 1977; Frederiksen & Simon, 1978) have been very impressive. There appear to be less attrition and better maintenance of controlled smoking at follow-ups than with most programs where abstinence is the goal. The long-term implications for controlled smoking are yet to be determined. While some stimulus control measures (places where one is permitted to smoke) are being forced upon smokers through legislation, controlled smoking may be an additional solution to drastically reducing the health risk imposed by tobacco. One possible line of future research would be to have controlled smoking function as the first stage of a comprehensive program aimed at abstinence. After functioning with controlled smoking for a while, subjects could then enter an abstinence treatment program (at their choice).

Not addressed by the controlled smoking approach is the problem of "offensive smoking." That is, a good many nonsmokers cheer anti-smoking efforts because of their intolerance (physical and otherwise) of tobacco smoke. As some problems of litter control might be best handled by large-scale stimulus control procedures, such as outlawing the use of nonreturnable bottles, similar efforts will help control cigarette smoking. Increased segregation of smokers and nonsmokers, or the outright prohibition of smoking in various public settings, will aid both the nonsmoker in attempts to avoid smoke and, probably, the smoker in efforts to quit smoking. Massive stimulus control procedures have been employed in France with a subsequent reduction in cigarette sales. Cigarette package warning labels in Sweden will point out specific risks such as cancer and cardiovascular disease (Ramstrom, 1976). Future research and efforts will determine how well similar attempts will do here. The business community has recently become interested in the problem of smoking cessation (Danaher & Lichtenstein, 1978). It only makes sense and good business for businesses to be interested in the health of their

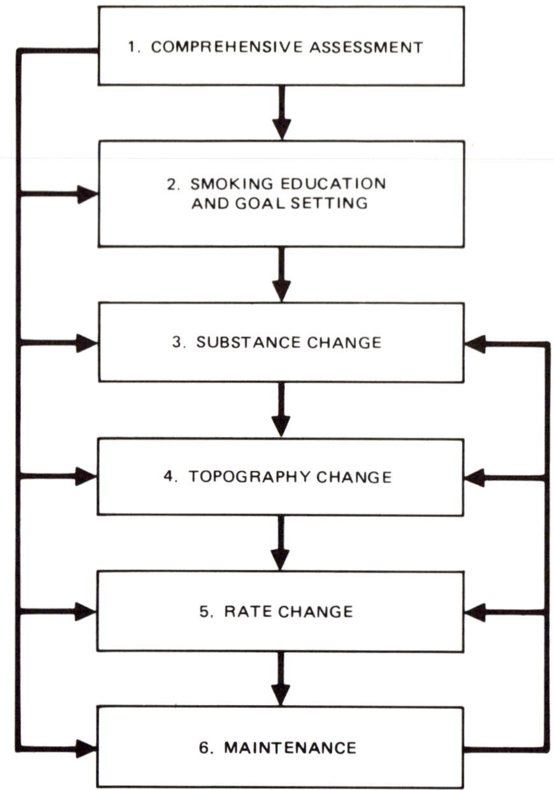

FIGURE 10-4. Flow chart of controlled smoking program. (From *"But I Don't Want to Quit Smoking": Alternatives to Abstinence,* by L. W. Frederiksen. Unpublished paper presented at the Association for Advancement of Behavior Therapy meeting, Atlanta, 1977. Reprinted by permission.)

employees. By using a variety of financial and fringe benefits, businesses could quite possibly alter the smoking habits of their employees. Like drinking, eating, and the abuse of drugs, tobacco addiction has several complex behavioral and physiological variables acting simultaneously upon the individual. Thus, simple behavior change programs of personal reinforcement and punishment may not produce the success rates we have had with other behavior problems.

Finally, as with the problem of obesity, self-help books on behavior change principles are becoming available in bookstores. Two of the better ones have been written by researchers who have had a history of conducting successful smoking cessation programs. These are *Become an Ex-Smoker* by Danaher and Lichtenstein (1978) and *Break the Smoking Habit* by Pomerleau and Pomerleau (1977). Again, we must question the validity of such self-help books. It is commendable that the

Pomerleaus' book addresses this issue, for a validity attempt reported that 11 of 22 subjects who read the book (with no outside professional help) were able to maintain benefits through one year later (18% quit, 32% reduced their rate).

ALCOHOL ABUSE

In the United States, somewhere between 80 and 90 million people drink alcoholic beverages (Miller & Eisler, 1976). There is some controversy concerning the number of these individuals who could be considered as alcohol abusers, problem drinkers, or alcoholics. These estimates run from 5 million (Brecher, 1972) to as many as 10 million (Knowles, 1977). Over 200,000 alcoholics are identified each year, and alcoholism now ranks as the fourth largest major health problem in our country (Ullmann & Krasner, 1975; O'Leary & Wilson, 1975). Since at least 40% of all arrests are for driving while under the influence of alcohol or for being drunk in a public place, alcohol abuse is by far the biggest law enforcement problem we have in the United States. Smolensky (1977) has stated that alcoholism and alcohol abuse costs the United States approximately 25 billion dollars each year.

There has been considerable controversy about a definition of alcoholism or alcohol abuse, as well as much time and effort searching for the causes of the problem and characteristics of those afflicted. The search for personality or character differences has led to conclusions such as "alcoholics are different in so many ways that it makes no difference" (Keller, 1977, p. 63); the only characteristic alcoholics share in common is that they *drink excessively* with the result that their personal, social, and economic functioning is seriously impaired (O'Leary & Wilson, 1975). Rather than debating about definitions and causes it seems more fruitful to view alcohol use and abuse along a continuum and to realize that there may be many interrelated causes of problem drinking that may vary from person to person. To determine whether one is a problem drinker, it is necessary to examine the effects of alcohol on daily functioning. Someone who frequently has significant life problems after consuming alcohol is a problem drinker (Miller & Mastria, 1977). Surely the environmental variables that cause one person to drink differ from those causing another to drink.

Critical to determining if a client is a problem drinker, and for determining a suitable behavior change program, is a comprehensive behavioral assessment. Sobell and Sobell (1978) and Miller (1976) have written extensively on a functional or behavioral assessment of alcohol abuse. Basically, assessment has consisted of a detailed analysis of the specific antecedents and consequences associated with drinking. Miller (1976) has argued that this analysis should examine a wide variety of physiological, emotional, cognitive, social, and situational variables. Tables 10-3 and 10-4 from Miller and Mastria's *Alternatives to Alcohol Abuse* (1977) list some of the possible antecedents to and consequences of problem drinking based on such an analysis.

We cannot overstate the importance of behavioral assessment to the design of behavior change programs. There is no one type of person who is susceptible to problem drinking, and there is no one cause of problem drinking. As Sobell and

TABLE 10-3. Possible Antecedents of Alcohol Abuse

Factors	*Antecedent Events*
Social	1. Social isolation (boredom) 2. Interpersonal conflict and stress 3. Positive interpersonal situations requiring behaviors in which the individual is deficient (e.g., adequate sexual functioning) 4. Heavy drinking friends (modeling influences) 5. Group pressure to drink
Emotional	1. Unpleasant feelings (anxiety, anger, depression), especially when combined with inability to express them 2. Heightened emotional arousal (either positive or negative)
Situational	1. Observing alcohol advertisements 2. Passing by a bar 3. Observing others drinking 4. Hearing references to drinking
Cognitive	1. Negative self-reference thoughts 2. Retaliatory thoughts (e.g., "I'll show her!") 3. Guilt-related thoughts
Physiological	1. Pain or physical discomfort 2. Decreases in blood/alcohol level 3. Withdrawal symptoms

From *Alternatives to Alcohol Abuse,* by P. M. Miller and M. A. Mastria. Copyright 1977 by Research Press. Reprinted by permission.

Sobell (1978) have stated, *"any person who uses alcohol could under appropriate circumstances develop serious alcohol problems"* (p. 10). Use of a behavioral assessment of antecedents and consequences of alcohol consumption will lead to a variety of possible treatment strategies. Likewise, points of intervention during the course of treatment may be multiple. In the end, treatment must be both effective (resolving current problems and promising maintenance of behavior change) and efficient (involving the least possible change in life style) for long-term success (Sobell & Sobell, 1978).

Applications of behavior change principles to alcohol abuse have involved three different treatment strategies (although some investigators have employed more than one of these strategies in their treatment programs). First, most of the early work involved the use of aversive conditioning procedures. A second approach has been more multimodal and has focused on learning alternative or incompatible behaviors. It has included the teaching of self-management techniques, coping skills, assertion, and relaxation. Finally, several investigators have focused on manipulation of the problem drinker's natural environment. We will now consider each of these strategies and try to come to some conclusions about the use of behavior change techniques for alcohol abuse.

Aversive conditioning techniques have included the use of electric shock, nausea-producing chemicals, and covert sensitization. Electric shock has been used in the form of an avoidance conditioning paradigm (Hsu, 1965; MacCulloch, Feldman, Orford, & MacCulloch, 1966; Moroski & Baer, 1970; Chapman, Burt, & Smith, 1972) or an escape conditioning paradigm (Blake, 1965, 1967; Vogler,

TABLE 10-4. Possible Consequences of Alcohol Abuse

Factors	*Positive Consequences*	*Negative Consequences*
Social	1. Enhanced behavioral repertoire 2. Attention and encouragement from friends	1. Decreased behavioral functioning 2. Confrontation or withdrawal of attention by others
Emotional	1. Enhanced ability to express feelings 2. Decreases in anxiety, boredom, depression, worry	1. Tendency to overreact emotionally (overly sensitive, hostile) 2. Increases in anxiety and depression
Cognitive	1. Increases in positive self-reference thoughts 2. Decreases in negative self-reference thoughts	1. Increases in negative self-reference or guilt-related thoughts
Physiological	1. Decreases in pain and physical discomfort 2. Decreases in withdrawal symptoms	1. Increased possibility of physical withdrawal symptoms and chronic physical disabilities (e.g., cirrhosis of the liver)

From *Alternatives to Alcohol Abuse*, by P. M. Miller and M. A. Mastria. Copyright 1977 by Research Press. Reprinted by permission.

Lunde, Johnson, & Martin, 1970; Miller & Hersen, 1972). In avoidance conditioning, clients are subjected to electric shock contingent upon consumption of alcoholic beverages. Situations are arranged whereby they must choose between alcoholic and nonalcoholic beverages; thus they may avoid shock if they make the right choice. In some studies (MacCulloch et al., 1966), photographs rather than actual beverages are used in choice situations. In escape conditioning studies, subjects are typically shocked while consuming alcohol and terminate the shock when they spit out the alcohol. Two of the more successful studies by Blake (1965, 1967) and Vogler, Lunde, Johnson, and Martin (1970) have been questioned on methodological grounds in a comprehensive review of behavioral treatment of alcoholism by Nathan (1976). Further, some researchers (Rachman & Teasdale, 1969; Nathan & Briddell, 1977) have questioned whether successful conditioning with the use of electric shock might not be due to other variables. We share these reservations and see a need for more definitive research; however, it is most likely that the use of electric shock in aversive conditioning would be most appropriate as a part of a multimodal broad spectrum treatment approach. As Nathan (1976) has said, "any unidimensional approach to a maladaptive behavior as complex as alcoholism is bound to fail" (p. 18). Certainly problem drinking involves such a complex interrelationship between physiological and multiple stimulus control factors that any kind of simple, in-office, conditioning procedure would be predicted to have weak or transient effects at best.

Similar conclusions can be drawn about the use of chemicals or covert sensitization. A variety of chemicals, all of which produce nausea or vomiting, have been used in aversive conditioning paradigms (Voetglin, 1940; Lemere, Voetglin, Broz, & O'Hallaran, 1942). The use of covert sensitization (Cautela, 1966; Ashem & Donner, 1968) has associated imagined scenes involving nausea and vomiting with drinking alcohol. Frequently, relief scenes are also used, which pair relaxation with nondrinking behavior. Nathan (1976) suggested that, while much more data are needed on chemical aversive conditioning, it has more promise than shock or covert sensitization because nausea is more central to drinking. Too little research has been conducted on covert sensitization techniques to draw any firm conclusions. In sum, the aversive conditioning techniques will probably be most effective as a part of a more comprehensive treatment program.

Behavior change programs for alcohol abuse that involve the teaching of alternative and/or incompatible behaviors have been extremely varied. Two recent books, *How to Control Your Drinking* by W. R. Miller and Munoz (1976) and *Alternatives to Alcohol Abuse* by P. M. Miller and Mastria (1977), provide excellent examples of this broad-spectrum approach. The Miller and Munoz program focuses mainly on self-control techniques. This includes learning to set limits, self-monitoring of alcohol consumption, learning how to reduce the rate of drinking, learning to refuse drinks, and self-reinforcement techniques. Strategies for the control of antecedents include monitoring of people, places, and times associated with drinking. Activities and emotional factors related to drinking are also identified. Alternative and/or incompatible behaviors are developed through learning relaxation, learning to deal with anxiety, training in problem solving, assertion training, and learning how to handle family conflicts, depression, and boredom. All in all, this program is extremely comprehensive. However, since the Miller and Munoz book is written for problem drinkers, its validity as a self-help manual, as stated elsewhere in this chapter and in this book, must be documented. The Miller and Mastria book, on the other hand, is written for therapists and counselors involved in the treatment of problem drinkers. The program outlined in the book is a broad-spectrum behavior change approach which includes training of relaxation, assertion, social skills, marital skills, self-control, and occupational skills (job seeking). Sexual counseling is also addressed.

Several excellent research studies, evaluating broad-spectrum behavior change programs that focus on the teaching of alternative behaviors, have been conducted. Lazarus (1965) described a case study that was one of the first presentations of this type of model treatment program. Lanyon, Primo, Terrell, and Wener (1972) provided an experimental framework for the comparison of multimodal with unimodal approaches (although their study does have some methodological problems). Other successful comprehensive behavioral treatment programs have been reported by McBrearty, Dichter, Garfield, and Heath (1968), Rozynko, Flint, Hammer, Swift, Kline, and King (1971), and Miller, Stanford, and Hemphill (1974). Most of these programs have included aversive conditioning and/or covert sensitization, relaxation training, assertion training, and self-control components. Treatment has been inpatient, and has lasted for up to 17 weeks, with up to 62% success at follow-ups of up to two years. Other investigators who have demonstrated superior effectiveness of multimodal programs focusing on the training of alternative behaviors include Vogler, Compton, and Weissbach (1975) and Caddy and Lovibond (1976).

Finally, one behavior change approach to alcohol abuse has concentrated on altering the problem drinker's natural environment. Representative of this approach is the community-reinforcement program developed by Hunt and Azrin (1973).

This program was intended to rearrange the vocational, family, and social reinforcers so that they would be withdrawn (timeout) contingent upon drinking alcohol. Eight hospitalized alcoholics were accepted into the program. Participants were told that sobriety depended upon having satisfying employment and good family and social adjustment. If they had any special problems (such as legal ones), appropriate referrals were made. The manner and sequence in which other program elements were implemented was dependent upon a behavioral assessment of each participant. Only those components identified as necessary were included for a given subject. Specific program elements are described below (adapted from Hunt & Azrin, 1973):

1. *Vocational Counseling.* Patients without employment were instructed in how to prepare a resume and in other job-seeking skills. Counselors assisted through role playing and by being present with the subjects during many job-seeking activities. These procedures followed empirically based procedures described in Chapter 4 (Jones & Azrin, 1973).

2. *Marital and Family Counseling.* The function of this counseling was to reinforce subjects for being a functional marital partner, to reinforce spouses for upholding the marital relationship, and to render alcohol abuse incompatible with subjects' improved marital relationships. These sessions continued for some time after discharge from the hospital. Communication about sexual interactions was also facilitated. Other aspects of marital counseling were based on the work of Stuart (1969) described in Chapter 12. For unmarried patients, "synthetic" families were created, consisting of relatives, employees, or clergymen. Maintenance of this family reinforcement system was contingent upon continued sobriety.

3. *Social Counseling.* This aspect of the program focused on improving the patients' social relationships and making their continuation contingent upon remaining sober. They were advised to avoid interaction with individuals who were likely to precipitate drinking and to associate with friends with whom alcohol abuse was not tolerated.

4. *Reinforcer-Access in Counseling.* It frequently became necessary to prime certain vocational, social, and marital activities. These included assisting patients in obtaining radios and televisions, helping them to subscribe to newspapers, and arranging for telephone installation. The counselor frequently arranged for the initial payment involved with some of these. The rationale for this was that it would be difficult to obtain work without access to newspapers and a telephone. Conversation skills and other social skills could be improved through reading newspapers, listening to the radio, and watching television.

After discharge from the hospital, the subjects were visited by their counselor once or twice each week for the first month. These sessions were used for problem solving, for reminding subjects of the contingent availability of family, work, and social life participation, and for monitoring progress. After this initial post-discharge month, visits were gradually faded out to once per month. Figures 10-5 and 10-6 present data for the community-reinforcement group and a matched control group. Further data collected revealed that, over a six-month period, the community-reinforcement group had a mean income of $355 per month and spent a mean of 13 weekends out of their homes engaging in some social activity. Control group subjects averaged a monthly income of only $190, and spent only four weekends on such activities.

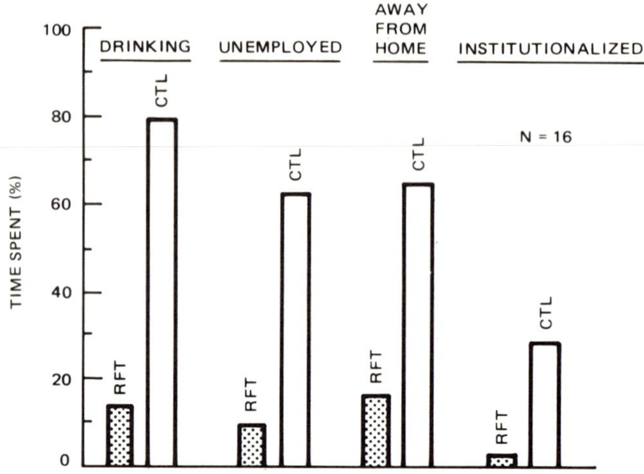

FIGURE 10-5.   A comparison of the key dependent measures for the reinforcement and control groups since discharge: Mean percentages of time spent drinking, unemployed, away from home, and institutionalized. (From "A Community-Reinforcement Approach to Alcoholism," by G. M. Hunt and N. H. Azrin. In *Behaviour Research and Therapy*, 1973, *11*, 91–104. Reprinted by permission of Pergamon Press, Ltd.)

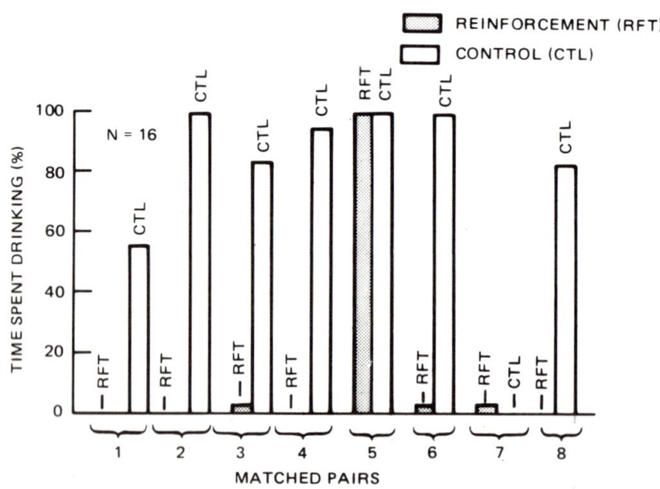

FIGURE 10-6.   Sobriety: A comparison of matched pairs. (From "A Community-Reinforcement Approach to Alcoholism," by G. M. Hunt and N. H. Azrin. In *Behaviour Research and Therapy*, 1973, *11*, 91–104. Reprinted by permission of Pergamon Press, Ltd.)

More recently, Azrin (1976) has reported that the gains of the community-reinforcement group were maintained at a two-year follow-up. He also modified the initial program to include several new components, including the use of Disulfiram (a drug that interacts with alcohol to produce nausea and vomiting) to control impulsive drinking, provision of a peer advisor, written contracts, group counseling, and self-monitoring of stressful situations that might precipitate drinking. While Azrin has provided a treatment program that has produced rather remarkable results, the number of participants has been, perhaps, too small to evaluate what impact this might have upon alcohol abuse programs. A second caution has to do with the cost-effectiveness of this program. Certainly a significant amount of time and effort was spent on the community-reinforcement group—much more than on the control group and, indeed, on treatment groups in other settings. Finally, what the active elements of Azrin's program are is, as yet, unclear. A component analysis of the many program elements is definitely needed. Despite these concerns, the Hunt and Azrin approach may turn out to be the most effective, since it is based on a plan of total environmental restructuring and promotes maintenance of treatment gains. Other investigators (Miller, Hersen, Eisler, & Watts, 1974; Miller, 1975; Miller, 1972) have also made use of the rearrangement of environmental contingencies. Frequently this has been accomplished through contingency contracting; however, we must consider most of these successful attempts as too narrow in focus to be applicable to the larger population of alcohol abusers.

We cannot leave the problem of alcohol abuse without some mention of the controversy over abstinence versus controlled drinking as treatment goals and the excellent long-term research project on controlled drinking conducted by the Sobells (see Sobell & Sobell, 1978, for a detailed discussion). The traditional model for the treatment of alcoholism is based upon a disease model and the belief that abstinence is the sole treatment goal; the problem drinker or alcoholic *cannot* drink socially or in moderation (Jellinek, 1960; Gitlow, 1973). Innumerable research studies have demonstrated that it is possible for some alcoholics to drink in moderation and exhibit self-control over their drinking. Many reviews of the literature (Lloyd & Salzberg, 1975; Sobell & Sobell, 1975; Pattison, 1976; Marlatt, 1979) have come to the same conclusion, as did the controversial ''Rand Report'' (Armor, Polich, & Stambul, 1976). An excellent book, *Emerging Concepts of Alcohol Dependence* (Pattison, Sobell, & Sobell, 1977), provides an extensive examination of these issues and argues strongly for nonabstinence treatment goals. It is necessary to state that a nonabstinence treatment goal is not appropriate for *every* person with a drinking problem (Miller & Munoz, 1976; Nathan & Goldman, 1979). Rather, nonabstinence outcomes should be seen as a possibility for some alcohol abusers. Even Sobell (1978) has said that nonabstinence outcomes are more probable with problem drinkers who: (1) have not yet become physically dependent upon alcohol; (2) have an environment that can reinforce a nonabstinence outcome; (3) consume less alcohol than the average chronic alcoholic; and (4) do not believe they need a total abstinence program.

The possibility of controlled drinking as an acceptable outcome first came from Davies (1962) when he reported a follow-up of alcoholics treated at Maudsley Hospital in London. Davies discovered seven former alcoholics who had been drinking in a moderate or controlled manner from seven to eleven years after treatment had ended. This report led to a number of attempts to produce controlled drinking via a treatment program. In 1970, Lovibond and Caddy described a procedure for teaching alcoholics to discriminate blood alcohol levels. Clients were first given feedback on their blood alcohol level during the course of two hours of drinking. Thereafter, three conditioning sessions were held with five to seven days' separation. After drinking until they reached a blood alcohol level of 0.065%, clients were required to continue to drink and were intermittently shocked with a total of eight to ten shocks delivered each session. Several more conditioning sessions were conducted (spaced further apart). Clients received from 30 to 70 shocks in from 6 to 12 sessions. Follow-up data were collected from four months to one year later and 75% were found to be drinking only moderately. While these data are quite remarkable, they are subject to question because of the fact that they are based on self-report. Despite this, Lovibond and Caddy's work is important because it did also demonstrate that clients can learn to discriminate blood alcohol levels quite accurately (within $\pm 0.01\%$). A similar procedure was used by Silverstein, Nathan, and Taylor (1974) to produce controlled drinking. In contrast to Lovibond and Caddy (1970), subjects in this study had an extremely difficult time discriminating blood alcohol levels. It appears that they may have learned to control their drinking through the use of other methods such as counting their drinks and pacing themselves. Schaefer, Sobell, and Mills (1971) produced controlled drinking by administering electric shock to patients contingent upon ordering a straight (unmixed) drink or *gulping* (more than one-seventh of the total volume) of a mixed drink. Finally, Miller and Becker (1975) have produced controlled drinking through the use of instructions, modeling, and feedback. Subjects were able to alter the volume of their sips, their intersip intervals, and to dilute somewhat the alcohol concentration of their drinks.

As previously stated, Mark and Linda Sobell (1973a, 1973b, 1976, 1978) have the most dramatic evidence for the efficacy of controlled drinking as a legitimate outcome. Their long-term project (definitely multimodal) involved hospitalized chronic alcoholics at Patton State Hospital in California. Seventeen "treatment sessions focused directly on drinking behavior and emphasized helping the subject to identify functions served by his problem drinking and to develop alternative, more appropriate (self-defined) ways of dealing with those situations" (Sobell & Sobell, 1978, p. 88). Figure 10-7 outlines the experimental design of this treatment program. Subjects were all alcoholics who had had some withdrawal symptoms and had damaged their health, finances, and social skills through alcohol abuse (Sobell & Sobell, 1973a).

The research project was conducted at the alcohol research unit at Patton State Hospital. This unit contained a simulated home environment as well as simulated bar and cocktail lounge. The two control groups of subjects, controlled drinker control (CD-C) and nondrinker control (ND-C), received a typical hospital treatment program including large therapy groups, Alcoholics Anonymous meetings, and so on. The other two groups, controlled drinker experimental (CD-E) and nondrinker experimental (ND-E), received 17 individualized behavior therapy sessions. These focused directly on drinking behavior, sought to identify the function

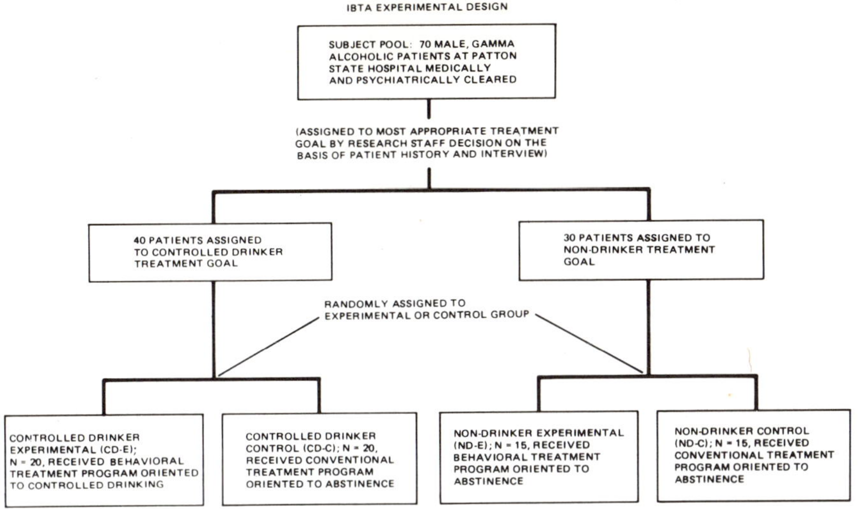

FIGURE 10-7.   Experimental design used to evaluate individualized behavior therapy for alcoholics. (From "Alcoholics Treated by Individualized Behavior Therapy: One Year Treatment Outcome," by M. B. Sobell and L. C. Sobell. In *Behaviour Research and Therapy*, 1973, *11*, 599–618. Reprinted by permission of Pergamon Press, Ltd.)

of this drinking, and developed alternative ways of handling these situations. The only difference between CD-E and ND-E groups was that CD-E group members were trained in controlled drinking and permitted to practice this during certain sessions. All sessions were 90 minutes long (except the first two) and were conducted in one of the simulated environments (Sobell & Sobell, 1978).

During Sessions 1 and 2, CD-E and ND-E subjects were permitted to drink as much as they wished and staff discussed with them possible setting events for excessive drinking. These sessions were videotaped. Session 3 focused on presenting the treatment plan to CD-E and ND-E subjects. In addition, they were trained to refuse drinks, and instructed that during some sessions they would be shocked for inappropriate drinking behavior, while in other (probe) sessions there would be no possibility of shock. Sessions 4 and 5 were used to play back the videotapes from Sessions 1 and 2. Staff members pointed out behavioral excesses, deficits, and setting events. Session 6 was devoted to the subjects' handling of an artificially arranged failure experience. Past and present failure experiences were explored and maladaptive responses were examined (Sobell & Sobell, 1978).

Ten sessions (7 through 16) were devoted to stimulus control procedures and problem-solving skills training. During these sessions, CD-E subjects were shocked whenever they exhibited uncontrolled drinking (ordering a straight drink, taking too large a sip, ordering more than one drink in a 20-minute period, and ordering more than three drinks per 90-minute session). ND-E subjects were shocked whenever they drank at all. Sessions 8, 12, and 16 were probe sessions and no electric shocks were administered. Stimulus control and problem-solving aspects of these sessions included the following: (1) training to identify situations and events that led to problem drinking in the past; (2) enumeration of alternative responses to problem drinking; (3) evaluation of each of these alternative responses for possible outcomes or results; (4) learning to use the alternative behaviors that had the best possible total outcome (Sobell & Sobell, 1973a, 1978).

During Session 17, videotapes of Sessions 1 and 2 were contrasted with Session 16. Progress was discussed, and each patient in CD-E and ND-E groups were given a wallet-sized card that contained a list of "dos" and "don'ts" related to their specific drinking problem.

A vast amount of follow-up data have been collected on the patients who composed this research project. Data are available from six months (Sobell & Sobell, 1973a), one year (Sobell & Sobell, 1973b), and two years (Sobell & Sobell, 1976). On numerous measures, both CD-E and ND-E groups were functioning much better than their two control groups at six months and one year. After two years, the controlled drinker experimental group continued to function significantly better than their control group; however, the nondrinker experimental group was no longer doing significantly better than their control group. An independent follow-up at three years (Caddy, Addington, & Perkins, 1978) continued to show the superiority of the controlled drinker experimental group. This long-term study has provided rather dramatic evidence for controlled drinking as a possible outcome for some problem drinkers.

Before leaving the Sobells' research project, we must mention that there have been some questions about the interpretation of these results (Nathan, 1976; Miller, 1976). These include the necessity for a component analysis to identify active elements of the program, a need to cautiously accept the self-reported drinking data that were collected by one of the principal investigators (although this is no longer true given the third year follow-up), and the difficulty in comparing some of the data with previous work because of the very different methods used for data analysis by the Sobells. These questions aside, the Patton State Hospital project has provided an excellent model for producing successful controlled drinking in alcoholics.

In closing this section on the use of behavior change techniques for the treatment of problem drinking, we are optimistic. Progress is being made with an extremely difficult-to-treat problem. The programs of Azrin and the Sobells appear particularly encouraging. Further research is definitely needed, perhaps most in the area of behavioral assessment and the prediction of treatment outcomes. More definite information is needed on which individuals are the best candidates for controlled drinking outcomes. Further research is needed with specific population groups such as women, American Indians, Skid Row residents, and business executives. Are specialized programs needed for specialized groups? Also, we can expect better research and media techniques in advertising and education in the prevention of alcoholism, although, as we have seen, these techniques produce difficult-to-evaluate and questionable results. We need to develop strategies for encouraging alcoholics to seek treatment (Craigie & Ross, 1980). Finally, Sobell and Sobell (1978) have discussed follow-up as a form of continuing care. This is a familiar thought, which we have discussed in the previous chapters on health care and earlier in this chapter. The Sobells even had some control group subjects tell them that they felt that continued follow-up might prevent or minimize their drinking. Chronic problems may need "chronic" treatment.

DRUG ABUSE

Compared to the numbers of individuals with personal problems related to obesity, smoking, or excessive drinking, the problem of drug abuse is relatively minor in actual occurrence. Yet drug abuse is still a severe and quite complex issue in our society today. It is obvious that strict laws and harsh punishment have not proven a successful deterrent; quite the contrary, drug abuse may be spreading (or at least be a bigger problem than we thought, given our crude data collection methods). Attempts at using behavior change techniques to alter drug abuse have been limited, but the number of such attempts is on the increase. Ross (1977) has estimated that approximately 30 programs in the United States use behavioral techniques as a part of treatment.

A number of writers have attempted behavior analyses of drug abuse and in doing so have emphasized the role of learning principles. These include Wikler (1965, 1971), who has proposed a classical or respondent conditioning model, and Cahoon and Crosby (1972), who have focused on an operant conditioning model. Cahoon and Crosby (1972) sought to account for the acquisition and maintenance of drug abuse as follows:

1. Positive reinforcement and social support received from a peer group
2. Positive reinforcement received directly from the drug which makes the user feel "good"
3. Negative reinforcement produced as the result of the drug's ability to terminate aversive stimuli in the environment (for example, may allow the user to escape the reality of poor living conditions)
4. Negative reinforcement received through the termination of aversive internal stimuli (for example, anxiety, depression, sleeplessness)
5. Negative reinforcement received through the termination of aversive internal stimuli related to drug use (real physical dependence)

The implication of this analysis is that drug abuse may be under the control of several variables. Variables that were important in the early phases of drug abuse may not presently be maintaining this behavior. These are extremely important considerations when devising treatment programs for drug abusers. A detailed behavior analysis is absolutely necessary. Treatment packages that are uniformly applied to heterogeneous groups of drug abusers will probably fail.

An excellent review of the behavioral treatment of drug abuse has been written by Callner (1975). He has stated that there have been three main treatment approaches: (1) counterconditioning (for example, aversion therapy, systematic desensitization, covert sensitization); (2) contingent delivery of reinforcers (for example, token economies, contingency contracting); and (3) treatments combining both contingent reinforcement and counterconditioning methods. Both chemical (Thomson & Rathod, 1968; Raymond, 1964; Liberman, 1968) and electric shock (Lesser, 1967; O'Brien & Raynes, 1972) aversion therapy have been used. Covert sensitization procedures have involved pairing images of drug taking and vomiting (Anant, 1968; Steinfeld, 1970). With systematic desensitization, drug abusers have been taught to relax in the presence of environmental stimuli that might normally precipitate drug use (Kraft, 1968, 1969).

Typical of the contingency contracting approach has been the work of Boudin (1972) with a young female graduate student. She was a heavy user of amphetamines (60–70 mg per day) and also used barbiturates. A three-month contract was drawn up between Boudin and the young woman. Although she tried to withdraw from the contract after three days, she had only two drug-use episodes (leading to a loss of $50 each time) during the three-month contract. Both instances were related to life crises (romantic and school related). Use of the shock apparatus was unreliable (it did not function properly and was unwieldy). At the end of the three-month period, the woman left for Africa for one year. A follow-up, conducted upon her return, indicated that she had remained drug free. A large community-based drug rehabilitation program making use of contingency contracting has been reported by Boudin and Valentine (1973). Hospital-based token economy programs have been described by Glicksman, Ottomanelli, and Cutler (1971) and O'Brien, Raynes, and Patch (1972). The opportunity to take methadone doses outside a clinic has been used as a reinforcer that increased attendance in counseling sessions (Sitzer, Bigelow, Lawrence, Cohen, D'Lughoff, & Hawthorne, 1977).

Typical of treatment programs combining contingency management with counterconditioning, O'Brien, Raynes, and Patch (1972) have used relaxation training, shock aversion therapy, and covert sensitization in treating heroin addicts. It should be noted that the focus in a number of drug treatment programs has been problem behaviors other than drug abuse. Obviously, the drug abuser presents a complex subject for treatment and large behavioral and environmental changes are often necessary, as in the treatment of alcohol abuse.

Callner's literature review (1975) provides a useful summary of the current status and future needs in the application of behavior change techniques to drug abuse. Nearly 75% of all studies reviewed were individual case reports. Over half relied on self-report for treatment and follow-up data. Obviously more research is needed with larger samples and other sources of data. Callner (1975) also suggested that investigators need to begin to conduct studies using drug abusers more typical of those found in most drug abuse programs. More often than not, the drug abusers in the single-case reports have been quite atypical. Some method of describing or quantifying the nature and extent of drug abuse is also necessary. A broad-based data collection system during treatment and follow-up, much in the manner of Sobell and Sobell (1978) with alcoholics, would prove extremely helpful. Finally, there is a need for a real, broad-spectrum approach to the treatment of drug abuse that can produce drug-free outcomes and good maintenance data. At the present time, the use of behavior change principles with drug abusers is in its infancy; thus, treatment procedures should not be limited. Rather, it is best for now to try to combine many different methods since this broad-spectrum approach is most likely to be successful. Researchers should look to the more successful alcohol abuse programs (Hunt & Azrin, 1973; Sobell & Sobell, 1978) for their models. When good outcome data have been produced, then investigators can conduct the necessary component analyses to determine the active elements in a complex treatment program.

CONCLUSIONS

While we must be optimistic about the potential of behavior change techniques for altering such addictive behaviors as obesity, smoking, alcoholism, and drug abuse, we must also be candid and point out that most successes have been short-term. Permanent behavior change in any of these areas has yet to be demonstrated with a rigorous experimental design, except for a relatively few exceptions. Researchers working on obesity and smoking are currently focusing on the problem of maintenance of behavior change. In the area of alcohol abuse, much controversy still exists concerning nonabstinence outcomes. While model programs devised by Hunt and Azrin (1973) and Sobell and Sobell (1978) are extremely promising, this controversy within the field of alcoholism may need to be settled before a significant impact can be made. Much research is still necessary before anything definitive can be said concerning the behavioral treatment of drug abuse. However, researchers have the advantage of adopting successful models from the treatment of other addictive behaviors.

Common to all four personal problems covered in this chapter is their complexity. A multiplicity of variables is involved with each individual in our society who has one or more of these problems. We are concerned about the development of treatment packages aimed at eradicating any of these addictive behaviors because of the possibility of neglecting individual behavior analysis. We are also concerned about the proliferation of self-help books for the same and other reasons. If persons using behavior change techniques are to have the maximum impact on the many problems of our society, then our major concern should be toward preserving an individual behavior analysis that can *then* lead to valid, reliable intervention strategies.

REFERENCES

Abrahms, J. L., & Allen, G. J. Comparative effectiveness of situational programming, financial pay-offs, and group pressure in weight reduction. *Behavior Therapy*, 1974, *5*, 391–400.

Abrams, D. B. Clinical developments in the behavioral treatment of obesity. *Clinical Behavior Therapy Review*, 1979, *1*(2), 1–14.

Abramson, E. E. A review of behavioral approaches to weight control. *Behaviour Research and Therapy*, 1973, *11*, 547–556.

Abramson, E. E. Behavioral approaches to weight control: An updated review. *Behaviour Research and Therapy*, 1977, *15*, 355–363.

Anant, S. S. Treatment of alcoholics and drug addicts by verbal aversion techniques. *International Journal of the Addictions*, 1968, *3*, 381–388.

Aragona, J., Cassady, J., & Drabman, R. S. Treating overweight children through parental training and contingency contracting. *Journal of Applied Behavior Analysis*, 1975, *8*, 269–278.

Armor, D. J., Polich, J. M., & Stambul, H. B. *Alcoholism and treatment*. Report R–1739–NIAAA. Santa Monica, Calif.: Rand Corporation, 1976.

Ashem, B., & Donner, L. Covert sensitization with alcoholics: A controlled replication. *Behaviour Research and Therapy*, 1968, *6*, 7–12.

Azrin, N. H. Improvements in the community-reinforcement approach to alcoholism. *Behaviour Research and Therapy*, 1976, *14*, 339–348.

Azrin, N. H. *Behavioral methodology: Research design vs. field testing*. Paper presented at the 86th Annual Convention of the American Psychological Association, Toronto, September 1978.

Ball, M. F. Seven major hazards for obese patients. In F. J. Stare (Ed.), *Obesity: Data and directions for the 1970s*. Richmond, Va.: A. H. Robins Company, 1973.

Bellack, A. S. Behavior therapy for weight reduction. *Addictive Behaviors*, 1975, *1*, 73–82.

Bellack, A. S., Schwartz, J., & Rozensky, R. H. The contribution of external control to self-control in a weight reduction program. *Journal of Behavior Therapy and Experimental Psychiatry*, 1974, *5*, 245–250.

Berecz, J. Modification of smoking behavior through self-administered punishment of imagined behavior: A new approach to aversive therapy. *Journal of Consulting and Clinical Psychology*, 1972, *38*, 244–250. (a)

Berecz, J. Reduction of cigarette smoking through self-administered aversive conditioning: A new treatment model with implications for public health. *Social Science and Medicine*, 1972, *6*, 57–66. (b)

Bernstein, D. A. Modification of smoking behavior: An evaluative review. *Psychological Bulletin*, 1969, *71*, 418–440.

Bernstein, D. A. The modification of smoking behavior: A search for effective variables. *Behaviour Research and Therapy*, 1970, *8*, 133–146.

Bernstein, D. A., & Glasgow, R. E. Smoking. In O. F. Pomerleau & J. P. Brady (Eds.), *Behavioral medicine: Theory and practice*. Baltimore: Williams and Wilkins, 1979.

Bernstein, D. A., & McAlister, A. The modification of smoking behavior: Progress and problems. *Addictive Behaviors*, 1976, *1*, 89–102.

Bjorgaard, M., Capell, J., & Martin, J. A study of a multidisciplinary approach to the treatment and prevention of obesity in a pediatric rehabilitation program. *Association of Rehabilitation Nurses Journal*, 1977, *2*, 12–16.

Blake, B. G. The application of behaviour therapy to the treatment of alcoholism. *Behaviour Research and Therapy*, 1965, *3*, 75–85.

Blake, B. G. A follow-up of alcoholics treated by behaviour therapy. *Behaviour Research and Therapy*, 1967, *5*, 89–94.

Boudin, H. M. Contingency contracting as a therapeutic tool in the deceleration of amphetamine use. *Behavior Therapy*, 1972, *3*, 604–608.

Boudin, H. M., & Valentine, V. E. *Behavioral techniques as an alternative to methadone maintenance*. Unpublished manuscript, University of Florida, 1973.

Brecher, E. M., & Editors of *Consumer Reports. Licit and illicit drugs*. Mt. Vernon, N.Y.: Consumers Union, 1972.

Brightwell, D. R., & Sloan, C. L. Long-term results of behavior therapy for obesity. *Behavior Therapy*, 1977, *8*, 898–905.

Caddy, G. R., Addington, H. J., & Perkins, D. *Individualized behavior therapy for alcoholics: A third year independent double-blind follow-up*. Unpublished manuscript, 1978.

Caddy, G. R., & Lovibond, S. H. Self-regulation and discriminated aversive conditioning in the modification of alcoholics' drinking behavior. *Behavior Therapy*, 1976, *7*, 223–230.

Cahoon, D. D., & Crosby, C. C. A learning approach to chronic drug use: Sources of reinforcement. *Behavior Therapy*, 1972, *3*, 64–71.

Callner, D. A. Behavioral treatment approaches to drug abuse: A critical review of research. *Psychological Bulletin*, 1975, *82*, 143–164.

Cautela, J. R. Treatment of compulsive behavior by covert sensitization. *Psychological Records,* 1966, *16,* 33–41.

Cautela, J. R. Covert sensitization. *Psychological Reports,* 1967, *20,* 459–468.

Chapman, R. F., Burt, D. W., & Smith, J. W. *Electrical aversion conditioning to alcohol: Individual measurement.* Paper presented at Western Psychological Association Convention, April 1972.

Cooke, C. J., & Meyers, A. The role of predictor variables in the behavioral treatment of obesity. *Behavioral Assessment,* 1980, *2,* 59–69.

Craigie, F. C., & Ross, S. M. The use of a videotape pretherapy training program to encourage treatment-seeking among alcohol detoxification patients. *Behavior Therapy,* 1980, *11,* 141–147.

Curtis, B., Simpson, D. D., & Cole, S. G. Rapid puffing as a treatment component of a community smoking program. *Journal of Community Psychology,* 1976, *4,* 186–193.

Danaher, B. G. Research on rapid smoking: Interim summary and recommendations. *Addictive Behaviors,* 1977, *2,* 151–166.

Danaher, B. G., & Lichtenstein, E. *Become an ex-smoker.* Englewood Cliffs, N.J.: Prentice-Hall, 1978.

Davies, D. L. Normal drinking in recovered alcohol addicts. *Quarterly Journal of Studies on Alcohol,* 1962, *23,* 94–104.

Dericco, D. A., Brigham, T. A., & Garlington, W. K. Development and evaluation of treatment paradigms for the suppression of smoking behavior. *Journal of Applied Behavior Analysis,* 1977, *10,* 173–181.

Ferster, C. B., Nurnberger, J. I., & Levitt, E. B. The control of eating. *Journal of Mathetics,* 1962, *1,* 87–109.

Flaxman, J. Quitting smoking. In W. E. Craighead, A. E. Kazdin, & M. J. Mahoney (Eds.), *Behavior modification: Principles, issues, and applications.* Boston: Houghton Mifflin, 1976.

Flaxman, J. Quitting smoking now or later: Gradual, abrupt, immediate, and delayed quitting. *Behavior Therapy,* 1978, *9,* 260–270.

Frederiksen, L. W. *"But I don't want to quit smoking": Alternatives to abstinence.* Paper presented at Association for the Advancement of Behavior Therapy meeting, Atlanta, 1977.

Frederiksen, L. W., Miller, P. M., & Peterson, G. L. Topographical components of smoking behavior. *Addictive Behaviors,* 1977, *2,* 55–61.

Frederiksen, L. W., & Peterson, G. L. *Controlled smoking: The case for a new treatment goal.* Paper presented at Association for Advancement of Behavior Therapy meeting, New York, 1976. (a)

Frederiksen, L. W., & Peterson, G. L. Controlled smoking: Development and maintenance. *Addictive Behaviors,* 1976, *1,* 193–196. (b)

Frederiksen, L. W., & Simon, S. J. Modification of smoking topography: A preliminary analysis. *Behavior Therapy,* 1978, *9,* 946–949.

Fremouw, W. J., & Zitter, R. E. Individual and couple behavioral contracting for weight reduction and maintenance. *The Behavior Therapist,* 1980, *3*(1), 15–16.

Gitlow, S. E. Alcoholism: A disease. In P. B. Bourne & R. Fox (Eds.), *Alcoholism—Progress in research and treatment.* New York: Academic Press, 1973.

Glasgow, R. E. *The effects of a self-control manual and amount of therapist contact in the modification of smoking behavior.* Unpublished doctoral dissertation, University of Oregon, 1977.

Glasgow, R. E., & Rosen, G. M. Behavioral bibliotherapy: A review of self-help behavior therapy manuals. *Psychological Bulletin,* 1978, *85,* 1–23.

Glicksman, M., Ottomanelli, G., & Cutler, R. The earn-your-way credit system: Use of a token economy in narcotic rehabilitation. *International Journal of the Addictions,* 1971, *6,* 525–531.

Goldiamond, I. Singling out self-administered behavior therapies for professional overview. *American Psychologist,* 1976, *31,* 142–147.

Grimaldi, K. E., & Lichtenstein, E. Hot, smoky air as an aversive stimulus in the treatment of smoking. *Behaviour Research and Therapy,* 1969, *7,* 275–282.

Hagen, R. L. Group therapy versus bibliotherapy in weight reduction. *Behavior Therapy,* 1974, *5,* 222–234.

Hall, S. M., & Hall, R. G. Outcome and methodological considerations in behavioral treatment of obesity. *Behavior Therapy,* 1974, *5,* 352–364.

Harris, M. B. Self-directed program for weight control: A pilot study. *Journal of Abnormal Psychology,* 1969, *74,* 263–270.

Harris, M. B., & Bruner, C. G. A comparison of a self-control and a contract procedure for weight control. *Behaviour Research and Therapy,* 1971, *9,* 347–354.

Harris, M. B., & Hallbauer, E. S. Self-directed weight control through eating and exercise. *Behaviour Research and Therapy,* 1973, *11,* 523–529.

Hsu, J. J. Electroconditioning therapy of alcoholics: A preliminary report. *Quarterly Journal of Studies on Alcohol,* 1965, *26,* 449–459.

Hunt, G. M., & Azrin, N. H. A community-reinforcement approach to alcoholism. *Behaviour Research and Therapy,* 1973, *11,* 91–104.

Hunt, W. A., & Matarazzo, J. D. Three years later: Recent developments in the experimental modification of smoking behavior. *Journal of Abnormal Psychology,* 1973, *81,* 107–114.

Jeffrey, D. B. *Some methodological issues in obesity research.* Paper presented at Association for Advancement of Behavior Therapy meeting, New York, 1972.

Jeffrey, D. B. A comparison of the effects of external control and self-control on the modification and maintenance of weight. *Journal of Abnormal Psychology,* 1974, *83,* 404–410.

Jeffrey, D. B. Behavioral management of obesity. In W. E. Craighead, A. E. Kazdin, & M. J. Mahoney (Eds.), *Behavior modification: Principles, issues, and applications.* Boston: Houghton Mifflin, 1976. (a)

Jeffrey, D. B. A proposal for a macro environmental analysis in the prevention and treatment of obesity. In B. J. Williams, S. Martin, & J. P. Foreyt (Eds.), *Obesity: Behavioral approaches to dietary management.* New York: Brunner/Mazel, 1976. (b)

Jeffrey, D. B., & Katz, R. C. *Take it off and keep it off.* Englewood Cliffs, N.J.: Prentice-Hall, 1977.

Jellinek, E. M. *The disease concept of alcoholism.* New Brunswick, N.J.: Hillhouse Press, 1960.

Jones, R. J., & Azrin, N. H. An experimental application of a social reinforcement approach to the problem of job-finding. *Journal of Applied Behavior Analysis,* 1973, *6,* 345–353.

Keller, M. The oddities of alcoholics. In E. M. Pattison, M. B. Sobell, & L. C. Sobell (Eds.), *Emerging concepts of alcohol dependence.* New York: Springer, 1977.

Kingsley, R. G., & Shapiro, J. A comparison of three behavioral programs for the control of obesity in children. *Behavior Therapy,* 1977, *8,* 30–36.

Knowles, J. H. (Ed.). *Doing better and feeling worse: Health in the United States.* New York: Norton, 1977.

Kraft, T. Successful treatment of a case of Drinamyl addiction. *British Journal of Psychiatry,* 1968, *114,* 1363–1364.

Kraft, T. Successful treatment of a case of chronic barbiturate addiction. *British Journal of Addictions,* 1969, *64,* 115–120.

Lanyon, R. I., Primo, R. V., Terrell, F., & Wener, A. An aversion-desensitization treatment for alcoholism. *Journal of Consulting and Clinical Psychology,* 1972, *38,* 394–398.

Lazarus, A. A. Towards the understanding and effective treatment of alcoholism. *South African Medical Journal,* 1965, *39,* 736–741.

Lemere, F., Voegtlin, W. L., Broz, W. R., & O'Hallaran, P. Conditioned reflex treatment of alcohol addiction. V. Type of patient suitable for this treatment. *Northwestern Medicine,* 1942, *4,* 88–89.

Leon, G. R. Current directions in the treatment of obesity. *Psychological Bulletin*, 1976, *83*, 557–578.

Leon, G. R., & Roth, L. Obesity: Psychological causes, correlations and speculations. *Psychological Bulletin*, 1977, *84*, 117–139.

Lesser, E. Behavior therapy with a narcotics user: A case report. *Behaviour Research and Therapy*, 1967, *5*, 251–252.

Levitz, L. S., & Stunkard, A. J. A therapeutic coalition for obesity: Behavior modification and patient self-help. *American Journal of Psychiatry*, 1974, *131*, 423–427.

Liberman, R. Aversive conditioning of drug addicts: A pilot study. *Behaviour Research and Therapy*, 1968, *6*, 229–231.

Lichtenstein, E., & Danaher, B. G. Modification of smoking behavior: A critical analysis of theory, research, and practice. In M. Hersen, R. M. Eisler, & P. M. Miller (Eds.), *Progress in behavior modification* (Vol. 3). New York: Academic Press, 1976.

Lichtenstein, E., & Glasgow, R. E. Rapid smoking: Side effects and safeguards. *Journal of Consulting and Clinical Psychology*, 1977, *45*, 815–821.

Lichtenstein, E., Harris, D. E., Birchler, G. R., Wahl, J. M., & Schmahl, D. P. Comparison of rapid smoking, warm smoky air, and attention placebo in the modification of smoking behavior. *Journal of Consulting and Clinical Psychology*, 1973, *40*, 92–98.

Lichtenstein, E., & Penner, M. P. Long-term effects of rapid smoking treatment for dependent cigarette smokers. *Addictive Behaviors*, 1977, *2*, 109–112.

Lloyd, R. W., & Salzberg, H. C. Controlled social drinking: An alternative to abstinence as a treatment goal for some alcohol abusers. *Psychological Bulletin*, 1975, *82*, 815–842.

Loro, B. Bibliography of behavioral approaches to weight reduction and obesity from 1962 through 1976. *Professional Psychology*, 1978, *9*, 278–289.

Lovibond, S. H., & Caddy, G. Discriminated aversive control in the moderation of alcoholics' drinking behavior. *Behavior Therapy*, 1970, *1*, 437–444.

Lutzker, J. R., & Lutzker, S. Z. A two-dimensional contract: Weight loss and household responsibility performance. In E. E. Abramson (Ed.), *Behavioral approaches to weight control*. New York: Springer, 1977.

MacCulloch, M. J., Feldman, M. P., Orford, J. F., & MacCulloch, M. L. Anticipatory avoidance learning in the treatment of alcoholism: A record of therapeutic failure. *Behaviour Research and Therapy*, 1966, *4*, 187.

Mahoney, M. J. Self-reward and self-monitoring techniques for weight control. *Behavior Therapy*, 1974, *5*, 48–57.

Mahoney, M. J., & Mahoney, K. *Permanent weight control: A total solution to the dieter's dilemma*. New York: Norton, 1976.

Mahoney, M. J., Moura, N. G., & Wade, T. C. Relative efficacy of self-reward, self-punishment, and self-monitoring techniques for weight loss. *Journal of Consulting and Clinical Psychology*, 1973, *40*, 404–407.

Mann, R. A. The behavior-therapeutic use of contingency contracting to control an adult behavior problem: Weight control. *Journal of Applied Behavior Analysis*, 1972, *5*, 99–109.

Marlatt, G. A. Alcohol use and problem drinking: A cognitive-behavioral analysis. In P. C. Kendall & S. D. Hollon (Eds.), *Cognitive-behavioral interventions*. New York: Academic Press, 1979

Marston, A. R., & McFall, R. M. Comparison of behavior modification approaches to smoking reduction. *Journal of Consulting and Clinical Psychology*, 1971, *36*, 153–162.

Mausner, B., & Platt, E. S. *Smoking: A behavioral analysis*. New York: Pergamon Press, 1971.

McAlister, A. Helping people quit smoking: Current perspective. In A. Enelow (Ed.), *Applying behavioral science to cardiovascular disease*. New York: American Heart Association, 1975.

McBrearty, J. T., Dichter, M., Garfield, Z., & Heath, G. A. A behaviorally oriented treatment program for alcoholism. *Psychological Reports*, 1968, *22*, 287–298.

Miller, P. M. The use of behavioral contracting in the treatment of alcoholism: A case study. *Behavior Therapy,* 1972, *3,* 593–596.

Miller, P. M. A behavioral intervention program for chronic public drunkenness offenders. *Archives of General Psychiatry,* 1975, *32,* 915–918.

Miller, P. M. *Behavioral treatment of alcoholism.* New York: Pergamon Press, 1976.

Miller, P. M., & Becker, J. *The effects of instructions on alcoholic drinking behavior.* Paper presented at meeting of Southeastern Psychological Association, Atlanta, 1975.

Miller, P. M., & Eisler, R. M. Alcohol and drug abuse. In W. E. Craighead, A. E. Kazdin, & M. J. Mahoney (Eds.), *Behavior modification: Principles, issues, and applications.* Boston: Houghton Mifflin, 1976.

Miller, P. M., & Hersen, M. Quantitative changes in alcohol consumption as a function of electrical aversion conditioning. *Journal of Clinical Psychology,* 1972, *28,* 590–593.

Miller, P. M., Hersen, M., Eisler, R., & Hemphill, D. P. Electrical aversion therapy with alcoholics: An analogue study. *Behaviour Research and Therapy,* 1973, *11,* 491–497.

Miller, P. M., Hersen, M., Eisler, R. M., & Watts, J. G. Contingent reinforcement of lowered blood/alcohol levels in an outpatient chronic alcoholic. *Behaviour Research and Therapy,* 1974, *12,* 261–263.

Miller, P. M., & Mastria, M. A. *Alternatives to alcohol abuse.* Champaign, Ill.: Research Press, 1977.

Miller, P. M., Stanford, A. G., & Hemphill, D. P. A comprehensive social learning approach to alcoholism treatment. *Social Casework,* 1974, *55,* 279–284.

Miller, W. R., & Munoz, R. F. *How to control your drinking.* Englewood Cliffs, N.J.: Prentice-Hall, 1976.

Moroski, T. E., & Baer, P. E. Avoidance conditioning of alcoholics. In R. Ulrich, T. Stachnich, & J. Mabry (Eds.), *Control of human behavior* (Vol. 2). Glenview, Ill.: Scott, Foresman, 1970.

Nathan, P. E. Alcoholism. In H. Leitenberg (Ed.), *Handbook of behavior modification.* New York: Appleton-Century-Crofts, 1976.

Nathan, P. E., & Briddell, D. W. Behavior assessment and treatment of alcoholism. In B. Kissin & H. Begleiter (Eds.), *The biology of alcoholism* (Vol. 5). New York: Plenum Press, 1977.

Nathan, P. E., & Goldman, M. S. Problem drinking and alcoholism. In O. F. Pomerleau & J. P. Brady (Eds.), *Behavioral medicine: Theory and practice.* Baltimore: Williams and Wilkins, 1979.

Ober, D. C. Modification of smoking behavior. *Journal of Consulting and Clinical Psychology,* 1968, *32,* 543–549.

O'Brien, J. S., & Raynes, A. E. Treatment of heroin addiction with behavioral therapy. In W. Keup (Ed.), *Drug abuse: Current concepts and research.* Springfield, Ill.: Charles C Thomas, 1972.

O'Brien, J. S., Raynes, A. E., & Patch, V. D. Treatment of heroin addiction with aversion therapy, relaxation training, and systematic desensitization. *Behaviour Research and Therapy,* 1972, *10,* 77–80.

O'Leary, K. D., & Wilson, G. T. *Behavior therapy: Application and outcome.* Englewood Cliffs, N.J.: Prentice-Hall, 1975.

Pattison, E. M. A conceptual approach to alcoholism treatment goals. *Addictive Behaviors,* 1976, *1,* 117–192.

Pattison, E. M., Sobell, M. B., & Sobell, L. C. (Eds.). *Emerging concepts of alcohol dependence.* New York: Springer, 1977.

Pechacek, T. F. Strategies for the modification of smoking behavior: A synoptic review. *Behavioral Medicine Update,* 1980, *2*(1), 16–18.

Pechacek, T. F., & Danaher, B. G. How and why people quit smoking: A cognitive-behavioral analysis. In P. C. Kendall & S. D. Hollon (Eds.), *Cognitive-behavioral interventions.* New York: Academic Press, 1979.

Penick, S. B., Filion, R., Fox, S., & Stunkard, A. J. Behavior modification in the treatment of obesity. *Psychosomatic Medicine,* 1971, *33,* 49–55.

Pomerleau, O. F., & Pomerleau, C. *Break the smoking habit*. Champaign, Ill.: Research Press, 1977.

Rachman, S., & Teasdale, J. *Aversion therapy and behavior disorders: An analysis*. Coral Gables: University of Miami Press, 1969.

Ramstrom, L. M. New ideas in Sweden's tobacco labeling act. *World Smoking and Health*, 1976, *1*, 28–31.

Raymond, M. J. The treatment of addiction by aversion conditioning with apomorphine. *Behaviour Research and Therapy*, 1964, *1*, 287–291.

Rosen, G. M. The development and use of nonprescription behavior therapies. *American Psychologist*, 1976, *31*, 139–141.

Rosen, G. M. Nonprescription behavior therapies and other self-help treatments: A reply to Goldiamond. *American Psychologist*, 1977, *32*, 178–179.

Ross, S. M. Behavioral treatment of drug abuse. *Association for the Advancement of Behavior Therapy Newsletter*, 1977, *4*(5), 11.

Rozynko, V. V., Flint, G. A., Hammer, C. E., Swift, K. D., Kline, J. A., & King, R. M. *An operant behavior modification program for alcoholics*. Paper presented at Western Psychological Association meeting, April 1971.

Sachs, L. B., Bean, H., & Morrow, J. E. Comparison of smoking treatments. *Behavior Therapy*, 1970, *1*, 465–472.

Schaefer, H. H., Sobell, M. B., & Mills, K. C. Some sobering data on the use of self-confrontation with alcoholics. *Behavior Therapy*, 1971, *2*, 28–39.

Schmahl, D. P., Lichtenstein, E., & Harris, D. E. Successful treatment of habitual smokers with warm, smoky air, and rapid smoking. *Journal of Consulting and Clinical Psychology*, 1972, *38*, 105–111.

Silverstein, S. J., Nathan, P. E., & Taylor, H. A. Blood alcohol level estimation and controlled drinking by chronic alcoholics. *Behavior Therapy*, 1974, *5*, 1–15.

Sitzer, M., Bigelow, G., Lawrence, C., Cohen, J., D'Lugoff, B., & Hawthorne, J. Medication take-home as a reinforcer in a methadone maintenance program. *Addictive Behaviors*, 1977, *2*, 9–14.

Smolensky, J. *Principles of community health* (Fourth edition). Philadelphia: Saunders, 1977.

Sobell, M. B. Alternatives to abstinence: Evidence, issues and some proposals. In P. E. Nathan & G. A. Marlatt (Eds.), *Experimental and behavioral approaches to alcoholism*. New York: Plenum Press, 1978.

Sobell, M. B., & Sobell, L. C. Individualized behavior therapy for alcoholics. *Behavior Therapy*, 1973, *4*, 49–72. (a)

Sobell, M. B., & Sobell, L. C. Alcoholics treated by individualized behavior therapy: One year treatment outcome. *Behaviour Research and Therapy*, 1973, *11*, 599–618. (b)

Sobell, M. B., & Sobell, L. C. The need for realism, relevance, and operational assumptions in the study of substance dependence. In H. D. Cappell & A. E. LeBlanc (Eds.), *Biological and behavioral approaches to drug dependence*. Toronto: Addiction Research Foundation, 1975.

Sobell, M. B., & Sobell, L. C. Second year treatment outcome of alcoholics treated by individualized behavior therapy: Results. *Behaviour Research and Therapy*, 1976, *14*, 195–215.

Sobell, M. B., & Sobell, L. C. *Behavioral treatment of alcohol problems*. New York: Plenum Press, 1978.

Steinfeld, G. J. The use of covert sensitization with institutionalized narcotic addicts. *International Journal of the Addictions*, 1970, *5*, 225–232.

Stuart, R. B. Behavioral control of overeating. *Behaviour Research and Therapy*, 1967, *5*, 357–365.

Stuart, R. B. Operant-interpersonal treatment for marital discord. *Journal of Consulting and Clinical Psychology*, 1969, *33*, 675–682.

Stuart, R. B. A three-dimensional program for the treatment of obesity. *Behaviour Research and Therapy*, 1971, *9*, 177–186.

Stuart, R. B. *Act thin, stay thin*. New York: Norton, 1978.

Stuart, R. B., & Davis, B. *Slim chance in a fat world: Behavioral control of obesity*. Champaign, Ill.: Research Press, 1972.

Stunkard, A. J. The management of obesity. *New York Journal of Medicine*, 1958, *58*, 79–87.

Stunkard, A. J. New therapies for the eating disorders. *Archives of General Psychiatry*, 1972, *26*, 391–398.

Stunkard, A. J., & Mahoney, M. J. Behavioral treatment of the eating disorders. In H. Leitenberg (Ed.), *Handbook of behavior modification and behavior therapy*. Englewood Cliffs, N.J.: Prentice-Hall, 1976.

Terry, L. L. Foreword. In O. F. Pomerleau & C. S. Pomerleau, *Break the smoking habit*. Champaign, Ill.: Research Press, 1977.

Thomson, I. G., & Rathod, N. H. Aversion therapy for heroin dependence. *The Lancet*, 1968, *2*, 382–384.

Ullmann, L. P., & Krasner, L. *A psychological approach to abnormal behavior*. Englewood Cliffs, N.J.: Prentice-Hall, 1975.

U.S. Public Health Service. *Adult use of tobacco—1975*. Atlanta: CDC, 1976.

Voegtlin, W. L. The treatment of alcoholism by establishing a conditioned reflex. *American Journal of Medical Science*, 1940, *199*, 802–809.

Vogler, R. E., Compton, J. V., & Weissbach, T. A. Integrated behavior change techniques for alcoholics. *Journal of Consulting and Clinical Psychology*, 1975, *43*, 233–243.

Vogler, R. E., Lunde, S. E., Johnson, G. R., & Martin, P. L. Electrical aversion conditioning with chronic alcoholics. *Journal of Consulting and Clinical Psychology*, 1970, *34*, 302–307.

Wald, N. J. Mortality from lung cancer and coronary heart disease in relation to changes in smoking habits. *The Lancet*, 1976, *1*, 136–138.

Wheeler, M. E., & Hess, K. W. Treatment of juvenile obesity by successive approximation control of eating. *Journal of Behavior Therapy and Experimental Psychiatry*, 1976, *7*, 235–241.

Whitman, T. L. Aversive control of smoking behavior in a group context. *Behaviour Research and Therapy*, 1972, *10*, 97–104.

Wikler, A. Conditioning factors in opiate addiction and relapse. In D. M. Wilner & G. G. Kassebaum (Eds.), *Narcotics*. New York: McGraw-Hill, 1965.

Wikler, A. Some implications of conditioning theory for problems of drug abuse. *Behavioral Science*, 1971, *16*, 92–97.

Winett, R. A. Parameters of deposit contracts in the modification of smoking. *Psychological Record*, 1973, *23*, 49–60.

Wollersheim, J. P. Effectiveness of group therapy based upon learning principles in the treatment of overweight women. *Journal of Abnormal Psychology*, 1970, *76*, 462–474.

Wooley, S. C., Wooley, O. W., & Dyrenforth, S. R. Theoretical, practical, and social issues in behavioral treatments of obesity. *Journal of Applied Behavior Analysis*, 1979, *12*, 3–25.

Wyden, P. *The overweight society*. New York: Morrow, 1965.

Yates, A. J. *Theory and practice in behavior therapy*. New York: Wiley, 1975.

Zifferblatt, S. M., & Wilbur, C. S. Maintaining a healthy heart: Guidelines for a feasible goal. *Preventative Medicine*, 1977, *6*, 514–525.

Zuti, W. B., & Golding, L. A. Comparing diet and exercise as weight reduction tools. *Physician and Sportsmedicine*, 1976, *4*, 45–53.

CHAPTER 11

Personal Problems: Anxiety and Depression

With some reluctance and discomfort, we devote this chapter to the problems of anxiety and depression. It is not that behavior change techniques have been unsuccessful with these problems; quite the contrary, they have been more successful than other approaches. The problem is in the necessity for defining anxiety and depression. If you are going to change or alter something, there must be some agreement about what that something is. We all know many people whom we would consider to be suffering from anxiety or depression, yet we would probably have some difficulty agreeing on who those people are.

Unfortunately, we can't decide not to write about anxiety and depression merely because of our uncertainty, for both anxiety and depression incapacitate a large segment of our society. Checking people's medicine cabinets in both urban and rural homes would surely reveal untold numbers of tranquilizers and antidepressants that reflect the enormity of the problems.

ANXIETY, FEARS, AND PHOBIAS

It is our opinion that anxiety and fear are quite closely related. The major difference may be in the salience of the stimulus that gives rise to each. With anxiety, one senses an unpleasant emotional state associated with an impending danger or difficulty, a state that would not be obvious to an outside observer. Fear, on the other hand, is a similar unpleasant state due to a more obvious threat or danger (Marks, 1978). Anxieties or fears become targets for behavior change only when they interfere with normal day-to-day functioning and/or when they are exaggerated beyond normalcy.

One way to deal with the difficulty in defining anxiety is to focus on a method for measuring it. Most researchers would agree that there are three distinct ways in which anxiety manifests itself: cognitively (what a person says to himself or reports to others); behaviorally (what a person does); and physiologically (increased heart rate, blood pressure, respiration, muscle tension, and so on). Unfortunately, these three methods of measuring anxiety do not correlate well with one another (Lang, 1969; Borkovec, Weerts, & Bernstein, 1977; Lick & Katkin, 1976). A person may verbally report that he experiences severe anxiety (cognitive anxiety) while riding in elevators; however, behaviorally he may continue to ride in elevators, and physiological measures of anxiety (heart rate, respiration rate) may not be indicative of increased anxiety. The reasons for this lack of correlation are probably complex, but a major factor is likely the differential control that various environmental stimuli have over each of the three ways anxiety manifests itself. In addition to the feared object or stimulus, other variables may also be controlling behavior such that anxiety or fear may be inhibited cognitively, behaviorally, and/or physiologically. For example, social pressure or sanctions may control avoidance of feared stimuli; that is, a person may choose not to avoid a feared stimulus as he does not wish to appear too deviant or strange.

The problem of asynchrony of different measures of anxiety obviously does not help in producing a definition, but it does point out the necessity for assessment in all three ways (Lick & Katkin, 1976). Since the initial severity of anxiety or fear may vary across the three measures, and because the response of each measure to intervention may vary, continuous measurement and follow-up across response measures may be needed.

Phobias are exaggerated fears that a person cannot control and that lead the person to avoid the feared situation (Marks, 1978). Fensterheim and Baer (1977) have classified fear and phobias into five different categories as follows: (1) things and places (for example, animals, heights, closed spaces); (2) social and interpersonal (for example, rejection, failure, anger); (3) internal fears (for example, fear of fear, or agoraphobia); (4) thoughts (for example, obsessive ruminations); and (5) derivative fears (for example, secondary fears that may develop because of the stress of an unrelated matter). The most common kind of phobia is agoraphobia, which accounts for between 50% and 60% of all phobic patients (Marks, 1970). While agoraphobia literally means fear of open or public places, it has been more accurately conceptualized as the fear of feelings within oneself when one is in open or crowded places (Weekes, 1976). Agoraphobia, then, is the fear of having a panic attack or of fear (Fensterheim & Baer, 1977). Other major phobias include illness and injury phobia, social phobia, and animal phobias (Marks, 1969).

While several different behavior change techniques have been used to eliminate different phobias, Marks (1978) has suggested that all contain a common element—exposure to the feared object or situation until one gets used to it. Confrontation often diminishes fear. Perhaps the major behavior change technique that has been used is systematic desensitization as developed by Joseph Wolpe (1958).

Systematic Desensitization

Wolpe (1958) has stated that the basic assumption behind teaching patients relaxation is that it is impossible to relax and be anxious at the same time (this is called reciprocal inhibition). Wolpe adapted the use of relaxation in systematic desensitization from earlier work of Jacobson (1938). While Jacobson's original work on progressive relaxation involved a great many training sessions, Wolpe developed a much more efficient way of teaching relaxation (Bernstein & Borkovec, 1973). Clients were systematically taught to alternatively tense and relax different muscle groups of the body. This procedure was followed until clients were able to voluntarily relax all of the major muscle groups simultaneously, thus achieving a state of deep muscle relaxation. The behavior change professional is quite active in this entire process by verbally directing the client during training and providing appropriate feedback.

The next step in systematic desensitization involves the construction of anxiety hierarchies, or lists of stimuli that would gradually elicit more fear from the client. Tables 11-1 and 11-2 provide examples of the two types of hierarchies, thematic and spatial-temporal (Paul, 1969a). Thematic hierarchies are based upon particular events in time or space, such as height in skyscrapers, talking to physicians, or swimming in the ocean. Paul (1969a) also states that combined hierarchies (thematic and spatial-temporal) are frequently necessary. Hierarchies are constructed through mutual agreement of the client and behavior change agent. The items contained in a hierarchy should be realistic, concrete situations closely related to the client's specific phobia. They can be either situations the client has experienced or ones he expects to experience (Rimm & Masters, 1974).

TABLE 11-1. Thematic Hierarchy (Fear of Opposite Sex)

 1. Attending outdoor athletic event where members of opposite sex will be present
 2. Entering a room where members of opposite sex will be present
 3. Anticipating social event where members of opposite sex will be present
 4. Saying "Hello" to known member of opposite sex
 5. Saying "Hello" to stranger of opposite sex
 6. Sitting next to someone of opposite sex in a public place
 7. Initiating conversation with known member of opposite sex
 8. Initiating conversation with stranger of opposite sex
 9. Asking person of opposite sex for date over telephone
10. Asking person of opposite sex for date in person

TABLE 11-2. Spatial-Temporal Hierarchy (Fear of Public Speaking)

 1. Four days before speech
 2. Three days before speech
 3. Two days before speech
 4. One day before speech
 5. Night before the speech
 6. Morning of the day of the speech
 7. Driving to place where speech will be given
 8. Entering room where speech is to be given
 9. Waiting to speak
10. Standing up to start speaking

Before beginning actual systematic desensitization, clients may need some practice at imagery (visually imagining certain scenes or occurrences). When the therapist has determined that the client can adequately visualize scenes, the two begin to move slowly through the hierarchy of feared situations. The client is told to relax and then to imagine the first scene in the hierarchy as clearly as possible. Clients are supposed to signal (usually by raising a finger) whenever they feel any anxiety at all. If no anxiety is signaled during the visualization, then the client rests and relaxes for a brief time before the second scene is presented. If the client signals anxiety during the first item on the hierarchy (or any successive item), the client is told to stop imagining the scene and to focus on relaxing. Thereafter, the item or scene may be altered in a way expected to diminish the anxiety, or a lower hierarchy scene may be re-presented. Progress through the hierarchy continues until all items have been successfully completed. Each session should end with a successfully completed scene, and the succeeding session should begin where the previous one ended (Paul, 1969a).

Following completion of the hierarchy (without any anxiety), it is obviously time to get out of the therapist's office or setting and into the real world. Hopefully, the client will have already experienced some fear-related changes in the outside world. The therapist may have to grade the client's exposure to feared objects or situations in the real world. This real-life *(in vivo)* process can uncover situations that were not dealt with in imagery, and so additional hierarchies may need to be created and dealt with. Systematic desensitization seems to be an extremely effective behavior change procedure for eliminating fears and phobias. Numerous excellent reviews of it are available for the interested student (Bandura, 1969; Lang, 1969; Paul, 1969a, 1969b). A classic, group design outcome study documenting the effectiveness of systematic desensitization with speech anxiety has been conducted by Paul (1966, 1968, 1969b). On multiple outcome measures, systematic desensitization was found to be more effective than insight-oriented psychotherapy, an attention-placebo treatment, a no-treatment waiting list, and a no-contact control group. A two-year follow-up revealed that systematic desensitization was still the superior treatment method. Others have also attempted comparative studies (Gelder & Marks, 1966; Gelder, Marks, Wolff, & Clarke, 1967) with results generally favorable to systematic desensitization; however, most have lacked the elegance of Paul's research design and his use of multiple outcome measures.

Although it is now generally accepted that systematic desensitization is an extremely effective method of behavior change, there is considerable controversy about how it works. This issue has been neatly addressed by Yates (1975). A review of the literature reveals an astonishing number of variants to the standard systematic desensitization procedure. Paul (1969b) has identified four distinct identifiable "treatment packages" as used by (1) Wolpe, (2) Lazarus and Rachman, (3) Lang and his associates, and (4) Paul and Shannon. These packages vary across procedures used during relaxation training, hierarchy construction, and desensitization proper. Even more discomforting is the presence of research (Agras et al., 1971) that demonstrated that relaxation training is not necessary for systematic desensitization to be effective. The necessity for rigidly adhering to the construction of hierarchies (from least to most anxiety-producing) has been questioned. For example, Bandura (1969) has shown that hierarchies that decrease in anxiety production work as effectively as those that increase. The fact of the matter is that systematic desensitization works when altered in numerous ways, and that the specific set procedure advocated by Wolpe (1958) is unnecessary. Why, then, does it work? Current thinking (Kazdin & Wilcoxon, 1976) is that the client's expectation of improvement and the "directiveness" of behavior therapy may be the common, most active ingredients in all of the different variants of systematic desensitization. Since the elaborate methodology of systematic desensitization may be unnecessary, behavior change professionals have looked for other techniques that might treat phobias equally effectively and more efficiently.

Other Techniques for Eliminating Phobias

Participant modeling is a technique developed by Bandura and his colleagues (Bandura, Grusec, & Menlove, 1967; Bandura & Menlove, 1968; Bandura, Jeffrey, & Wright, 1974). Its major component is the client's observation of the therapist or model exhibiting nonphobic behavior in the presence of the feared stimuli or situation. These observations are graded in much the same ways as hierarchy construction in systematic desensitization. While the early work of Bandura and associates consisted of observation alone, more recently the client has been required to take a more active role by copying the behavior of the model. This is done in a gradual, step-by-step fashion with the client receiving encouragement, reassurance, and social reinforcement (Bandura, Blanchard, & Ritter, 1969; Ritter, 1969a, 1969b; Blanchard, 1970). We see examples of this all of the time in our day-to-day living. Many of us become much braver and will engage in feared acts *after* we have observed someone we like, admire or respect exhibit the act. While the breadth of applications of participant modeling may be limited to relatively concrete social stimuli or physical settings (Bernstein, 1976), it has proven to be a much more rapid method of treatment than systematic desensitization, and it can be more effective (Bandura, Blanchard, & Ritter, 1969). However, it should be noted that nonclinical phobics (for example, volunteers who were afraid of snakes, dogs, and so on) were used in the majority of research on participant modeling. The utility of the procedure yet needs to be examined in a clinical situation where persons with severe phobias are seeking assistance.

Leitenberg and his colleagues have systematically examined the treatment of phobias by a procedure he has called *reinforced practice* (Leitenberg, Agras, Thomson, & Wright, 1968; Leitenberg, Agras, Allen, Butz, & Edwards, 1975). It involves the gradual exposure to fear-provoking stimuli while providing reinforcement for the client. The client is encouraged to proceed along this graded approach while keeping anxiety to a minimum. In practice, the procedure is equivalent to shaping or successive approximation as described in Chapter 1. In general, the results of using this procedure have been very favorable in the treatment of clinical phobias (for example, agoraphobia, fear of closed rooms, fear of crowded places), and in a thorough review of the experimental literature on reinforced practice, Leitenberg (1976) has concluded that it is a viable alternative to systematic desensitization.

Flooding and *implosion* are two other procedures that have been used to eliminate phobias (Marks, Boulougouris, & Marset, 1971; Stampfl & Levis, 1967). Flooding may involve both the imagination of stressful stimuli and confronting these stimuli *in vivo*. On the other hand, implosion is restricted to imagery based on exaggerated phobic stimuli laced with psychodynamic elements (for example, sex, hostility, death, and so on). Currently, there exists a great deal of controversy about flooding and implosion techniques. Their effectiveness has not been conclusively documented (Morganstern, 1973) and there is a legitimate concern over the potential harmfulness of the procedures to the client (Bandura, 1969), especially when less stressful (and perhaps more effective) techniques are available.

Three other types of behavior change techniques have been used in the treatment of anxiety—relaxation, cognitive behavior modification, and assertion training. In the main, these strategies have been used to treat anxiety of unidentifiable origin and/or lesser anxieties that cannot be called real phobias (active escape and avoidance of certain situations or objects are missing). The teaching of progressive relaxation has proven to be a very effective technique for helping clients deal with general anxieties of day-to-day living. At times, some behavior change agents may use EMG biofeedback as an adjunct in teaching relaxation. However, there is no evidence that this procedure is superior to more traditional ways of teaching progressive relaxation (Blanchard & Epstein, 1977).

A number of cognitive behavior modification strategies, such as RET, or rational-emotive therapy (Ellis & Harper, 1975), cognitive restructuring (Goldfried & Davison, 1976), and stress inoculation (Meichenbaum, 1977), have been proposed as useful for the treatment of anxieties and fears. RET focuses on the alteration of irrational or self-defeating beliefs. Cognitive restructuring involves clients' thoughts or self-talk. Stress inoculation combines the teaching of coping self-talk with a graded exposure to stressful situations. These strategies, then, attempt to change overt behavior (a person's actions) through altering a person's thoughts, beliefs, or cognitions (in contrast to most behavior change techniques, which try to change behavior more directly). While cognitive behavior modification fascinates us, we must remember that the current enthusiasm for these techniques far exceeds the clinical research data. Ledwidge (1978) has reviewed studies that compared cognitive behavior modification with more typical behavior change procedures (for example, systematic desensitization, implosion) and found them to be equally effective. However, none of these comparative studies used clinical populations (rather, those treated had milder problems, such as test-taking anxiety or animal phobias). There is a tremendous amount of research that documents the effectiveness of behavior change techniques with both mild and severe anxieties. Based upon a literature review, Wilson (1978) has concluded that performance-based treatment (for example, participant modeling and other *in vivo* techniques) is superior to imaginal techniques (for example, systematic desensitization, flooding). This would indicate that one should not expect cognitive behavior modification techniques to be any more effective than the other imaginal techniques (and so, also less effective than more direct performance-based treatments). In summary, despite the fact that cognitive behavior modification has produced a deluge of books (Mahoney, 1974; Meichenbaum, 1977; Foreyt & Rathjen, 1978; Kendall & Hollon, 1979), we will be reluctant to jump on the bandwagon until there is considerably more research with clinical populations. Cognitive behavior modification may be most useful with less serious problems faced by normal people rather than with clinical problems such as severe anxieties or fears. Thus, it may have the potential of providing help for the many thousands of people each year who are involved in counseling or psychotherapy for problems of daily living.

Assertion Training

Assertion training has been one of the most popular movements within psychology (and perhaps society) in the 1970s. We see assertion training as *one part* of a social skills package that can be taught to certain individuals and groups with certain deficits. With regard to anxiety, the teaching of social skills may be very useful with individuals who have difficulty and anxiety in interpersonal relationships. They can be taught in a manner quite similar to methods used with psychiatric patients (Chapter 9). Typical anxiety-related problems treated by assertion or social skills training include minimal dating (MacDonald, Lindquist, Kramer, McGrath, & Rhyne, 1973), job interviews (McGovern, Tinsley, Liss-Levinson, Laventure, & Britton, 1975) and marital interactions (Eisler, Miller, Hersen, & Alford, 1974). Social skills training appears to offer hope for individuals with certain types of interpersonal anxieties (not phobias).

While we have noted that assertiveness training may be a part of a social skills training package used in the treatment of anxiety, it has also been offered to many "normal people." Salter (1949) first suggested that individuals could benefit from learning to be more assertive. Specific training in assertiveness was largely ignored by behavior change professionals until Alberti and Emmons published their classic book, *Your Perfect Right* (1970). This led to a flurry of other self-help books that claimed to teach individuals to be more assertive (Smith, 1975; Fensterheim & Baer, 1975; Lazarus & Fay, 1975). None of these books, unfortunately, have been validated, and so we cannot be certain that they teach anyone anything.

Actually, there is considerable disagreement as to the procedures that constitute assertiveness training. Lange and Jakubowski (1976) have written thoughtfully on this problem and we find ourselves in general agreement with their views on assertion training. They see it as a "semistructured training approach which is characterized by its emphasis on acquiring assertive skills through practice" (Lange & Jakubowski, 1976, pp. 2–3). Training may involve role playing and/or observing models. It incorporates four major components as follows: (1) teaching people the differences between aggression and assertiveness (and between politeness and non-assertiveness); (2) teaching people to recognize and accept personal rights (their own and others); (3) diminishing the cognitive and affective barriers to acting assertively (for example, anxiety, anger, irrational beliefs); and (4) using active practice methods to develop assertive skills (Jakubowski-Spector, 1973; Jakubowski, 1977).

As with other behavior change techniques, assertiveness training is best done by those who are trained. Unfortunately, we are aware that a lot of training is currently being done by those with little training. We believe that this is unfortunate since, in the long run, assertiveness training may die out because of its relative ineffectiveness in the hands of untrained trainers. Lange and Jakubowski (1976) have written an excellent book for trainers and we see this book as a step in the right direction, as is their book (Jakubowski & Lange, 1978) that focuses much more on specific techniques that can be used to change behavior and become more assertive.

There are a number of critical issues that need to be addressed in future research on assertiveness training (see Heimberg, Montgomery, Madsen, & Heimberg, 1977, for a more extensive review). First of all, we would like to see assessment and outcome data that indicate that significant numbers of any population (for example, psychiatric patients, college sophomores, secretaries) have problems relating to assertion alone, and that these problems can be alleviated through assertion training alone. (Does it make people happier?) There is a definite need to assess whether assertiveness training generalizes to the wide variety of social and professional settings in which most of us interact. Finally, as with other behavior change techniques, long-term follow-up studies are needed. After individuals have been taught to be more assertive, does this skill endure or fade in time?

Obsessive-Compulsive Behavior

Somewhat related to phobias and fears are obsessive-compulsive behaviors. Obsessions are repetitive thoughts usually of a frightening nature. The most common kinds have to do with illness and doing injury to others (Leitenberg, 1976). Compulsions are repetitive actions of a ritualistic nature. Common compulsions have to do with cleanliness (such as repetitive handwashing) for fear of being contaminated. Just as there is a wide variety of obsessive and compulsive behaviors, the severity of each may vary. Occasionally, a person may be totally nonfunctional as a result of obsessive-compulsive behavior.

Since obsessive-compulsive behaviors may be a function of fears, they have been treated in much the same way as other fears and phobias. Thus far, systematic desensitization has not proven to be very effective (Cooper, Gelder, & Marks, 1965). Flooding and participant modeling have been successfully used by Rachman, Hodgson, and Marks (1971) with obsessive-compulsives. Perhaps the most effective behavior change procedure for eliminating obsessive-compulsive behaviors was developed by Meyer (1966). This procedure involves placing the client in situations or settings that are likely to provoke obsessive-compulsive behavior and then blocking the client's compulsive rituals. Since that time, many investigators (Levy & Meyer, 1971; Hodgson, Rachman, & Marks, 1972; Mills, Agras, Barlow, & Mills, 1973) have based their behavior change programs on these two key elements. While most of these treatment programs must, by necessity, be inpatient based, it may be possible with highly motivated and cooperative clients to design a more *in vivo* treatment program in certain instances. For example, Devine (1973) has successfully treated "cleanliness" types of compulsions by having a treatment team check into a motel for a weekend. In this semi-restricted setting, then, clients can be exposed to obsession-evoking situations and be prevented from engaging in their rituals.

DEPRESSION

Depression is certainly one of the major problems in our society today. Unfortunately, like anxiety, it is difficult to define. It is estimated that 5% to 10% of all people will be seriously (clinically) depressed once or more during their lifetimes. Women may run an even higher risk (Klerman & Barrett, 1973; Woodruff, Goodwin, & Guze, 1974). These figures, however, may underestimate the problem, for other estimates indicate that up to 25% of the population may need clinical intervention because of depression (Schwab, Brown, Holzer, & Sokolof, 1968). Beck (1967) has defined depression as characterized by: (1) a specific change in mood, such as apathy or sadness; (2) a negative self-concept; (3) self-punitive desires and wishes to escape or die; (4) changes in eating, sleeping, and sexual habits; (5) changes in activity level (either increased or decreased). Davison and Neale (1978) have defined depression as an emotional state in which apprehension and sadness are exhibited, a withdrawal from other people can be observed, loss of appetite, sleep, and sexual desire are seen, and lethargy or agitation is present. Lewinsohn, Youngren, and Grosscup (in press) have described depression as a syndrome that includes dysphoric statements, self-deprecation, social isolation, guilt, material burden, somatic complaints, and a reduction in overt behavior. Despite the fact that depression has been recognized for over 2000 years (Beck, 1967), Lewinsohn (1975) has argued that the classification of people as depressed remains very confused and unsettled. Further, depression includes a very long list of behaviors and any two depressed clients probably exhibit different symptoms. There is not one symptom that directly leads to a diagnosis of depression. Depression is polydimensional, involving cognitive, physiological, and overt somatic motor behaviors (Craighead, 1980). You will soon be aware that this is a relatively new area of research and clinical endeavor. Much more has been written about the causes of depression (from a functional analytic viewpoint) than has been determined by research about a definitive treatment.

Reinforcement Model

Charles Ferster (1965), in addressing the issue of the classification of behavior pathology, first proposed a reinforcement model for the etiology of depression. Viewing depression from a functional analysis approach, he focused on the obviously lowered rate of behavior of depressed individuals, which he attributed to a reduction in positive reinforcement. Ferster (1965, 1966, 1973, 1974) noted at least three different behavioral processes that can lead to depression and a reduction in behavior. First, the schedule of reinforcement for nondepressed behavior was too lean (for example, reinforcement was not delivered frequently enough). Second, there was some significant change in the environment, such as the death of a family member or close friend. Any change or act that leads to a disruption of a predictable source of reinforcement will likely reduce nondepressed behavior. Finally, it is likely that much of a depressed person's behavior occurred under inappropriate circumstances or in inappropriate settings. This occurred because of an inaccurate observation of the environment by the depressed person or, as Ferster (1966) says, "the environment does not control the performances appropriate to activating it." As a result, a large portion of the depressed person's behavior goes unreinforced. The depressed person is, according to Lazarus (1968), on an extinction schedule of reinforcement. Costello (1972) has postulated that depression is due to a loss of reinforcer effectiveness rather than a loss of reinforcers. This view has merit, for it is parsimonious with either a biochemically and/or neurophysiologically based depression or a behaviorally based depression resulting from the disruption of a chain of behaviors.

Major research with the reinforcement model of depression has been conducted by Dr. Peter Lewinsohn and his colleagues at the University of Oregon (Lewinsohn, 1974, 1975; Lewinsohn, Biglan, & Zeiss, 1976). Lewinsohn and his associates (Lewinsohn, Weinstein, & Shaw, 1969; Lewinsohn, 1974) have stated that a low rate of response-contingent reinforcement is enough to explain depression (including the low rate of behavior, dysphoria, and somatic complaints). Further, Lewinsohn (1974) has suggested that the reduced rate of response-contingent reinforcement may occur for three reasons: (1) the overall number of potentially reinforcing stimuli may be reduced, much as Costello (1972) has proposed; (2) certain reinforcing events may be unavailable because of a physical injury, loss of a loved one, and so on; and (3) the individual may lack the necessary skill or repertoire to elicit the reinforcers. The role of enabling, sympathy, or concern by persons in the depressed individual's immediate environment is also critical. Eventually this reinforcement will be reduced because people will find the behavior of the depressed individual more and more aversive. The escape or avoidance behavior of these people will be negatively reinforced when they interact less and less with the depressed individual. Depression will be further accentuated due to this additional decrease in response-contingent reinforcement (Lewinsohn, 1975). Figure

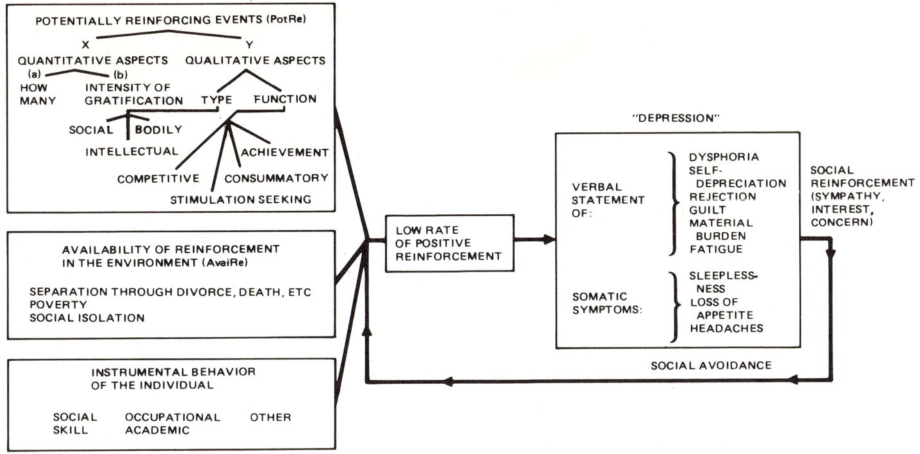

FIGURE 11-1.   Schematic representation of the causation and maintenance of "depressive" behavior. (From "The Behavioral Study and Treatment of Depression," by P. M. Lewinsohn. In M. Hersen, R. M. Eisler, and P. M. Miller (Eds.), *Progress in Behavior Modification* (Vol. 1). Copyright 1975 by Academic Press. Reprinted by permission of author and publisher.)

11-1 is a schematic representation of the Lewinsohn reinforcement model of depression. In summary, depression is viewed to be a function of the reduction in the occurrence of response-contingent reinforcement or, equally, when reinforcement is delivered noncontingently or independent of nondepressed behavior (Lewinsohn, 1975).

As a result of this theory of the etiology of depression, Lewinsohn and his associates have developed a comprehensive treatment program (Lewinsohn & Grosscup, 1978) and evaluated it through numerous research studies (Lewinsohn & Graf, 1973; Lewinsohn & Libet, 1972; Lewinsohn, Sullivan, & Grosscup, 1978; Lewinsohn, Youngren, & Grosscup, in press). Intake assessment may include observations at the depressed person's home and in other interpersonal settings. The symptoms of depression are seen as falling into five categories as follows: (1) dysphoria (for example, feelings of sadness); (2) behavioral deficits (for example, decreased sexual activity); (3) behavioral excesses (for example, verbal complaints about material problems); (4) somatic symptoms (for example, insomnia); and (5) "cognitive" manifestations (for example, negative self-statements). In addition to evaluating change in general depression level, specific problems should be monitored also (Lewinsohn, Biglan, & Zeiss, 1976). General depression is evaluated (and clients are screened for treatment) through ratings based on an interview (see Grinker, Miller, Sabshin, Nunn, & Nunally, 1961, for criteria and basis of ratings) and selected scales from the Minnesota Multiphasic Personality Inventory (MMPI).

Because clients are expected to actively participate in the Lewinsohn treatment program (Lewinsohn, Biglan, & Zeiss, 1976), various contingencies have been arranged to increase the probability of treatment-relevant activities. These include:

(1) making the subsequent appointment contingent upon completion of certain tasks; (2) earning credit toward one's bill by completing homework assignments; (3) increasing the length of therapy time in proportion to a rating of the patient's activity level; (4) having friends or relatives deliver social and/or other reinforcement; and (5) awarding points for progress, which can be exchanged for items on a "self-reward" menu (things patients like to do).

The major goals of Lewinsohn's treatment program are as follows: (1) to decrease the occurrence of unpleasant events; (2) to lessen the client's experienced aversiveness of unpleasant events; (3) to increase the client's rate of engaging in pleasant activities; (4) to enhance the client's enjoyment of pleasant activities; and (5) to provide both a maintenance and prevention program that the client can use to maintain an improved mood and to avoid future depression (Lewinsohn & Grosscup, 1978).

This treatment program is based on research that has demonstrated relationships between a depressed client's mood and the rate at which the client engages in pleasant and unpleasant activities (Lewinsohn & Libet, 1972; Lewinsohn & Graf, 1973; Lewinsohn & MacPhillamy, 1974; MacPhillamy & Lewinsohn, 1974; Lewinsohn & Amenson, 1978; Lewinsohn, Youngren, & Grosscup, in press).

Treatment consists of 12 sessions, with the first five sessions devoted to decreasing the frequency and the aversiveness of unpleasant events. The next five sessions in turn focus on increasing the frequency and the enjoyment of pleasant events, while the last two sessions are devoted to the development of maintenance and prevention strategies (Lewinsohn & Grosscup, 1978). Clients complete both a Pleasant Events Schedule (MacPhillamy & Lewinsohn, 1971) and an Unpleasant Events Schedule (Lewinsohn, 1975). From these, a personal Activity Schedule is constructed that consists of the 80 most enjoyable activities and the 80 most aversive activities. The client is then instructed to monitor the daily frequency of each of these 160 items as well as record his or her daily mood (using either a checklist or a 1 to 9 rating). Twenty-one days of baseline-type data are collected to determine which of the 160 items correlate with differing moods. With this information, clients are guided to minimize the rate of engaging in certain unpleasant activities and to maximize the rate of engaging in certain pleasant activities (Lewinsohn & Grosscup, 1978). Tables 11-3 and 11-4 provide examples of these two different schedules.

TABLE 11-3. Example of Pleasant Events Schedule

Being in the country.
Wearing expensive or formal clothes.
Making contributions to religious, charitable, or other groups.
Talking about sports.
Meeting someone new of the same sex.
Taking tests when well prepared.
Going to a rock concert.
Playing baseball or softball.
Planning trips or vacations.
Buying things for myself.

From *Pleasant Events Schedule,* by D. J. MacPhillamy and P. M. Lewinsohn. Unpublished manuscript, 1971. Reprinted by permission of Rev. D. J. MacPhillamy.

TABLE 11-4. Example of Unpleasant Events Schedule

Listening to people complain.
Being talked down to.
Being in very hot weather.
Having to obtain the assistance of a lawyer.
Talking with an unpleasant person (stubborn, unreasonable, aggressive, conceited, etc.).
Being alone.
Having a relative or friend living in unsatisfactory surroundings.
Being hungry or thirsty.
Having my belongings stolen.
Getting separated or divorced from my spouse.

From *Unpleasant Events Schedule,* by P. M. Lewinsohn. Unpublished manuscript, 1978. Reprinted by permission of Peter Lewinsohn.

Other parts of the treatment program include: (1) relaxation training to help clients deal with anxiety and tenseness, which may alter the aversiveness of the unpleasant events; (2) teaching the use of a variety of behavioral and cognitive skills (for example, assertion training, self-instructional training) to increase pleasant events and decrease unpleasant events; and (3) developing a maintenance and prevention plan, which might include periodic monitoring of events and mood- and stress-inoculation training (Lewinsohn & Grosscup, 1978).

This treatment program is probably the major reinforcement approach to the treatment of depression, although other programs (McLean, 1976; Rehm, 1977) do exist. Lewinsohn and his associates have written a self-help book, *Control Your Depression* (Lewinsohn, Munoz, Youngren, & Zeiss, 1978), based on their treatment program. (It has not yet been field-tested or validated.) The reinforcement model is highly attractive and well systematized. However, questions still exist about the exact mechanisms involved in the model (for example, response-contingent reinforcement versus reinforcer effectiveness). Comparative outcome studies have yet to be completed (Costello, 1972; McLean, 1976).

Cognitive Distortion Model

Dr. Aaron Beck at the University of Pennsylvania has developed a strong competitor to the reinforcement model of depression (Beck, 1967, 1970, 1974, 1976; Beck, Rush, Shaw, & Emery, 1979). He believes that distorted cognitions lead to depression. Specifically, Beck (1967, 1970) has described depression in terms of three different types of cognitive distortions (the "primary triad"). First, depressed persons view their experiences in the world in a negative way (for example, life is a burden, there are too many obstacles). Second, such people have negative views of themselves (for example, they see themselves as inadequate, deficient, unworthy). Finally, depressed persons see their future in a negative way (for example, they anticipate their current suffering will continue). Table 11-5 describes the relationship between the primary triad and the resulting symptoms.

Beck conceptualizes depressed individuals as arriving at that state as the result of developmental experiences (Beck, 1967, 1974; Beck & Rush, 1978). Certain people become vulnerable to depression as a result of negative concepts obtained while growing up. Later in life, a traumatic event (losing a job, loss of a loved one) might precipitate depression in such a person, while a person who grew up with

TABLE 11-5. Primary Triad and Resulting Symptoms

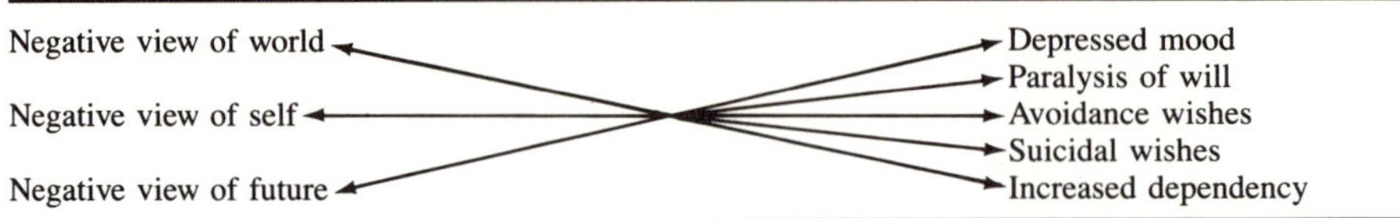

From *Depression: Causes and Treatment,* by A. T. Beck. Copyright 1967 by University of Pennsylvania Press. Reprinted by permission.

a more positive self-concept would respond less abnormally. Table 11-6 outlines several of the cognitive distortions that Beck described. The treatment for depression within the cognitive distortion model is aimed directly at altering these distortions (Beck, 1976; Beck & Burns, 1978; Beck et al., 1979).

Specific aspects of Beck's treatment model may be broken into behavioral and verbal components (Beck & Burns, 1978). In the former, attempts to change irrational ideas are made through changing behavior. Patients are challenged to engage in real-life behaviors (through successive approximation, if necessary), and successful behaviors are reinforced. Patients are taught to identify negative thoughts and cognitive distortions and to test their validity. Next, patients learn to substitute interpretations that are reality-oriented for their cognitive distortions. Finally, the patient is taught to describe and change the dysfunctional beliefs that make him susceptible to distortion and negative self-evaluations (Beck, 1976; Rush & Beck, 1978; Beck et al., 1979).

Beck's model has been the subject of a study (Rush, Beck, Kovacs, & Hollon, 1977) involving pharmacotherapy as a comparison group. Severely depressed subjects were randomly assigned to one of the two groups and treated for 12 weeks. Table 11-7 and Figure 11-2 show data from this study for both groups. The cognitive behavior therapy method proved to be the superior treatment. One must be cautious in interpreting these results and jumping to conclusions. While the results are extremely encouraging, they are based on one sample of severely depressed patients. Yet, this is the first time that any treatment approach has demonstrated superiority to drug treatment for depression (Hollon & Beck, 1979). It has been rightly argued that there have been improvements in pharmacotherapy since the study was con-

TABLE 11-6. Cognitive Distortions

Negative View of World
Life is a burden.
There are too many obstacles to happiness.
Positive or neutral events are discounted.

Negative View of Self
I am unattractive and unpopular.
I can't live up to people's expectations.
I am unintelligent and inferior to almost everyone.

Negative View of the Future
Things will not get better.
If things do improve, it will be temporary.
I will suffer forever.

TABLE 11-7. Clinical Status of Patients at the End of Treatment

Status[a]	Cognitive therapy	Pharmacotherapy
Markedly or completely improved (0–9)	15	5
Partially improved (10–15)	2	6
Not improved (≥ 16)	1	3
Dropouts[b]	1	8
Total assigned treatment	19	22

[a] Numbers in parentheses indicate Beck Depression Inventory cut-off scores.

[b] According to their Beck Depression Inventory scores, all dropouts had a "not improved" clinical status classification at the time of termination.

From "Comparative Efficacy of Cognitive Therapy and Pharmacotherapy in the Treatment of Depressed Outpatients," by A. J. Rush, A. T. Beck, M. Kovacs, and S. Hollon. In *Cognitive Therapy and Research*, 1977, *1*, 17–37. Reprinted by permission of Plenum Publishing Corporation.

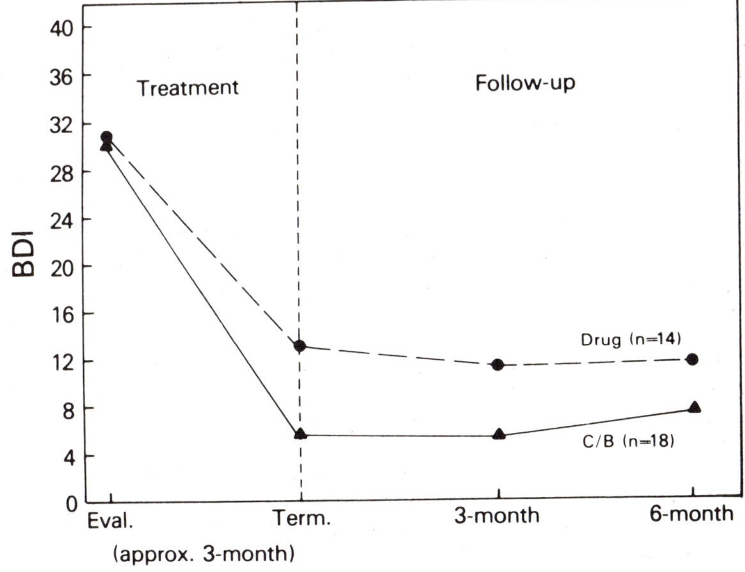

FIGURE 11-2.   Self-reported level of depression: Completers only. (From "Comparative Efficacy of Cognitive Therapy and Pharmacotherapy in the Treatment of Depressed Outpatients," by A. J. Rush, A. T. Beck, M. Kovacs, and S. Hollon. In *Cognitive Therapy and Research*, 1977, *1*, 17–37. Reprinted by permission of Plenum Publishing Corporation.)

ducted, that different results might be obtained with varying degrees of depression, and that it is important to identify variables that will predict which patients will respond to which type of treatment (Becker & Schuckit, 1978; Rush, Hollon, Beck, & Kovacs, 1978). Future examinations of the cognitive distortion model are likely and should be enhanced by the development of treatment manuals for individuals and groups (Shaw, 1975; Beck, Rush, Shaw, & Emery, 1979). We would hope for controlled comparisons with the reinforcement model.

Learned Helplessness Model

Seligman (1973, 1975, 1976) has outlined a model of depression based on the concept of learned helplessness. This model was developed based on experimental work with animals (Seligman & Maier, 1967; Overmier & Seligman, 1967; Seligman & Groves, 1970) and more recently with humans (Miller & Seligman, 1976; Klein & Seligman, 1976; Klein, Fencil-Morse, & Seligman, 1976). Based on his research and criticism from several directions (Bandura, 1977; Tennen & Eller, 1977; Hanusa & Schulz, 1977), Seligman and his associates (Abramson, Seligman, & Teasdale, 1978) have reformulated their model of depression. The original learned helplessness model was based on the tenet that experimentally produced helplessness is the result of learning that one is unable to exert control over important events. Thus, the belief that behavior and reinforcement are independent results in three basic behavioral patterns similar to depression: (1) there is a decrease in the number of responses initiated to gain reinforcement; (2) correlating successful responding with consequent reinforcement becomes increasingly difficult; and (3) anxiety and a depressive-like affect occurs (Seligman, 1976). The reformulated model of learned helplessness (Abramson, Seligman, & Teasdale, 1978) can be seen in Table 11-8, while Table 11-9 outlines the treatment strategies and tactics based on this model.

It is gratifying to see a treatment strategy for the learned helplessness model, for up until this time this was a major criticism. What needs to be done is to carefully delineate the differences between the reinforcement model, the cognitive distortion model, and the learned helplessness model, and then plan a carefully designed comparative outcome study. It may be, however, that depression is such a multifaceted phenomenon that *no one treatment modality will prove superior for any large proportion of depressed clients*. In fact, Zeiss, Lewinsohn, and Munoz (in press) have recently compared three treatment groups: a cognitive training group,

---

TABLE 11-8. Reformulated Learned Helplessness Model

---

1. Upon discovering that one is helpless, one tries to determine the reason why.
2. As a result, one makes an attribution about the cause.
3. This attribution determines one's expectations about the future outcomes of one's responses.
4. These expectations affect both the intensity and chronicity of helplessness behavior.
5. Attributions related to helplessness may have widespread or specific effects.
6. Self-esteem is eventually affected.

Adapted from "Learned Helplessness in Humans: Critique and Reformulation," by L. Y. Abramson, M. E. P. Seligman, and J. D. Teasdale, *Journal of Abnormal Psychology*, 1978, 87, 49–74.

TABLE 11-9. Treatment, Strategies, and Tactics Implied by the Reformulated Learned Helplessness Hypothesis

A. Change the estimated probability of the relevant event's occurrence: Reduce estimated likelihood for aversive outcomes and increase estimated likelihood for desired outcomes.
  a. Environmental manipulation by social agencies to remove aversive outcomes or provide desired outcomes, for example, rehousing, job placement, financial assistance, provision of nursery care for children.
  b. Provision of better medical care to relieve pain, correct handicaps, for example, prescription of analgesics, provision of artificial limbs and other prostheses.

B. Make the highly preferred outcomes less preferred.
  a. Reduce the aversiveness of highly aversive outcomes.
    1. Provide more realistic goals and norms, for example, failing to be top of your class is not the end of the world—you can still be a competent teacher and lead a satisfying life.
    2. Attentional training and/or reinterpretation to modify the significance of outcomes perceived as aversive, for example, you are not the most unattractive person in the world. "Consider the counterevidence" (Beck, 1976; Ellis, 1962).
    3. Assist acceptance and resignation.
  b. Reduce the desirability of highly desired outcomes.
    1. Assist the attainment of alternative available desired outcomes, for example, encourage the disappointed lover to find another boy or girl friend.
    2. Assist reevaluation of unattainable goals.
    3. Assist renunciation and relinquishment of unattainable goals.

C. Change the expectation from uncontrollability to controllability.
  a. When responses are not yet within the person's repertoire but can be, train the necessary skills, for example, social skills, child management skills, skills of resolving marital differences, problem-solving skills, and depression-management skills.
  b. When responses are within the person's repertoire, modify the distorted expectation that the responses will fail.
    1. Prompt performance of relevant, successful responses, for example, graded task assignment (Burgess, 1968).
    2. Generalized changes in response–outcome expectation resulting from successful performance of other responses, for example, prompt general increase in activity; teach more appropriate goal-setting and self-reinforcement; help to find employment.
    3. Change attributions for failure from inadequate ability to inadequate effort (Dweck, 1975), causing more successful responding.
    4. Imaginal and miniaturized rehearsal of successful response–outcome sequences: Assertive training, decision-making training, and role playing.

D. Change unrealistic attributions for failure toward external, unstable, specific; change unrealistic attributions for success toward internal, stable, global.
  a. For failure
    1. External: for example, "The system minimized the opportunities of women. It is not that you are incompetent."
    2. Unstable: for example, "The system is changing. Opportunities that you can snatch are opening at a great rate."
    3. Specific: for example, "Marketing jobs are still relatively closed to women, but publishing jobs are not" (correct overgeneralization).
  b. For success
    1. Internal: for example, "He loves you because you are nurturant not because he is insecure."
    2. Stable: for example, "Your nurturance is an enduring trait."
    3. Global: for example, "Your nurturance pervades much of what you do and is appreciated by everyone around you."

a group focused on increasing pleasant activities, and a group aimed at improving assertiveness and social interactions. Because each of these three treatments was aimed at specific classes of behavior, it was expected that there would be related specific changes in depression. Rather, all patients improved, but they did not improve differentially dependent upon which treatment they received. They all improved on outcome measures related to specific treatment modalities (for example, cognitive variables, pleasant events variables, interpersonal skills variables). There were no differences across treatment modalities! Zeiss, Lewinsohn, and Munoz (in press) speculate that these results may be related to Bandura's concept of self-efficacy (Bandura, 1977). Success in therapy may be related not to the specific skills taught in treatment but, instead, to renewed positive personal experiences that patients relate to increased competency or self-efficacy. It may be that the content of therapy for depression (and other personal problems) is less important than believed; additional comparative outcome research similar to that described above is needed. We are pleased that a number of methods and behavior change models have been developed for depression and look forward to the day when depression is no longer a major problem in our society.

CONCLUSIONS

The use of a wide variety of behavior change techniques for treating the personal problems of anxiety and depression has been examined in this chapter. Rather than asking if their treatment methods are effective, behavior change professionals and researchers have started to compare different treatment techniques. Since we have sufficiently demonstrated the effectiveness of a number of techniques, this is the next step and one that will receive much attention in the future. Additionally, we would expect to see a continued expansion of the use of cognitive behavior modification techniques; hopefully, they will be subjected to the same rigid experimental analysis that has been the strength of the behavior change field. As in most areas, good long-term follow-up studies are needed to evaluate the true effectiveness of our techniques when used to treat anxiety and depression. Finally, a relatively unexplored topic is that of preventive mental health. An extremely exciting venture would be to teach individuals (in school and work settings) skills to prevent or minimize anxiety or depression. Additionally, we think it would be particularly important to focus on people who might be at risk of either anxiety or depression (for example, those with stressful jobs, those with a previous history of either problem). A shift in emphasis toward preventing or minimizing anxiety and depression may provide a valuable opportunity for behavior change professionals to have a major impact on the mental health of our society.

REFERENCES

Abramson, L. Y., Seligman, M. E. P., & Teasdale, J. D. Learned helplessness in humans: Critique and reformulation. *Journal of Abnormal Psychology,* 1978, *87,* 49–74.
Agras, W. S., Leitenberg, H., Barlow, D. H., Curtis, N. A., Edwards, J., & Wright, D. Relaxation in systematic desensitization. *Archives of General Psychiatry,* 1971, *25,* 511–514.

Alberti, R. E., & Emmons, M. L. *Your perfect right: A guide to assertive behavior*. San Luis Obispo, Calif.: Impact, 1970.

Bandura, A. *Principles of behavior modification*. New York: Holt, Rinehart & Winston, 1969.

Bandura, A. Self-efficacy: Toward a unifying theory of behavior change. *Psychological Review*, 1977, *84*, 191–215.

Bandura, A., Blanchard, E. B., & Ritter, B. The relative efficacy of desensitization and modeling approaches for inducing behavioral, affective, and attitudinal changes. *Journal of Personality and Social Psychology*, 1969, *13*, 173–199.

Bandura, A., Grusec, J. E., & Menlove, F. L. Vicarious extinction of avoidance behavior. *Journal of Personality and Social Psychology*, 1967, *5*, 16–23.

Bandura, A., Jeffery, R. W., & Wright, C. L. Efficacy of participant modeling as a function of response induction aids. *Journal of Abnormal Psychology*, 1974, *83*, 56–64.

Bandura, A., & Menlove, F. L. Factors determining vicarious extinction of avoidance behavior through symbolic modeling. *Journal of Personality and Social Psychology*, 1968, *8*, 99–108.

Beck, A. T. *The diagnosis and management of depression*. Philadelphia: University of Pennsylvania Press, 1967.

Beck, A. T. *Depression: Causes and treatment*. Philadelphia: University of Pennsylvania Press, 1970.

Beck, A. T. The development of depression: A cognitive model. In R. J. Friedman & M. M. Katz (Eds.), *The psychology of depression: Contemporary theory and research*. New York: Wiley, 1974.

Beck, A. T. *Cognitive therapy and the emotional disorders*. New York: International Universities Press, 1976.

Beck, A. T., & Burns, A. T. Cognitive therapy of depressed suicidal outpatients. In J. O. Cole et al. (Eds.), *Depression: Biology, psychodynamics, and treatment*. New York: Plenum Press, 1978.

Beck, A. T., & Rush, A. J. Cognitive approaches to depression and suicide. In G. Serban (Ed.), *Cognitive defects in the development of mental illness*. New York: Brunner/Mazel, 1978.

Beck, A. T., Rush, A. J., Shaw, B. F., & Emery, G. *Cognitive therapy of depression*. New York: Guilford Press, 1979.

Becker, J., & Schuckit, M. A. The comparative efficacy of cognitive therapy and pharmacotherapy in the treatment of depression. *Cognitive Therapy and Research*, 1978, *2*, 193–197.

Bernstein, D. A. Anxiety management. In E. Craighead, A. E. Kazdin, & M. J. Mahoney (Eds.), *Behavior modification: Principles, issues, and applications*. Boston: Houghton Mifflin, 1976.

Bernstein, D. A., & Borkovec, T. D. *Progressive relaxation: A manual for therapists*. Champaign, Ill.: Research Press, 1973.

Blanchard, E. B. The relative contributions of modeling, informational influences, and physical contact in the extinction of phobic behavior. *Journal of Abnormal Psychology*, 1970, *76*, 55–61.

Blanchard, E. B., & Epstein, L. H. The clinical utility of biofeedback. In M. Hersen & P. M. Miller (Eds.), *Progress in behavior modification* (Vol. 3). New York: Academic Press, 1977.

Borkovec, T. D., Weerts, T. C., & Bernstein, D. A. Assessment of anxiety. In A. R. Ciminero, K. S. Calhoun, & H. E. Adams (Eds.), *Handbook of behavioral assessment*. New York: Wiley, 1977.

Cooper, J. E., Gelder, M. G., & Marks, I. M. Results of behavior therapy in 77 psychiatric patients. *British Medical Journal*, 1965, *1*, 1222–1225.

Costello, C. G. Depression: Loss of reinforcers or loss of reinforcer effectiveness? *Behavior Therapy*, 1972, *3*, 240–247.

Craighead, W. E. Away from a unitary model of depression. *Behavior Therapy*, 1980, *11*, 122–128.

Davison, G. C., & Neale, J. M. *Abnormal psychology: An experimental clinical approach.* New York: Wiley, 1978.

Devine, V. T. *Severe obsessive-compulsive reactions.* Paper presented at Minnesota Association for Behavior Analysis meeting, St. Paul, November 1973.

Eisler, R. M., Miller, P. M., Hersen, M., & Alford, H. Effects of assertive training on marital interaction. *Archives of General Psychiatry,* 1974, *30,* 643–649.

Ellis, A., & Harper, R. A. *A new guide to rational living.* Hollywood, Calif.: Wilshire, 1975.

Fensterheim, H., & Baer, J. *Don't say yes when you want to say no.* New York: Dell, 1975.

Fensterheim, H., & Baer, J. *Stop running scared!* New York: Dell, 1977.

Ferster, C. B. Classification of behavioral pathology. In L. Krasner & L. P. Ullmann (Eds.), *Research in behavior modification.* New York: Holt, Rinehart & Winston, 1965.

Ferster, C. B. Animal behavior and mental illness. *Psychological Record,* 1966, *16,* 345–356.

Ferster, C. B. A functional analysis of depression. *American Psychologist,* 1973, *28,* 857–870.

Ferster, C. B. Behavioral approaches to depression. In R. J. Friedman & M. M. Katz (Eds.), *The psychology of depression: Contemporary theory and research.* New York: Wiley, 1974.

Foreyt, J. P., & Rathjen, D. P. (Eds.), *Cognitive behavior therapy: Research and applications.* New York: Plenum Press, 1978.

Gelder, M. G., & Marks, I. M. Severe agoraphobia: A controlled prospective trial of behavior therapy. *British Journal of Psychiatry,* 1966, *112,* 309–319.

Gelder, M. G., Marks, I. M., Wolff, H. E., & Clarke, M. Desensitization and psychotherapy in the treatment of phobic states: A controlled inquiry. *British Journal of Psychiatry,* 1967, *113,* 53–73.

Goldfried, M. R., & Davison, G. C. *Clinical behavior therapy.* New York: Holt, Rinehart & Winston, 1976.

Grinker, R. R., Miller, J., Sabshin, M., Nunn, R., & Nunally, J. C. *The phenomena of depression.* New York: Harper & Row, 1961.

Hanusa, B. H., & Schulz, R. Attributional mediators of learned helplessness. *Journal of Personality and Social Psychology,* 1977, *35,* 602–611.

Heimberg, R. G., Montgomery, D., Madsen, C. H., & Heimberg, J. S. Assertion training: A review of the literature. *Behavior Therapy,* 1977, *8,* 953–971.

Hodgson, R., Rachman, S., & Marks, I. M. The treatment of chronic obsessive-compulsive neurosis: Follow-up and further findings. *Behaviour Research and Therapy,* 1972, *10,* 181–189.

Hollon, S. D., & Beck, A. T. Cognitive therapy of depression. In P. C. Kendall & S. D. Hollon (Eds.), *Cognitive-behavioral interventions.* New York: Academic Press, 1979.

Jacobson, E. *Progressive relaxation.* Chicago: University of Chicago Press, 1938.

Jakubowski, P. Assertive behavior and clinical problems of women. In D. Carter & E. Rawlings (Eds.), *Psychotherapy for women: Treatment towards equality.* Springfield, Ill.: Charles C Thomas, 1977.

Jakubowski, P., & Lange, A. J. *The assertive option.* Champaign, Ill.: Research Press, 1978.

Jakubowski-Spector, P. *An introduction to assertive training.* Washington, D.C.: American Personnel and Guidance Association, 1973.

Kazdin, A. E., & Wilcoxon, L. A. Systematic desensitization and nonspecific treatment effects: A methodological evaluation. *Psychological Bulletin,* 1976, *83,* 729–758.

Kendall, P. C., & Hollon, S. D. (Eds). *Cognitive-behavioral interventions: Theory, research and procedures.* New York: Academic Press, 1979.

Klein, D. C., Fencil-Morse, E., & Seligman, M. E. P. Learned helplessness, depression, and the attribution of failure. *Journal of Personality and Social Psychology,* 1976, *33,* 508–516.

Klein, D. C., & Seligman, M. E. P. Reversal of performance deficits in learned helplessness and depression. *Journal of Abnormal Psychology,* 1976, *85,* 11–26.

Klerman, G. L., & Barrett, J. E. The affective disorders: Clinical and epidemiological aspects. In S. Gershon & B. Shopsin (Eds.), *Lithium: Its role in psychiatric treatment and research*. New York: Plenum Press, 1973.

Lang, P. J. The mechanics of desensitization and the laboratory study of human fear. In C. M. Franks (Ed.), *Behavior therapy: Appraisal and status*. New York: McGraw-Hill, 1969.

Lange, A. J., & Jakubowski, P. *Responsible assertive behavior*. Champaign, Ill.: Research Press, 1976.

Lazarus, A. A. Learning theory and the treatment of depression. *Behaviour Research and Therapy*, 1968, *6*, 83–89.

Lazarus, A. A., & Fay, A. *I can if I want to*. New York: Morrow, 1975.

Ledwidge, B. Cognitive behavior modification: A step in the wrong direction? *Psychological Bulletin*, 1978, *85*, 353–375.

Leitenberg, H. Behavioral approaches to treatment of neuroses. In H. Leitenberg (Ed.), *Handbook of behavior modification and behavior therapy*. Englewood Cliffs, N.J.: Prentice-Hall, 1976.

Leitenberg, H., Agras, W. S., Allen, R., Butz, R. R., & Edwards, J. Feedback and therapist praise during treatment of phobia. *Journal of Consulting and Clinical Psychology*, 1975, *43*, 396–404.

Leitenberg, H., Agras, W. S., Thomson, L. E., & Wright, D. E. Feedback in behavior modification: An experimental analysis in two phobic cases. *Journal of Applied Behavior Analysis*, 1968, *1*, 131–137.

Levy, R., & Meyer, V. Ritual prevention in obsessional patients. *Proceedings Royal Society of Medicine*, 1971, *64*, 1115–1118.

Lewinsohn, P. M. A behavioral approach to depression. In R. J. Friedman & M. M. Katz (Eds.), *The psychology of depression: Contemporary theory and research*. New York: Wiley, 1974.

Lewinsohn, P. M. The behavioral study and treatment of depression. In M. Hersen, R. M. Eisler, & P. M. Miller (Eds.), *Progress in behavior modification* (Vol. 1). New York: Academic Press, 1975.

Lewinsohn, P. M., & Amenson, C. S. Some relations between pleasant and unpleasant events and depression. *Journal of Abnormal Psychology*, 1978, *87*, 644–654.

Lewinsohn, P. M., Biglan, A., & Zeiss, A. M. Behavioral treatment of depression. In P. O. Davison (Ed.), *The behavioral management of anxiety, depression and pain*. New York: Brunner/Mazel, 1976.

Lewinsohn, P. M., & Graf, M. Pleasant activities and depression. *Journal of Consulting and Clinical Psychology*, 1973, *41*, 261–268.

Lewinsohn, P. M., & Grosscup, S. J. *Decreasing unpleasant events and increasing pleasant events: A treatment manual for depression*. Unpublished manuscript, 1978.

Lewinsohn, P. M., & Libet, J. Pleasant events, activity schedules, and depressions. *Journal of Abnormal Psychology*, 1972, *79*, 291–295.

Lewinsohn, P. M., & MacPhillamy, D. J. The relationship between age and engagement in pleasant activities. *Journal of Gerontology*, 1974, *29*, 290–294.

Lewinsohn, P. M., Munoz, R. F., Youngren, M. A., & Zeiss, A. M. *Control your depression*. Englewood Cliffs, N.J.: Spectrum, 1978.

Lewinsohn, P. M., Sullivan, J. M., & Grosscup, S. J. *Changing reinforcing events: An approach to the treatment of depression*. Unpublished manuscript, 1978.

Lewinsohn, P. M., Weinstein, M. S., & Shaw, D. A. Depression: A clinical research approach. In R. D. Rubin & G. M. Franks (Eds.), *Advances in behavior therapy, 1968*. New York: Academic Press, 1969.

Lewinsohn, P. M., Youngren, M. A., & Grosscup, S. J. Reinforcement and depression. In R. A. Depue (Ed.), *The psychobiology of the depressive disorders: Implications for the effects of stress*. New York: Academic Press, in press.

Lick, J. R., & Katkin, E. S. Assessment of anxiety and fear. In M. Hersen & A. S. Bellack (Eds.), *Behavioral assessment: A practical handbook*. New York: Pergamon Press, 1976.

MacDonald, M. L., Lindquist, C. U., Kramer, J. A., McGrath, R. A., & Rhyne, L. L. *Social skills training: The effects of behavior rehearsal in groups on dating skills.* Unpublished manuscript, 1973.

MacPhillamy, D. J., & Lewinsohn, P. M. *Pleasant events schedule.* Unpublished manuscript, 1971.

MacPhillamy, D. J., & Lewinsohn, P. M. Depression as a function of desired and obtained pleasure. *Journal of Abnormal Psychology,* 1974, *83,* 651–657.

Mahoney, M. J. *Cognition and behavior modification.* Cambridge, Mass.: Ballinger, 1974.

Marks, I. M. *Fears and phobias.* New York: Academic Press, 1969.

Marks, I. M. Agoraphobic syndrome (phobic anxiety state). *Archives of General Psychiatry,* 1970, *23,* 539–553.

Marks, I. M. *Living with fear.* New York: McGraw-Hill, 1978.

Marks, I., Boulougouris, J., & Marset, P. Flooding versus desensitization in the treatment of phobic patients: A crossover study. *British Journal of Psychiatry,* 1971, *119,* 353–375.

McGovern, T. V., Tinsley, D. J., Liss-Levinson, N., Laventure, R. O., & Britton, G. Assertion training for job interviews. *Counseling Psychologist,* 1975, *5,* 65–68.

McLean, P. Therapeutic decision-making in the behavioral treatment of depression. In P. O. Davidson (Ed.), *The behavioral management of anxiety, depression, and pain.* New York: Brunner/Mazel, 1976.

Meichenbaum, D. *Cognitive-behavior modification: An integrative approach.* New York: Plenum Press, 1977.

Meyer, V. Modification of expectations in cases with obsessional rituals. *Behaviour Research and Therapy,* 1966, *4,* 273–280.

Miller, W. R., & Seligman, M. E. P. Learned helplessness, depression, and the perception of reinforcement. *Behaviour Research and Therapy,* 1976, *14,* 7–17.

Mills, H. L., Agras, S., Barlow, D. H., & Mills, J. R. Compulsive rituals treated by response prevention. *Archives of General Psychiatry,* 1973, *28,* 524–529.

Morganstern, K. P. Implosion therapy and flooding procedures: A critical review. *Psychological Bulletin,* 1973, *79,* 318–334.

Overmier, J. R., & Seligman, M. E. P. Effects of inescapable shock upon subsequent escape and avoidance learning. *Journal of Comparative and Physiological Psychology,* 1967, *63,* 23–33.

Paul, G. L. *Insight versus desensitization in psychotherapy.* Stanford: Stanford University Press, 1966.

Paul, G. L. Two-year follow-up of systematic desensitization in therapy groups. *Journal of Abnormal Psychology,* 1968, *73,* 119–130.

Paul, G. L. Outcome of systematic desensitization I: Background, procedures, and uncontrolled reports of individual treatment. In C. M. Franks (Ed.), *Behavior therapy: Appraisal and status.* New York: McGraw-Hill, 1969. (a)

Paul, G. L. Outcome of systematic desensitization II: Controlled investigations of individual treatment, technique variations, and current status. In C. M. Franks (Ed.), *Behavior therapy: Appraisal and status.* New York: McGraw-Hill, 1969. (b)

Rachman, S., Hodgson, R., & Marks, I. M. The treatment of chronic obsessive-compulsive neurosis. *Behaviour Research and Therapy,* 1971, *9,* 237–247.

Rehm, L. P. A self-control model of depression. *Behavior Therapy,* 1977, *8,* 787–804.

Rimm, D. C., & Masters, J. C. *Behavior therapy: Techniques and empirical findings.* New York: Academic Press, 1974.

Ritter, B. Treatment of acrophobia with contact desensitization. *Behaviour Research and Therapy,* 1969, *7,* 41–45. (a)

Ritter, B. The use of contact desensitization, demonstration-plus-participation, and demonstration alone in the treatment of acrophobia. *Behaviour Research and Therapy,* 1969, *7,* 157–164. (b)

Rush, A. J., & Beck, A. T. Adults with affective disorders. In M. Hersen & A. S. Bellack (Eds.), *Behavior therapy in the psychiatric setting.* Baltimore: Williams and Wilkins, 1978.

Rush, A. J., Beck, A. T., Kovacs, M., & Hollon, S. Comparative efficacy of cognitive therapy and pharmacotherapy in the treatment of depressed outpatients. *Cognitive Therapy and Research*, 1977, *1*, 17–37.

Rush, A. J., Hollon, S. D., Beck, A. T., & Kovacs, M. Depression: Must pharmacotherapy fail for cognitive therapy to succeed? *Cognitive Therapy and Research*, 1978, *2*, 199–206.

Salter, A. *Conditioned reflex therapy*. New York: Creative Age Press, 1949.

Schwab, J. J., Brown, J. M., Holzer, C. E., & Sokolof, M. Current concepts of depression: The sociocultural. *International Journal of Social Psychiatry*, 1968, *14*, 226–234.

Seligman, M. E. P. Fall into helplessness. *Psychology Today*, 1973, *7*, 43–48.

Seligman, M. E. P. *Helplessness*. San Francisco: W. H. Freeman, 1975.

Seligman, M. E. P. Learned helplessness and depression in animals and men. In J. T. Spence, R. C. Carson, & J. W. Thibaut (Eds.), *Behavioral approaches to therapy*. Morristown, N.J.: General Learning Press, 1976.

Seligman, M. E. P., & Groves, D. No-transient learned helplessness. *Psychonomic Science*, 1970, *19*, 191–192.

Seligman, M. E. P., & Maier, S. F. Failure to escape traumatic shock. *Journal of Experimental Psychology*, 1967, *74*, 1–9.

Shaw, B. F. *Group therapy manual for cognitive behavior therapy of depression*. Unpublished manuscript, 1975.

Smith, M. J. *When I say no I feel guilty*. New York: Bantam, 1975.

Stampfl, T. G., & Levis, D. J. Essentials of implosive therapy: A learning-theory based psychodynamic behavioral therapy. *Journal of Abnormal Psychology*, 1967, *72*, 496–503.

Tennen, H., & Eller, S. J. Attributional components of learned helplessness and facilitation. *Journal of Personality and Social Psychology*, 1977, *35*, 265–271.

Weekes, C. *Simple effective treatment of agoraphobia*. New York: Hawthorne Books, 1976.

Wilson, G. T. Cognitive behavior therapy: Paradigm shift or passing phase? In J. Foreyt & D. P. Rathjen (Eds.), *Cognitive behavior therapy: Research and applications*. New York: Plenum Press, 1978.

Wolpe, J. *Psychotherapy by reciprocal inhibition*. Stanford: Stanford University Press, 1958.

Woodruff, R. A., Goodwin, D. W., & Guze, S. B. *Psychiatric diagnosis*. New York: Oxford University Press, 1974.

Yates, A. J. *Theory and practice in behavior therapy*. New York: Wiley, 1975.

Zeiss, A. M., Lewinsohn, P. M., & Munoz, R. F. Nonspecific improvement effects in depression using interpersonal skills training, pleasant activity schedules, or cognitive training. *Journal of Consulting and Clinical Psychology*, in press.

CHAPTER 12

Relationships and Sexual Behavior

AT least 15 years before behavior change principles were being applied in a systematic way (see Chapter 1), B. F. Skinner described a community in which people got along nearly perfectly in an environment of carefully arranged physical and behavioral events. In his novel, *Walden Two* (1948), Skinner describes the relationships among members of the community as entirely cooperative. This pleasant state of affairs is brought about through positive reinforcement and an avoidance of aversive control tactics by the residents of Walden Two. Since no one has really been brought up in an ideal community like Walden Two, many people enter adult life finding it difficult to maintain or even achieve successful communications or mutually satisfying (reinforcing) relationships with others. However, one of the advances in the application of behavior change procedures to complex human problems has been the use of these techniques in the treatment of family and partnership relationships. The purpose of this chapter is to review the work that has been done in the areas of family communications, marital problems, and sexual behavior.

COMMUNICATIONS IN FAMILIES

Communication is a term that has been thrown around fairly casually by the psychological community. Its meaning seems to range from direct verbal exchanges between people to a more general state of "getting along" among family members. One of the earliest reports of behavioral family therapy was provided by Dr. Richard Stuart (1971). He described the use of a behavioral contracting system within the families of delinquent youth. Stuart asserted that "the family plays a critical role in the etiology of delinquency" (p. 2). He believed that the family contributes to delinquency in two ways: (1) by modeling and differentially reinforcing antisocial behavior, and (2) by failing to reinforce prosocial behavior. In the contracts Stuart mediates, he organizes an exchange of reinforcement between, say, parents and their teenage children in what has been referred to as a *quid pro quo* arrangement (Jackson, 1965). *Quid pro quo* means "this for that" and thus literally refers to contracts in which "you do this for me and I'll do that for you." The contract structures these reciprocal changes by specifying the conditions under which exchanges occur, when they occur, for what they occur, and for whom they occur. Table 12-1 details Stuart's (1971) five components of good contracts. Dr. Stuart describes an example of a contract system in the case of Candy, a 16-year-old girl who had been referred by a juvenile court for alleged promiscuity (a term that may have less significance in the 1980s than the early 1970s), exhibitionism, drug abuse, and home truancy. Her parents were in their sixties and physically ill. Some of the reciprocal arrangements that Stuart helped negotiate were: (1) in exchange for the privilege of riding the bus directly from school into town after school, Candy agreed to phone her father by 4:00 P.M. to tell him that she was safe and she was to return home by 5:15 P.M.; (2) in exchange for the privilege of going out at 7:00 P.M. on one weekend evening without having to account for her whereabouts, Candy agreed

This chapter is adapted from "Deviant Family Systems," by J. R. Lutzker. In B. B. Lahey and A. E. Kazdin (Eds.), *Advances in Clinical Child Psychology* (Vol. 3). Plenum Press, 1980. Reprinted by permission.

that she must have a "B" grade average in all her academic classes and be home on that weekend night by 11:30 P.M. In exchange for the privilege of having Candy complete her household chores and maintain her curfew, her parents agreed to pay her $1.50 on the morning following days on which the money was earned. Some of the bonuses and sanctions built into the contract were: if Candy was 1–10 minutes late, she had to come home early the next day an amount of time equal to the number of minutes she was late the previous day; if she was 31–60 minutes late, she lost the privilege of going out the next day and forfeited her money that day; if Candy abided by the terms of her contract for one week with a tardiness total not exceeding 30 minutes, she was allowed to go out on Sunday evening from 7:00 to 9:00 P.M. Candy's parents monitored her behavior by keeping track of her compliance to the agreements. They did this by posting a form on which all agreed behaviors were listed and performance was checked off when it occurred. Stuart describes this system as greatly improving the family "climate." He further reports that, most importantly, the family complied with the contract. In a contract such as the one negotiated with Candy and her parents, negative emotional behavior is often reduced because everyone's responsibilities are clearly negotiated and backed up by fair and mutually agreeable contingencies. The room for bickering and bitterness is substantially reduced. You will remember similar tactics used in Achievement Place, the program for predelinquent youth (see Chapter 7).

TABLE 12-1. Five Components of Good Contracts

1. Detail the privileges each person expects to gain after fulfilling the agreed-upon responsibilities.
2. Detail the responsibilities essential for securing the privilege.
3. Include responsibilities that can be appropriately monitored by parents.
4. Include sanctions for failure to meet responsibilities.
5. Include bonus clauses providing for positive reinforcement for compliance to the terms of the contract.

From "Behavior Contracting within Families of Delinquents," by R. B. Stuart, *Journal of Behavior Therapy and Experimental Psychiatry*, 1971, *2*, 1–11.

Research on short-term interventions with families with delinquent adolescents was described in 1973 by Alexander and Parsons. Their research was designed to assess and evaluate the behaviors that maintain delinquent behavior in the family, to modify family communication patterns, and to include a contingency contract program aimed at modifying inappropriate family interactions and increasing functional ones. The several families who served in this study all had at least one adolescent who had been referred by the juvenile court for offenses such as running away, being declared ungovernable, truancy, shoplifting, or possession of alcohol, drugs, or tobacco. Since prior research and clinical efforts had determined that deviant behavior was a function of a deviant family system (Alexander, 1973; Lutzker, 1980) in which members were more silent (in other words, less communicative) and showed a lack of reciprocity (Patterson & Reid, 1970), treatment emphasized modeling and prompting by therapists of clear communication of "substance," feelings, demands, alternative solutions, and negotiations. In attempting to negotiate problem solving, the therapists socially reinforced interruptions for clarification, interruptions for increasing information about how the questioning family member fit into the topic, and interruptions designed to provide constructive feedback to other family members. Comparison groups received client-centered or psychodynamic therapy (neither of these latter therapies can usually be considered "behavioral"). In the clinic, direct behavioral observations were taken during a situation in which the family was given three tasks: (1) a behavioral specificity phase; (2) a vignette phase; (3) an interaction phase. The behavioral specificity phase involved each family member independently writing down three behaviors they would like to see changed in them. The vignette phase involved each family member writing down responses calling for parental action in relation to the adolescent's behavior. Finally, the interaction phase involved a 20-minute discussion of the first two phases by the members of the family. The families who received this short-term behavioral intervention did significantly better on all three measures than families who received either of the two nonbehavioral therapies. Of course, an important question is whether delinquent behaviors were reduced. Unfortunately, those results are somewhat more equivocal, but it did seem that the families who received the behavioral interventions tended to have fewer subsequent delinquency problems than the families who received either the client-centered or psychodynamic therapy. This study, while having some shortcomings, did provide a framework and a model for the study and modification of family communication problems.

If families are to learn how to resolve conflicts on their own, it needs to be shown that they can be trained to do so effectively. A group of researchers at the University of Kansas (Bob Kifer, Martha Lewis, Don Green, and Elery Phillips) studied the training and generality of conflict negotiating skills. They defined conflict situations as interpersonal situations in which youths and authority figures have opposing desires. There were two purposes to their 1974 research: one was the emphasis on having the families learn new adaptive behaviors rather than focusing on the elimination of problem behavior; the second was to make the training "educational." Negotiating skills were analyzed and broken into components through a task analysis. Further, instructions, practice, and feedback were used to train negotiation. The final goal was to have families be able to resolve their own conflicts without outside intervention, thus creating generality of training. Two mother-daughter pairs and one father-son pair in which the youths had juvenile court contacts were subjects of this study. The age range of the youths was 13–17 years. One week before training, home observations were made by observers who recorded the parent-youth pairs' responses in discussing conflict situations. Further observations occurred in classroom sessions in which the members of the dyads were taught negotiation skills. In the next phase of the study there were more home observations of the parent-youth pairs attempting conflict solving. These observations were made in order to determine whether generalization of training from the classroom (clinic) to the home had occurred. The classroom sessions involved a "presession" simulation in which the trainer instructed the parent-child pair to play a hypothetical conflict situation. Next there was a discussion phase in which a model was provided that made use of situations, options, consequences, and simulation (Roosa, 1973). During this phase each parent-child pair were given the same situation as they had just simulated, but were presented with a list of response options and a list of consequences. Each option was reviewed with the trainer for a match to a probable consequence. The example provided was a situation in which "you have worked all summer for money and your mother insists that you spend it on clothes, but you want to spend it on something else" (p. 359). Some of the possible options are "tell her it is your money and it is none of her business what you spend it on, do not spend it on anything, put it in a savings account and let it collect interest, or sell the clothes to a friend after you buy them." Some of the possible consequences would be, "get mad at her and maybe have the money taken away, end up with more money than you originally had, never learn how to negotiate" (p. 359). After all of the probable consequences were matched to the options, the parent-youth pair role-played the selected option. Finally, a postsession simulation identical to the presession simulation was then conducted. The behavior of the parent-youth pairs was scored according to complete communications, identification of issues, suggestion of options, and agreements. The data from this study showed that under training all three parent-youth pairs increased their use of negotiation over baseline presession simulations. Probably the most encouraging result was that the pairs showed generalization of their conflict negotiation skills from the classroom to their homes. Of course, cautious enthusiasm is warranted here in that Kifer et al. (1974) fail to report what kind of "clinical" changes occurred within the families; that is, were the youths' delinquent behaviors reduced?

The "family council" was described by Phillips in 1975 as another method for improving family communication. The council involves a highly structured group interaction in order to produce an increase in communication among families who show reluctance to be communicative. The "council" comprises a therapist, the adolescent, and the parents. Importantly, included in the council are "significant others" such as grandparents, babysitters, or other parent-surrogates. The therapist acts as a referee, model, teacher, and social reinforcer. The "council" follows 11 rules which include respect, reciprocity, statements of feelings, limitations, and definitions. In her description of the family council, Phillips reports seven cases in which problems such as drugs, affairs, and alcoholism were either reduced or eliminated.

Twenty-eight recidivistic (frequent, repeated offenders) delinquent adolescents and their parents were the benefactors of contingency contracting described by Weathers and Liberman (1975). These researchers utilized contingency contracting along with communication skills training and videotape feedback to modify school attendance, compliance with curfew and chores, and verbal abusiveness to parents. The authors report moderate successes with verbal abusiveness, but surprisingly report mostly failures with the other problems. They suggest that the problems of delinquency might require a whole variety of behavioral treatment procedures.

A comprehensive and detailed analysis of deviant parent-youth communication patterns was provided by Lysaght and Burchard (1975). The subject was a 12-year-old boy who had not been to school for three months. He was severely deficient in academic and social skills. The behavior analysis was accomplished by tape recording structured discussions between the boy and his mother. Discussion "A" revolved around three point gains and three point losses that the boy had received the previous week at the weekday residential setting at which he had been living. Discussion "B" involved an essay that he was required to write each week. Responses in discussions "A" and "B" were recorded, such as praise, criticism, relevancy, and so on. A multiple baseline design showed that therapist feedback was functional in increasing relevant communication and praise, and decreasing irrelevant remarks and criticism.

In what Mealiea (1976) called conjoint behavior therapy of family constellations, we find a multifaceted approach to the treatment of family relationship problems. Mealiea believes that quite often a child's deviant behavior is a side effect of inappropriate interactions between the parents. The nine objectives of conjoint behavior therapy are: (1) identifying behavioral excesses and skill deficits in the children: (2) the observation and recording of targeted problem behavior; (3) a behavior analysis to determine the contingencies that are maintaining the problem behavior; (4) the development of a treatment strategy that makes use of the behavior analysis; (5) making the parents understand that their behavior as a couple affects their children; (6) identifying existing positive reinforcers; (7) identifying new areas for reinforcement in the relationship; (8) identifying problem areas that lack reciprocity; and (9) establishing awareness of one another as persons, allowing for changes and "growth," and forming a broad base of reinforcement. The three-phase therapy makes use of audio and videotapes in the analysis of the family's performance. Mealiea points out that this therapy takes considerable time and effort, but contends that the outcomes make it all worthwhile.

A very popular nonbehavioral approach to parent-child relationships is Parent Effectiveness Training, or P.E.T., which was originally described by Dr. Thomas Gordon (1970). P.E.T. has been combined with a behavioral approach by Martin and Twentyman (1976). They suggest that there are two important components to parent-child interactions: (1) how parents and children talk about problems, and (2) what they do about the problems. Direct behavioral measures are taken on how parents and children talk to one another in attempting to solve problems. The important aspect of the Martin and Twentyman work is that they have been reliably able to quantify nine areas of parent-child interactions. Detailed outcome data are not available from these authors, but they contend that through this behavioral-expressive therapy a durable generalized improvement in families with conflict is produced.

The reports of communication-skill training must be examined with mixed reactions. The data (which are sometimes quite limited) tend to show that communication patterns in families can, indeed, be altered by using behavioral training procedures. The problem, however, is that there are limited data showing that improved communications, ability to negotiate, problem solve, and so on, lead to behavior change. That is, just because a teenager has been taught to express concerns and feelings and the parents have, in turn, been taught to react in a nonreactionary fashion, does that mean that drug abuse, truancy, or other problems will necessarily be changed? Our best guess is no. Probably, the most logical approach to relationship problems involves a combination of communication-skill training, carefully monitored behavioral contracting, and a rearrangement of the ecosystem (the families' environmental support system). This very model is described in the next section in reporting the work of Azrin, Naster, and Jones (1973).

MARITAL RELATIONSHIPS

One of the earliest descriptions of a behavioral approach to the treatment of marital problems was provided by Dr. Israel Goldiamond (1965). What Dr. Goldiamond's case study report lacked in empirical data, it made up for in creative, behavioral solutions to a young couple's problems.

The couple's complaints revolved around the husband's constant brooding and scolding of his wife over an extramarital affair that she had two years prior to treatment. Goldiamond explained to the couple that he saw no reason to "treat" the affair since it was long since over and that the problem at hand was to stop the husband's sulking and scolding, and to get the couple to enjoy each other's company again. A stimulus control procedure was aimed at reducing the sulking. This was done by arranging for the husband to use a "sulking stool" in the garage. Whenever he felt like sulking, the only place it was allowable for him to do so was on his stool in the garage. Needless to say, this procedure fairly quickly eliminated the sulking. Another stimulus control procedure involved having the couple rearrange the furniture in their apartment. This was done because the old arrangement probably was setting the occasion for their problems and a new arrangement would be associated with their attempts at resolving their problems. When the couple felt amorous toward each other, they were instructed to turn a yellow light on in their bedroom. This changed the "atmosphere" of the bedroom and, thus, again changed the stimulus control.

Finally, the couple was instructed to go out in public once a week. This was done to increase the likelihood that they would communicate with each other, because, as Goldiamond reasoned, the husband was less likely to berate the wife in public. In order to further the likelihood of communication, the husband had been instructed to carry with him an index card on which he had written a word that might trigger a harmless topic of conversation. These procedures were quite successful in reducing the husband's sulking and scolding and increasing the couple's communication and marital satisfaction. A lengthy follow-up showed the couple to be as happy as they were prior to the wife's affair. The uniqueness of this report was the focus on environmental rearrangement rather than insight-oriented psychotherapy in producing marital behavior change.

In 1970, Dr. Robert Liberman, a behaviorally oriented psychiatrist, outlined the three components of behavioral family therapy as: (1) the creation and maintenance of a trusting therapeutic relationship; (2) a behavioral analysis involving specification of problem behavior; and (3) the utilization of behavioral procedures such as modeling, social reinforcement, and contingency contracting to remediate the identified problem behaviors. Two case studies exemplify Liberman's work. In the first study, the subjects were a 30-year-old housewife, who had a 15-year history of severe migraine headaches, and her family. Medical examinations had determined no organic basis for the headaches, so it was suggested that the attention she received from her family might be reinforcing complaining and putting herself to bed. Thus, the family was taught to ignore the wife when she complained of headaches, and the husband was taught to provide considerably more attention contingent upon the wife's homemaking efforts. The wife, in turn, was also taught to provide additional attention to her husband, in response to the new attention he gave her. As a result, not only did the wife report many fewer headaches, but there appeared to be a generalization of treatment effects in that the couple reported using more reinforcement procedures with their children, an improved sex life, and new employment for the wife. A one-year follow-up showed continued improvement.

In another case report, Liberman describes the treatment of depression in a 34-year-old mother of five children. Dr. Liberman had the husband and wife engage in more reciprocity of reinforcement and taught the wife to be more assertive with her mother-in-law. An eight-month follow-up in this case showed the couple to be happier than they had ever been before. These case reports by Goldiamond (1965) and Liberman (1970) have not provided a strong research base, but they have laid the groundwork for both clinical and research advances in behavior analysis of marriage.

In 1973, research appeared in the form of an analysis of corrective feedback and instruction in the modification of problematic marital communication. Carter and Thomas (1973) utilized a behaviorally specific inductive identification of problematic verbal interactions between nine couples who had been referred from a private family service agency. During a couple's first session, they were familiarized with the procedures and rationale for the study. In order for them to have some practice using the signalling device that was going to be used by them throughout the study, they were asked to briefly discuss a noncontroversial topic. They were then asked to spend 20 minutes on each of two topics: (1) problems they have in their marriage, and (2) the expectations each had of the other as a partner. The second session involved having the couple discuss the same two topics with a modification in the device that signalled to the partners what kind of feedback they were providing. The tape-recorded discussions in the first two sessions were used by the therapist for a "prefeedback analysis," which was provided to the couple during the third session. Also begun during the third session were corrective feedback and instructions involving a brief description of the positive aspects of the couple's first two discussion sessions, a detailed analysis of the most important communication problems noted in the first two sessions, and a recommendation as to what steps might be taken to alleviate the problems. Examples of problems included not maintaining specificity and diverting the focus of the discussion. The third session typically involved having the couples discuss a new topic, "problems you have in communication with each other." This conversation was used to see if the feedback and instructions improved their communications. Twenty-seven categories in communication were determined in this research. The major feature that Carter and Thomas discuss in their work is that couples are provided with feedback and direction based on an empirical baseline of their communication problems. These authors further report encouraging results in improving communication, but as with the studies we reviewed in the previous section, there was a failure to report on overall clinical behavior change.

As we have reported so often in this book, the work of Dr. Nathan Azrin and his colleagues offers major breakthroughs in several areas. Undoubtedly the most comprehensive treatment approach to marital problems was initially described in 1973 by Azrin, Naster, and Jones. They describe a rapid learning-based procedure for marital counseling, which they labeled "reciprocity counseling." Their treatment model stemmed from a view that marital discord is the result of nonreciprocated reinforcement. Their procedures are utilized to teach couples reciprocity in several problem areas. Twelve couples participated in the first study which utilized a control procedure of catharsis-type (traditional) counseling compared to three to four weeks of reciprocity counseling. The reciprocity counseling procedures increased marital happiness in 96% of the clients while the catharsis counseling produced no increases in marital happiness. Azrin, Naster, and Jones (1973) suggested that the best way to assure marital reinforcers for the partners is to teach each how to provide the reinforcers to the other.

These researchers listed nine sources of marital discord, which are shown in Table 12-2.

TABLE 12-2. Nine Sources of Marital Discord

1. Too little reinforcement in the marriage.
2. The existing reinforcers are for only one or two states of need such as sex or financial concerns.
3. The spouse is taken for granted.
4. Previous reinforcers no longer provide reinforcement.
5. New desires and their reinforcers are not recognized.
6. More satisfactions are given than are received.
7. Poor communication.
8. Marriage interferes with external sources of reinforcement.
9. Aversive control is used as the primary behavior change procedure.

From "Reciprocity Counseling: A Rapid Learning-Based Procedure for Marital Counseling," by N. H. Azrin, B. J. Naster, and R. Jones, *Behaviour Research and Therapy,* 1973, *11,* 365–382.

Every day for a seven-week period, a marital adjustment scale was administered to each of the twelve couples. This provided a continuous measure of change in marital adjustment. During the catharsis counseling period, clients were encouraged by the therapist to talk about their problems and feelings about their marriage. After the catharsis period, the reciprocity awareness procedure was initiated; this procedure involved having the spouses make each other aware of the reciprocity that already existed in the marriage. This was accomplished by having them list at least ten satisfactions they found in their marriage. These lists were read by the counselor to the couple. The next step was the perfect marriage procedure, which meant that each spouse was to list fantasies that would make each of the nine problem areas into a perfect marriage for that partner.

The following step in the reciprocity counseling procedure was the appreciation reminder, which consisted of each partner reminding the other of any novel, unusual, unanticipated, or unscheduled satisfactions that had been provided by the other (for example, the husband brings the wife flowers). Next, the fantasy fulfillment procedure involved the counselor instructing each spouse to decide what the other partner could do to increase the spouse's own happiness in each of the first three problem areas. After the fantasy fulfillment procedure came the frequency fulfillment procedure. For this, with the help of the counselor, compromises were negotiated by the couple on how to reach some agreeable frequency of fantasy fulfillment.

Another aspect of this complex treatment model was the happiness contract in which current satisfactions given and received were listed along with new satisfactions from the fantasy fulfillment list. Contingencies were arranged as to what would happen if there was a failure to comply to these agreements. If agreements were not met, the spouse discontinued all new and old satisfactions for a 24-hour period. In Session Two of the first week, a happiness contract was reviewed for reevaluation by the couple and a fantasy fulfillment home assignment was made.

The first session of Week Two brought the positive statement procedure, which was used throughout the remainder of the counseling program. This taught the partners to preface any negative or corrective remark with a positive note. At this time in counseling, a sex feedback component was also introduced. In order to avoid some initial embarrassment by the pairs, the counselor underscored certain aspects of a marriage manual and had each spouse independently (separately) rate on a 10-point scale the degree of desire for the various underscored sexual activities. Later on in counseling the ratings were shared and discussed.

After all of these procedures were in effect, the counselor gradually withdrew involvement, thereby letting the couple have more responsibility in trying the procedures on new problems. A once-a-month follow-up was conducted by sending the couples marital happiness scales.

The results of reciprocity counseling showed considerable improvements on the Marital Happiness Scales. Follow-up after one month from the end of treatment showed continued improvement. The reciprocity counseling procedures were clearly responsible for the dramatic improvements whereas the catharsis counseling control periods effected no changes. This innovative, extensive program has been replicated with many more subjects showing similar improvements. Longer than one-month follow-up data will add to the credibility of these procedures. Outcome data on divorce rates of the participating clients would also be noteworthy.

A further analysis of reciprocity counseling was provided by Wolf and Etzel (1976), who also found considerable improvements on the Marital Happiness Scale. They found, however, that the exchange of the scale by partners did not appear to be a very important component of reciprocity counseling since equal improvements were noted when the scale was not exchanged. This study served two important purposes by replicating the Azrin et al. (1973) results and providing a partial component analysis of reciprocity counseling procedures.

Another reciprocity approach was reported by Weiss and Margolin (1975). They saw twelve couples in one-hour sessions twice a week. As in the Azrin et al. (1973) study, the first three weeks acted as a "control" time to look at the effects, if any, of catharsis-style counseling. During treatment, the marital pairs received training in learning to respond reciprocally to the positive and satisfying behaviors of their spouses. In addition to the reciprocity procedures developed by Azrin et al. (1973), these couples were provided with training in negotiating their own contracts. The self-report data showed considerable improvement for all 12 couples.

A group comparison study was conducted by Jacobson (1977). He compared a minimal-treatment, waiting-list control group to a treatment group receiving pinpointing, communication training, negotiation training, and contracting. A within-subjects single-subject design provided further assessments of the treatment effects. The treatment group showed significant improvements in reducing negative behaviors and increasing positive behaviors. The control group did not show similar improvements.

Lutzker (1980) has stated that the treatment of marital problems needs to focus more regularly on some of the more mundane, everyday aspects of the marital relationship, such as attention to the family budget, attention to the children, and the performance of household duties. Tearnan and Lutzker (1980) used contracting and negotiation training to improve the marital satisfaction of a couple and to directly change three pairs of problem behaviors in their relationship.

The couple, Bob and Mary, were asked to identify three behaviors in the partner they wanted increased. In a *quid pro quo* arrangement, they paired the behaviors so that as each partner increased the target behavior, so did the other partner. A multiple baseline across the three pairs of behaviors showed this contract to be the functional variable in producing the increases in the desired behaviors, which were for Bob: (1) that Mary would help more with the children (both Bob and Mary felt that the other did not help enough with the children); (2) that Mary show more positive emotion toward Bob; and (3) that Mary display more physical affection toward Bob. For Mary, the three behaviors she wanted increased in Bob were: (1) more positive emotion; (2) more help with the children; and (3) more help with household chores. Considerable improvements occurred in all three pairs of behaviors. The Locke-Wallace Marital Satisfaction Inventory scores for Bob and Mary improved greatly between pre- and posttreatment and were maintained in a follow-up. These procedures were based on a 1977 report by Lutzker and Lutzker, which outlines contracting procedures for nondistressed couples and partners in any dyadic relationships.

A preventative approach to marital and other two-party relationships was described by Margolin and Louscher (1978). They saw two groups of three couples for six-week treatment periods that consisted of behavioral group training in attentive listening, emotional clarification, anger management, the formulation of requests, and problem solving. The couples, all of whom were nondistressed as measured by the Dyadic Adjustment Scale, were also instructed to practice the skills at home and to tape record a problem-solving discussion in which they implemented the new behaviors. A multiassessment package was used to evaluate the effects of the behavioral group training. The results showed an interesting dichotomy. For those couples who were compliant, that is, attended regularly and did their "homework," there were considerable positive changes in most measures of communications. For couples that Margolin and Louscher labeled "noncompliant," that is, couples who did not attend regularly and/or did not do their home assignments, there were no changes in positive communication.

Thus, since Goldiamond's early case study, behavioral approaches to marital communication training and behavioral improvements in the marital relationship have flourished. New assessment techniques, along with more elaborate treatment procedures, have been reported. The next decade will undoubtedly see further replications of these procedures, an increase in multimodal assessment procedures, and the further expansion of an overall "family systems" (Lutzker, 1980) approach that includes more attention to the more mundane, basic aspects of everyday relationships.

SEXUAL BEHAVIOR

Clearly, some of the significant clinical achievements in behavior change technology have been in the treatment of heterosexual behavior disorders. Prior to the work of Masters and Johnson (1966) and behavior therapists such as LoPiccolo and Lobitz (1972), sexual dysfunction was thought of as symptomatic of deep-seated psychological disease, the "cure" for which could only occur after years of psychotherapy. However, relatively simple behavior change techniques have been applied with remarkable success to the three most common heterosexual disorders: impotence, premature ejaculation, and frigidity. The high degree of success of the behavioral treatment of sexual dysfunction is not surprising when viewed from the logic of stimulus control. While problems of obesity, smoking, drinking, drugs, and communications in relationships are a function of the highly complex relationship between the person and the environment, sexual behavior really involves rather discrete (technically and socially speaking), comparatively simple behaviors that occur in fairly well-established (discriminated) stimulus situations. Thus, whereas the treament of problems such as obesity or alcoholism necessarily involves a rearrangement of many aspects of an individual's environment, the treatment of a sexual problem can be expected to generalize more easily from a relaxed, informative clinical situation to the sexual encounter in the natural environment. Despite our emphasis on sex in advertising and the fact that we might feel that it is frequently "on our minds," the actual performance of sexual behavior takes up very little of most people's time compared to the time that most other activities take. These therefore may be contributing factors to the successes of behavioral sexual therapies.

Impotence is the inability of a male to achieve or maintain an erection. While it can be caused by alcohol or drug consumption, its most common cause is anxiety, usually anxiety or fear of being unable to perform. There are two types of impotence: primary and secondary, the latter being by far the most common. Primary impotence is descriptive of a male who has never been able to achieve or maintain an erection. More often than not, this is due to organic factors. Secondary impotence is more often behaviorally based and is descriptive of a male who has had a history of being able to achieve and maintain erections, but is currently unable to do so. Secondary impotence is the kind frequently reported in the behavioral treatment literature.

The most frequently utilized treatment procedure for the treatment of secondary impotence has been a variation of what has been called "sensate focus" (Kaplan, 1975; Masters & Johnson, 1970; Wolpe & Lazarus, 1966). A couple is asked to assume a relaxed position. The female is told to stimulate the male in a gentle, non-anxiety-producing fashion. Oils, lotions, vibrators, heat, or oral stimulation may be used to produce erection. If the presence of the female is initially too anxiety-provoking for the man, he might be asked to fantasize and/or masturbate in order to achieve and maintain an erection. In this case, the female is gradually introduced into the situation. The primary goal is for the male to achieve and maintain an erection without concentrating on it and becoming anxious about its subsiding or his failing in a copulation attempt. Obviously, considerable patience is required of the partner.

When a maintained erection has become a routine phenomenon in this situation, brief vaginal penetration is advised. It is generally recommended that the female maintain the superior coital position so that the male is allowed to relax and focus on the enjoyment and presumably suffer less anxiety about performance (Redd, Porterfield, & Anderson, 1979). If the male loses the erection, the female dismounts, stimulates the male to full erection again and gently, gradually conducts another penetration attempt. After the couple has engaged in this sequence several times and the male is able to achieve and maintain erections, penetration and thrusting to orgasm is recommended. Systematic desensitization (Wolpe, 1958) may also be used to augment this *in vivo* process.

The "squeeze technique" has come to be known as the treatment of choice for premature ejaculation (Masters & Johnson, 1970). Premature ejaculation involves the male ejaculating prior to or immediately after vaginal penetration. The technique is considered behavioral in that it attacks the problem directly without looking toward "internal" causative factors and a clear shaping process is involved. With the squeeze technique, the female stimulates the male until he reports that he is going to ejaculate. When this occurs, the female forcefully squeezes the penis just below the glans with her thumb and forefinger for a few seconds. This simple procedure inhibits ejaculation and the male begins to learn to develop control. After this becomes a practiced sequence of four or five trials, the couple is told to engage in brief lateral coital penetration with the male removing his penis prior to feeling as though he is going to ejaculate, again learning to control the response. This relatively simple procedure has "liberated" countless men who might otherwise not be able to be enriched by a sexual life they desire.

What was previously called "frigidity" in women can be better described as sexual dysfunction. Two types of the most common forms of female sexual dysfunction are sexual arousal deficits and orgasmic dysfunction. The former often involves failure by the female to achieve appropriate vaginal lubrication, the latter involves the female having difficulty or never having had orgasms. A combination of sensate focus, and systematic and *in vivo* desensitization procedures have been effective in treating these problems for females. Also, video desensitization involves the use of graphic aids such as slides or films depicting anxiety-free sexual encounters. In a 1976 study, Wincze and Caird treated 21 women complaining of sexual dysfunctions. Video desensitization was more effective in reducing heterosexual anxiety compared to no-treatment control subjects; however, only 25% of the nonorgasmic subjects were orgasmic at the conclusion of the study. It would seem that a combination of sensate focus and video desensitization would have produced a higher percentage of orgasmic subjects.

Quantitative measures of sexual arousal in women have only recently been achieved. Cerny (1978) studied 30 women who were shown an erotic videotape while vaginal blood volume and pulse pressure were monitored. The women concurrently subjectively rated their arousal states. One group of women received accurate feedback about blood volume changes while a second group received inaccurate feedback. A third group acted as controls and received no feedback. The women had been instructed to increase their sexual arousal on two experimental trials and to suppress their arousal on two experimental trials. The women were able to exercise voluntary control of their physiological measures related to sexual arousal. The results imply that biofeedback itself does not enhance or suppress vaginal vasocongestion (an increase in bloodflow to the labia), but knowing that females can voluntarily control vasocongestion may lead to further advances in the treatment of female sexual dysfunctions. Further exploring the measurement of female sexual arousal, Henson, Rubin, Henson, and Williams (1977) have determined that temperature change of the labia minor can be used as an objective measure. These Southern Illinois University researchers developed a device that allowed for the objective assessment of female eroticism. Female volunteer subjects were exposed to erotic motion pictures. Nine of the ten subjects showed increases in labial temperature during the film as compared to baseline temperature measures. As a further control, upper chest temperature was measured during all conditions and showed no changes similar to those generated from the labia. Subjective measures of arousal that correlated with the labial temperature changes were obtained from the women. Thus, it appears that female eroticism can be measured best by this labial technique. This means that more work, using similar techniques, can be expected in the areas of explaining the human female sexual response and providing objective measurement in some types of behavioral sexual therapy.

The effects of three different behavioral strategies in treating 36 couples who presented a variety of sexual dysfunctions was reported by Mathews, Bancroft, Whitehead, Hackmann, Julier, Bancroft, Gath, and Shaw (1976). Some of the complaints of the males included erectile failure and premature ejaculation. The females reported frigidity, lack of interest, or vaginismus. The three treatments compared were systematic desensitization plus counseling that addressed attitudes and beliefs about sexual behavior, directed practice as recommended by Masters and Johnson (1970) along with counseling, and directed practice with minimal therapist contact and discussion. These British researchers found all three approaches functional in improving the couples' sexual adjustment, with no one treatment mode statistically significantly more effective than another. The trends, however, suggested the direct practice plus counseling approach to be the most effective. Once again, what we are seeing here is that almost any behavioral approach seems to have a high probability of success in the treatment of sexual dysfunction. And, once again, we might speculate that it is the direct nature of behavior change techniques that functions as the effective element of the successes.

Objective measurement of male eroticism has a longer history than the measurement of female eroticism. In 1969, Laws and Rubin described the achievement of instructional control of erectile responding in males viewing erotic films. The device used to measure eroticism was something called a strain gauge, which is a device worn around the penis that measures any engorgement. Later, Henson and Rubin (1971) provided further utility for the device in their study objectifying men's voluntary control of eroticism.

Modification of penile erectile response in six males with impotency problems was achieved through either fantasy, fantasy with graphic feedback (as measured by a strain gauge), erotic pictures, or pictures plus feedback (Csillag, 1976). The men who experienced these conditions showed considerable improvement, which led the author of the study to suggest that a variety of rather simple procedures might be available in the treatment of impotence.

While no behavior therapist necessarily promotes promiscuity, the fact is that many people seek sexual relations with more than one partner. An important issue of generalization of therapeutic gains was addressed by Sergio Yulis of the University of Chile (1976). He saw 37 men who had complained of premature ejaculation. The men were treated using the squeeze technique described earlier in this chapter. Further, the single men were given assertiveness training, specifically dealing with interactions with women. Twenty-three of the men reported successful generalization of therapeutic gains in achieving ejaculatory control with women other than the partners who had gone through the treatment with them. Yulis suggests that the assertiveness training may have greatly enhanced this generalization.

An unusual case study was reported by Sharpe and Meyer (1973), who treated a 25-year-old man who complained of unbearable pain in the tip of his penis during thrusting motions and ejaculating during intercourse. A physical condition treated surgically early in the man's life apparently had produced a sort of "conditioned pain." By distracting the husband with pornography and gradually stimulating more and more sensitive areas of his penis, the couple was able to "countercondition" the pain. Over time, the distraction was discontinued and a three-month follow-up showed the man to be pain-free while enjoying frequent intercourse with his wife. An interesting sidelight to this report is the issue of "operant pain," which we touched on in Chapter 5. Pain may be maintained by consequences even though the original organic cause for the pain may have long ago disappeared.

There are a few ethical questions for the behavior therapist dealing with heterosexual dysfunction, but most issues are fairly clearcut. The waters become muddier, however, when the behavior therapist is faced with dealing with problems considered deviant or with new issues dealing with behavior formerly labeled as deviant—for example, homosexuality. Among the so-called deviancies treated by behavior therapists have been fetishes (sexual attractions to inanimate objects) (Rachman, 1966), exhibitionism (Brownell & Barlow, 1976), and sadistic fantasies (Davison, 1973).

Variations in sexual behavior can still be seen as deviancies if the behavior infringes on the rights of others. For example, pedophilia, sexual attraction to and molestation of children, is generally considered a serious problem. Pedophilia has been treated by aversion therapies (Barlow, Leitenberg, & Agras, 1969) and by orgasmic reconditioning (VanDeventer & Laws, 1978). The latter authors treated two male pedophiles who had been convicted of sexual encounters with children. Using both self-reports and physiological measures, it was determined that both young men showed high sexual arousal to pictures of young boys. Neither subject showed the same responsiveness to pictures of adult males or females. Training in orgasmic reconditioning frequently involves the subject masturbating to "deviant" fantasies and being asked to switch to a "nondeviant" fantasy just prior to and during orgasm. In the VanDeventer and Laws study, treatment involved having the subjects spend alternating weeks masturbating to fantasies about boys and fantasies about women. Further, the subjects were instructed to speak their fantasies aloud where therapists monitored them in adjoining rooms. Several hours after these masturbation sessions, the subjects were evaluated on their arousal to deviant slides (boys) and nondeviant slides (women). For one subject, sexual arousal to both kinds of slides decreased. For the other subject, arousal to adults increased whereas arousal to children decreased. Follow-up showed continued improvements for both subjects after two months.

While studies such as these hold promise for the treatment of sexual deviancies, it would nevertheless seem only logical that a variety of "support" techniques in the subjects' natural communities would contribute to maintained therapeutic gains. These "support" techniques might include assertiveness training as in the Yulis (1976) study, community-based (friend- or relative-implemented) reinforcement programs for maintaining treatment gains, and knowledge by the subjects that they will be carefully monitored for "violations." "Booster" treatment sessions might also be in order.

Only recently in Western culture has homosexuality ceased to be regarded by the majority as legally deviant. Also, until recently, homosexuality was regarded clinically as deviant by the American Psychological Association and the American Psychiatric Association. However, as gay people began to come forth demanding their rights, both of these professional organizations changed their official stands on homosexuality, no longer regarding it necessarily as evidence of poor mental health.

Prior to 1974, many behavior therapists were involved in clinical attempts to change the sexual preferences of homosexuals to heterosexual. Most of these attempts were made through a variety of aversive conditioning procedures whereby the gay client gained relief from shock by turning off slides showing provocative same-sexed nudes. However, in his presidential address before the Association for the Advancement of Behavior Therapy in 1974, Dr. Gerald Davison, of the State University of New York at Stony Brook, urged behavior therapists to stop their attempts to change the sexual preference of homosexuals and instead to provide behavioral counseling to gay individuals who might have adjustment problems because of their sexual preferences. This bold move by Dr. Davison was only logical behaviorally. The mounting evidence to support the theory that sexual preference is learned and that homosexuality is not deviant could scarcely be overlooked. Recently, Masters and Johnson (1970) have provided further evidence for this notion. Since Davison's charge to his colleagues, few articles have appeared describing behavioral attempts at sexual preference change in adults.

CONCLUSIONS

The treatment of sexual dysfunction has seen relative success using behavior change strategies. Treatment for female sexual dysfunction, vaginismus, premature ejaculation, and impotency has become fairly standard. More equivocal results have been presented in the treatment of sexual deviancies.

In the area of relationships, several advances have also been made, although the empiricism we have seen in other behavior change applications is still frequently missing in the complex realm of human relationships.

REFERENCES

Alexander, J. R. Defensive and supportive communications in normal and deviant families. *Journal of Consulting and Clinical Psychology*, 1973, *40*, 223–231.

Alexander, J., & Parsons, B. Short-term behavioral intervention with delinquent families: Impact on family process and recidivism. *Journal of Abnormal Psychology*, 1973, *81*, 219–225.

Azrin, N. H., Naster, B. J., & Jones, R. Reciprocity counseling: A rapid learning-based procedure for marital counseling. *Behaviour Research and Therapy*, 1973, *11*, 365–382.

Barlow, D. H., Leitenberg, H., & Agras, W. S. The experimental control of sexual deviation through manipulation of the noxious scene in covert sensitization. *Journal of Abnormal Psychology*, 1969, *74*, 596–601.

Brownell, K. D., & Barlow, D. H. Measurement and treatment of two sexual deviations in one person. *Journal of Behavior Therapy and Experimental Psychiatry*, 1976, *7*, 349–354.

Carter, R. D., & Thomas, E. J. Modification of problematic marital communication using corrective feedback and instruction. *Behavior Therapy*, 1973, *4*, 100–109.

Cerny, J. A. Biofeedback and the voluntary control of sexual arousal in women. *Behavior Therapy*, 1978, *9*, 847–855.

Csillag, E. R. Modification of penile erectile response. *Journal of Behavior Therapy and Experimental Psychiatry*, 1976, *7*, 27–29.

Davison, G. C. Elimination of a sadistic fantasy by a client-controlled counterconditioning technique: A case study. *Journal of Abnormal Psychology*, 1973, *81*, 60–73.

Davison, G. C. *Homosexuality: The ethical challenge.* A presidential address at the 8th Annual Convention of the Association for the Advancement of Behavior Therapy, Chicago, November 1974.

Goldiamond, I. Self-control procedures in personal behavior problems. *Psychological Reports*, 1965, *17*, 851–868.

Gordon, T. *Parent effectiveness training.* New York: Wyden, 1970.

Henson, D. E., & Rubin, H. B. Voluntary control of eroticism. *Journal of Applied Behavior Analysis*, 1971, *4*, 37–44.

Henson, D. E., Rubin, H. B., Henson, C., & Williams, J. R. Temperature change of the labia minora as an objective measure of female eroticism. *Journal of Behavior Therapy and Experimental Psychiatry*, 1977, *8*, 401–410.

Jackson, D. D. Family rules. *Archives of General Psychiatry*, 1965, *12*, 589–594.

Jacobson, N. S. Problem solving and contingency contracting in the treatment of marital discord. *Journal of Consulting and Clinical Psychology*, 1977, *45*, 92–100.

Kaplan, H. S. *The new sex therapy.* New York: Brunner/Mazel, 1975.

Kifer, R., Lewis, M., Green, D., & Phillips, E. L. Training predelinquent youths and their parents to negotiate conflict situations. *Journal of Applied Behavior Analysis*, 1974, *7*, 357–364.

Laws, D. R., & Rubin, H. B. Instructional control of an autonomic sexual response. *Journal of Applied Behavior Analysis*, 1969, *2*, 93–99.

Liberman, R. Behavioral approaches to family and couple therapy. *American Journal of Orthopsychiatry*, 1970, *40*, 106–118.

LoPiccolo, J., & Lobitz, W. C. The role of masturbation in the treatment of primary orgasmic dysfunction. *Archives of Sexual Behavior*, 1972, *2*, 163–171.

Lutzker, J. R. Deviant family systems. In B. B. Lahey & A. E. Kazdin (Eds.), *Advances in clinical child psychology* (Vol. 3). New York: Plenum Press, 1980.

Lutzker, J. R., & Lutzker, S. Z. A two-dimensional marital contract: Weight loss and household responsibility performance. In E. Abramson (Ed.), *Behavioral approaches to weight control*. New York: Springer, 1977.

Lysaght, T. V., & Burchard, J. D. The analysis and modification of a deviant parent-youth communication pattern. *Journal of Behavior Therapy and Experimental Psychiatry*, 1975, *6*, 339–342.

Margolin, G., & Louscher, K. *Communication training for marital couples: A preventative approach*. Paper presented at the Association for the Advancement of Behavior Therapy, Chicago, 1978.

Martin, B., & Twentyman, C. Teaching conflict resolution skills to parents and children. In E. J. Mash, L. C. Handy, & L. A. Hamerlynck (Eds.), *Behavior modification approaches to parenting*. New York: Brunner/Mazel, 1976.

Masters, W. H., & Johnson, V. E. *Human sexual response*. Boston: Little, Brown, 1966.

Masters, W. H., & Johnson, V. E. *Human sexual inadequacy*. Boston: Little, Brown, 1970.

Mathews, A., Bancroft, J., Whitehead, A., Hackmann, A., Julier, D., Bancroft, J., Gath, D., & Shaw, P. The behavioral treatment of sexual inadequacy: A comparative study. *Behaviour Research and Therapy*, 1976, *14*, 427–436.

Mealiea, W. L. Conjoint-behavior therapy: The modification of family constellations. In E. J. Mash, L. C. Handy, & L. A. Hamerlynck (Eds.), *Behavior modification approaches to parenting*. New York: Brunner/Mazel, 1976.

Patterson, G. R., & Reid, J. B. Reciprocity and coercion: Two facets of social systems. In C. Neuringer & J. Michael (Eds.), *Behavior modification in clinical psychology*. New York: Appleton-Century-Crofts, 1970.

Phillips, D. The family council: A segment of adolescent treatment. *Journal of Behavior Therapy and Experimental Psychiatry*, 1975, *6*, 283–287.

Rachman, S. Sexual fetishism: An experimental analogue. *The Psychological Record*, 1966, *16*, 293–296.

Redd, W. H., Porterfield, A. L., & Anderson, B. L. *Behavior modification: Behavioral approaches to human problems*. New York: Random House, 1979.

Roosa, J. B. *SOCS: Situations, options, consequences and simulation: A technique for teaching social interaction*. Unpublished paper presented at the American Psychological Association, Montreal, August 1973.

Sharpe, R., & Meyer, V. Modification of "cognitive sexual pain" by the spouse under supervision. *Behavior Therapy*, 1973, *4*, 285–287.

Skinner, B. F. *Walden two*. New York: Macmillan, 1948.

Stuart, R. B. Behavior contracting within families of delinquents. *Journal of Behavior Therapy and Experimental Psychiatry*, 1971, *2*, 1–11.

Tearnan, B. H., & Lutzker, J. R. A contracting "package" in the treatment of marital problems: A case study. *American Journal of Family Therapy*, 1980, *8*, 24–31.

VanDeventer, A. D., & Laws, D. R. Orgasmic reconditioning to redirect sexual arousal in pedophiles. *Behavior Therapy*, 1978, *9*, 748–765.

Weathers, L., & Liberman, R. P. Contingency contracting with families of delinquent adolescents. *Behavior Therapy*, 1975, *6*, 356–366.

Weiss, R. L., & Margolin, G. Marital conflict and accord. In A. K. Ciminero, K. S. Calhoun, & H. F. Adams (Eds.), *Handbook for behavioral assessment*. New York: Wiley, 1975.

Wincze, J. P., & Caird, W. K. The effects of systematic desensitization and video desensitization in the treatment of essential sexual dysfunction in women. *Behavior Therapy*, 1976, *7*, 335–342.

Wolf, S. S., & Etzel, B. C. *A behavioral analysis of reciprocity marital counseling procedures*. Paper presented at the Annual Meeting of the Association for Advancement of Behavior Therapy, New York, December 1976.

Wolpe, J. *Psychotherapy by reciprocal inhibition*. Stanford, Calif.: Stanford University Press, 1958.

Wolpe, J., & Lazarus, A. A. *Behavior therapy techniques*. Oxford: Pergamon Press, 1966.

Yulis, S. Generalization of therapeutic gain in the treatment of premature ejaculation. *Behavior Therapy*, 1976, *7*, 355–358.

CHAPTER 13

Training, Ethics, and the Future

s you have seen, behavior change technology has been applied to almost every conceivable dimension of human development. The applications seem almost unlimited, but some issues remain. What does it take to train behavior change skills to professionals, paraprofessionals, parents, teachers, and all of those people who could benefit from being able to utilize this technology? Further, what ethical issues need to be considered in the development and dissemination of this vast technology? Do behavior change professionals or behavior change procedures need to be certified or licensed? Finally, what lies ahead in this field? What areas as yet untapped or barely examined today can we expect to see new work on in the 1980s and beyond? These are the issues of this final chapter.

TRAINING

Not much to our surprise, we have discovered that in the training of behavior change skills we must apply the same logic and many of the same principles as we do in any other of the areas of applications covered in this book. We have found that feedback and other reinforcers and punishers are necessary in training behavior change skills. We have also discovered the necessity to model and shape, fade, make use of stimulus control procedures, and so on, in teaching behavior change skills. A brief review of this literature ensues.

The early work in the training of behavior change skills to others focused on two areas: staff training and parent training. One of the first studies involving staff at a residential treatment facility was reported by Panyan, Boozer, and Morris (1970). They showed that feedback could act as a reinforcer that served to increase staff performance of routines related to residents' activities. Similarly, Gardner (1972) used trading stamps to increase the number of training sessions conducted by nonprofessionals at an institution. As we noted in Chapter 4, Quilitch (1975) compared three procedures aimed at increasing the frequency of staff engaging in activities with the residents of a mental health facility. He found that administrative memos, and even workshops, were not effective, but that scheduling and (public) feedback of activities greatly increased the number of activities conducted by the staff. While these studies shed light on some variables that influence staff behavior, none of them directly assessed resident (client) benefits from increased staff performance. Without these assessments, the "data" are not complete on the overall impact of behavior change training procedures.

Recently, however, a study was reported that measured client gains from staff-implemented programs (Greene, Willis, Levy, & Bailey, 1978). Their study took place in the Sunland Hospital in Tallahassee, Florida, an institution for the mentally retarded. The "subjects" in the first of two experiments were six afternoon staff members who were responsible for toilet training four severely retarded residents. Baseline measures reflected the percent of client participation in toilet training. (These staff members had participated in a workshop on toilet training.) The baseline data showed participation to be low and sporadic. After baseline, a "public posting" procedure was implemented that involved the program director posting a large graph that showed the percent of clients participating in the toilet training program. The graph also displayed the names of the therapists (staff members) involved in each training session. The results showed a graphic increase in the percent of clients participating in toilet training, but no direct measures assessed the quality or success of the toilet training, so in a second experiment Greene et al. (1978) designed staff feedback procedures that were made contingent upon client performance. The training under study in this case involved a rather complex ambulation training program of previously nonambulatory clients. Public feedback was again provided graphically, but this time contained client progress and the therapists responsible for each session. The results showed feedback and public posting to be responsible for considerable improvements in clients' ambulation and range of motion. Very importantly, too, the staff expressed satisfaction with the program. This study demonstrates that behavior change techniques can be successfully implemented to produce client improvement through simple contingencies on staff behavior that do not violate civil service or union regulations governing "contingencies" on staff behavior. Further research should demonstrate that similar procedures can be effective with more staff members and different client behaviors over a lengthy follow-up period.

In another study with state hospital staff, Katz and Lutzker (in press) found modeling and modeling plus incentives to be superior to lectures in producing accurate timeout procedures. Three groups of staff from a state hospital treating developmental disabilities and mental illness served as subjects. All three groups received personalized instruction plus lectures on timeout procedures. Also, all three groups were tested on a "paper-and-pencil" measure assessing their knowledge of timeout procedures. All staff members of all three groups scored very well on the "paper-and-pencil" timeout tests. The groups experienced differences in their training. One group had more lecture than the other two groups. The other two groups had a modeling and role-playing component to their training. That is, the experimenters actually demonstrated the use of timeout procedures and had the staff members practice. Subjects in all three groups were also tested by having them actually demonstrate the use of timeout procedures in a simulation wherein one of the experimenters acted as a problem child. Subjects in both the modeling and modeling plus incentive groups passed this "hands-on" test, whereas the staff who experienced lectures only did not pass the test. Of course, the true test of training would have been to see how well the staff members used timeout procedures on the hospital units, but, unfortunately, this was not possible.

Another study (Hursh, Schumaker, Fawcett, & Sherman, 1973) showed that direct training (modeling and feedback) was superior to indirect training (written instructions) in training high school student volunteers to teach some simple skills to retarded children.

Thus, we see three trends in the literature on staff training. It appears that contingencies are necessary to improve performance, that performance (rate of responding) is not necessarily related to treatment change for clients without contingencies specifically designed to do that, and that "hands-on" training is superior to didactic training.

Parent Training

We reviewed parent training to some extent in Chapter 7, but we would like to extend that review somewhat here in order to present a broader picture of the issue of training behavior change techniques.

Similar results to those obtained with mental hospital staff were obtained by Nay (1975) in looking at some of the parameters involved in training mothers to use timeout procedures with their children. Seventy-seven mothers served as subjects in Nay's study. Each mother was put into one of four experimental groups: (1) written presentation; (2) lecture; (3) modeling plus role playing; (4) videotaped modeling; also, there was a no-treatment control group. As in the Katz and Lutzker study (in press), the mothers' proficiency in the use of timeout procedures was assessed through a written test and a simulation. In this case, the simulation involved the mothers' ability to describe what should be done with a problem child heard on an audio tape recording. The results were also very similar to those of Katz and Lutzker. All groups except the no-treatment control did well on the written tests, but only the groups that experienced some kind of modeling did well on the simulation test. The Nay (1975) study provides further support for the importance of modeling in the training of behavior change skills.

An important issue in the whole field of behavior change applications is that of generalization. Specific to training, we are concerned with how well hospital staff, parents, or teachers might generalize their newly learned behavior change skills. For example, will a mother who has learned to use rapid toilet training with her 2½-year-old son apply some of her newly learned skills to teaching him proper mealtime behavior or to teaching him to tie his shoes? Dr. Robert Koegel and his colleagues at the University of California at Santa Barbara have addressed this issue in looking at generalization of parent-training results with the parents of autistic children (Koegel, Glahn, & Nieminen, 1978). They found that if parents were trained on how to teach specific skills to their children such as stacking blocks or putting on a coat, they (the parents) showed little generalization in being able to teach their child another skill without specific instructions on how to do so. More generalization of teaching skill by the parents was shown when they were taught less specific, more general behavior change skills. These results should prove valuable to professionals involved in training behavior change skills. It would seem that if only a few specific skills need to be taught to clients or children, specific staff or parent training might be in order; however, if the goal is to try to have staff or parents be able to carry out their own behavior change programs with a variety of behaviors, then more general training would appear to be the way to go.

Further research in parent training by Rincover, Koegel, and Russo (1978) has provided the "basic recipe" for what the parents should learn. Parents should learn to give instructions correctly, how to use reinforcers effectively, how to use shaping procedures, how to use physical prompting and fading techniques, and to use discrete trials—that is, to present one instruction at a time, wait for the response, and apply the proper consequence, before moving on to the next instruction. It seems as though we are beginning to get a clearer picture of some of the critical elements of successful behavior change skill training.

Dr. Rob Hawkins (1974) suggested that we focus on preventative rather than remedial programs in the area of child-rearing training, as it is more humane and less costly. A preventive program may be accomplished in one of three ways: (1) supplementing the work of the parents (for example, day care & TV), (2) placing the task of all child rearing in the hands of a "well-qualified expert" (for example, a kibbutz), or (3) training the parents themselves to become such "experts." Hawkins favors this latter method. He suggests the most logical place is the school, since some "living skills" are already taught there. In most classes that teach this information the educator has no occasion to observe the student practicing these skills. Hawkins suggests that there should be a nursery school or day care center as an integral part of every high school and junior high school. There should be a one-year course *required* for *all* students. The course should place major emphasis on: (1) how children typically develop, (2) what behaviors to develop in a child, and (3) how to develop these behaviors. These three elements can best be taught through the integration of reading, discussions, field trips, and laboratory experiences, according to Hawkins. It is not too unlikely that much of Hawkins suggestions will come to pass.

Training Centers

During the 1950s aspiring behavioral psychologists came directly from Skinner's laboratory at Harvard. As we mentioned in Chapter 1, the "hotbeds" of behaviorism in the early sixties were the University of Washington, Southern Illinois University at Carbondale, and Arizona State University. No one program specialized in behavior change technology. From the late sixties until now (and maybe forever), the University of Kansas Department of Human Development has been the Mecca of applied behavior analysis. The department offers M.A. programs and a Ph.D. The "apostles" from Kansas have gone all over to "spread the behavioral word."

By the mid-sixties, master's degree programs specializing in behavior modification were developed. Among the earliest and most enduring have been the programs at Drake University, Southern Illinois University at Carbondale, Western Michigan University, and West Virginia University. The latter three have also developed doctoral programs. Other Ph.D. "hotbeds" now include the State University of New York at Stony Brook, Florida State University, the University of Georgia, Georgia State University, the University of Hawaii, the University of Illinois, the State University of New York at Binghamton, and others. New master's programs have appeared, and behaviorally oriented programs have also begun to appear in diverse areas, such as social work at the University of Chicago. Finally, postdoctoral training centers have become noteworthy, such as Johns Hopkins University School of Medicine, the John F. Kennedy Institute, and the University of Mississippi Medical Center. This growth of behavioral enclaves will surely continue throughout the next decade.

ETHICAL ISSUES

The 1970s brought the law into psychology, including behavior change technology. Courts mandated "right to treatment" while they also tried to articulate clients' rights in treatment. These legal issues came at a time when the term *behavior modification* was being applied to techniques that did not justifiably fit within the purview of behavior change technology as described in this book. Some of these techniques included psychosurgery, chemotherapy, and cruel aversion therapies. Rather than become very defensive and challenge all legal issues, behavior change professionals looked to their own field and began an intense self-behavior analysis to determine how to comply with recent legal decisions without reducing the technology's effectiveness. And they began a long series of discussions that led to actions protecting the field from an improper image while also protecting the public's rights. The interested reader should examine Reed Martin's book *Legal Challenges to Behavior Modification* (1975).

One of the first of these self-analyses occurred at the First Drake Conference on Professional Issues in Behavior Analysis held in 1974. Discussed at the conference were whether certification or licensure would help protect the field and its consumers, and the reminders that behaviorism's main strength, accountability, would always allow us to answer to the kinds of challenges that were being considered.

To a large extent, the issue of certification has been settled from both sides of the argument. Many behavior change professionals feel that licensure or certification reflects anachronistic procedures. To meet licensure or certification requirements in most fields, a professional is tested once, usually in writing and by oral examination, and no actual measures of performance competency at the time of testing or thereafter occur. Continuing education requirements in most fields are even more lax than the original certification procedures for the professionals. Thus, for many behavior change professionals, licensure or certification represents all we know to be ineffective and inefficient. Another question in certifying individuals is whom to certify—psychologists? Social workers? Teachers? Parents? As we have seen, a great variety of individuals utilize behavior change procedures.

One alternative to certifying professionals is to certify procedures or training centers. But there are cogent arguments against this proposal. Would the certification of procedures stifle the creative development of new procedures? Who would do the certifying? What about well-trained, highly respected professionals who do not teach at behavioral enclaves? Would their students be precluded from being certified? These are difficult issues.

One of the most "behavioral" compromises to this whole question was offered by Beth Sulzer-Azaroff, Jack Thaw, and Carol Thomas (1975). They proposed developing competencies required for a range of titles within the field. These titles included Behavior Analyst, Behavior Technology Coordinator, Behavior Technologist Engineer, and Behavior Co-Technician. Various training experiences and demonstrated competencies would be necessary for any individual to earn one of these labels. Sulzer-Azaroff et al. (1975) polled 92 well-known and highly regarded professionals in order to come up with these competencies. Their work did not go for naught. Stimulated by this issue of certification through competencies, professionals in Minnesota expanded the Sulzer-Azaroff et al. (1975) survey and through tireless efforts, managed to produce a whole civil service career ladder for "behavior analysts" for the state of Minnesota (Thomas, 1979). This was a major breakthrough accomplishment, which can be expected to be imitated by other states and provinces. It is also testimony to the wide recognition of behavior change technology as an entire field or discipline, rather than a small set of tools embedded in some other discipline.

Sajwaj (1977) has reminded us that self-scrutiny will mean self-protection, for as he has put it, ". . . it is critical that guidelines be written by acknowledged leaders of the field and not by anonymous, inexperienced bureaucrats" (p. 538). The rights of clients and the responsibilities of therapists have been well articulated by Hare-Mustin, Marecek, Kaplan, and Liss-Levinson (1979). They have carefully pointed out that protecting client rights helps protect therapists, and thus, the field. Further, they have provided some guidelines for establishing contracts between private patients (clients) and their therapists. These issues will continue to be discussed throughout the next decade.

Before leaving the area of ethics, we cannot overlook the important contribution of Dr. Montrose Wolf (1978). He has charged the behavior change field with providing "social validation" for what we do. By this, Wolf means that formal survey data should be gathered from all "consumers" related to a behavior change project. For example, if a parent-child training program has been effected, information about satisfaction with the results, ease of implementation of the procedures, and such should be gleaned from parents, perhaps the children themselves, siblings, teachers, and others who intimately know the family. In the case of a health-related intervention, not only the client, but medical personnel and, perhaps, family, should provide the social validation. Providing social validation is a way to maintain public visibility and accountability and, again, to provide self-scrutiny within the field.

TOMORROW

In most of the chapters of this book, we have already made some suggestions regarding future directions of each particular area of application. Here, briefly, we would like to mention some of them again and add a few more.

Certainly in the next decade we will see an expansion of an ecobehavioral approach (Rogers-Warren & Warren, 1977; Lutzker, 1980) to the treatment and analysis of many problems. An ecobehavioral approach involves looking at the many ways the environment contributes to behavior. For example, in looking at child abuse, Lutzker, Frame, and Greene (1980) have discussed 12 components in treating the problem. Child abuse not only involves (1) poor parent-child relations, but involves problems (2) in parent education about children, (3) in handling stress, (4) in managing the family budget, (5) in providing the family with productive leisure-time activities, (6) in marital relations, (7) in drinking (alcoholism), (8) in self-control, (9) in social support, (10) in respite (day care), (11) in preventing problems in high-risk families, and (12) in teaching abused or neglected children many of the skills we have described earlier. Thus, all of these components are treated in dealing with the global child abuse label.

Many critics of behavior change technology have accurately pointed their fingers at a "sore spot" in the field—generalization. More studies need to describe carefully programmed generalization of responses across settings and procedures across several subjects. Stokes and Baer (1977) have suggested that to date we have had a tendency to "train and hope," and they have provided several suggestions for advancing beyond this "stage." A durable technology will depend on this kind of advancement.

Similar to the need to document more systematic attempts to produce generalization, there is a need to produce more and longer follow-up data. Whether in children or impotent adult males, or in reporting community litter control or trash-packaging programs, data need to be presented on the long-term results of the behavior change interventions. It appears that a trend for better follow-up has already begun to appear. We are sure that this will continue.

As demonstrations of the success of behavior change applications appear over and over again, we can expect to see more large group studies comparing a particular behavioral approach to some other approach(es). We have begun to see some of these comparisons in the more "clinical" treatments and will undoubtedly see them in many of the other application areas.

With our growing problems and concerns about the environment, energy conservation, energy sources, and economic conditions, we can surely expect to see many more applications of behavior change technology emerge in these areas.

Another "natural" area for involvement of behavior change professionals is the area of community planning on a much larger scale than reported by Briscoe, Hoffman, and Bailey (1975). Perhaps entire new communities will be built utilizing innovative behavior change technology, including architecture.

In the next decade we can expect a continuation of an interdisciplinary involvement among professionals. The most clearcut example we have seen of this is in the health care fields where medical personnel, allied medical personnel, and behavior change professionals have joined forces in combatting health problems. In doing this, we can also be expected to continue to define our own limits and to learn where behavior change technology belongs and can be helpful and where it does not belong and may be of little or no help.

In family relations, we can expect to see increased development of parent training programs, premarital behavioral counseling, and training for single parents. We hope to see a much greater focus on preventing family problems through exposing school children to behavioral training procedures. Such preventive programs should help reduce the occurrence of child abuse and delinquency. Also, we can expect to see more large-scale stimulus control procedures in health-related applications such as the public segregation of smokers, exercise clubs, increased availability of healthful food, and maybe insurance plans that reduce premiums for good health.

One thing we can be sure of is that behavior change technology will continue to move forward. Of course, our bias has shown throughout this book in that we feel that this may be the most important technology in humankind's history.

REFERENCES

Briscoe, R. V., Hoffman, D. B., & Bailey, J. S. Behavioral community psychology: Training a community board to problem solve. *Journal of Applied Behavior Analysis*, 1975, *8*, 157–168.

Gardner, J. M. Teaching behavior modification to nonprofessionals. *Journal of Applied Behavior Analysis,* 1972, *5,* 517–521.

Greene, B. F., Willis, B. S., Levy, R., & Bailey, J. S. Measuring client gains from staff-implemented programs. *Journal of Applied Behavior Analysis,* 1978, *11,* 395–412.

Hare-Mustin, R. T., Marecek, J., Kaplan, A. G., & Liss-Levinson, N. Rights of clients, responsibilities of therapists. *American Psychologist,* 1979, *34,* 3–16.

Hawkins, R. P. Universal Parenthood Training: A proposal for preventive mental health. In Ulrich, R., Stachnik, T., & Mabry, J. *Control of human behavior* (Vol. 3). Glenville, Ill.: Scott, Foresman, 1974, 187–192.

Hursh, D. E., Schumaker, J. B., Fawcett, S. B., & Sherman, J. A. *Training behavior modifiers: A comparison of written and direct instructional methods.* Paper presented at the American Psychological Association Convention, Montreal, 1973.

Katz, R. C., & Lutzker, J. R. Comparison of three methods for training the use of timeout. *Behavior Research of Severe Developmental Disabilities,* in press.

Koegel, R. L., Glahn, T. J., & Nieminen, G. S. Generalization of parent-training results. *Journal of Applied Behavior Analysis,* 1978, *11,* 95–109.

Lutzker, J. R. Deviant family systems. In B. B. Lahey & A. E. Kazdin (Eds.), *Advances in clinical child psychology* (Vol. 3). New York: Plenum Press, 1980.

Lutzker, J. R., Frame, R. E., & Greene, B. F. *An ecobehavioral approach to child abuse and neglect.* An invited address to the 6th Annual Convention of the Association for Behavior Analysis, Dearborn, Michigan, May 1980.

Martin, R. *Legal challenges to behavior modification.* Champaign, Ill.: Research Press, 1975.

Nay, W. R. A systematic comparison of instructional techniques for parents. *Behavior Therapy,* 1975, *6,* 14–21.

Panyan, M., Boozer, H., & Morris, M. Feedback to attendants as a reinforcer for applying operant techniques. *Journal of Applied Behavior Analysis,* 1970, *3,* 1–4.

Quilitch, H. R. A comparison of three staff-management procedures. *Journal of Applied Behavior Analysis,* 1975, *8,* 59–66.

Rincover, A., Koegel, R. L., & Russo, D. C. Some recent behavioral research on the education of autistic children. *Education and Treatment of Children,* 1978, *1,* 31–45.

Rogers-Warren, A., & Warren, S. *Ecological perspectives in behavior analysis.* Baltimore: University Park Press, 1977.

Sajwaj, T. Issues and implications of establishing guidelines for the use of behavioral techniques. *Journal of Applied Behavior Analysis,* 1977, *10,* 531–540.

Stokes, T. F., & Baer, D. M. An implicit technology of generalization. *Journal of Applied Behavior Analysis,* 1977, *10,* 349–367.

Sulzer-Azaroff, B., Thaw, J., & Thomas, C. Behavioral competencies for the evaluation of behavior modifiers. In S. Wood (Ed.), *Issues in evaluating behavior modification.* Champaign, Ill.: Research Press, 1975.

Thomas, D. R. Certification of behavior analysis in Minnesota. *Behavior Analyst,* 1979, *2,* 1–13.

Wolf, M. M. Social validity: The case for subjective measurement or how applied behavior analysis is finding its heart. *Journal of Applied Behavior Analysis,* 1978, *11,* 203–214.

SUBJECT INDEX